THE REBEL PUBLISHING HOUSE

Editing by Ma Prem Gitika, M.A., B.Sc., Ma Deva Sarito
Typing by Ma Prem Praveeta, Ma Deva Anupo, M.S.W.
Design by Ma Dhyan Amiyo
Calligraphy by Ma Deva Satyama
Production by Ma Prem Arya
Published by The Rebel Publishing House GmbH, Cologne, West Germany

Copyright © Neo-Sannyas International
First Edition

Typesetting by Photon Graphics Pvt. Ltd, Poona, India
Printing by Mohndruck, Guetersloh, West Germany

Distributed in the U.S.A. by
Chidvilas, Boulder, Colorado

Distributed in Europe by
The Rebel Publishing House GmbH, Cologne, West Germany

Quotations from *The Zen Teaching of Bodhidharma*
(complete version available in a bilingual,
Chinese/English, edition from Empty Bowl,
P.O. Box 646, Port Townsend, WA 98368, USA)
Translation by Red Pine
Copyright © Red Pine 1987
Reproduced by permission

ISBN 3-89338-025-6

Bhagwan Shree Rajneesh

Commentaries on the Teachings of the Messenger of Zen from India to China

BODHIDHARMA

達磨

**In
loving
gratitude
to
Bhagwan**

**Swami
Anand
Vibhavan**

TABLE OF CONTENTS

Talks
given
to
the
Rajneesh
International
University
of
Mysticism
in
Chuang Tzu
Auditorium
Poona
India

EARLY THIS MORNING, every bit of aerial space in the garden was crisscrossed with the rainbow-colored threads of spiders. Right near my face, suspended from an iridescent superstructure four meters wide, were sixty concentric rings making up a web the size of a dinner plate. In the faintest movements of air, the web billowed and sparkled. At the center of the web was the spider, unbelievably small for the amount of web supporting her. She was the size of the pupil through which I was closely observing her.

In the slanting shafts of sunlight little whorls of midges rose and fell, tantalizingly close to her web. I found I was willing her to jump on them, or sweep her web like a fishing net, do something – but no, she remained perfectly still. The midges finally ascended to the treetops and I withdrew, shocked that my mind had so wanted to interfere with her spider-nature.

In a world where all man's actions however well intentioned are bringing him to the verge of annihilation, this book comes at a moment of existential need.

Bhagwan Shree Rajneesh is talking to his disciples explaining and expanding into twentieth century language the insights that Bodhidharma communicated in the sixth century to his disciples.

Bodhidharma is one of the giants of the Buddha's inheritance. Bhagwan is a seer who spans all traditions and all times. A book of two such men, in dialogue as it were, is a survival handbook of a new dimension.

There used to be a confidence amongst humanity that rational men could put together rational solutions for the well-being of the species. Now doubt has arisen as to whether there is such a thing as a rational man and whether, if there is, he even wants to solve the problems facing him. With the advent of the phrase "global suicide" the concept of global self-extinction becomes accepted currency.

All the world's problems are man-made. They are a

product of man's awareness – or as the book will show, man's unawareness. For in unawareness man is overpopulating the planet, he is amassing nuclear weapons, he is dividing himself into ever more fanatic parts.

As the discourses unfold we begin to glimpse Bhagwan's penetrating insights into the normal aberrations of human behavior.

He draws attention to the subtle methods of division and control practiced by man on man and man on himself.

He demonstrates that political, social and religious freedoms are not real freedoms because they can be taken away.

He shows how all our miseries are nothing but attachments.

And he exposes the root of all blindness and aunawareness as attachment to the mind.

Recognition of the symptoms is nine-tenths of the way to cure. And that includes recognition of some symptoms that even Bodhidharma displays, of a conditioned Buddhist-mind.

In the splendor of these totally unscripted discourses Bhagwan goes on to unravel the thread that leads to the natural man, the true man, the new man for this age.

"The greatest delusion, according to those who have reached the highest peak of awareness, is searching and seeking outside of yourself."

"In meditation, *dhyan,* mind simply disappears. Dhyan is a silence beyond mind."

In that silence is the source of all true action and all true non-action: the spider's weaving of her web and the spider's stillness.

Swami Deva Rashid

1

TO SEEK NOTHING IS BLISS

達磨

2 —— CHA: TEA

Beloved Bhagwan,

Bodhidharma's Outline of Practice

Many roads lead to the Path, but basically there are only two: reason and practice. To enter by reason means to realize the essence through instruction and to believe that all living things share the same true nature, which isn't apparent because it's shrouded by sensation and delusion. Those who turn from delusion back to reality, who meditate on walls, the absence of self and other, the oneness of mortal and sage, and who remain unmoved, even by scriptures, are in complete and unspoken agreement with reason.

Without moving, without effort, they enter, we say, by reason.

To enter by practice refers to four all-inclusive practices: suffering injustice, adapting to conditions, seeking nothing and practicing the Dharma.

First, suffering injustice. When those who search for the Path encounter adversity, they should think to themselves, "In countless ages gone by, I've turned from the essential to the trivial and wandered through all manner of existence, often angry without cause and guilty of numberless transgressions. Now, though I do no wrong, I'm punished by my past. Neither gods nor men can foresee when an evil deed will bear its fruit. I accept it with an open heart and without complaint of injustice."

The sutras say, "When you meet with adversity, don't be upset. Because it makes sense." With such understanding, you're in harmony with reason. And by suffering injustice, you enter the Path.

Second, adapting to conditions. As mortals, we're ruled by conditions, not by ourselves. All the suffering and joy we experience depend on conditions. If we should be blessed by some great reward, such as fame or fortune, it's the fruit of a seed planted by us in the past. When conditions change, it ends. Why delight in its existence? But while success and failure depend on conditions, the mind neither waxes nor wanes. Those who remain unmoved by the wind of joy silently follow the Path.

Third, seeking nothing. People of this world are deluded. They're always longing for something, always, in a word, seeking. But the wise wake up. They choose reason over custom. They fix their minds on the sublime and let their bodies change with the season. All phenomena are empty. They contain nothing worth desiring. Calamity forever alternates with Prosperity.

To dwell in the three realms is to dwell in a burning house. To have a body is to suffer. Does anybody with a body know peace?

Fourth, practicing the Dharma. The Dharma is the truth that all natures are pure. By this truth, all appearances are empty. Defilement and attachment, subject and object don't exist. The sutras say, "The Dharma includes no being because it's free from the impurity of being. And the Dharma includes no self, because it's free from the impurity of self." Those wise enough to believe and understand this truth are bound to practice according to the Dharma. Since the embodiment of the Dharma contains nothing worth begrudging, they give their body, life and property in charity, without regret, without the vanity of giver, gift or recipient, and without bias or attachment. And they take up transforming others to eliminate impurity but without becoming attached to form. Thus, through their own practice, they're able to help others and glorify the Way of Enlightenment. And as with charity, they also practice the other virtues. But while practicing the six virtues to eliminate delusion, they practice nothing at all. This is what's meant by practicing the Dharma.

Those who understand this detach themselves from all that exists and stop imagining or seeking anything. The sutras say, "To seek is to suffer. To seek nothing is bliss." When you seek nothing, you're on the Path.

I HAVE A very soft corner in my heart for Bodhidharma. That makes it a very special occasion to speak about him. Perhaps he is the only man whom I have loved so deeply that speaking on him I will be almost speaking on myself. That also creates a great complexity, because he never wrote anything in his life. No enlightened being has ever written. Bodhidharma is not an exception, but by tradition these three books that we are going to discuss are attributed to Bodhidharma.

The scholars reason that because there is no contrary evidence – and for almost one thousand years, these books have been attributed to Bodhidharma – there is no reason why we should not accept them. I am not a scholar, and there are certainly fragments which must have been spoken by Bodhidharma, but these are not books written by him. These are notes by his disciples. It was an ancient tradition that when a disciple takes notes from the master he does not put his own name on those notes, because nothing of it belongs to him; it has come from the master.

But knowing Bodhidharma as intimately as I know him... There are so many fallacies which are possible only if somebody else was taking notes and his own mind entered into it; he has interpreted Bodhidharma – and with not much understanding.

Before we enter into these sutras, a few things about Bodhidharma will be good to know. That will give you the flavor of the man and a way to understand what belongs to him in these books and what does not belong to him. It is going to be a very strange commentary.

Bodhidharma was born fourteen centuries ago as a son of a king in the south of India. There was a big empire, the empire of Pallavas. He was the third son of his father, but seeing everything – he was a man of tremendous intelligence – he renounced the kingdom.

He was not against the world, but he was not ready to waste his time in mundane affairs, in trivia. His whole concern was to know his self-nature, because without knowing it you have to accept death as the end.

All true seekers in fact, have been fighting against death. Bertrand Russell has made a statement that if there were no death, there would be no religion. There is some truth in it. I will not agree totally, because religion is a vast continent. It is not only death, it is also the search for bliss, it is also the search for truth, it is also the search for the meaning of life; it is many more things. But certainly Bertrand Russell is right: if there were no death, very few, very rare people would be interested in religion. Death is the great incentive.

Bodhidharma renounced the kingdom saying to his father, "If you cannot save me from death, then please don't prevent me. Let me go in search of something that is beyond death." Those were beautiful days, particularly in the East. The father thought for a moment and he said, "I will not prevent you, because I cannot prevent your death. You go on your search with all my blessings. It is sad for me but that is my problem; it is my attachment. I was hoping for you to be the successor, to be the emperor of the great Pallavas empire, but you have chosen something higher than that. I am your father so how can I prevent you?

"And you have put in such a simple way a question which I had never expected. You say, 'If you can prevent my death then I will not leave the palace, but if you cannot prevent my death, then please don't prevent me either.'" You can see Bodhidharma's caliber as a great intelligence.

And the second thing that I would like you to remember is that although he was a follower of Gautam Buddha, in some instances he shows higher flights than Gautam Buddha himself. For example, Gautam Buddha was afraid to initiate a woman into his commune of sannyasins but Bodhidharma got initiated by a woman who was enlightened. Her name was Pragyatara. Perhaps people would have forgotten her name; it is only because of Bodhidharma that her name still remains, but only the name – we don't know anything else about her. It was she who ordered Bodhidharma to go to China. Buddhism had reached China six hundred years before Bodhidharma. It was something magical; it had never happened anywhere, at any time – Buddha's message immediately caught hold of the whole Chinese people.

The situation was that China had lived under the influence of Confucius and was tired of it. Because Confucius is just a moralist, a puritan, he does not know anything about the inner mysteries of life. In fact, he denies that there is anything inner. Everything is outer; refine it, polish it, culture it, make it as beautiful as possible.

There were people like Lao Tzu, Chuang Tzu, Lieh Tzu, contemporaries of Confucius, but they were mystics not masters. They could not create a counter movement against Confucius in the hearts of the Chinese people. So there was a vacuum. Nobody can live without a soul, and once you start thinking that there is no soul, your life starts losing all meaning. The soul is your very integrating concept; without it you are cut away from existence and eternal life. Just like a branch cut off from a tree is bound to die – it has lost the source of nourishment – the very idea that there is no soul inside you, no consciousness, cuts you away from existence. One starts shrinking, one starts feeling suffocated.

But Confucius was a very great rationalist. These mystics, Lao Tzu, Chuang Tzu, Lieh Tzu, knew that what Confucius was doing was wrong, but they were not masters. They remained in their monasteries with their few disciples.

When Buddhism reached China, it immediately entered to the very soul of the people...as if they had been thirsty for centuries, and Buddhism had come as a rain cloud. It quenched their thirst so immensely that something unimaginable happened.

Christianity has converted many people, but that conversion is not worth calling religious. It converts the poor, the hungry, the beggars, the orphans, not by any spiritual impact on them but just by giving them food, clothes, shelter, education. But these have nothing to do with spirituality. Mohammedanism has converted a tremendous amount of people, but on the point of the sword: either you be a Mohammedan, or you cannot live. The choice is yours.

The conversion that happened in China is the only religious conversion in the whole history of mankind. Buddhism simply explained itself, and the beauty of the message was understood by the people. They were thirsty for it, they were waiting for something like it. The whole country, which was the biggest country in the world, turned to Buddhism. When Bodhidharma reached there six hundred years later, there were already thirty thousand Buddhist temples, monasteries, and two million Buddhist monks in China. And two million Buddhist monks is not a small number; it was five percent of the whole population of China.

Pragyatara, Bodhidharma's master, told him to go to China because the people who had reached there before him had made a great impact, although none of them were enlightened. They were great scholars, very disciplined people, very loving and peaceful and compassionate, but none of them were enlightened. And now China needed another Gautam Buddha. The ground was ready.

Bodhidharma was the first enlightened man to reach China. The point I want to make clear is that while Gautam Buddha was afraid to initiate women into his commune, Bodhidharma was courageous enough to be initiated by a woman on the path of Gautam Buddha. There were other enlightened people, but he chose a woman for a certain purpose. And the purpose was to show that a woman can be enlightened. Not only that, her disciples can be enlightened. Bodhidharma's name stands out amongst all the Buddhist enlightened people second only to Gautam Buddha.

There are many legends about the man; they all have some significance. The first legend is: When he reached China – it took him three years – the Chinese emperor Wu came to receive him. His fame had reached ahead of him. Emperor Wu had done great service to the philosophy of Gautam Buddha. Thousands of scholars were translating Buddhist scriptures from Pali into Chinese and the emperor was the patron of all that great work of translation. He had made thousands of temples and monasteries, and he was feeding thousands of monks. He had put his whole treasure at the service of Gautam Buddha, and naturally the Buddhist monks who had reached before Bodhidharma had been telling him that he was earning great virtue, that he will be born as a god in heaven.

Naturally, his first question to Bodhidharma was, "I have made so many monasteries, I am feeding thousands of scholars, I have opened a whole university for the studies of Gautam Buddha, I have put my whole empire and its treasures in the service of Gautam Buddha. What is going to be my reward?"

He was a little embarrassed seeing Bodhidharma, not thinking that the man would be like this. He looked very ferocious. He had very big eyes, but he had a very soft heart – just a lotus flower in his heart. But his face was almost as dangerous as you can conceive. Just the sunglasses were missing; otherwise he was a mafia guy!

With great fear, Emperor Wu asked the question, and Bodhidharma said, "Nothing, no reward. On the contrary, be ready to fall into the seventh hell."

The emperor said, "But I have not done anything wrong – why the seventh hell? I have been doing everything that the Buddhist monks have been telling me."

Bodhidharma said, "Unless you start hearing your own voice, nobody can help you, Buddhist or non-Buddhist. And you have not yet heard your inner voice. If you had heard it, you would not have asked such a stupid question.

"On the path of Gautam Buddha there is no reward because the very desire for reward comes from a greedy mind. The whole teaching of Gautam Buddha is desirelessness and if you are doing all these so-called virtuous acts, making temples and monasteries and feeding thousands of monks, with a desire in your mind, you are preparing your way towards hell. If you are doing these things out of joy, to share your joy with the whole empire, and there is not even a slight desire anywhere for any reward, the very act is a reward unto itself. Otherwise you have missed the whole point."

Emperor Wu said, "My mind is so full of thoughts. I have been trying to create some peace of mind, but I have failed and because of these thoughts and their noise, I cannot hear what you are calling the inner voice. I don't know anything about it."

Bodhidharma said, "Then, four o'clock in the morning, come alone without any bodyguards to the temple in the mountains where I am going to stay. And I will put your mind at peace, forever."

The emperor thought this man really outlandish, outrageous. He had met many monks; they were so polite, but this one does not even bother that he is an emperor of a great country. And to go to him in the darkness of early morning at four o'clock, alone.... And this man seems to be dangerous – he always used to carry a big staff with him.

The emperor could not sleep the whole night, "To go or not to go? Because that man can do anything. He seems to be absolutely unreliable." And on the other hand, he felt deep down in his heart the sincerity of the man, that he is not a hypocrite. He does not care a bit that you are an emperor and he is just a beggar. He behaves as an emperor, and in front of him you are just a beggar. And the way he has said, "I will put your mind at peace forever."

"Strange, because I have been asking," the emperor thought, "of many many wise people who have come from India, and they all gave me methods, techniques, which I have been practicing, but nothing is happening – and this strange fellow, who looks almost mad, or drunk, and has a strange face with such big eyes that he creates fear.... But he seems to be sincere too – he is a wild phenomenon. And it is worth to risk. What can he do – at the most he can kill me." Finally, he could not resist the temptation because the man had promised, "I will put your mind at peace forever."

Emperor Wu reached the temple at four o'clock, early in the morning in darkness, alone, and Bodhidharma was standing there with his staff, just on the steps, and he said, "I knew you would be coming, although the whole night you debated whether to go or not to go. What kind of an emperor are you – so cowardly, being afraid of a poor monk, a poor beggar who has nothing in the world except this staff. And with this staff I am going to put your mind to silence."

The emperor thought, "My God, who has ever heard that with a staff you can put somebody's mind to silence! You can finish him, hit him hard on the head – then the whole man is silent, not the mind. But now it is too late to go back."

And Bodhidharma said, "Sit down here in the courtyard of the temple." There was not a single man around. "Close your eyes, I am sitting in front of you with my staff. Your work is to catch hold of the mind. Just close your eyes and go inside looking for it – where it is. The moment you catch hold of it, just tell me, 'Here it is.' And my staff will do the remaining thing."

It was the strangest experience any seeker of truth or peace or silence could have ever had – but now there was no other way. Emperor Wu sat there with closed eyes, knowing perfectly well that Bodhidharma seems to mean everything he says.

He looked all around – there was no mind. That staff did its work. For the first time he was in such a situation. The choice...if you find the mind, one never knows what this man is going to do with his staff. And in that silent mountainous place, in the presence of Bodhidharma, who has a charisma of his own.... There have been many enlightened people, but Bodhidharma stands aloof, alone, like an Everest. His every act is unique and original. His every gesture has his own signature; it is not borrowed.

He tried hard to look for the mind, and for the first time he could not find the mind. It is a small strategy. Mind exists only because you never look for it; it exists only because you are never aware of it. When you are looking for it you are aware of it, and awareness surely kills it completely. Hours passed and the sun was rising in the silent mountains with a cool breeze. Bodhidharma could see on the face of Emperor Wu such peace, such silence, such stillness as if he was a statue.

He shook him and asked him, "It has been a long time. Have you found the mind?"

Emperor Wu said, "Without using your staff, you have pacified my mind completely. I don't have any mind and I have heard the inner voice about which you talked. Now I know whatever you said was right. You have transformed me without doing anything. Now I know that each act has to be a reward unto itself; otherwise, don't do it. Who is there to give you the reward? This is a childish idea. Who is there to give you the punishment? Your action is punishment and your action is your reward. You are the master of your destiny."

Bodhidharma said, "You are a rare disciple. I love you, I respect you, not as an emperor but as a man who has the courage just in a single sitting to bring so much awareness, so much light, that all darkness of the mind disappears."

Wu tried to persuade him to come to the palace. He said, "That is not my place; you can see I am wild, I do things I myself don't know beforehand. I live moment to moment spontaneously, I am very unpredictable. I may create unnecessary trouble for you, your court, your people; I am not meant for palaces, just let me live in my wildness."

He lived on this mountain whose name was Tai... The second legend is that

Bodhidharma was the first man who created tea – the name 'tea' comes from the name *tai,* because it was created on the mountain Tai. And all the words for tea in any language, are derived from the same source, tai. In English it is tea, in Hindi it is *chai.* That Chinese word tai can also be pronounced as *cha.* The Marathi word is exactly *cha.*

The way Bodhidharma created tea cannot be historical but is significant. He was meditating almost all the time, and sometimes in the night he would start falling asleep. So, just not to fall asleep, just to teach a lesson to his eyes, he took out all his eyebrow hairs and threw them in the temple ground. The story is that out of those eyebrows, the tea bushes grew. Those were the first tea bushes. That's why when you drink tea, you cannot sleep. And in Buddhism it became a routine that for meditation, tea is immensely helpful. So the whole Buddhist world drinks tea as part of meditation, because it keeps you alert and awake.

Although there were two million Buddhist monks in China, Bodhidharma could find only four worthy to be accepted as his disciples. He was really very choosy. It took him almost nine years to find his first disciple, Hui Ko.

For nine years – and that is a historical fact, because there are ancientmost references, almost contemporary to Bodhidharma which all mention that fact although others may not be mentioned – for nine years, after sending Wu back to the palace, he sat before the temple wall, facing the wall. He made it a great meditation. He would just simply go on looking at the wall. Now, looking at the wall for a long time, you cannot think. Slowly, slowly, just like the wall, your mind screen also becomes empty.

And there was a second reason. He declared, "Unless somebody who deserves to be my disciple comes, I will not look at the audience."

People used to come and they would sit behind him. It was a strange situation. Nobody had spoken in this way; he would speak to the wall. People would be sitting behind him but he would not face the audience, because he said, "The audience hurts me more, because it is just like a wall. Nobody understands, and to look at human beings in such an ignorant state hurts deeply. But to look at the wall, there is no question; a wall, after all is a wall. It cannot hear, so there is no need to be hurt. I will turn to face the audience only if somebody proves by his action that he is ready to be my disciple."

Nine years passed. People could not find what to do – what action would satisfy him. They could not figure it out. Then came this young man, Hui Ko. He cut off one of his hands with the sword, and threw the hand before Bodhidharma and said, "This is the beginning. Either you turn, or my head will be falling before you. I am going to cut my head too."

Bodhidharma turned and said, "You are really a man worthy of me. No need to cut the head, we have to use it." This man, Hui Ko, was his first disciple.

Finally when he left China, or intended to leave China, he called his four disciples – three more he had gathered after Hui Ko. He asked them, "In simple words, in small sentences, telegraphic, tell me the essence of my teachings. I intend to leave tomorrow morning to go back to the Himalayas, and I want to choose from you four, one as my successor."

The first man said, "Your teaching is of going beyond mind, of being absolutely silent, and then everything starts happening of its own accord."

Bodhidharma said, "You are not wrong, but you don't satisfy me. You just have my skin."

The second one said, "To know that I am not, and only existence is, is your fundamental teaching."

Bodhidharma said, "A little better, but not up to my standard. You have my bones; sit down."

And the third one said, "Nothing can be said about it. No word is capable of saying anything about it."

Bodhidharma said, "Good, but you have said already something about it. You have contradicted yourself. Just sit down; you have my marrow."

And the fourth was his first disciple, Hui Ko, who simply fell at Bodhidharma's feet, without saying a word, tears rolling down from his eyes. Bodhidharma said, "You have said it. You are going to be my successor."

But in the night Bodhidharma was poisoned by some disciple as a revenge, because he had not been chosen as the successor. So they buried him, and the strangest legend is that after three years he was found by a government official, walking out of China towards the Himalayas with his staff in his hand and one of his sandals hanging from the staff – and he was barefoot.

The official had known him, had been to him many times, had fallen in love with the man, although he was a little eccentric. He asked, "What is the meaning of this staff, and one sandal hanging from it?" Bodhidharma said, "Soon you will know. If you meet my people just tell them that I'm going into the Himalayas forever."

The official reached immediately, as fast as he could, the monastery on the mountain where Bodhidharma had been living. And there he heard that he had been poisoned and he had died...and there was the tomb. The official had not heard about it, because he was posted on the boundary lines of the empire. He said, "My God, but I have seen him, and I cannot be deceived because I have seen him many times before. He was the same man, those same ferocious eyes, the same fiery and wild outlook, and on top of it, he was carrying on his staff one sandal."

The disciples could not contain their curiosity, and they opened the tomb. All that they could find there was only one sandal. And then the official understood why he had said, "You will find out the meaning of it; soon you will know."

We have heard so much about Jesus' resurrection. But nobody has talked much of the resurrection of Bodhidharma. Perhaps he was only in a coma when they buried him, and then he came to his senses, slipped out of the tomb, left one sandal there and put another sandal on his staff, and according to the plan, he left.

He wanted to die in the eternal snows of the Himalayas. He wanted that there should be no tomb, no temple, no statue of him. He did not want to leave any footprints behind him to be worshiped; those who love him should enter into their own being – "I am not going to be worshiped." And he disappeared almost in thin air.

Nobody heard anything about him – what happened, where he died. He must be buried in the eternal snows of the Himalayas somewhere.

This is the man, and there are these three small collections which we are taking as one whole book. These are not his writings, because they don't show any quality of the man. They are notes of scholarly disciples; hence they are bound to have fundamental and essential faults, misunderstandings, misinterpretations. They are not people of no-mind. Their minds are taking the notes; their minds are choosing the words.

Bodhidharma was not a man of words, he was a man of action.

There is no possibility of him writing a book. A man who never wanted to be worshiped, a man who never wanted to leave any footprints behind him to be followed, is not going to write a book either, because that is leaving footprints to be followed.

But I have chosen to speak on them because these three small collections are the only writings which for centuries have been believed to be Bodhidharma's. They contain here and there, in spite of the people who were taking the notes, something of Bodhidharma – something has entered. The task is difficult for any scholar to make a distinction as to which part is Bodhidharma's and which part is the note taker's. It is not a problem for me.

I know from my own experience what can be unpolluted Bodhidharma, and what can be only the mind of a scholar interpreting him. So these are not ordinary commentaries. In a way this is the first effort about Bodhidharma to sort out the wheat from the chaff.

The first statement: *Many roads lead to the Path*. This cannot be said by Bodhidharma. He cannot even say that even a single path leads to the truth; his whole approach was that you are the truth, you are not to go anywhere. You have to stop going, so that you can remain at home where the truth is. It is not a question of following a path; on the contrary it is a question of not following any path, not going anywhere, so you can be here – so that you can be now, just within yourself. Every path leads astray, that was Bodhidharma's approach. This is a scholarly way.

Many roads lead to the Path, but basically there are only two: reason and practice.

It is not possible for Bodhidharma to say that. Certainly not that reason can lead you to the ultimate reality of your being. Reason is part of the mind. And even more wrong is the path of practice. That means it should be based on belief and you have to practice and discipline yourself according to it. You will become an imitator, but you will not be able to come to your original face.

No practice is needed. You are really where you need to be. It is just that you go on and on, round and round, but never settle down into your own being. That settling down into your being has neither many paths nor two paths.

To enter by reason, means to realize the essence through instruction...

That means the information comes from somebody else.

...and to believe that all living things share the same true nature...

Bodhidharma cannot use the word 'believe.' He is the last person to use the word believe, because belief only creates blind people. Belief never becomes your eyes; it never brings light to you but only prejudices, opinions, ideologies. But they are not the experience and Bodhidharma is fundamentally interested only in experience.

...which is not apparent because it is shrouded by sensation and delusion.

These are ordinary statements, far below the outlandish caliber of Bodhidharma.

*Those who turn from delusion back to reality, who meditate on walls...*perhaps this small fragment.... *Those who turn from delusion back to reality, who meditate on walls, the absence of self and other, the oneness of mortal and sage, and who remain unmoved, even by scriptures, are in complete and unspoken agreement with reason.*

Just the last part of the statement has to be changed. Instead of "with reason" it should be "with existence."

This piece I can say with absolute guarantee, comes from Bodhidharma. Try to understand it.

Those who meditate on walls means those who start dropping thoughts, dropping mind, whose screen of the mind becomes just like a wall – no movement, pure stillness. They come to understand the absence of self, that there is no ego within you, that there is nobody who can say, "I am."

"Existence is, I am not."

No-selfness is one of the fundamentals of Gautam Buddha. And Bodhidharma will certainly agree with it because it is the very foundation of the whole revolution that Gautam Buddha created.

...the oneness of mortal and sage... That even Gautam Buddha cannot say – only Bodhidharma, a single man in the whole world, in the whole history – that the ordinary man and the sage are not different. They only have different personalities, facades, but in the innermost part of their subjectivity they are just the same. The sinner and the saint are the same. The sinner is suffering unnecessarily from guilt and the saint is suffering unnecessarily from the ego, that "I am holier than thou." But both are basically the same – no-self, just a pure nothingness.

...and who remain unmoved, even by scriptures.... Whatever the scriptures may say cannot change these people, these meditators, who have come to know the nothingness, who have come to know the selflessness, who have come to know pure consciousness without any contamination by ego. Even if all the scriptures say this is not right, they are not going to be moved by it. No scriptures can disturb them.

...are in complete and unspoken agreement with existence, *not with reason.* That small part of the statement is not from Bodhidharma. That is added by the person who is writing the book.

Without moving, without effort, they enter, we say, by reason. Again, the statement certainly seems to be from Bodhidharma. *Without moving,* because there is nowhere to go. To find yourself you have to be in a state of unmoving silence. Without moving, and of course without any effort because the effort will bring movement. You simply have to be effortless and unmoving and just silent, as if you are not. They enter into the very heart of existence.

To enter by practice refers to four all-inclusive practices.

I don't think these statements are coming from Bodhidharma, although they are coming from Buddhist scriptures. So we will have a little look into them.

Suffering injustice... That is coming from Buddhist scriptures. The first thing Bodhidharma cannot say but Gautam Buddha can say. And it is a very complex statement: *Suffering injustice, adapting to conditions...* It can help a person to be contented but it takes away all rebelliousness from him.

Suffering injustice has to be looked at from both sides. One side is to suffer injustice just as part of the law of karma: your past life's evil acts have created it; it is just a punishment – suffer it without complaining, without revolting. It will certainly create a superficial contentment but it will destroy something very beautiful – your individuality. It will destroy the rebel in you; it is a kind of suicide of the rebel.

This has certainly been taught by Gautam Buddha, and hence I have always been saying that in India's poverty, two thousand years of slavery, Gautam Buddha has some hand. When you teach people to suffer injustice without complaining against it, and to adapt to any conditions that you find happening around you, for example slavery – adapt to it... Gautam Buddha's influence was great. It went deep into India's very heart and that was the cause of its poverty, its long slavery. No country has lived for two thousand years in slavery, and even today when so-called freedom has come, the Indian mind is still psychologically a slave.

For example when Rabindranath Tagore got the Nobel prize for his book of songs, *Gitanjali,* "Offering of Songs," the book had already been in existence for twenty years in Bengali and in Hindi. Nobody even bothered about it. But when it got the Nobel prize, when it was translated into English, immediately Rabindranath Tagore became a world figure. He lived in Calcutta and the Calcutta University wanted to confer on him an honorary doctorate, but he refused. In his refusal he wrote, "You are not conferring the doctorate on me, you are conferring the doctorate on the Nobel prize. Your minds are so enslaved. My book has been in existence for twenty years and the translation is not so beautiful as my original." The translation is a faraway echo, and it is true the original has a beauty which the translation cannot have.

Poetry cannot be translated from one language to another; only prose can be translated, because every language has its own nuances and in poetry those nuances play such a major role that you cannot take them easily into another language.

Gautam Buddha is certainly responsible for India's slavery, poverty, by giving such a teaching of adapting to the conditions, that whatsoever the conditions are – it is our fate. And even suffering injustice you are not supposed to complain. This kills the very rebel in your being and without a rebel you are almost dead.

Your rebelliousness is your very life stream.

I cannot think that a man like Bodhidharma, so outrageous in his statements, can make these two things significant practices. Yet the third thing certainly comes from him: *Seeking nothing and practicing the Dharma.*

You have to understand the word *dharma*. It has not been translated but it can be translated very easily. Dharma means self-nature. For example, to be hot is the dharma of fire; to be cold is the dharma of ice, the self-nature. What is the self-nature of man? No-selfness, silence, and suddenly an upsurge of compassion. This can be said by Bodhidharma, it must have been said. And before it, is a condition: seeking nothing. Every seeking is going to take you away from yourself, so non-seeking is one of the essentials of Bodhidharma's teaching.

Don't go anywhere. Pull all your energy inwards. Close all your petals and just be in. And you will experience what dharma is, what self-nature is. Then practice it. Then act as if you are nobody.

Then act with great compassion.

Then let your whole life be simply a presence, but not a person because there is no self inside you.

First, suffering injustice. When those who search for the Path encounter adversity, they should think to themselves, "In countless ages gone by, I have turned from the essential to the trivial and wandered through all manner of existence, often angry without cause and guilty of numberless transgressions. Now, though I do no wrong, I am punished by my past."

These words are from the person who is writing the notes.

"Neither gods nor men can foresee when an evil deed will bear its fruit. I accept it with an open heart and without complaint of injustice."

These words certainly are not from Bodhidharma.

The sutras say, "When you meet with adversity, don't be upset. Because it makes sense." With such understanding you are in harmony with reason. And by suffering injustice, you enter the Path.

No signature of Bodhidharma on these words.

Second, adapting to conditions. As mortals, we are ruled by conditions, not by ourselves.

Again, it is not from Bodhidharma. Bodhidharma cannot say that we are ruled by conditions and not by ourselves. In the first place, we are not. We are only pure nothingness, and who can rule the pure nothingness? As a person you can be ruled, but as a presence you cannot be ruled. And making conditions more important than yourself is again supporting the vested interests, the exploiters, the parasites. Bodhidharma is one of the greatest rebellious souls of the world.

If we should be blessed by some great reward, such as fame or fortune, it is the fruit of a seed planted by us in the past.

Again, it is not Bodhidharma. Bodhidharma does not believe in the past or in the future; his trust is only in the present.

And whatever you do, the consequence of it will immediately follow the action just like the shadow follows you. That which brings rewards is virtue and that which brings suffering is sin. He is a simple man; he is not a complicated philosopher and he is not in any way in support of the vested interests.

When conditions change, it ends. Why delight in its existence? But while success and failure depend on conditions, the mind neither waxes nor wanes. Those who remain unmoved by the wind of joy silently follow the Path.

Perhaps, I say perhaps these words can be Bodhidharma's. Neither by success nor by failure should you be affected. They are not more than dreams, they come and go. You should remain in your witnessing self. *Those who remain unmoved by the wind of joy silently follow the Path.*

Third, seeking nothing. People of this world are deluded. They are always longing for something, always, in a word, seeking. But the wise wake up. They choose reason over custom. They fix their minds on the sublime and let their bodies change with the season. All phenomena are empty. They contain nothing worth desiring. Calamity forever alternates with Prosperity. To dwell in the three realms is to dwell in a burning house. To have a body is to suffer. Does anybody with a body know peace?

In this passage a few things certainly give the flavor of Bodhidharma, but a few things look not of the same quality. For example, *seeking nothing* is Bodhidharma. *The wise wake up...* this is Bodhidharma. *They choose reason over custom.* I would like to change the word reason to meditation. They choose meditation over custom. They choose their own intelligence over custom and tradition.

This certainly cannot be from Bodhidharma. *They fix their minds on the sublime and let their bodies change with the season.* The man who is saying that the sinner and the saint are the same, the ordinary man and the sage are not different, cannot make this statement – because for him the mundane and the sublime are not different, they cannot be different.

Yes, this statement can be confirmed as Bodhidharma's: *All phenomena are empty.* Whatever happens outside you in life is just empty, as empty as dreams; it is made of the same stuff. *The wise wake up* and see the whole of life as a long series of dreams – sometimes good, sometimes bad, sometimes sweet, sometimes nightmarish, but they are all dreams. The awakened one neither dreams in his sleep nor is deluded by the dreams of the outside world while he is awake. They contain nothing worth desiring.

Calamity forever alternates with Prosperity. To dwell in the three realms is to dwell in a burning house. The three realms are of the body, of the mind and of the heart. To dwell in the fourth, the *turiya,* is to be at peace with existence.

Fourth, practicing the Dharma. The Dharma is the truth that all natures are pure. By this truth all appearances are empty. Defilement and attachment, subject and object don't exist.

This can be said to be purely Bodhidharma.

The sutras say, "The Dharma includes no being because it is free from the impurity of being. And the Dharma includes no self, because it is free from the impurity of self." Those wise enough to believe and understand this truth are bound to practice according to the Dharma.

These are additions by the people who are taking notes.

Since the embodiment of the Dharma contains nothing worth begrudging, they give their body, life and property in charity, without regret, without the vanity of giver, gift or recipient, and without bias or attachment. And they take up transforming others to eliminate impurity but without becoming attached to form. Thus, through their own practice, they are able to help others and glorify the Way of Enlightenment. And as with charity, they also practice the other virtues. But while practicing the six virtues to eliminate delusion, they practice nothing at all.

All the statements above this sentence cannot be authentically said to be from Bodhidharma. But this sentence, *they practice nothing at all...*

The people who are practicing all these things recorded before, are practicing nothing, because if the world is only a dream land, then whether you are a thief or a great man of charity, makes no difference. In a dream, if you are a thief or a man of charity, will it make any difference when you wake up? Will you feel good that you were such a great man of charity? Or will you feel ashamed that in the dream you were a thief? Both were dreams, soap bubbles; they don't mean anything.

Knowing Bodhidharma, I can say exactly what are his words. *They practice nothing at all* – the people who are practicing the abovementioned things... *This is what is meant by practicing the Dharma.*

Bodhidharma is saying: Knowing this – that whatever you are practicing is nothing at all – *this* knowing, this understanding is called practicing the dharma.

Those who understand this detach themselves from all that exists and stop imagining or seeking anything. The sutras say, "To seek is to suffer. To seek nothing is bliss." This is pure Bodhidharma. When you seek nothing, you are on the Path.

So it is going to be a continuous effort to draw lines, between what exactly are Bodhidharma's statements and what are statements by the writers of these books, these notes. But I can say it with authority, because this is my own understanding and experience too: I agree with Bodhidharma on each and every point. In other words, Bodhidharma agrees with me on each and every point.

Scholars have been talking about these books. I am not a scholar. I am a Bodhidharma. I will recognize what is my statement and what is not my statement.

Get it?

Okay, Maneesha?

Yes, Bhagwan.

達磨

Beloved Bhagwan,

Bodhidharma's Bloodstream Sermon

Everything that appears in the three realms leads back to the mind. Hence, buddhas of the past and future teach mind to mind without bothering about definitions.
But if they don't define it, what do they mean by mind?
You ask. That's your mind. I answer. That's my mind. If I had no mind, how could I answer? If you had no mind, how could you ask? That which asks is your mind. Through endless *kalpas* without beginning, whatever you do, wherever you are, that's your real mind, that's your real buddha. *This mind is the buddha,* says the same thing. Beyond this mind you'll never find another buddha. To search for enlightenment or nirvana beyond this mind is impossible. The reality of your own self-nature, the absence of cause and effect, is what's meant by mind. Your mind is nirvana. You might think you can find a buddha or enlightenment somewhere beyond the mind, but such a place doesn't exist.

Trying to find a buddha or enlightenment is like trying to grab space. Space has a name but no form. It's not something you can pick up or put down. And you certainly can't grab it. Beyond this mind, you'll never see a buddha. The buddha is a product of your mind. Why look for a buddha beyond this mind?

Buddhas of the past and future only talk about this mind. The mind is the buddha. And the buddha is the mind. Beyond the mind there's no buddha. And beyond the buddha there's no mind. If you think there's a buddha beyond the mind, where is he? There's no buddha beyond the mind, so why envision one? You can't know your real mind as long as you deceive yourself. As long as you're

ENSŌ: CIRCLE __ 23

enthralled by a lifeless form, you're not free. If you don't believe me, deceiving yourself doesn't help. It's not the buddha's fault. People, though, are deluded. They're unaware that their own mind is the buddha. Otherwise, they wouldn't look for a buddha outside the mind.

Buddhas don't save buddhas. If you use your mind to look for a buddha, you won't see the buddha. As long as you look for a buddha somewhere else, you'll never see that your own mind is the buddha. And don't use a buddha to worship a buddha. And don't use the mind to invoke a buddha. Buddhas don't recite sutras. Buddhas don't keep precepts. And buddhas don't break precepts. Buddhas don't keep or break anything. Buddhas don't do good or evil.

To find a buddha, you have to see your nature. Whoever sees his nature is a buddha. If you don't see your nature, invoking buddhas, reciting sutras, making offerings and keeping precepts are all useless. Invoking buddhas results in good karma. Reciting sutras results in a good memory. Keeping precepts results in a good rebirth. And making offerings results in future blessings. But no buddha.

THE REALIZATION OF enlightenment, or buddhahood, is difficult. And it is also not difficult. It is difficult if you start looking for it. It is not difficult if you simply sit down, settling within yourself in calmness, quietness, being just purely aware. Then you are the buddha, then you are the enlightenment. It is not that you become enlightened, it is not your becoming. It is your very being, it is you in your simplest, spontaneous nature.

Enlightenment is your self-nature.

Once somebody attains to enlightenment, the greatest difficulty is to convey it to those who are living in darkness and who have never seen any light. It is almost like talking about light to blind people. One enlightened master has been reported to have said, "My whole effort of conveying my experience is just like selling glasses to blind people."

Hence, many of those who have attained have remained silent, and those very few who have spoken, know that their words cannot carry their enlightenment, its beauty, its joy, its fragrance; that the moment the experience is translated into words, something essential dies. Only a corpse reaches to the other person.

But out of compassion, hoping against hope, a few enlightened people down the ages have made every effort to convey to you that life is not all that you think it is. It is much more, infinitely much more.

But no enlightened man has ever written a single word, for the simple reason that the spoken word has a certain warmth, and the written word is absolutely cold. The spoken word has the presence of the master, but the written word has no presence of the master. The spoken word is not just a word; there are so many other things which may be indirectly conveyed to you. The presence of the master, the blissfulness of the master, the grace of the master, his inviting eyes, his heart calling you, invoking you for a journey, for a pilgrimage to your own being...all this is absent in the written word.

Hence, no enlightened man has ever written anything. But disciples have taken notes. All the literature that exists in the name of enlightened people is nothing but disciples' notes. The problem becomes more and more complicated because the disciple is writing something which he does not understand. He loves the master, he has fallen into a deep love affair, but he does not understand the mystery of the master. He is under his magical influence, but he does not know his secret. Unless he knows his own secret he will never know the secret of the master, because they are not two things.

The disciple thinks, has been thinking for ages, that the words of the master should not be lost; they are so precious, they are pure gold. At least something for the future generations should be collected. But his understanding is very small, and he writes according to his understanding. First, much is lost when the master speaks; then much is lost when the disciple hears; then much is lost when the disciple writes. And the disciple writes in one language, and then it goes on being translated into other languages. It becomes a faraway echo of the original.

For example, Bodhidharma spoke in Chinese, which was not his mother tongue. He was born in India. He learned Chinese. Even in your own mother tongue, to give expression to the experiences of your innermost life sources, silences of your heart, and blissfulness of your being, is difficult – even in your mother tongue. But to speak in a language which he has just learned, and Chinese is not a simple language.... If one really wants to be a scholar it needs at least thirty years, because it has no alphabet, it is a pictorial language. It is a very primitive sort of language.

The alphabet brings language to a very simple phenomenon. But a non-alphabetical language, like Chinese, or Korean, or Japanese, is very difficult for one who is not born in those lands. You have to remember thousands of pictures. Those languages are pictorial. Each thing has a certain symbolic picture and unless you remember thousands of symbolic pictures, it is impossible to speak, it is impossible to write. Bodhidharma had only three years while he was moving towards China to learn as quickly as possible before he reached there. He did in three years, almost thirty years' work.

Naturally, what he has said is far from his experience. And the difficulty is again multiplied because these sutras are translated from Chinese into English. For example, I will just give you one word which is very central to these sutras, the word 'mind'.

Anybody reading these sutras is going to understand exactly the opposite of what Bodhidharma must have meant, and the reason is the word 'mind'.

In English there is only one word for your thinking process, and that is 'mind'. And in the English language there is no word which can denote something beyond the thinking process. The whole philosophy of Gautam Buddha and Bodhidharma is how to go beyond the thinking process. In Sanskrit, in Pali, there are different words: *manus,* which is the root of the English word 'mind', exactly means *thinking process;* then *chitta* means *consciousness beyond the thinking process.*

Those who are very alert, and those who have not only been just scholars but have also experienced something about meditation – wherever in these sutras you find the word 'mind', a meditator would put just its opposite, 'no-mind'. English has no word for no-mind, so it is just an arbitrary creation. Everywhere in these sutras, where mind is mentioned, please read no-mind. Otherwise you will go absolutely on a wrong track.

The sutras: *Everything that appears in the three realms leads back to the no-mind.*

The translator says, "to the mind." Mind is something to be transcended, mind is a disease; meditation is an effort to go beyond it. Hence, I will read everywhere instead of 'mind', 'no-mind', to correct the translation. The translation is done by somebody who understands language but who does not understand meditation.

Everything that appears in the three realms... Which are the three realms? The body, the mind, the heart...leads to the fourth, *turiya,* which can be translated only as no-mind; leads to a silence where there is no ripple of thought, where time disappears, space disappears and just a pure consciousness, not conscious of any thing, but conscious of itself...a self-luminous awareness remains. Everything leads to this self-luminous awareness.

The people who understand meditation have always translated the word *chitta* as 'no-mind'.

Hence, buddhas of the past and future teach mind to mind, without bothering about definitions. This is so ridiculous, but scholars are really doing something that they are not prepared for. The right thing would be to say, "Buddhas of the past and future, teach no-mind to no-mind, from silence to silence, from presence to presence. And naturally, in that transfer from silence to silence, in that transmission from being to being, there is no place for definitions."

Definitions are part of the mind. The moment you transcend mind, you transcend all definitions. Now the disciple's mind comes in: *But if they don't define it, what do they mean by mind?* This is so stupid, it is unbelievably ridiculous. The disciple himself who has taken these notes is puzzled. He asks, *But if they don't define it, what do they mean by mind?* And he answers to satisfy himself: *You ask. That's your mind. I answer. That's my mind.* It is true about the disciple, but not true about the enlightened being, who does not express himself through the words. Even if he uses the words, that is only a device to create moments of silence.

The real transfer happens in the gaps. Nothing is said, and nothing is heard, and yet the message takes a quantum leap from one being to another being. This is the beauty and the miracle and the magic that happens between the master and the disciple.

The disciple quotes Bodhidharma as saying, *If I had no mind, how could I answer? If you had no mind, how could you ask? That which asks is your mind. Through endless kalpas,* through endless ages, *without beginning, whatever you do, wherever you are, that is your real mind, that is your real buddha.*

He is getting really confused. But anybody will be in the same position, not knowing that meditation is a transcendence, a freedom from mind. It is a beyond space, where no functioning of the mind can ever reach.

And that is your true nature, that is your enlightenment, that is your buddhahood. And out of that silence, whatever you do is enlightened. Out of that silence, whatever grows is a lotus of paradise. Out of that silence you cannot do anything wrong. In fact, out of that silence the very idea, the distinction between wrong and right, good and bad, disappears. Whatever you do out of that silence is simply existential, the way it should be. It is not your effort, it is not your thought-out, pre-planned act; it is simply your spontaneous outpouring.

This mind is the buddha. Let me correct it.

This no-*mind is the buddha. Beyond this* no- *mind, you will never find another buddha. To search for enlightenment or nirvana, beyond this* no-*mind, is impossible. The reality of your own self-nature, the absence of cause and effect, is what is meant by* no-*mind. Your* no-*mind is nirvana* – but remember wherever I am saying no-mind, in the sutra itself is written mind. I disagree with it totally, and Bodhidharma would disagree with it, and Buddha would disagree with it, and anybody who has even a little glimpse of meditation will disagree with it.

You might think you can find a buddha or enlightenment somewhere beyond no-*mind, but such a place doesn't exist.*

Trying to find a buddha or enlightenment is like trying to grab space. Space has a name but no form. It's not something you can pick up or put down. And you certainly can't grab it. Beyond this no-*mind you'll never see a buddha. The buddha is a product of your* no-*mind.*

In fact no-mind and buddha are synonymous. But the poor disciple who has taken these notes goes on using the word 'mind' which is absolutely absurd.

Why look for a buddha beyond this no-*mind?*

Buddhas of the past and future only talk about this no-*mind. This* no-*mind is the buddha. And the buddha is the* no-*mind. Beyond the* no-*mind there is no buddha. And beyond the buddha there is no* no-*mind. If you think there is a buddha beyond the* no-*mind, where is he?*

The same mistake continues all along the sutra. It is the ancientmost sutra about Bodhidharma, and for almost fourteen centuries it has been accepted as Bodhidharma's teaching. And the reason is that nobody tries to understand the experience by experiencing it. People simply read scriptures, they become knowledgeable, but deep inside the ignorance prevails. They start talking about light, but their blindness continues. That's why he says, *You think there is a buddha beyond the mind.* There is the buddha *only* beyond the mind; it is not a question of thinking, but this stupid disciple says there is no buddha beyond the mind. He has made it a point that buddha and mind are synonymous. Then what is the need of meditation? You all have minds; you have enough of buddha – do you need more mind?

You need freedom from the mind, freedom from all the fetters of thought, emotions, moods, sentiments; they all constitute your mind. And beyond them there is a witness, a watcher.

That watcher is the buddha.

I have to be hard on this disciple, although he has done a service to humanity. He has kept a record of Bodhidharma's words, although he is not capable of keeping the record in a right way. But still, his record can be corrected by anybody of the same state as Bodhidharma. So there is no problem. He has done a great service, although he is stupid.

Once in a while, he repeats Bodhidharma: *You can't know your real no-mind as long as you deceive yourself. As long as you are enthralled by a lifeless form, you are not free.*

What is your imprisonment? Your mind is your prison. There are different prisons, but they are all prisons. The Hindu has a different kind of prison, different architecture; the Mohammedan has a different prison, different architecture; the Christian has a different prison, and so on and so forth. But they differ only in their architecture. As far as the prisoner is concerned, they are all prisons. And people move from one prison to another prison in the hope that perhaps they will find freedom. The Christian becomes the Hindu, the Hindu becomes the Buddhist, the Buddhist becomes the Mohammedan and they are simply changing prisons. From one program they move to another program, and what is needed is a deprogramming. That's what, in scientific terms is the meaning of the word 'meditation' – deprogramming.

If your mind can be completely deprogrammed, it can become a completely erased tabula rasa, a clean slate from which every knowledge has been erased. This innocence is the beginning of no-mind. This innocence is the birth of the buddha in you.

If you don't believe me, deceiving yourself doesn't help. It is not the buddha's fault. People, though, are deluded. They're unaware that their own no-mind is the buddha. Otherwise, they wouldn't look for a buddha outside the no-mind.

The greatest delusion according to those who have reached to the highest peak of awareness, is searching and seeking outside yourself for the truth, the meaning of existence, or the deathless, eternal current of life. Mind always tries to look outside, because the very function of the mind is to work in the world. That's why mind is perfectly okay in science, in business, in economics. In everything that is outside you, then mind is perfectly the right means.

But that which is within you is beyond mind's reach. You will have to leave the mind, and move above and away. The moment you become only a witness, watching the mind as something outside you, you have come home. But the man who took the notes and the man who translated them into English...perhaps neither had experience of meditation. They go on repeating the word 'mind' where only 'no-mind' is ever possible.

Buddhas don't save buddhas. Now this I can say must have come from Bodhidharma. This is such a tremendously meaningful statement, and so outrageous that it is beyond the capacity of the poor disciple, who cannot even understand it. He has simply written it, he must have heard it. Perhaps Bodhidharma was again and again repeating it. This is one of the most essential teachings of Gautam Buddha, that nobody can save you.

Jesus says, "I am the savior." If you compare Jesus and Bodhidharma, you will be in for a great surprise. Jesus says, "You are the sheep, I am the shepherd and if you get lost, I will find you." And it looks, for those who don't understand, to be a great compassionate ideology. Jesus seems to be of great compassion, love, kindness. In fact Christians say that he sacrificed himself to save humanity, but nobody asks why humanity is not saved. The poor fellow died unnecessarily.

I have always been wondering.... I have been listening to Christians, and without feeling any embarrassment they go on saying that Jesus gave up his life to save humanity. I used to be very friendly with a preacher, Stanley Jones, who was a reknowned Christian missionary and had a very philosophical bent of mind. Whenever he used to come into the city where I was, I always used to go to listen to him. One day it was too much; he was continuously repeating that "Jesus is the only savior."

I had to stand up. I said, "It is not my business, I am not a Christian and in fact, I should not create any disturbance in the church; I don't belong to the congregation. But you are repeating such nonsense. You go on saying that he saved humanity by giving up his life on the cross. But I don't see humanity saved anywhere. He could not even save himself."

But all the religions born outside India have the idea of the savior. Mohammedanism, Judaism, Christianity – three religions are born outside India and all three have the idea of the savior. In India there are four religions: Hinduism, Sikhism, Jainism, Buddhism. Jainism and Buddhism are the only two religions which simply deny the very concept of saving anybody, because they say – and I agree with their concept – that it is condemnatory, it is humiliating. The very idea that "I will save you" makes me higher than you, and holier than you. I become special. I am the only begotten son of God, or I am the only prophet of God, or the only messenger of God, and you are just ordinary human beings.

Bodhidharma's statement is, *Buddhas don't save buddhas.* He is saying you are all buddhas whether you know it or not, and how can anybody save you? How can one buddha save another buddha? All that a buddha can do is to wake you up. That is not much of a saving. When you wake somebody up, do you think you are holier, and special, and you have done a great service to humanity, by waking a poor fellow who was sleeping?

Buddhas don't save buddhas. This is a very pregnant statement. It gives equality to every being. The only difference, which is not much of a difference, is...everybody is a buddha; a few are asleep and are unaware of who they are, and a few have become awakened and know who they are. But essentially, there is no difference at all, and there is no question of saving anybody. It is his right if somebody wants to continue to sleep; it is his birthright. You cannot forcibly wake up somebody because that is interfering with his freedom.

It happened: I was sitting on the banks of the Ganges in Allahabad. I had gone to speak in a Christian college in Allahabad, and the Christian college is just on the bank of the Ganges on a very beautiful spot just near the railway bridge. I was sitting on the bank, and there was nobody for miles and suddenly a man came and jumped. I thought perhaps he was taking a bath, and as he jumped, he started shouting, "Help me, help me." He was just close to me.

For a moment I thought, "What is the matter? If he wanted to be helped, why has he jumped?" But I thought it is better to first bring him out. If I start thinking about it, by that time he will be finished. So I jumped. He was a heavy man but I pulled him out somehow, and I felt a certain resistance. It became even more puzzling, he was shouting, "Save me, I am drowning." But when I was trying to bring him out, I felt that he was not being helpful, he was resisting my effort.

I said, "You seem to be mad. Do you want to be saved or not?"

He said, "Please save me." So I pulled him out. And when he was out, he started becoming very angry at me saying, "Can't you understand? I was committing suicide."

I said, "You should have said so before. So why were you shouting, 'Save me'?"

He said, "It is natural. I wanted to commit suicide but deep down somewhere there was still a desire to live. That's why I started shouting."

I said, "Okay." I simply pushed him back. I said, "If this is the case, then I will not do anything against you."

He started shouting again, "Are you mad or what? Do you want to kill me?"

I said, "Now I have nothing to do with you. Whatever I have done, I have undone it. Now I will sit silently here and watch."

Somebody else came by and jumped in and took him out. This time he did not give any resistance but he went on looking at me. I said, "What is the matter, where are you going?"

He said, "Is it compulsory to commit suicide?"

I said, "It is not; I have never told you to commit suicide. You were committing suicide; have you forgotten?"

He said, "You seem to be a strange man. When somebody commits suicide, or tries to commit suicide, people prevent him – but you help them."

I said, "I am ready to help in any way. If you want to get out of the river, I am ready to help. If you want to go in the river, I am ready to help. I don't want to interfere in your lifestyle whatever you want to do."

He said, "I don't want to die."

I said, "That's perfectly okay. You can go, but think twice. You may have to come back again."

He said, "I am not going to come back."

I said, "It is up to you. I am just reminding you that the idea of suicide will come again to you, and this is a good chance. Don't miss it. Ordinarily, there are so many people on the bank. Just by chance there is nobody – only a man who is ready to help in any way, this way or that."

He said, "As long as you are here, I am not going to come back!"

I said, "It is up to you. Without me you will be in difficulty."

Bodhidharma is saying, *Buddhas don't save buddhas.* Buddhas simply make every effort to wake people to their own reality, but it is not a question of saving. They are buddhas already, nothing has to be added. This is one of the greatest contributions of Buddhism and Jainism. But again and again that disciple is bound to commit mistakes; he is simply helpless. This sentence he has put exactly as it should be.

But again he starts: *If you use your mind to look for a buddha, you won't see the buddha. As long as you look for a buddha somewhere else, you will never see that your own* no-*mind is the buddha.* He is saying mind, I am reading no-mind.

And don't use a buddha to worship a buddha. Again, this statement I can say with absolute authority, comes from Bodhidharma. *Don't use a buddha to worship a buddha.* Just as a buddha cannot save another buddha, so it is absolutely idiotic that one buddha should worship another buddha. Buddhism is against worship.

The last words of Gautam Buddha were, "Don't make my statues, don't make my temples, because my whole life I have been teaching you that you are a buddha, and you don't have to worship another buddha." And particularly if a stone buddha is being worshiped by a living buddha; this is sheer absurdity.

And don't use the mind to invoke a buddha. Buddhas don't recite sutras. Buddhas don't keep precepts. And buddhas don't break precepts. Buddhas don't keep or break anything. Buddhas don't do good or evil.

These statements must be coming directly from Bodhidharma because it is beyond the capacity of the disciple to say such great things. Bodhidharma is saying that buddhas don't follow any discipline except their own awareness. They don't follow any scriptures except their own light. Neither do they follow anything nor do they break anything. They do neither good nor evil. They simply act out of spontaneity which is beyond good and evil.

Buddhas are not puritans or moralists. They act out of pure consciousness and their actions are not decided by any ideals, by any precepts, by any sutras. They don't recite any sutras. They don't bother about holy scriptures because they know their own awareness is enough to show them the path and to lead them to their ultimate destiny.

To find a buddha, you have to see your nature. Whoever sees his nature is a buddha. If you don't see your nature, invoking buddhas, reciting sutras, making offerings and keeping precepts are all useless.

These words certainly have the ring and the sound of a man of awareness. They must be coming from Bodhidharma. But the disciple is not satisfied, he must be feeling a little uneasy. The whole idea that reciting sutras, making offerings, and keeping precepts are all useless...he must be feeling uneasy because these are all irreligious ideas. No ordinary religion is going to accept them.

Hence, the disciple immediately puts his own ideas. *Invoking buddhas results in good karma.* Now this is his addition. Just now it was *useless,* but he could not feel at ease with the word useless. He had to write it because Bodhidharma must have been saying it, but he is free to dilute it. In fact, he starts changing its whole tone.

Invoking buddhas results in good karma. Reciting sutras results in a good memory. Keeping precepts results in a good rebirth. And making offerings results in future blessings. But no buddha.

The disciple has been trying hard to put the words of Bodhidharma exactly, but it must have been a great effort and a great tension for him because what Bodhidharma is saying can be understood only by people of great meditation. It is not possible for it to be understood by so-called ordinary humanity. It goes against all ordinary religions, ordinary prophets, ordinary messengers of God, ordinary holy scriptures.

Feeling uneasy, the disciple makes some additions on his own part. Now if a man reads these sutras without having a taste of meditation, he is bound to be in confusion, and he is bound to be misled by the additions. The disciple is mixing, and polluting the pure crystal clear water of Bodhidharma with all kinds of crap, because he cannot tolerate such a crystal clear approach, so refined.

Although there have been many enlightened people in the lineage of Gautam

Buddha, Bodhidharma became the most famous. He is not the founder of Zen Buddhism; the founder of Zen is Mahakashyapa. But even Mahakashyapa has faded. Bodhidharma is not the founder but he has become the most important enlightened person after Gautam Buddha just because of his outrageousness, his non-compromising approach. He is not going to console anybody; he is simply going to say the truth. Whether it hurts you or heals you it is up to you, but he is not going to add a single word just to console you, because every consolation is putting you into sleep. Every consolation is a kind of opium.

Bodhidharma is absolutely strict. That's why he is painted as a ferocious looking man. It does not mean that he was like that. He was a prince, and I don't think that the way he has been painted down the centuries is his actual photograph. It is rather the experience of those who had to deal with him – he was ferocious. And he was ferocious because he would not say any consolatory words, he would simply say the naked truth. If it hurts you, good. Perhaps you need to be hurt and only that will awaken you. You don't need any consolation, because that will put you into a deeper sleep.

Bodhidharma is unique, and I can understand why his disciple could not understand. That must have been the case with many people who heard him. At the last moment when he wanted to choose a successor – he had chosen only four disciples, and from four he was going to choose one successor. He was really strict; perhaps the most strict master the world has ever known, but the most compassionate, because his strictness is nothing but his compassion.

Okay, Maneesha?

Yes, Bhagwan.

BEYOND THIS NATURE THERE'S NO BUDDHA

達磨

36 __ SAN SUI: MOUNTAIN-WATER

Beloved Bhagwan,

If you don't understand by yourself, you'll have to find a teacher to get to the bottom of life and death. But unless he sees his nature, such a person isn't a teacher. Even if he can recite the Twelvefold Canon, he can't escape the Wheel of Birth and Death. He suffers in the three realms without hope of release.

Long ago, the monk Good Star was able to recite the entire Canon. But he didn't escape the Wheel because he didn't see his nature. If this was the case with Good Star, then people nowadays who recite a few sutras or shastras and think it's the Dharma are fools. Unless

you see your mind, reciting so much prose is useless.

To find a buddha, all you have to do is see your nature. Your nature is the buddha. And the buddha is the person who's free, free of plans, free of cares. If you don't see your nature and run around all day looking somewhere else, you'll never find a buddha. The truth is, there's nothing to find. But to reach such an understanding you need a teacher. And you need to struggle to make yourself understand. Life and death are important. Don't suffer them in vain. There's no advantage in deceiving yourself. Even if you have mountains of jewels and as many servants as there are grains of sand along the Ganges, you see them when your eyes are open. But what about when your eyes are shut? You should realize then that everything you see is like a dream or illusion.

If you don't find a teacher soon, you'll live this life in vain. It's true, you have the buddha-nature. But without the help of a teacher you'll never know it. Only one person in a million becomes enlightened without a teacher's help.

If though, by the conjunction of conditions, someone understands what the Buddha meant, that person doesn't need a teacher. Such a person has a natural awareness superior to anything taught. But unless you're so blessed, study hard. And by means of instruction, you'll understand.

People who don't understand and think they can do so without study are no different from those deluded souls who can't tell white from black. Falsely proclaiming the Buddhadharma, such persons, in fact, blaspheme the Buddha and subvert the Dharma. They preach as if they were bringing rain. But theirs is the preaching of devils not of buddhas. Their teacher is the King of Devils. And their disciples are the Devil's minions. Deluded people who follow such instruction unwittingly sink deeper in the Sea of Birth and Death.

Unless they see their nature, how can people call

themselves buddhas? They're liars who deceive others into entering the realm of devils. Unless they see their nature, their preaching of the Twelvefold Canon is nothing but the preaching of devils. Their allegiance is to Mara, not to the Buddha. Unable to distinguish white from black, how can they escape birth and death?

Whoever sees his nature is a buddha. Whoever doesn't is a mortal. But apart from our mortal nature if you can find a buddha-nature somewhere else, where is it? Our mortal nature is our buddha-nature. Beyond this nature there's no buddha. The buddha is our nature. There's no buddha besides this nature. And there's no nature besides the buddha.

SANSKRIT, PRAKRIT, AND Pali, three languages used in the past by the enlightened people of this land, have a very rich vocabulary as far as inner experiences are concerned. The West today has a very exact language to express scientific research, discoveries, inventions and technologies, but the Eastern languages don't have this. However, as far as the interior experience is concerned, the Eastern languages are immensely rich while the Western languages are absolutely poor. Of these three languages, Sanskrit has been used by the Upanishads and the Hindu mystics, Prakrit has been used by Mahavira and all the Jaina mystics and masters, and Pali has been used by Gautam Buddha.

Just for the word 'teacher', they have many words, all with slight differences. The first word is *sikshak;* that means a man who only imparts information. He may know, he may not know – that is irrelevant. But his information is correct; he is a man of the mind.

The second word, which goes a little deeper into experience, not just information, is *adhyapak.* That teacher is not only an informer but he himself is informed. It is not only a mental thing for him; it is part – but only a part – of his heart, too.

And the third word is *upadhyay* which goes a little more deeper into experience. This teacher's information is more alive than the previous two. He has traveled the path, but he has not reached the goal.

And then finally the *acharya,* who has reached the goal, and the information that he imparts is his own experience. He is his own authority, his own argument; his own presence is the whole evidence.

But in English there is only one word, teacher, which is used for all kinds of people. The other word is master, which is not used very much by the English speaking people themselves. But I would like to use the word master, equivalent to the word acharya: One who knows, not only through mind, but through experience.

Most of the sutras in this part are unpolluted. The disciple has simply noted them down as Bodhidharma must have spoken them.

If you don't understand by yourself, you will have to find a teacher.

Instead of teacher, the word master would be right because a teacher is one who teaches you about things of the outside world. Even if he teaches about the inner experiences, it is borrowed. He may be knowledgeable but he is not knowledge itself. To make the distinction, the translator has made the point in a different way.

If you don't understand by yourself, you will have to find a teacher to get to the bottom of life and death. But unless he sees his nature, such a person is not a teacher.

It is better to call a man who has reached to the highest peaks of experience a master, and leave the word teacher for those who impart knowledge from one generation to another. And master, also has a dignity of its own.

The teacher is almost like a computer. He has read, he has studied, he may have crammed all scriptures but his presence does not indicate that he knows anything. His actions are not arguments for what he says. His sayings come only from the superficial layer of the mind; they are not coming from the innermost core of his being. The teacher cannot teach without words. But the master, on the contrary, cannot teach without silences. If he uses words, it is only to create silence.

The master is a living example of what he is saying. The teacher simply shows a very well-versed, educated mind. The master shows a transformed being, a luminous presence. Anybody who has eyes can see it...his grace, his beauty, his blissfulness, his laughter; even in his silence much is said, without words. Even his silence is a song of the ultimate; even unmoving, he is a dance expressing the dance of the whole universe. The master is so far away from the teacher that it is better to use the word separately.

I would prefer to say: If you don't understand by yourself, you will have to get a master, because the master knows his own nature. And by knowing his own nature, he also knows the nature of every living being because it is the *same* nature. By knowing himself, he knows you too. His knowledge, his knowing, is a bridge between him and his disciples.

Even if the teacher can recite the Twelvefold Canon, he can't escape the Wheel of Birth and Death. He suffers in the three realms without hope of release.

Just knowledgeability is not going to give you the experience of your immortality or your eternity or your oneness with the whole. It fills your mind with many words, but it leaves your being empty and hollow. You don't know anything firsthand, and truth can only be known firsthand. The moment it is secondhand, it is no longer truth; it is just a dead word, with no life.

The man of great knowledge, a scholar, a pundit, a rabbi, is not going to get free from the wheel of birth and death. And he is not going to be free from the suffering in the three realms. According to Gautam Buddha, heaven, the earth, and hell, all three are nothing but different kinds of sufferings. Buddhism reaches to the highest peak, because even heaven is not considered to be the ultimate home. It is still a suffering – very refined suffering, but suffering all the same. One has to be free from all three; then it is nirvana, then it is enlightenment.

Long ago, the monk Good Star was able to recite the entire Canon. But he did not escape the Wheel because he did not see his nature. If this was the case with Good Star, then people nowadays who recite a few sutras or shastras and think it's the Dharma are fools.

It can be taken for granted that Bodhidharma must have said this. It is beyond the capacity of a disciple to call knowledgeable people who can recite all the Buddhist sutras, fools. Only Bodhidharma can do that, not out of any arrogance, not out of any ego, not to condemn them, not to humiliate or insult them, but for Bodhidharma, it is simply the fact.

And the fact has to be stated. He is not a man of manners and etiquette and all that rubbish. He simply says whatsoever is the truth. I absolutely agree with him. My own experience with great learned scholars is that they are learned fools. They have big degrees, great honors from universities, but as far as their own consciousness is concerned, it is of the same quality as anybody else's. They are just parrots.

And perhaps parrots are more intelligent than your pundits.

I have heard about a parrot: It was wintertime and the lady to whom the parrot belonged used to cover the parrot and his cage with a thick blanket so that he would not feel cold. In the day she used to remove the blanket. One day she removed the blanket as the sun was rising and the parrot started singing, the way all parrots sing, not a song taught to him, but a song that is natural and spontaneous to all the parrots even if they are wild – meaningless to us, but tremendously joyful to them. And just then the lady heard her husband's car stopping near the porch. Her husband was on an emergency army duty, so once in a while he used to come home without notice.

She immediately put the blanket back on the parrot and went to her bed. The parrot said, "My God, today's day has been very short." Now nobody has taught him this. This was coming out of his own intelligence. It was strange…every day the blanket was removed in the morning, and in the evening the blanket was put back. What happened today? The day had been really too short.

But your so-called learned people around the world don't have even that much intelligence, for the simple reason that their knowledge becomes mountainous and every possibility of intelligence becomes lost in their knowledge. The burden of knowledge is too heavy. They cannot afford to be intelligent against their knowledge.

They are certainly fools – fools because they are not only deceiving others by talking to them about things they know nothing of, but because they are also deceiving themselves. And they are wasting their life in mere words.

Authentic life consists of experiences, not mere words. You can go on repeating "love, love, love," your whole life, and still you will not have an experience of love. And the moment you have the experience of love, you will be suddenly surprised that the experience is so vast that the word 'love' cannot contain it; it is too small.

If this is the case with love, what will be the case with truth? – because truth is infinite, eternal. To know it means to become silent.

Just the presence of truth, the feeling of it, leaves you in a state of awe. All words fall short.

Unless you see your no-*mind*…. Here the disciple falls back to his own understanding; he again uses the word 'mind'.

Unless you see your no-*mind, reciting so much prose is useless.*

And if you know your no-mind, then too reciting so much prose is useless because then there is no point in reciting it. You have come to the very source from which every buddha has spoken. Now there is no meaning in scriptures, sutras, and shastras. The holy books can't give you more than you know already.

To find a buddha, all you have to do is to see your nature.

That's what I have been telling you again and again. The only way out of ignorance and out of this dark night of the soul is to be aware of your own being, aware of your own awareness. In that moment when you are aware of your own awareness, everything stops, time stops. Suddenly you are beyond time and beyond space, and a door opens which makes you part of the whole. This is the inner mathematics, that the part of the whole is not smaller than the whole. That will be difficult to understand. The part of the whole is equal to the whole, because the whole cannot be divided into parts. Division is not possible.

That's why we call the real authentic being in you 'individual'. Individual means indivisible – that which cannot be divided. So the moment you feel yourself part of the whole, that is the beginning – the first encounter with the whole. Soon you will realize you are not the part, you are the whole because there is no possibility of any division.

Your nature is the buddha. And the buddha is the person who is free, free of plans, free of cares. If you don't see your nature and run around all day looking somewhere else, you will never find enlightenment.

The truth is, there is nothing to find so all your running is useless. I can testify this statement must be coming from Bodhidharma himself.

There is nothing to find. You are all.

The finder itself is the treasure; there is nothing else to find. Hence, I have told you that Jesus' statement, "Seek, and ye shall find, knock and the door shall be opened unto you, ask and it shall be given," is beautiful, poetic, impressive, but not true.

If you follow Bodhidharma, he will say, "Seek, and you shall never find," because every seeking takes you away from yourself. Who are you trying to find? You are the one, you are the buddha. Where are you going?

Do not knock, otherwise the door will be closed because your very knocking is a desire, is a demand – and a buddha has no desire, no demand. That's why the door is always open for him.

Do not ask, otherwise you will go on missing. Who are you asking? There is no one to give it to you. You have already got it. In asking you are wandering away, you are looking up to somebody else. And nobody can give it to you. There is no question of giving it to you, you have got it already.

So all that is needed is neither seeking, nor knocking, nor asking. All that is needed is to be aware of your own nature and you have found it. There is nothing to find. But to reach such an understanding you need a master.

Why do you need a master? Because you already have the truth within you, why can't you just relax and become conscious of it?

The problem is that for ages your consciousness has been wandering all over the world. It has forgotten the way to come home. It has been a long, long time since you left home and now you don't know whether you have a home or whether you ever had a home. Your remembrance of home seems to be as if you have seen it in a movie or in a dream, or you have read about it somewhere.

It is a faraway echo in the valleys; it does not give you a certainty.

Hence, the need of a master. The master is nothing but a certainty. His presence makes it absolutely certain that there is much more within you than you ever dreamt of. His eyes give you a glimpse of your own possibility. His silence provokes a silence in you and his authority triggers a process in you.

Bodhidharma is right:

But to reach such an understanding you need a teacher. And you need to struggle to make yourself understand. Life and death are important. Don't suffer them in vain. There is no advantage in deceiving yourself.

And everybody is deceiving: a few are deceiving by earning money and thinking that when they are super-rich they will have reached to the realization of their potential; a few are deceiving by accumulating knowledge; a few are deceiving by becoming powerful, respectable; a few are even deceiving by becoming saints, ascetics. But whatever you do, unless it leads to awareness of your nature, it is a deceiving.

Even if you have mountains of jewels and as many servants as there are grains of sand along the Ganges, you see them when your eyes are open. But what about when your eyes are shut?

They all disappear. Bodhidharma is saying that this is just a small experiment for you. As you close your eyes, your palaces disappear, your whole world disappears almost in the same way as when in the morning, you open your eyes, all your dreams disappear. And have you ever watched one very strange thing? In the day sometimes, you can suspect perhaps it is not real because there is no way to be certain about its reality. You are sitting here – can't you think it is just a dream? It is possible that you are dreaming. How do you know that it is true and not a dream? The only difference is that your eyes are open. But in a dream in the night – you never suspect in a dream that it may be a dream. This is one of the strangest mysteries. In real life, fully awake, you can doubt its reality; in a dream nobody ever doubts the reality of the dream. Nobody thinks it is a dream. It is so real.

Bodhidharma is trying to give you an example. When you die, your eyes will be closed.... In the East it is a tradition: the moment somebody dies, immediately his eyes are closed. From my very childhood I have been interested in the idea – why? Let him die if he wants to die with open eyes. Why should others be interfering – you cannot even allow him a little freedom of keeping his eyes open after death? I asked everybody, because whenever somebody died I was always present. The moment I heard somebody had died in the neighborhood or somewhere, I immediately went to see the whole thing, what was happening. And I have asked many but nobody was able to answer why it mattered, why they closed the eyes.

Most often people die with open eyes. It is very rare to die with closed eyes for the simple reason that for closing the eyelids, you need life energy; just as you cannot die with a fist, because to keep your hand as a fist you need a certain life energy. Everybody dies with an open hand; now there is no more energy, how can you keep the fist? In the same way almost everybody dies with open eyes.

And my own understanding is, although nobody has been able to tell me.... I have asked great saints and they said, "You bring such strange questions. We have never thought about it and there is no mention of it in any scriptures. It is just convention."

But I said, "It goes on and on. I cannot accept that it is absolutely meaningless because I can see the meaning. When a man dies, his eyes turn upwards. In a dead man's open eyes you will see only the white – all the black part, the real eye, turns upwards. That creates fear in people. Just to see somebody's eyes open and all white gives them fear. It also happens in your sleep; your eyes turn up. That is a rest for the eyes. And now the eyes have gone into complete rest and so as not to provoke fear in people, the eyes are immediately closed."

And in a philosophical sense, the eyes are closed because now the world no longer exists for you to see. You are not; the world has disappeared for you. The moment a man dies he cannot take his empire with him, he cannot take his knowledge with him, he cannot take his prestige, respectability, honor with him. All that he can take with himself is his awareness of his own nature. That is your only wealth. And if you are not earning that wealth, you are wasting a tremendous opportunity.

You should realize then that everything you see is like a dream or illusion, because death is going to take it all away. That which death cannot take is the only criterion for reality.

If you don't find a master *soon, you will live this life in vain. It is true, you have the buddha-nature. But without the help of a* master *you will never know it. Only one person in a million becomes enlightened without a* master's *help.*

This I can say is coming directly from Bodhidharma. This is beyond the capacity of an ordinary recorder of notes; a disciple, however learned, cannot manage to say this: *Only one person in a million becomes enlightened without a* master's *help.* Even Bodhidharma has not become enlightened without a master's help.

But the possibility remains because it is your self-nature. In fact, there is no need at all of any master. If you are courageous enough to enter within yourself without bothering whether you are going to find something there or not, you will find it without the help of the master.

What is the help of the master? He only gives you a certainty, because you are not adventurous – otherwise, what is the need of certainty? It is *your* life and you have the right – and you should have a longing – to know what it is all about.

I had no master in my life. Many times I have come across enlightened people, but I simply told them to just leave me alone. What can their help do? Just give me a certainty. But I was capable of going without certainty. In fact it is more juicy to go without any certainty, not knowing at all where you are going, whether you are going to find anything or not.

When you go with certainty it is as if you are seeing a film twice. Everything is certain, you know exactly now what is going to happen. The new man I have been talking about all my life will not need masters, because he will be so full of adventurous spirit that he would like to go within himself just out of sheer adventure, to see what is there at the very source of life.

But up to now it has been happening: *Only one person in a million becomes enlightened without a teacher's help.* Perhaps I am that one person, because I don't know of any enlightened people in the whole history of mankind who have not had a master. But Bodhidharma recognized the fact and the possibility, although he himself had a master. And I am fulfilling his statement: *Only one person in a million becomes enlightened without a teacher's,* a master's *help.*

If though, by the conjunction of conditions, someone understands what the Buddha meant, that person does not need a master. *Such a person has a natural awareness superior to anything taught. But unless you are so blessed, study hard. And by means of instruction, you'll understand.*

These last sentences cannot be from Bodhidharma. First, knowing your nature does not come by studying. You can go on studying all the scriptures of the world and still you will not know yourself. Nor does it come by instruction; instruction means information from outside. Then how does it come?

It comes through communion with the master, through falling in love with someone who has reached, seeing in him your own future. You are just a seed and he has come to blossom. That gives you a longing to move upwards and to become a flower yourself. It is not a question of study, it is not a question of instruction; it is a question of deep love for the master.

Hence I say these statements are not from Bodhidharma; they cannot be. Even if Bodhidharma were here and even if he were to say that they are his statements, I will refuse to believe it. They are not his statements. A man like

Bodhidharma cannot say such rubbishy things.

People who don't understand and think they can do so without study are no different from those deluded souls who can't tell white from black.

These are the disciple's notes. He is again emphasizing the fact of studying.

You all know people of great learning, great knowledge, but in whom deep down, there is no light; they don't radiate a blissfulness. In fact, their studies make them serious. Rather than making them light, they make them burdened. They know too much without knowing anything and it becomes a great tension in their being, because actually they know nothing but they have accumulated so much information. People worship them, people respect them, so they cannot accept the fact that all our knowledge is superficial. It has not grown within our own being, it has no roots in us. All these flowers have been purchased from the marketplace. They have not grown in our own being.

I have heard about a man who had gone fishing. The whole day he tried and could not get a single fish. Now he was worried about his wife so he went to the fish market and purchased three beautiful big fish, but on a condition. The fisherman who was selling those fish could not understand the condition which was very strange, and it was the first time he had come across such a thing. The man was ready to pay the price, whatsoever the fisherman was asking, but the condition was that he had to throw the fish and the man would catch them. The fisherman said, "There is no problem. I will throw, you catch, but I don't understand…what is the point of it?"

The man said, "You don't understand but I don't like to lie. When I go home, my wife will ask how many fish I have got. I will show the three fish I have caught with my own hands. I want to be exactly true."

Such a man can deceive his wife, but can he deceive himself? And is this really true or just a falseness covered with the name of truth? And that is the situation of all your so-called learned people. They have caught fish, not from the lake but from a fisherman and his shop in the market, and they have certainly caught them. But they themselves know that they have not caught, they have purchased – and truth cannot be purchased.

You have to catch hold of your inner light with your own awareness. Other than that there is no way.

Falsely proclaiming the Buddhadharma, such persons, in fact, blaspheme the Buddha and subvert the Dharma. They preach as if they were bringing rain. But theirs is the preaching of devils not of buddhas. Their teacher is the King of Devils. And their disciples are the Devil's minions. Deluded people who follow such instruction unwittingly sink deeper in the Sea of Birth and Death.

Unless they see their nature, how can people call themselves buddhas? They're liars who deceive others into entering the realm of devils. Unless they see their nature, their preaching of the Twelvefold Canon is nothing but the preaching of devils. Their allegiance is to Mara... Mara is the buddhist equivalent of the devil. *Their allegiance is to Mara, not to the Buddha. Unable to distinguish white from black, how can they escape birth and death?*

Whoever sees his nature is a buddha. Whoever doesn't is a mortal. But apart from our mortal nature if you can find a buddha-nature somewhere else, where is it? Our mortal nature is our buddha-nature.

It only needs recognition. There is no other difference. One who recognizes and is aware of his nature is a buddha. One who does not recognize his own self-nature, who has never gone inwards, is a mortal. But the difference is only of recognition, of awareness; there is no qualitative difference between you and the enlightened man. The difference is only that he knows it and you are unaware of your own treasures.

Hence, Bodhidharma declares: *Our mortal nature is our buddha-nature. Beyond this nature there's no buddha. The buddha is our nature,* but unless we are aware we will remain mortals. *There's no buddha besides this nature. And there's no nature besides the buddha.*

The word 'buddha' will be repeated again and again by Bodhidharma so you have to understand what it means. It is not a personal name of anybody. Buddha simply means one who is awakened. Gautam Buddha is the most famous awakened person but that does not mean that he is the only awakened person. There have been many buddhas before him and there have been many buddhas after him and as long as every human being can become a buddha, there will go on springing up new buddhas in the future.

Because everybody has the potentiality...it is only for a time, the right time that you are waiting. Some day, tortured by the outside reality, in despair of having seen everything and found nothing, you are bound to turn inwards.

Gautam Buddha's personal name was Siddhartha. Gautama is his family name so his name was Gautama Siddhartha. Buddha is not his name, it is his awakening. Because I have named our discos *Zorba the Buddha,* the ambassador of Sri Lanka – Sri Lanka is a Buddhist country – the ambassador wrote a letter to me, saying, "It is very disrespectful and it hurts our religious feelings that you have given the name *Zorba the Buddha* to discos. Please take the Buddha out of it."

I wrote him a letter saying, "Perhaps you are a born Buddhist, but I am a buddha. And I have every right to call the discos, *Zorba the Buddha;* it has nothing to do with your Buddha...you can be satisfied. If I were calling it 'Zorba the Siddhartha', there would be a point to your being disturbed. But buddha is not a personal name; Gautam Buddha is only one of the buddhas amongst millions. And Zorba has every potential to become a buddha. I cannot prevent it and neither can you. And you are only a Buddhist, just a follower, an imitator. You don't even know exactly the meaning of the word 'buddha'. You have never experienced what self-awareness is. So write to me again what you want."

He has been silent, he has not answered. And I don't think he has shown the letter to anybody else.

So whenever Bodhidharma uses the word buddha, remember he is not mentioning Gautam Buddha. He is saying awareness, enlightenment, liberation, total freedom – all those qualities are in that word buddha. It is nobody's name and it is everybody's potential.

Okay, Maneesha?

Yes, Bhagwan.

達磨

Beloved Bhagwan,

But suppose I don't see my nature, can't I still attain enlightenment by invoking buddhas, reciting sutras, making offerings, observing precepts, practicing devotions, or doing good works?

No, you can't.

And why not?

If you attain anything at all it's conditional, it's karmic. It results in retribution. It turns the Wheel. And as long as you're subject to birth and death, you'll never attain enlightenment. To attain enlightenment you have to see your nature. Unless you see your nature, all this talk about cause and effect is nonsense. Buddhas don't practice nonsense. A buddha is free of karma, free of cause and effect. To say he attains anything at all is to slander a buddha. What could he possibly attain? Even focusing on a mind, a power, an understanding or a view is impossible for a buddha. A buddha isn't one-sided. The nature of his mind is basically empty, neither pure nor impure. He's free of practice and realization. He's free of cause and effect.

A buddha doesn't observe precepts. A buddha doesn't do good or evil. A buddha isn't energetic or lazy. A buddha is someone who does nothing, someone who can't even focus his mind on a buddha. A buddha isn't a buddha. Don't think about buddhas. If you don't see what I'm talking about, you'll never know your own mind.

People who don't see their nature and imagine they can practice doing nothing all the time are liars and fools. They fall into endless space. They're like drunks. They can't tell good from evil. If you intend to practice doing nothing, you have to see your nature before you can put an end to rational thought. To attain enlightenment without seeing your nature is impossible.

Still others commit all sorts of evil deeds,

claiming karma doesn't exist. They erroneously maintain that since everything is empty, committing evil isn't wrong. Such persons fall into a hell of endless darkness with no hope of release. Those who are wise hold no such conception.

But if our every movement or state, whenever it occurs, is the mind, why don't we see this mind when a person's body dies?

The mind is always present. You just don't see it.

But if the mind is present, why don't I see it?

Do you ever dream?

Of course.

When you dream, is that you?

Yes, it's me.

And is what you're doing and saying different from you?

No, it isn't.

But if it isn't, then this body is your real body. And this real body is your mind. And this mind, through endless kalpas without beginning, has never varied. It has never lived or died, appeared or disappeared, increased or decreased. It's not pure or impure, good or evil, past or future. It's not true or false. It's not male or female. It doesn't appear as a monk or a layman, an elder or a novice, a sage or a fool, a buddha or a mortal. It strives for no realization and suffers no karma. It has no strength or form. It's like space. You can't possess it. And you can't lose it. Its movements can't be blocked by mountains, rivers or rock walls. Its unstoppable powers penetrate the Mountain of Five Skandhas and cross the River of Samsara. No karma can restrain this real body. But this mind is subtle and hard to see. It's not the same as the sensual mind. Everyone wants to see this mind. And those who move their hands and feet by its light are as many as the grains of sand along the Ganges. But ask them. They can't explain it. They're like puppets. It's theirs to use. Why don't they see it?

I FEEL EXTREMELY sad and sorry because Bodhidharma has the wrong kind of people taking the notes of his statements; they are mixing in their own confusions. They are trying hard to make it appear as if what they are saying is said by Bodhidharma. And the people who do not understand existentially what enlightenment is, are bound to fall into their trap. They will not be able to discriminate what belongs to Bodhidharma and what belongs to the people who have taken these notes.

Seeing the situation, I am reminded of one instance I have told you about, but it needs to be repeated. Rabindranath Tagore, one of the greatest poets of this country, translated his own book of poems, *Gitanjali,* into English. Although he was educated in England…he belonged to a very super-rich family of Bengal; his grandfather was given the title of king by the British empire.

He had all the best education possible in the world, but still a mother tongue is a mother tongue. He had written all his poems in Bengali, but a few friends suggested that *Gitanjali* has such a grandeur that if it is translated into English there is every possibility of it getting a Nobel prize. But who should translate it except Rabindranath himself? Who could be a better translator?

So he translated it, but he was still hesitant. He asked a great Christian missionary of those days, C.F. Andrews – a great scholar and very influential, a world famous figure – to go through the translations because he could also understand Bengali. He was living in Bengal as a missionary; he was working amongst Bengalis and had learned their language. So he was the right person to go through the translation and to look at the original. He approved the whole book except at four points, just four words scattered through the book. He said, "They are not grammatically correct, and I would suggest different words meaning almost the same, but grammatically correct."

And Rabindranath was convinced that C.F. Andrews was right as far as language was concerned. So he changed those four words and replaced them with the words suggested by C.F. Andrews. In England he had friends among all the English poets, so he went to London where he was a guest of one of the great poets of those days, Yeats. And Yeats called a meeting of only English poets to listen to the recitation of Rabindranath's *Gitanjali.* He was convinced that the book was so rare and so unique that it could be proposed for a Nobel prize, but it would be good to have the opinion of many Nobel prize winning poets.

So nearabout twenty or twenty-five poets gathered in Yeats' house to listen to Rabindranath's recitation. They were all immensely impressed, and unanimously they wanted to make an appeal to the Nobel prize committee that the book should be honored by a Nobel prize. But Yeats himself had a little reservation. He said, "Everything is perfectly right, except for four words." Rabindranath could not believe it – these were exactly the four words that C.F. Andrews had suggested!

Yeats said, "They are perfectly grammatical, but they are not poetic. They look as if somebody else has interfered; they prevent the flow of poetic beauty. Rather than being a help, they are hindrances and I would suggest that you change these words. Where did you get them? Because I have every certainty in my being that they are not your words. No poet can use those words in the places where they have been used. A linguist, yes; a man who wants to be perfect in grammar and language will use them. But a poet has a certain freedom; he has a poetic license to go a little off the track with grammar because poetry is a higher value than prose. For prose, grammar is okay, but for poetry, grammar can be a disturbance."

Rabindranath could not believe it, but he said, "You are right, these are not my words; these words are from C.F. Andrews. I will tell you the words that I originally used."

And he gave his words and Yeats was immensely happy. He said, "Now everything is okay. Those four rocks are removed from the river-like flow. Your words are not grammatical but they are poetic, and they are coming from your very heart."

Grammar is a game of the mind and poetry is not part of the mind; mind is essentially prose, poetry belongs to the heart.

Grammatically wrong, but poetically right, *Gitanjali* was presented to the Nobel prize committee and was accepted unanimously for the prize.

This instance shows that the people who have been writing these sutras of Bodhidharma were good as far as language was concerned, but they were not at all in tune with the experience of enlightenment – not at all. So there are many false statements, very confused statements, along with absolutely right statements from Bodhidharma.

So one has to read with a very sharp awareness; otherwise it is very difficult to find where Bodhidharma ends and the disciple comes in, and where the disciple ends and Bodhidharma comes in. It is so mixed, and I feel sad because Bodhidharma deserves better disciples. He is one of the greatest masters the world has known. But perhaps he was so great a master that very few disciples could even reach close to him. And those who reached close to him have not written any notes.

Hui Ko, whom he had chosen as his successor, when asked by Bodhidharma, "What is my essential teaching?" simply fell to his feet, tears rolling down from his eyes, not uttering a single word. Bodhidharma helped him to stand up and said, "Although you have not answered, I accept your answer. Although you have not said a single word, your tears are enough to convey the message. You have understood me and I can understand why you are silent. Your silence is saying more than you could have managed by saying anything. You are my very soul; you will represent me when I am gone."

But Hui Ko has not written a single word. So it is a strange fate: those who can understand find it hard to make anything but a confused statement. They would prefer to remain silent rather than commit a mistake. And those who do not understand fear nothing. They don't know that they are committing mistakes, mistakes of profound meaning and significance.

And I will show you that on the surface the notes look perfectly right, but just underneath, in many places they cannot be the statements of Bodhidharma. They cannot be the statements of anyone who has attained to ultimate consciousness, of one who has reached to the destiny of self-realization.

The sutras: *But suppose I don't see my nature, can't I still attain enlightenment by invoking buddhas, reciting sutras, making offerings, observing precepts, practicing devotions, or doing good works?*

No, you can't.

This *no* is certainly from Bodhidharma. The statement above is what all the religions are doing in the world. The so-called religious people are doing all these things; they are invoking God, they are invoking buddhas, they are invoking jinnahs, they are invoking prophets, messiahs, saviors. They are reciting sutras, holy *Koran, Holy Bible,* holy *Gita,* holy *Dhammapada.* They are making offerings in temples, in mosques, in churches, in synagogues, in *gurudwaras.* They are observing precepts, fasting, not eating in the night, not drinking in the night. Thousands of different kinds of precepts are being followed by different religions.

Just the other day I was looking at the *Talmud,* the holy scripture of the Jews, and I could not believe…. Many times before I have also opened it and closed it, because just to read one paragraph is enough to see the stupidity. You open anywhere and things are said which seem to have no relevance at all to any spirituality. For example, on the holy day of the sabbath you can go to your farm or your garden or your field, but not to the very end. You can go very close to the end, but not to the very end. And this is part of a holy scripture! And then there are commentaries on it; one rabbi says, "Why is it said?" Then another rabbi says something else. Then another rabbi.... Hundreds of commentaries on such a stupid statement.

Or...that you should have one door and only one window and the question is whether the window should be on the right side of the door or on the left side of the door. And there are great rabbis discussing the point that it has to be on the right or it has to be on the left, and they are giving great arguments why. And it has not to be big, it has to be small – how small...?

In the name of precepts, disciplines, all kinds of nonsense is being practiced – devotions, or doing good works, opening hospitals, schools, orphanages. Only a man like Bodhidharma can say, "No, you cannot attain to enlightenment or buddhahood by such stupid things." There is only one way and that is to know your being, that is to know your self-nature.

And why not?

If you attain anything at all it's conditional. Now this is very significant and you have to understand it. Anything that is conditional you can lose if the condition is removed. Enlightenment has to be unconditional for the simple reason that it cannot be taken away. Your life is conditional: anybody can murder you, you can commit suicide. But your enlightenment has to be unconditional.

You cannot do anything to demolish, to destroy anything that is unconditional. You cannot make any effort to go backwards, because there is no condition, there is no cause; it is free from being destroyed. For example, you are having a bonfire – but it is conditional. If you remove the wood, the fire will be gone. That wood was absolutely necessary for the fire to remain in existence. It was not unconditional, it was an effect of a cause. The cause removed, the effect disappears.

That is the difference between the spiritualist and the materialist. The materialist says in philosophical terms that life, consciousness, are all conditional, are all effects. When causes are removed they will disappear. When in death the five elements of which your body is made fall apart, back into their original sources – water into water, earth into earth, air into air, fire into fire, space, sky into sky – then nothing is left. There is no soul that survives; it was only an effect. If causes were present, the effect was present – when causes are removed, the effect disappears. In other words Karl Marx says, "Consciousness is only a by-product; in itself it has no existence."

Bodhidharma is saying: *If you attain anything at all, it's conditional, it's karmic. It results in retribution. It turns the Wheel. And as long as you're subject to birth and death, you'll never attain enlightenment.* Enlightenment has not to be an effect of some cause, not an effect of some practice, not an effect of some conditions that you have fulfilled. It has not to be an attainment, but only a discovery.

It is already there.

You are just keeping your eyes closed, so when you open your eyes and you see your buddhahood, you cannot say you have attained it. It was already there before you had even seen it. It is not your 'attainment', and the opening of your eyes is not a cause.

Whether you open your eyes or not, your buddhahood is intact. Even with closed eyes you are buddhas; with open eyes there will be no change – you will be buddhas. The only change will be in your understanding, not in your quality, not in your being. The only change will be in your understanding: "My God, I have been looking for enlightenment, for buddhahood, for lives altogether, searching and seeking everywhere and doing every kind of good act, observing precepts, making offerings, doing prayers, reciting sutras – and that was all foolish, because while I was reciting sutras I was a buddha. When I was offering flowers to a stone statue I was doing such an idiotic act because I was making a buddha touch the feet of a stone statue. I have always been the buddha; that is my unconditional nature."

That's why Bodhidharma's statement is of tremendous significance when he says, "No, you cannot find buddhahood by all these so-called things which religions go on preaching to people."

To attain enlightenment you have to see your nature.

And it is just language and the difficulty of language that one has to call it attainment; otherwise what attainment is there? It is really only a discovery.

The treasure is there, you simply uncover it.

You are not producing it, you are not creating it, it is not something new; it has always and always been there. And whether you discover it or not makes no difference to it. It is unconditionally eternal.

Unless you see your nature, all this talk about cause and effect is nonsense.

I can say that these harsh words can only come from Bodhidharma, not from any disciple who cannot have that much courage. Only a Bodhidharma can say: *Buddhas don't practice nonsense.* It is a lion's roar. It is a lion's roar, not an ordinary disciple's writing.

A buddha is free of karma, free of cause and effect. To say he attains anything at all is to slander a buddha.

There is no question of attainment, he only discovers. He only opens his eyes and sees himself.

What could he possibly attain? Even focusing on a mind, a power, an understanding, or a view is impossible for a buddha. A buddha is not one-sided.

Hence, he cannot focus on himself. He is multidimensional, he is universal. Only one-dimensional beings can focus. Your ordinary mind can focus; it can concentrate, but a buddha cannot concentrate. He is as open as the sky, in all directions, in all dimensions.

A buddha is not one-sided. The nature of his no-*mind...* the disciple is writing his *mind,* but I have to correct him. *The nature of his* no-*mind is basically empty, neither pure nor impure.* And you can see why I am correcting it because if it is mind, it cannot be empty. Mind is always full of thoughts; mind is nothing but a container of thoughts. Mind is another name for the thought process. In the day it is thinking, in the night it is dreaming, but it is always filled with something. It is never empty.

And mind is always either pure or impure. It depends on what kind of thoughts it has going through it. If you are thinking of murdering someone, or if you are thinking of stealing something, or you are thinking of helping someone.... If you are filled with a compassionate thought, a loving thought or a destructive thought...it will depend what kind of content is in your mind, and mind is never empty. Hence, either it will be pure or impure, or it will be both together. Because your mind is such a mess, impurity and purity, good thoughts and bad thoughts, all are standing there as a crowd. Hence, I want to change the word mind to no-mind. Then only can the statement become meaningful: *The nature of his* no-*mind is basically empty, neither pure nor impure* because the no-mind is beyond duality.

Mind can never be beyond duality. It is always thinking for or against, it is always divided and split, it is always schizophrenic; it is never total. A part of it is always hesitating. Whatever you do, a part of you will not be with you; it will go on saying, "Don't do it, you will repent if you do it."

That is one of the causes why every human being is in misery. Because whatever you do, it doesn't matter what, the part that has not cooperated is going to take revenge with vengeance. It will say to you, "Listen, now look, I have told you before, don't do this, but you never listened." If you had listened to it, then too the situation would not have been different because the other part that was saying, "Do it," will wait and watch for its opportunity to condemn you saying, "You never listen to me." You are always in such a catch-22: whether you do this or do that, you are always wrong.

Only no-mind can be without any duality, because it is empty. The no-mind is choicelessness. The no-mind is pure awareness. It is just the empty sky.

A buddha doesn't observe precepts.

Now this is a great statement. It should be written in gold letters everywhere around the earth for everyone to understand it.

A buddha doesn't observe precepts.

He does not follow any discipline. Why? Because he has no need to follow any discipline, any precepts; he has not to follow any morality for the simple fact that he lives in full awareness. Out of his full awareness comes the response – not from any precepts, any scriptures, any moral codes. No, he acts moment to moment out of his pure emptiness.

Just looking silently he allows his whole being to respond. He is just like a mirror; he reflects, he does not do anything else. His responses are his reflections.

A buddha doesn't do good or evil. A buddha is not energetic or lazy. A buddha is someone who does nothing, someone who can't even focus his mind on a buddha.

Even if God is standing before him, he cannot concentrate on him. He is just pure emptiness. He does not carry any tensions, because concentration is a tension, focusing is a tension. He is utterly relaxed.

Here Bodhidharma comes to his height when he says:

A buddha isn't a buddha.

Now this will be very difficult for people to understand – particularly those whose minds are prejudiced by so many religions in the world. *A buddha isn't a buddha.* It has to be understood, because it is so significant that if you miss it, you will miss everything.

Just take a few instances; perhaps that may help. A child who is just born is utterly innocent. But do you know or do you think he is aware that he is innocent? Can the innocent child know that he is innocent? If he knows that he is innocent, he is no longer innocent. The innocent child is innocent only if he does not know that he is innocent.

The buddha is a rebirth, the rebirth of consciousness. He is attaining a second childhood; he is born again. He is absolute consciousness, but he cannot be aware and he cannot say, "I am absolute consciousness." That statement will make the consciousness impure. His consciousness is just like the innocence of a child. It cannot be self-conscious. It is there and there is no space left for anything else, even for the thought, "I am a buddha."

A buddha isn't a buddha. Don't think about buddhas, because thinking about buddhas is an absurdity. You *are* a buddha. Why are you wasting your time thinking about buddhas? Why not simply open your eyes and be awake and be a buddha? What are you going to gain by thinking about buddhas?

If you don't see what I am talking about, you'll never know your own no-mind.

People who don't see their nature and imagine they can practice doing nothing all the time are liars and fools.

There is a danger – Bodhidharma is aware of it – that there can be cunning people, liars, fools, deceiving others, deceiving themselves. I have come to know many who, reading or listening to such great statements like Bodhidharma's, start pretending that for them there is nothing good, nothing bad, that they need not be concerned about discriminating between right and wrong. Because Bodhidharma and people like Bodhidharma declare that you are a buddha, they enjoy the idea without opening their eyes. It is so ego-fulfilling that they don't open their eyes. They don't experience their self-nature, but they start declaring that they're enlightened. Such people do immense harm to themselves and immense harm to others.

I have seen so many people who start declaring themselves enlightened and they are not even a little more conscious than you are. So these great statements can be dangerous. They are like great heights of the Himalayan peaks. From these heights, you can fall and you can destroy yourself. These secrets should be understood in a very sincere, honest way; they should not be used to exploit people and to enhance your ego.

These people *fall into endless space. They're like drunks. They can't tell good from evil. If you intend to practice doing nothing, you have to see your nature before you can put an end to rational thought. To attain enlightenment without seeing your nature is impossible.*

So it is up to each individual to continuously remember to remain sincere. Otherwise nobody can prevent you; you can declare you are enlightened but your life will show, your actions will show, your eyes will show, everything around you will show that you are not enlightened. And this is not going to help you in any way; this may even mislead a few people. And if you can get a few people to believe in your enlightenment, which is always possible because the world is so full of idiots that any idiot can find disciples.... And once you have found a few idiots as disciples, then you become absolutely certain that you must be enlightened; otherwise how can so many wise people believe in you?

Still others commit all sorts of evil deeds, claiming karma doesn't exist. They erroneously maintain that since everything is empty, committing evil isn't wrong. Such persons fall into a hell of endless darkness with no hope of release. Those who are wise hold no such conception.

It is a question of great individual responsibility; there is no other responsibility which is greater than this. Remember always – and don't forget for a single moment – don't say anything which you are not; otherwise you will be falling into a darkness from which it is very difficult to come out.

"But if our every movement or state, whenever it occurs, is no-*mind, why don't we see this* no-*mind when a person's body dies?"*

The no-*mind is always present. You just don't see it.*

No-mind is not a thing. It is not a commodity, it is not an object. No-mind is pure space. It is utter emptiness, it is silence. You cannot hear it. Have you ever thought about it, when you say it is absolutely silent? Do you hear silence? All that you hear is no noise. Because you are hearing no noise, you conclude it is silence.

Because you don't experience any worry, any anxiety, any tension, any misery, any suffering, you infer that this is the state of peace and bliss. But these are not things or objects that you can see. Or when a person dies, you cannot see his no-mind leaving the body.

Remember again, I am changing the statements – wherever there is mind, I am saying no-mind – because mind can be seen. You see it every day. There is no need to die to see it; even while living you see it. Just close your eyes and you will start seeing it.

"But if the no-*mind is present, why don't I see it?"*

The disciple is raising questions and trying to find Bodhidharma's answers. Perhaps he asked these questions...he must have received the answers, but he could not understand those answers. He has interpreted those answers in his own way. Bodhidharma has said: *The* no-*mind is always present. You just don't see it.* You cannot see it because it is pure space, it is not a thing. It is nothing; or better, it is a no-thing. It is not visible. But still the disciple goes on asking the same question in a different form. *If the mind* – if the no-mind – *is present, why don't I see it?*

It seems he has not written...he has forgotten, or he has not understood the answer given by Bodhidharma, because the question is there, but the answer is not there. The answer must have been: Because you *are* it, so you cannot see it.

You can see everything in the world except yourself. Obviously I can catch with my hand everything in the world except my hand itself. I can see with my eyes everything in the world except my own eyes.

No-mind is my nature.

I can feel it, I can live it, I can relish it, I can sing it, I can dance it, but I cannot see it. Because I *am* it. Something like this must have been the answer but it is not recorded.

And Bodhidharma must have tried hard so that the disciple could understand the distinction. He asks him:

Do you ever dream?

Of course.

When you dream, is that you?

But still the disciple does not get it. He answers: *Yes, it's me.*

And this goes against the whole philosophy of Bodhidharma and Gautam Buddha and all those who have ever become awakened. The answer should be, "No, it is not me." Because how can I be the dreams? The dreams float in front of me. I see them. Because I see them, obviously I am not them. I am the seer and they are the seen. I am the knower and they are the known. They are objects, I am the subject. Hence the right answer should be, not "Yes, it is me," but "No, it is not me."

And is what you're doing and saying different from you?

Again the same fallacy; the answer given is *No, it isn't.* It is not different from me – any doing or saying.... But it is so simple; particularly for you it must be so simple. Walking, you can see that it is an action of your body, but you are not it. You are not walking; your consciousness inside is exactly where it has always been. Whether you stand still or walk, it is always the same. The real answer will be, "Yes, it is different. It is not me. My action cannot be me, my doing cannot be me. I am always the watcher behind; I am always the witness beyond."

But if it is, then this body is not your real body. That's my correction. The notes themselves are just the opposite. The notes continue in the same way being wrong. The note is: *But if it isn't, then this body is your real body.* If you are not different from your actions, if you are not different from your dreams, then this is your real mind, this is your real body.

But this body is not your real body. Soon a day will come when this body will be burning on a funeral pyre. But you will not be burning. Your consciousness will have taken a new form – moved far away.

So I will go with my corrections: *But if it is, then this body is not your real body. And this real body is your no-mind. And this no-mind, through endless kalpas without beginning, has never varied. It has never lived or died....* Just see the confusion. If this body is real, then the later statements cannot be relevant...*through endless kalpas,* through endless ages, *without beginning, has never varied. It has never lived or died, appeared or disappeared, increased or decreased. It's not pure or impure, good or evil, past or future. It's not true or false. It's not male or female. It doesn't appear as a monk or a layman, an elder or a novice, a sage or a fool, a buddha or a mortal. It strives for no realization and suffers no karma. It has no strength or form. It's like space. You can't possess it.*

These statements are possible only if my corrections are made; otherwise these statements become absolutely impossible because your body has died many times, has been born many times, will die again, will be born again. This body is not your real body.

Your real body is your real being – which has never died, which has never been born, which has always continued eternally through many forms, but it has been the same. There is a statement of Gautam Buddha: "You can taste the ocean from anywhere, from any direction; its taste is always the same."

So whether in this body or in another, your consciousness is the same. And this body is certainly male or female; only your being is not male or female. So unless my corrections are there, all the statements following become absolutely irrelevant and diametrically opposite to the statements that the disciple has written.

And you can't lose it. Its movements can't be blocked by mountains, rivers or rock walls. Its unstoppable powers penetrate the Mountain of Five Skandhas... These five *skandhas* are what I have been calling the five elements. *Skandha* is the Buddhist word for element – the earth, the air, the water, the fire, and the sky. These are the five elements your so-called body is made of. But your real being is beyond all these *skandhas...the Mountain of Five Skandhas and cross the River of Samsara.* Your consciousness does not consist of these five elements and even if these five elements are mountainous, still they cannot prevent your consciousness from passing beyond to your real home.

Even oceans of this *samsara,* this world, cannot prevent you from reaching to your ultimate home. Because the ultimate home is already inside you, nothing can prevent you from reaching it. You are already there, just you are not aware of it.

No karma can restrain this real being, or *this real body. But this* no-*mind is subtle and hard to see. It's not the same as the sensual mind. Everyone wants to see this* no-*mind. And those who move their hands and feet by its light are as many as the grains of sand along the Ganges.*

Although you don't see it, everybody has it. You live in its light. Your very life belongs to your no-mind.

But ask them. They can't explain it.

You live, you know you are alive, but if somebody asks you what life is, or to define what you mean by living, you will be at a loss. It is just as if you taste something delicious; you know the taste, but is there any way to say what it is, how it is? The only way is for the other person to taste it. No explanation can help.

The man who has never tasted sweets...you cannot explain to him what sweetness is. You can bring all your articulateness, but you cannot explain a simple thing, sweetness. The only way is to offer him some sweets. That's what the masters have been doing all along. Rather than telling you what sweetness is, they offer it to you to taste. They themselves are offering their own being, their own presence for you to taste it.

Everybody has a buddha inside but because they are unaware they function like puppets. This buddha inside is theirs to use; why don't they see it? Why do they go on remaining like puppets? Why don't they become masters of their own being? And it is not a difficult task, in fact it is not a task at all. It is just a little knack of becoming aware, just shaking yourself and waking up. All the meditations are simply devices to shake you so that the deep spiritual sleep is disturbed. P.D. Ouspensky has offered and dedicated his book, *In Search of the Miraculous,* to his master, George Gurdjieff, with very beautiful words: "To George Gurdjieff, the disturber of my sleep." But that is the only function of a master: in some way to disturb you, in some way to shake and wake you up.

There is nowhere to go and there is nothing to attain.

You are already there where you need to be.

Seeking is the only sin.

Searching is the only way of going astray.

Just remaining within yourself, withdrawing yourself from everything, every energy, every ray of energy, and concentrating it at the very center of your being...Gurdjieff calls it 'crystallization'. And he was a man very much like Bodhidharma. If anybody can be put in the same category as Bodhidharma, then Gurdjieff is the man. What he calls crystallization of your being is called by Bodhidharma awakening of your being, or buddhahood.

Reading through these sutras, I have been thinking to have a look at other ancient sutras, because the same fallacies that I am seeing in these sutras are bound to be there. They are not written by enlightened people. And these confusions, these misstatements, without any intention, are doing immense harm to all those who are following them; they have to be corrected. So my commentaries are more corrections and critiques of all that is confused and wrong. I want to bring out Bodhidharma completely clearly, without any impressions left by these disciples who have written the sutras. It has always happened...the gospels of Jesus were written after three hundred years when Jesus was not there to correct them. And no Christian would like another Jesus to correct them. Otherwise...I am absolutely willing.

Gautam Buddha's sutras were written after his death. And there was so much quarreling amongst the disciples that immediately after his death there were thirty-two schools in conflict with each other. Somebody was saying, "This has been said by him," or "This has not been said." Thirty-two interpretations, contradicting each other, and poor Gautam Buddha was no longer alive and certainly he was not saying things which had thirty-two different interpretations. He was not a madman. His meaning was very clear, but that clarity is possible only to those who have gone beyond mind, because mind is confusion, and no-mind is clarity.

The silence of no-mind gives you the clarity. You can see immediately what is right and what is wrong; there is no question of any argumentation. Reading these sutras, I have not had to think for a single moment or hesitate for a single moment as to where it is wrong and where it is right. The moment I came to any place which was wrong, it was immediately and absolutely clear to me, without any hesitation.

Seeing these sutras, I have been thinking to have a look into all ancient scriptures which are written by unenlightened disciples and to correct them. Because it is time – they have lived for thousands of years without any correction.

But people become so obsessed and fanatic that they don't want any change. For example, my corrections will not be liked by the Buddhists. They will feel very much hurt – every line has to be right – but they don't see the point that these lines are not written by Bodhidharma; otherwise they would have been all right. They have been written by people who are not enlightened. Hence, it is absolutely certain that there are going to be fallacies, confusions, misstatements, many things missing and perhaps many things added by the disciples, just to make it a complete story, a complete system of philosophy. It is going to be a difficult job. It is going to annoy many more people. I have annoyed so many people that now I don't care anymore. It does not matter. I have annoyed millions of people, a few millions more – now it does not matter at all.

The future generations of the new man will feel grateful that at least there was one man who did not care about the whole world being annoyed with him. He went on discriminating between what is truth and what is not truth.

Okay, Maneesha?

Yes, Bhagwan.

SUCHNESS IS OUR SELF-NATURE

達磨

70 ___ SHIN-NYO: ETERNAL TRUTH

Beloved Bhagwan,

The Buddha said people are deluded. This is why when they act they fall into the River of Endless Rebirth. And trying to get out, they only sink deeper. And all because they don't see their nature. If people weren't deluded, why else would they ask about something right in front of them? Not one of them understands the movement of his own hands and feet. The Buddha wasn't mistaken. Deluded people don't know who they are. Something so hard to fathom is known by a buddha and no one else. Only the wise know this mind, this mind called dharma-nature, this mind called liberation. Neither life nor death can restrain this mind. Nothing can. It's also called the Unstoppable Tathagata, the Incomprehensible, the Sacred Self, the Immortal, the Great Sage. Its names vary but not its essence. Buddhas vary too, but none leaves his own mind.

The mind's capacity is limitless, and its manifestations are inexhaustible. Seeing forms with your eyes, hearing sounds with your ears, smelling

odors with your nose, tasting flavors with your tongue, every movement or mode, it's all your mind. At every moment, where languages can't go, that's your mind.

The sutras say, "A tathagata's forms are endless. And so is his awareness." The endless variety of forms is due to the mind. Its ability to distinguish things, whatever their movement or mode, is the mind's awareness. But the mind has no form and its awareness no limit. Hence, it's said, "A tathagata's forms are endless. And so is his awareness."

A material body of the four elements is trouble. A material body is subject to birth and death. But the real body exists without existing because a tathagata's real body never changes. The sutras say, "People should realize that the buddha-nature is something they have always had." Mahakashyapa only realized his own nature.

...The sutras say, "Everything that has form is an illusion." They also say, "Wherever you are, there's a buddha." Your mind is the buddha. Don't use a buddha to worship a buddha.

Even if a buddha or bodhisattva should suddenly appear before you, there's no need for reverence. This mind of ours is empty and contains no such form. Those who hold onto appearances are devils. They fall from the path. Why worship illusions born of the mind? Those who worship don't know. And those who know don't worship. By worshiping you come under the spell of devils. I point this out because I'm afraid you're unaware of it. The basic nature of a buddha has no such form. Keep this in mind, even if something unusual should appear. Don't embrace it, and don't fear it. And don't doubt that your mind is basically pure. Where could there be room for any such form? Also, at the appearance of spirits, demons, or divine beings, conceive neither respect nor fear. Your mind is basically empty. All appearances are illusions. Don't hold onto appearances.

I T IS ONE of the most strange coincidences that Gautam Buddha and Mahavira both revolted against the knowledgeable, the learned, the scholarly, the brahmins, the pundits, for a single reason – that by being knowledgeable, you simply cover up your ignorance. It is not dispelled out of your being.

It is just like on a dark night when you don't have even a lamp in your house. You may have as much information about light as you like, but your information about light is not going to bring light into the house. The house will remain dark. But one thing is possible: your information may create a delusion for you. You may become so engaged in the information about light that you forget about darkness. But darkness is there; whether you forget it or not makes no difference.

In fact it is better to know that the darkness is there, and something has to be done to create light, to destroy darkness. Knowing about light is of no help; real light is needed. The strange coincidence is that both Gautam Buddha and Mahavira were surrounded by brahmin scholars. And all that they have said has been compiled by the same people against whom they were speaking their whole lives.

Mahavira had eleven intimate disciples – they were all brahmin scholars of great integrity, of great learning, of great knowledge, but their ignorance was just the same as anybody else's. Ignorance can decorate itself with knowledge, but that only hides it; it does not destroy it.

One has to discover one's own light, one's own being, one's own self-nature. The moment one discovers one's inner being, all darkness starts disappearing, because at the very center of your being is nothing but pure light. But it has to be discovered.

The people who are interested in knowledge, or interested in scriptures, or interested in learning from other wise men, are not doing anything to reach to their own light, to the very source of enlightenment.

The same happened with Gautam Buddha. His closest disciples were brahmins and hence a great misunderstanding has arisen in their reportings. What they have reported about Gautam Buddha is mixed, polluted, corrupted by their own knowledgeability, by their own learning. Their minds have come in and interfered with the message that was given in silence – a message that was transmitted heart to heart, being to being, but not from mind to mind.

The same unfortunate situation has happened with Bodhidharma – even on a far greater scale because Bodhidharma was born in India, but he was teaching in China. The people who surrounded him, who became interested in him, were the people who were interested in knowledge. And certainly he had the golden key that opens all the mysteries of life. His every word comes from an authentic experience. He attracted thousands of monks, but the problem is that those were the people who crammed his words and forgot the phenomenal presence of Bodhidharma. And they have written these sutras. Naturally, there are great mistakes but even though there are many stones, there are a few diamonds, and we can find those diamonds.

Even though they were not able to experience in the same way as Bodhidharma, they were certainly impressed by his charismatic being. Just like moths come to the flame of a candle, they came from faraway provinces in China, just to sit at his feet. But it is not enough. It is a good beginning, but it is not the end of the journey. They could not forget their own minds. Even while listening to him, they were still thinking their own thoughts, they were still comparing whether it fits with their ideology or not. They were interpreting, giving new meanings, new colors to his words.

And because Bodhidharma has not written anything.... No enlightened being has written anything for the simple reason that the written word is a dead word. A spoken word has the warmth, the splendor, and the presence of the master. The spoken word is a totally different category from the written word. The written word is only a corpse; the spoken word is alive, it is still breathing. It has a heartbeat which the written word cannot have. That's why no enlightened man around the world, in any age, has ever written anything.

So you have to be very aware. I will point out where the minds of the disciples who are collecting these sutras have interfered and destroyed something immensely beautiful. But even though they could not report exactly what Bodhidharma was saying, here and there, perhaps by mistake, they have reported the actual words.

Even to find a few actual words spoken by Bodhidharma and give them again a heartbeat, is a great joy. My commentary is not just a commentary; it is giving life, a resurrection, to those beautiful words which have fallen in wrong hands. They have to be relieved and released from this confused, imprisoned corpse-like existence.

The sutras:

The Buddha said people are deluded. This is why when they act they fall into the River of Endless Rebirth. And trying to get out, they only sink deeper. And all because they don't see their nature. If people were not deluded, why else would they ask about something right in front of them? Not one of them understands the movement of his own hands and feet. The Buddha was not mistaken. Deluded people don't know who they are.

The first thing to be understood is that these are actual words of Bodhidharma with no interference from the people who have been collecting these words. The emphasis in these sutras is that people are deluded. What is their delusion? Their delusion is that they don't know who they are. Because they don't know who they are, they create false personalities around themselves – because it is impossible to live knowing that you don't know who you are; you would certainly go mad.

Just think for a moment: if you are aware that you don't know who you are, it will be such a shock, such a shattering of all your identity. You cannot live without knowing yourself, who you are. And if you cannot know, then you have to create something. It will be a false substitute, but it will take away the maddening situation of not knowing oneself.

Ask somebody who he is, and he will say he is a doctor, he is an engineer, he is a professor, he is a Christian, he is a Hindu, he is a Buddhist.... These are false identities. These are creating a false layer around yourself to forget the maddening situation that you don't know yourself.

You are getting identified with a thousand and one things. You are a husband, you are a wife...but these are not your nature. You were not born as a husband, and you were not born as an engineer; and you were not born as a doctor, or a professor. These are created by you and by the society so that you don't feel continuously in an emptiness, which can be dangerous and can create an insanity in you.

And people are not satisfied. They go on making the false layer thicker and thicker. They become members of political parties, they become members of religions, they become members of Rotary clubs, Lions clubs; they go on creating some idea of who they are. This is needed just to keep you in your normal insanity.

One has to face oneself in utter nudity, without all these clothes that you have covered over yourself.

This is the delusion, that everybody is living a life which is not coming out of his self-nature, which is more like acting than like an authentic living. Just watch yourself, and you will see the great insight in the very significant and meaningful statement, *people are deluded*. That's why their actions always go in wrong directions. That's why they live a life of misery, suffering, agony, anguish.

When Bodhidharma says that these people go on falling into darkness, he is saying that they go on becoming more and more deluded. They have to make the layer of their delusion as thick as possible so they can remain unaware of their reality. And out of this false layer, their love becomes false, their friendship becomes false, their whole life becomes just a drama.

They are doing everything, but it is not coming from their spontaneity. It is not coming from their individuality. It is not coming from their very being. Hence, they are always wishy-washy, they are always hesitant, they are always asking what is right, and what is wrong; they are always asking questions about everything.

The man who knows himself has no questions to ask. The man who knows himself knows exactly what has to be done, and there is no question of choosing. Whatever he does, is right. Out of your self-nature, only right arises. Just as out of a real rosebush, only authentic roses arise. It is a natural phenomenon.

I used to live for few months in Raipur and just by my side lived a retired professor of mathematics. I used to see him from my windows. He had a beautiful pot with beautiful flowers, and every day he used to bring water to shower on the pot. The first day there was no problem, but as days passed, I was surprised that those flowers went on being the same. Their petals didn't fall, they didn't disappear as is the natural way of life – that the old disappears to give place for the new. Finally I could not resist my temptation. I went close to his window and I was surprised. Those were not real flowers, they were plastic flowers. But to keep the illusion in the neighborhood that they were real, he was watering them. I knocked on the door, and asked the old man, "What are you doing? These flowers don't need watering."

He said, "I know it also, but the whole neighborhood does not know about it. I have to water them, just to keep up appearances."

Your false personality is just a plastic flower. It cannot give you fulfillment, it cannot give you enlightenment, it cannot give you liberation from misery.

It cannot take you from your agony into an ecstatic experience. It cannot take you away from darkness into light, from death into immortality. This is the delusion.

Something so hard to fathom is known by a buddha and no one else.

Remember, by 'buddha' is not meant any personal name. 'Buddha' simply means the awakened one. Anyone who becomes awakened, enlightened, is the buddha. You are also the buddha; the only difference is that you are not aware of it. You have never looked inside yourself and found the buddha there.

Your very life source is nothing but enlightenment.

Bodhidharma is saying: *Something so hard to fathom is known by a buddha and no one else.*

You will know only that you are deluded if you enter yourself and find your authentic individuality. Then there will be a comparison. The man who has never seen real roses may remain with plastic flowers his whole life, believing that these are real roses. To wake him up, you have to bring real roses so that he can compare and he can see the difference. The plastic flowers are dead; they don't have any fragrance. They have not grown up; they will not die.

The real flower is fragile. With the morning it comes into existence, dances in the rain, in the wind, in the sun, and by the evening it is gone. It comes from the unknown and moves back into the unknown. The same is the situation of our human life.

We come from the unknown and we go on moving into the unknown. We will come again; we have been here thousands of times, and we will be here thousands of times. Our essential being is immortal but our body, our embodiment, is mortal. Our frame in which we are, our houses, the body, the mind, they are made of material things. They will get tired, they will become old, they will die. But your consciousness, for which Bodhidharma uses the word 'no-mind' – Gautam Buddha has also used the word, 'no-mind' – is something beyond body and mind, something beyond everything; that no-mind is eternal. It comes into expression, and goes again into the unknown.

This movement from the unknown to the known, and from the known to the unknown, continues for eternity, unless somebody becomes enlightened. Then that is his last life; then this flower will not come back again. This flower that has become aware of himself need not come back to life because life is nothing but a school in which to learn. He has learned the lesson, he is now beyond delusions. He will move from the known for the first time not into the unknown, but into the unknowable.

If from the known you move to the unknown, you will be born again. But if you move from the known to the unknowable, to the mystery of existence, you become one with the universe; there is no coming back.

Only the wise know this no-*mind, this* no-*mind called dharma-nature, this* no-*mind called liberation.*

Here the person who has taken these notes has missed the point. Instead of saying no-mind, he says mind. Mind is not your ultimate reality. He has not understood Bodhidharma and it is a great sin to misrepresent a man of enlightenment because for centuries people will be confused.

Neither life nor death can restrain this no-*mind. Nothing can. It is also called the Unstoppable Tathagata, the Incomprehensible, the Sacred Self, the Immortal, the Great Sage.*

And the person who has taken these notes is not even intelligent enough to see the point that mind cannot be called *tathagata*. Mind cannot be called *the Incomprehensible*. The mind cannot be called *the Sacred Self, the Immortal, the Great Sage*.

The mind is very ordinary, mundane. It is useful for day-to-day work; its function is in the outside world. In the inner world it is absolutely useless. Those who want to know their inner being have to go beyond mind.

They have to leave the mind behind.

That is the whole process of meditation.

One word *tathagata* has to be understood. The translator could not find any word to translate it; perhaps he could not even understand the meaning of the word because in the West and in Western languages, no parallel word exists. Tathagata is specifically a Buddhist term. Gautam Buddha preached the philosophy of *tathata* and tathata is very close to the word 'suchness.' Whatever happens, Buddha says, such is the nature of things. There is no need to be happy, there is no need to be miserable, there is no need to be affected at all by anything that happens. Birth happens, death happens, but you have to remain in a suchness, remembering that this is how life functions.

This is the way of life.

You cannot do anything against it.

Just as rivers move towards the ocean, that is their suchness. Just as fire is hot, that is its suchness.

Suchness is our self-nature.

So whatever happens...somebody comes and insults Gautam Buddha, abuses him. He listens silently and when asked by his disciples, when the man went, "Why did you remain silent?" Buddha said, "That was his suchness, that was his way of behaving. It was my suchness to remain silent. I'm not holier than that man, I'm not higher than that man, just our suchness is different, our natures differ."

The word tathata is of great profundity. A man who understands what tathata is becomes undisturbed in every situation; nothing can disturb him, he becomes unperturbable. And *tathagat* means one who has been living moment-to-moment in tathata. Tathagat is one of the most beautiful words possible in any language: one who lives simply according to his nature without being bothered about other people's nature.

Gautam Buddha used to say, "Once I was passing through a forest, and a branch of a tree fell on me. What do you think? Should I beat that branch of the tree because it hurt me, it wounded me?" The person to whom he was talking said, "There is no question of beating the branch; it had no desire to hurt you, it had no desire to fall on you. It was just a natural accident that you happened to be under the tree when the branch fell."

Buddha said, "If somebody insults me, that is also the same. I simply happened to be there and that man was full of anger. If I had not been there he would have been angry with somebody else. It was his nature; he was following his nature. I followed my nature."

And to be in tune with your nature, you certainly become impenetrable, unperturbable.

You become so crystallized in yourself that nothing can disturb you.

Its names vary but not its essence. Buddhas vary too, but none leaves his own no-mind.

This is a significant statement to be understood. *Buddhas vary too....* Each awakened person has a uniqueness of his own. This has created great misunderstandings in people, because Christ does not behave like Gautam Buddha, Mahavira does not behave like Gautam Buddha, Krishna does not behave like Gautam Buddha. Even Bodhidharma, a disciple of Gautam Buddha, does not behave like Gautam Buddha. This has created a great confusion in the world. People think these people cannot all be right.

Buddhists think only Gautam Buddha is right; Christ cannot be right. The misunderstanding arises because they think every buddha down the ages is going to be the same.

In existence, nothing is the same. Every person has his own uniqueness.

And when he becomes enlightened, his uniqueness becomes even more unique. He becomes a Himalayan peak, like Gourishankar, standing aloof, alone, reaching to the stars. It is not like any other peak in the Himalayas, or like any other mountain. It is just itself.

That's why I have been speaking on so many awakened people. This has been done for the first time in the whole history of man. Hindus have been speaking on Krishna, on Rama; Buddhists have been speaking on Buddha, on Bodhidharma; Christians have been speaking on Christ, St. Francis, Meister Eckhart. Mohammedans have been speaking about Mohammed; Sufis have been speaking about Jalaluddin Rumi, Sarmad, Al-Hillaj Mansoor. But nobody has dared to bring all the enlightened people together.

My whole effort has been to make it clear to the world that all enlightened people, howsoever different in their behavior, howsoever different in their philosophies, howsoever different in their actions, howsoever different in their individualities, still have the same taste, still have the same no-mind. Their innermost core is the same. It is the same light.

Don't go according to the shape of the candle. The candle can have any kind of shape, but the flame in every candle – of different shapes, different sizes, different colors – is the same. Those who know the flame don't bother about the candles and their shapes and their sizes and their colors. What is important is not the candle; what is important is the flame.

No-mind is the flame of every awakened being. He functions out of his self-nature, not out of his mind.

The no-*mind's capacity is limitless, and its manifestations are inexhaustible. Seeing forms with your eyes, hearing sounds with your ears, tasting flavors with your tongue, every movement or mode, it's all your* no-*mind. At every moment, where language can't go, that's your* no-*mind.*

But the reporter of Bodhidharma's sayings goes on saying it is your mind. Now it is so stupid, so illogical, so irrational that one can not conceive what kind of disciple this was who could not see a simple contradiction. Language can't go to the mind...language *belongs* to the mind, there is no need to go. Language cannot go to the no-mind, to the silence beyond thoughts. Mind is full of thoughts and all thoughts are in the form of language.

The sutras say, "A tathagata's forms are endless. And so is his awareness."

Not understanding that the forms of tathagatas, of the buddhas, of the people, of awakening are endless, religions have been fighting about trivia. For example, Jainas don't accept Gautam Buddha as enlightened for a simple reason: because they accept Mahavira as enlightened, and Mahavira lived naked. Gautam Buddha did not live naked. Just the clothes.... Because Buddha used clothes, he is not enlightened. Mahavira lived naked; he is enlightened. And the same is the situation with Buddhist scholars. They don't accept Mahavira as enlightened because he lived naked.

Nobody is ready to accept the varieties. They want buddhas to be produced almost like cars on an assembly line. Every car looks the same. In the factories of Ford, every minute one Ford car comes out of the assembly line, and you cannot make any distinction between one Ford and the other. In one hour, sixty Ford cars will come out and they will be all similar.

A buddha is not a machine. Machines can be similar. Even people who are not enlightened are not similar. Here, five thousand people are here, and you cannot find two persons similar. Even twins are not exactly similar. Their mother recognizes them and slowly, slowly their friends start recognizing them. Although they look almost the same – but it is almost – there are slight differences even in twins. And these buddhas are not twins. Christ has his own flavor, Mahavira has his beauty, Buddha has his own splendor.

I want it to be impressed in you as deeply as possible that all over the world, in different ages, in different races, enlightened people have existed. And it is time that they should be recognized as belonging to the same category, although protecting their uniqueness. They have a certain oneness but that is their innermost core. On the periphery, they are as unique as you can conceive. And it is beautiful. Having all the buddhas like Jesus Christ, everybody carrying his cross on his shoulder, the world would be very poor. Wherever you go, you would meet a Jesus Christ carrying a cross. Or if all the enlightened people lived naked, like Mahavira, that would not be enriching the world.

Mahavira alone is perfectly good. He has his uniqueness, his beauty, his grandeur, and he is incomparable.

Every enlightened being is incomparable.

He is unparalleled by anybody else.

This is how things should be. The world should not have only roses, it should have all kinds of flowers, and it should have all kinds of fragrances. Only then existence becomes richer.

Its ability to distinguish things, whatever their movement or mode, is the no-mind's awareness. But the no-mind has no form and its awareness no limit. Hence, it is said, "A tathagata's forms are endless. And so is his awareness."

A material body of the four elements is trouble. A material body is subject to birth and death. But the real body – the real being – exists without existing, because a tathagata's real body never changes.

Within your so-called body there is an inner being, an inner body, the body of your awareness, the body of your flame of consciousness. That never changes.

The sutras say, "People should realize that the buddha-nature is something they have always had."

This is one of the most important emphases of Bodhidharma. That you all have – every human being has – the same space within you, the same no-mind, and the same potential to blossom into a unique flowering. Nobody is poor and nobody is rich as far as the inner being is concerned. You have always had it. Even this very moment you are all buddhas. But you have never looked into yourself, you have never discovered it.

Remember buddhahood, enlightenment, awakening, liberation, moksha, nirvana; all these words mean the same thing.

When you become enlightened, the first thing is to have a good laugh about yourself. And the second thing is to have a good hot cup of tea. A good laugh, because you have been searching for something which you always had within you. And a cup of tea...you are so tired, ages of search and seeking and finding nothing. And the problem was you could have gone searching for ages and you would not have found, because the searcher is himself your search. What you are trying to find outside in the world, you are not going to find because the searcher himself is the sought.

Once you discover yourself, you will be simply amazed – you have always been enlightened, just you were not aware of it. It's as if you had a diamond, a Kohinoor, in your pocket, and you were begging all your life, not knowing that in your pocket you have the most precious diamond in the world. The day you discover it, you are bound to be surprised that life has played a great joke with you.

Mahakashyapa only realized his own nature.

You need to be reminded about that story. Bodhidharma is not the founder of Zen. The real founder is Mahakashyapa. But because he never spoke, people have always forgotten him; he has fallen into shadows, but he was a tremendously beautiful man, a man of immense grace. And how he became the founder of Zen is something to be remembered.

One day, a poor man in Vaishali – he was a shoemaker – found in his pond, a lotus flower out of season. He was very happy that he could sell it for a good price because it was not the season, and it was a beautiful lotus flower. He took the flower, and as he was going towards the palace he saw the richest man of the city coming towards him in his golden chariot. Seeing the beautiful lotus flower, the super-rich man stopped the chariot and asked Sudas, "How much will you take for your untimely lotus flower?"

Poor Sudas could not conceive how much. He said, "Whatever you can give will be enough for me. I am a poor man." The rich man said, "Perhaps you don't know but I am going to see Gautam Buddha who is staying outside the city in a mango grove, and I would like this untimely lotus flower to put at his feet. Even he will be surprised with such a gift. I will give you five hundred gold coins."

Sudas could not believe it. He had never dreamt that he would ever have five hundred gold coins. But just then the king's chariot stopped, and the king said to Sudas, "Whatever that rich man is giving you, I will give you four times more. Don't sell it, wait."

Sudas could not believe what was happening. Five hundred gold coins, four times. Two thousand gold coins for a single flower.

He asked the king, "I don't understand. What is the reason why you are so interested?"

But the rich man was not to be defeated so easily. He was richer than the king; in fact the king owed much money to him. He said, "It is not right of you. You are the king, but right now we are competitors. I will give four times more than what the king is giving." And this way they went on four times, four times...and Sudas lost track of how much money. The poor man did not know much arithmetic either; it was going beyond his capacity to count. But one thing he suddenly understood. And he stopped both the men and said, "Wait, I am not going to sell it." They were both shocked and said, "What is the problem? Do you want more?"

He said, "I don't know how much the price has gone to. And I don't want more. I simply don't want to sell it for the simple reason that both of you are going to give it to Gautam Buddha. I don't know anything about him, I have just heard his name. If the man is such that you are fighting to give any amount of money, then I will not miss the chance. I will present the lotus flower to Gautam Buddha. Let him be doubly surprised." From a poor man, who was being offered uncountable money.... But he refused.

Sudas went. The king and the rich man had reached there before and they had already told the story: "We have been shocked by a shoemaker; we have been defeated. He refused to sell it at any price. I was ready to offer him my whole treasury." And then Sudas, walking, arrived, touched Gautam Buddha's feet, and offered his flower at his feet.

Gautam Buddha said, "Sudas, you should have accepted; they were giving you so much money. I cannot give you anything."

There were tears in the eyes of Sudas, and he said, "If you can just hold my flower in your hand, it is enough. It is far greater than the whole kingdom. It is far greater than the super-rich man's whole treasury. I am poor, but I am perfectly okay; I earn my livelihood. There is no need for me to be rich. But it will be a historical event remembered for centuries and centuries – as long as man remembers you, Sudas will be remembered and his flower will be remembered. You just take it in your hand."

Buddha took the flower in his hand...and this was the time of the morning when he used to give his morning sermon. Everybody was waiting for him to start but rather than starting the morning sermon, he simply went on looking at the lotus flower. Minutes passed, one hour passed. People started becoming restless, thinking, "What has happened? This flower seems to be something magical that he is simply looking at the flower."

At that moment Mahakashyapa, one of the disciples of Gautam Buddha – who had never spoken, and who had not been mentioned before this or again after this, in any scriptures – laughed. And Gautam Buddha called Mahakashyapa, and gave the flower to him.

And he said, "It is not only the flower that I am giving to you, I am transmitting to you my whole light, my whole fragrance, my whole awakening. It is a transmission in silence; this flower is only symbolic."

This is the beginning of Zen.

People asked Mahakashyapa, "What happened? Although we were present and we were eyewitnesses, we could not see anything except the flower being given to you. And you touched the feet of Gautam Buddha and went back to your seat again and closed your eyes. What happened?"

Mahakashyapa is reported to have said only one thing: "You ask my master. While he is alive, I have no right to answer." And Gautam Buddha said, "This is a new beginning, of transferring without words my whole experience. One just has to be receptive. And Mahakashyapa, by his laughter, showed his receptivity. You don't know why he laughed. He laughed because in that moment, he suddenly looked into himself and he found that he is also a buddha. And I offered the flower as a recognition – 'I accept your awakening.'"

This man Mahakashyapa was the founder of Zen – or this situation between Mahakashyapa and Gautam Buddha is the beginning of the river of Zen. But Bodhidharma was such a strong individual that he has almost become the founder, although he came one thousand years later than Mahakashyapa. But he is immensely articulate. He can say things which cannot be said. He can speak the unspeakable. He can find ways and means and devices to bring you back home, to awaken you to your self-nature.

Mahakashyapa only realized his own nature. Nothing was given to him; it was only a recognition from the master. The master never gives anything to the disciple except the final recognition. The disciple already has everything. He just has to be tricked in some way to look into himself. All the meditations are simply arbitrary methods to look into yourself. Once you look into yourself the master can give you the recognition.

...The sutras say, "Everything that has form is an illusion." They also say, "Wherever you are there is a buddha."

You are there: there may not be anybody else, but wherever you are, there is a buddha, because you are a buddha. Don't look all around for where the buddha is. Wherever you are, there is a buddha, because you are there.

Your no-mind is the buddha. Don't use a buddha to worship a buddha.

Hence, Buddha has not taught worshiping, because it is ugly. All are buddhas – a few are asleep, a few are awake, but that does not make much difference. Those who are asleep will become awake. Those who are awake have been asleep. There is no question of worshiping. There is no prayer as such in Buddha's teachings.

Even if a buddha or a bodhisattva should suddenly appear before you, there is no need for reverence.

Bodhidharma is saying something that can be misunderstood. In fact, everything that he is saying can be misunderstood, so you have to be very alert not to misunderstand him. To understand him is very difficult, to misunderstand him is very simple. If you can manage not to misunderstand him, there is a possibility for understanding him.

When he says *there is no* need *for reverence,* the sentence is clear. But it can be easily misunderstood. He is saying: *there is no need for reverence.* He is not saying that there is no possibility of a spontaneous reverence. There is no *need;* it is not a duty. You are not obliged to revere a buddha, but your whole being may feel to, although there is no need. Without any need, you may feel a great reverence, a great gratitude just because the buddha represents your future, reminds you of your self-nature.

He is a reminder. He is an arrow pointing towards you. So there is no need for reverence, but there may be a spontaneous feeling for reverence.

Even Mahakashyapa touched Gautam Buddha's feet; there was no need. Even Bodhidharma, every day – although Buddha had died one thousand years before – used to bow down from China, towards the direction of the place where Buddha became enlightened, near Bodh Gaya, by the bank of a small river, Niranjana.

He used to find on the map, the place where Buddha had become enlightened one thousand years before, and he would touch the earth in China with his head. And he is saying: *there is no need for reverence.*

Certainly there is no need. But there arises a spontaneous reverence, and that is authentic reverence. When you do it as a need, it is false. When you have to do it because it is expected of you, then it is hypocrisy. But when it has been said to you that there is no need and still it arises in you, then it has an authenticity, a sincerity, a love, a gratitude, a truth, a beauty of its own.

This no-*mind of ours is empty and contains no such form. Those who hold onto appearances, are devils.*

It has to be said to you that in Buddhism, neither God exists nor devils. God and the devil can exist only together. They are two sides of the same coin.

God cannot do without the devil, and the devil cannot do without God; they are partners in the same business – but both are hypothetical. So when Bodhidharma uses the word 'devil' he simply means darkness. It is a personalization of darkness. There is no person as devil; there is no person as God. There is godliness, and there is evil. These are qualities, not persons.

Those who hold onto appearances are devils.

They are living in darkness, they are living a life of evil.

They fall from the path. Why worship illusions born of the mind? Those who worship don't know.

These are very strong and very pregnant statements. *Those who worship don't know.* Certainly they are not aware that they are carrying within themselves the buddha himself. *And those who know don't worship.*

So in the temples, in the synagogues, in the mosques, in the churches, all that worshiping going on is utterly out of ignorance, out of darkness. *Those who know don't worship:* They live a life which itself is worship. They don't go to the church, they don't go to the temple. They live a life which is twenty-four hours nothing but a worship. They live a life which is nothing but a prayerfulness. They live a life of compassion and love and gratitude. Each of their actions shows their enlightenment.

By worshiping you come under the spell of devils. I point this out because I am afraid you are unaware of it. The basic nature of a buddha has no such form. Keep this in mind, even if something unusual should appear. Don't embrace it, and don't fear it. And don't doubt that your no-mind is basically pure. Where could there be room for any such form? Also, at the appearance of spirits, demons, or divine beings, conceive neither respect nor fear.

These are only fantasies of your mind; they are only hallucinations. There are people who see Krishna, there are people who see Christ, there are people who see ghosts. There are people, all kinds of people, seeing all kinds of illusions. They are your mind creations. There is no need either for respect or for fear.

Your no-mind is basically empty. All appearances are illusion. Don't hold onto appearances.

Remember only one thing: your basic nature is absolute silence, serenity, peace, almost a nothingness, an emptiness. And that is your buddha-nature, that is your nature awakened to its own potential. To be aware of it is the greatest experience of life, because it brings liberation from life, birth, death. It takes you out of the wheel that goes on eternally giving you birth and death, and all the agonies and the sufferings. It takes you out into the world of ecstasy, of eternal blissfulness.

These sutras are not just for your entertainment. They are for your enlightenment. And remember the enlightenment is not going to come from outside. It is already there. You just have to wake up. You have been asleep for millions of lives. How many more do you want to sleep? It is time. In fact, you have already overslept. Now be kind to yourself and wake up.

Okay, Maneesha?

Yes, Bhagwan.

達磨

Beloved Bhagwan,

If you envision a buddha, a dharma or a bodhisattva and conceive respect for them, you relegate yourself to the realm of mortals. If you seek direct understanding, don't hold onto any appearance whatsoever, and you'll succeed. I have no other advice.

...Don't cling to appearances, and you'll be of one mind with the buddha.

But why shouldn't we worship buddhas and bodhisattvas?

Devils and demons possess the power of manifestation. They can create the appearance of bodhisattvas in all sorts of guises. But they're false. None of them are buddhas. The buddha is your own mind. Don't misdirect your worship.

Buddha is Sanskrit for what you call *aware, miraculously aware*. Responding, perceiving, arching your brows, blinking your eyes, moving your hands and feet, it's all your miraculously aware nature. And this nature is the mind. And the mind is the buddha. And the buddha is the path. And the path is zen. But the word *zen* is one that remains a puzzle. Seeing your nature is Zen.

Even if you can explain thousands of sutras and shastras, unless you see your own nature, yours is the teaching of a mortal, not a buddha. The true Way is sublime. It can't be expressed in language. Of what use are scriptures? But someone who sees his own nature finds the Way, even if he can't read a word.... Everything the buddha says is an expression of his mind. But since his body and expressions are basically empty, you can't find a buddha in words.

...The Way is basically perfect. It doesn't require perfecting. The Way has no form or sound. It's subtle and hard to perceive. It's like when you drink water. You know how hot or cold it is. But you can't tell

others. Of that which only a tathagata knows, men and gods remain unaware. The awareness of mortals falls short. As long as they're attached to appearances, they're unaware that their mind is empty. And by mistakenly clinging to the appearance of things, they lose the Way.

If you know that everything comes from the mind, don't become attached. Once attached, you're unaware. But once you see your own nature, the entire Canon becomes so much prose. Its thousands of sutras and shastras only amount to a clear mind. Understanding comes in mid-sentence. What good are doctrines?

The ultimate Truth is beyond words. Doctrines are words. They're not the Way. The Way is wordless. Words are illusions. They're no different from things that appear in your dreams at night, be they palaces or carriages.... Don't conceive any delight for such things. They're all cradles of rebirth. Keep this in mind when you approach death. Don't cling to appearances, and you'll break through all barriers. A moment's hesitation and you'll be under the spell of devils. Your real body is pure and impervious. But because of delusions, you're unaware of it. And because of this, you suffer Karma in vain. Wherever you find delight, you find bondage. But once you awaken to your original body and mind, you're no longer bound by attachments.

THE UNDERSTANDING OF Bodhidharma and his insight into the secrets of human consciousness is so profound that it certainly can be said it is perfect. Nothing can be added to it and nothing can be edited out of it. He speaks telegraphically, uses only the most essential words.

You will see how a man can express something which eludes expression, something which has always been known as inexpressible. But Bodhidharma comes very close to expressing it. If you don't understand, it is your fault.

Otherwise it is very difficult to find a master of the stature of Bodhidharma. In the whole legendary past of masters, Bodhidharma stands very aloof, very alone; his way of life, his way of teaching, everything is his own. Never before was there anybody like Bodhidharma, and there has never been another after him who can be called exactly equal in insight, in understanding, in profundity. And yet he does not use a jargon; he is not a philosopher, not a theologian. He is a very simple man. He uses direct words that go just like arrows into your heart. All that is needed on your part is to keep the doors of your heart open. He will not come uninvited within you, but invited he is sure to reach to your heart. Your receptivity is ultimately going to be the decisive factor.

In the sutras this evening, except for a few mistakes by the disciples who have taken the notes, almost everything seems to be authentically Bodhidharma's.

If you envision a buddha, a dharma, or a bodhisattva, and conceive respect for them, you relegate yourself to the realm of mortals.

According to Bodhidharma, everybody is essentially a buddha. But if you start imagining buddhas and worshiping them, then you are doing tremendous harm to yourself. It means you have not understood the basic teaching. There is no one to be worshiped, no one to be envisaged, because you are a buddha yourself.

It is because of this point that Gautam Buddha denies the existence of one God. His denial is so great that its significance has not been understood. He denies one God, not because he is an atheist; he denies one God because he respects every living being as a god. There are as many gods as there are living beings. A few have attained to the realization of who they are, and most of the people among the living beings are still asleep. They do not know who they are but their ignorance does not change their nature.

So the first sutra is: *If you envision a buddha, you relegate yourself to the realm of the mortals.* You unnecessarily degrade yourself. Every worshiper in every temple, in every synagogue, in every church, is humiliating himself and is humiliating the god within. The god within needs no other god to be worshipped. All that it needs is an awakening, awareness, a consciousness of one's own being.

The moment one becomes conscious of himself, he is no longer a mortal; he becomes an immortal. He has always been an immortal but because of his misunderstanding, he degraded himself into being a mortal, into someone who is going to die. Although the life within you and the consciousness within you is eternal and immortal, still you go on being afraid of death because you see somebody dying every day. And everybody's death reminds you of your own death.

The poet sings, "Never ask for whom the bell tolls, the bell tolls for thee." In Christian villages, it is an ancient custom that when somebody dies, the church bell starts tolling, informing the whole village, the people who have gone to the farms, or the people who have gone to the orchards, or the people who have gone to their wine presses, to come back; somebody has died.

The poet is saying, "Never ask for whom the bell tolls, it always tolls for thee." He has some truth to convey to you. Every death is symbolic. It shows that you are standing in the same queue and the queue is becoming shorter and shorter. Every day you are coming closer and closer to death. In fact the day you were born was not the day of your birth; it was the day you started dying. And since then you have been dying every day. Every birthday, your death has come one year closer.

It is an absolutely certain fact that people die, animals die, trees die, birds die. How can you avoid the fact that you are also going to die – maybe tomorrow, maybe the day after tomorrow? It is only a question of time.

But still, those who are aware of their being know that nobody dies.

Death is an illusion.

You have seen people die; have you ever seen yourself dying? And when you see somebody dying, are you really seeing somebody dying? All that you are seeing, and all that your medical science can see is that the man has stopped breathing, that his pulse has disappeared, that his heart beats no more, and they declare that he is dead.

Just a few days ago, a man in the part of Kashmir occupied by Pakistan, for the third time deceived his friends, his colleagues, his family. At the age of one hundred and thirty-five, he died for the third time. People were very suspicious because two times before he had played the trick; he died. Diagnosed by the doctors as dead, certified as dead, he woke up, opened his eyes and started laughing. So when he died this time, people were very cautious. Doctors were very cautious, but there was every certainty of his death; there was no question.

They said, "Perhaps before he may have deceived you, but this time he is certainly dead. As far as medical science can know, he fulfills every requirement of a dead man." And the moment the certificate was signed by three doctors, the man opened his eyes, started laughing and said, "Listen, next time when I am going to die, I am going to *really* die. I just thought one time more...."

That part of Kashmir occupied by Pakistan has the longest living people in India and Pakistan. One hundred and twenty is very ordinary, normal. One hundred and fifty you can find; it is not so normal, but still there are hundreds of people who have passed one hundred and fifty. And there are a few rare cases who have reached one hundred and eighty years of age and they are still young; they are still working in their fields.

And this man has been questioned by newspapers, by journalists from all over the world, because he is a rare man; three times certified dead and three times he has defied all medical knowledge, all medical science. And they asked, "What have you been doing? What happens?"

He said, "Nothing – because I am not my body. I know it; and I am not my breathing, I know it; and I am not my heart, I know it – I am beyond all these. I simply slip into the beyond. The heart stops, the pulse stops, the breathing stops, and you are all befooled. Then I slip back again into the body, the blood starts running again, the pulse starts working again and the heart starts beating again."

He is a simple man, a farmer. He is not a yogi; he has never practiced anything. But just when he was a very young child, not more than seven or eight years old, he came in contact with a Sufi mystic who told him that death is an illusion. And he was so innocent that he accepted it.

The Sufi mystic said to him, "There is a very simple way to slip out of your body. Just watch it from inside; watch the body and suddenly there will come more and more distance between you and your body. Soon the body will be miles away. Watch the mind and the same will happen with the mind.

"You simply remain a watcher and you will be able to slip out of the body, out of the mind, out of this whole personality. And it is within your control to come back. Because you have slipped out, you know the way you slipped out. So you know the way to come back in. And the way is that by watching, you slipped out – now stop watching. Become identified with the body. Say, 'I am the body, I am the mind, I am the breathing, I am the heart beating.' Immediately the distance will disappear. You will come closer and soon you will slip back into the body."

Identifying yourself with the body, you become the body.

Then you are a mortal.

Then there is fear of death.

Non-identifying with the body, you are just a watcher, you are just a pure consciousness, a no-mind. And there is no death and there is no disease and there is no old age. As far as your witnessing is concerned, it is eternal and it is always fresh and young and the same.

The authentic religion does not teach you to worship. The authentic religion teaches you to discover your immortality, to discover the god within you. And that's what Bodhidharma is saying.

If you seek direct understanding, don't hold onto any appearance whatsoever, and you will succeed. I have no other advice.

His advice is very simple, but it never fails. He is advising not to get identified with any appearance: the body is an appearance, the mind is an appearance, the world is an appearance. The only thing that is absolutely real is your consciousness. Everything else goes on changing. That which goes on changing is an appearance – don't get identified with it. You are the unchanging divine, you are the unchanging godliness. And Bodhidharma says: *I have no other advice.*

...Don't cling to appearances, and you will be of one mind with the buddha.

The sutra says: *You will be of one mind with the buddha.* That is the misunderstanding of the person who has been taking notes of Bodhidharma's statements. I have to make the correction from "mind" to "no-mind."

As minds, you can never be one with the buddha. Just try to understand, because it is infinitely significant. Here, if you are all minds, then there are as many people as there are minds. But if you all become silent, with no thoughts, then there is only one no-mind – then all the distinctions disappear. Whether you are a man or a woman, a young child or old, educated or uneducated, rich or poor, it does not matter.

All distinctions disappear the moment mind is transcended. All distinctions are made by the mind. Beyond the mind is just a silent sky, a pure space. In that pure space with the buddha, you are all one with existence.

You are one with the whole.

I call this oneness with the whole, the only holiness.

The disciple asks Bodhidharma: *But why shouldn't we worship buddhas and bodhisattvas?*

The disciple seems to be of a very mediocre mind, because Bodhidharma has already answered. And now what he gives as Bodhidharma's answer, I deny absolutely that it can be the answer of Bodhidharma. It is so stupid that Bodhidharma cannot say it. So first I will read what the disciple writes, then I will tell you what exactly Bodhidharma must have said.

Devil and demons possess the power of manifestation. They can create the appearance of bodhisattvas in all sorts of guises. But they're false. None of them are buddhas. The buddha is your own mind. Don't misdirect your worship.

The disciple is saying that worshiping a buddha is denied because the devils can pretend to be buddhas. If you worship, the appearance will be of the buddha, and in fact there is a devil hiding behind the appearance. This cannot be the answer of Bodhidharma.

A man who does not believe in God cannot believe in devils. A man who is capable of denying God is certainly capable of denying all devils.

And his only answer could have been the one which he gave in the basic sutra. Without any doubt his answer would have been, "You should not worship any buddhas because you are a buddha. It is simply ridiculous that a buddha worships another buddha."

I am reminded of another Zen master. He must have been a man of some similar qualities to Bodhidharma; he was a disciple in the same lineage. He was staying in a Buddhist temple on a winter night – the priest, knowing that he was a great master had allowed him to stay in the temple. But in the middle of the night the priest woke up. Suddenly there was so much light. He looked inside the temple…because his room was by the side of the temple. The master he had allowed to stay in the temple was enjoying burning a beautiful statue, a wooden statue of Gautam Buddha.

The priest was simply mad. He said, "Are you insane or something? You have burnt the statue of Gautam Buddha."

The master took his staff and started searching for something in the ashes of the burned statue. The priest said, "What are you searching for?" He said, "I am looking for the bones."

Even the priest had to laugh, although he was angry and his most beautiful statue had been burned. But he said, "You are really insane. But how can a wooden statue have bones?"

The master said, "That's what I have been showing you; that if there are no bones inside it, it is not the statue of Buddha. It is not Buddha; it is just wood cut into a certain shape. Don't be deceived by it. The night is long and it is too cold and I am so tired of this long journey. If you can be of some help…you have still got three more statues. One is enough for worshiping, two you can give me. The night is really cold. Moreover I am a living buddha. For a living buddha it is absolutely right to burn a wooden buddha to have a little heat. It is too cold in this temple."

The priest became very afraid that this man seemed to be absolutely dangerous and thought, "If I go to sleep, he is going to burn all my statues." In the middle of the night he threw the master out of the temple. The master was insisting, "This is not right. Listen, you will repent of it. You are throwing a living buddha into the darkness of the night, into the cold winter night. And you are protecting wooden buddhas. Are you mad or something?"

The priest said, "I don't want to discuss it with you. I know who is mad. You just get out."

In the morning the priest opened the door to see at what had happened to the master. He was sitting by the side of the road. He had picked a few wild flowers and he had put those wildflowers on a milestone. He was worshiping, *"Buddham sharanam, gachchhami. Sangham sharanam gachchhami. Dhammam sharanam gachchhami."*

The priest could not believe it. "He is really mad. Last night he burned a buddha, so costly" – it was made of sandalwood – "and now that madman is worshiping a milestone as a buddha." The priest came close to him and said, "What are you doing?"

The master said, "My morning prayer." The priest said, "But you look a strange type. Last night you destroyed my buddha and now you are worshiping a milestone."

He said, "You don't understand. It is only our visualization. If you visualize that this is a buddha, this is a buddha. You visualized a buddha in the wooden statue – it became a buddha. It is all a mind game. I don't believe in prayers. It was just for you that I waited and was worshiping the milestone – just to show you that whatever you worship, you are worshiping something wrong, because you are the buddha. The worshiper is the buddha, not the worshiped. Can I come in the temple again tonight?"

The priest said, "No, although you appear to be right and perhaps I am wrong, I cannot follow your great understanding – it is dangerous. It will be good if you leave this place and do your act in some other temple. I am a poor priest; you have already destroyed one of my most beautiful buddhas; now I cannot – even though you convinced me – I cannot allow you inside the temple."

The master said, "It is not a question…but I can see that you have understood rightly, and one day you will come searching for me. I can see in your eyes the light of understanding, a ray of understanding. Don't let me in…but I am already within you."

And after two years the priest had to come to the master to give an apology, and he brought the remaining three statues, saying, "You can burn them whenever you need. I have understood. Since that night, I have not been able for a single moment to forget you – your beauty, your grace, your peace, your silence and your great effort to make me understand that what I had been doing was stupid.

"And I misbehaved with you; I threw you out in the dark night, on a cold night. Still you waited for me next morning, to give me another opportunity to understand. And I was so foolish that I missed that opportunity too. But two years are enough. You have been haunting me. Now I have come, knowing perfectly well that the buddha is within; he is not in the statues of the temples, and the statues of the temples and the milestones are not different."

That reminds me: when for the first time in India, the British government created the roads and put the milestones, they painted those milestones red, because red is a very brilliant color and you can see it from far away. Particularly in contrast to the greenery of the fields and the forest, it looks separate. Any other color may get mixed, but red stands absolutely separate.

The British engineers who were working on the roads were surprised that the villagers started worshiping them! They thought that these were statues of Hanuman. It was a great problem for the engineers to tell those villagers that they were just milestones. But the villagers insisted, "They may be milestones for you, but for us, it is perfectly good. They look so beautiful, and we are not doing any harm to you. We will just be worshiping them."

I have been reading the history…when the roads were first made in India, the British engineers were shocked. They could not prevent the villagers who had said, "You can think of them as milestones, but what is the harm if we worship them? To us they look just the statues of Hanuman."

Bodhidharma's answer cannot be what the disciple has noted here. His answer can only be: Remember your own buddhahood, awaken to your own buddhahood, and this awakening will make your no-mind one with the buddha. Don't misdirect your worship. You have to worship your own innermost consciousness. You are the temple, you are the worshiper, and you are the worshiped.

Buddha is Sanskrit for what you call aware, miraculously aware. Responding, perceiving, arching your brows, blinking your eyes, moving your hands and feet, it is all your miraculously aware nature. And this nature is the no-mind. And the no-mind is the buddha. And the buddha is the path. And the path is zen. But the word zen is one that remains a puzzle. Seeing your nature is Zen.

The word *zen* remains a puzzle because it comes from a Sanskrit root; it comes from the word *dhyan*. Buddha used the contemporary language of his people – which was a revolutionary step, because Sanskrit has always been the language of the scholars. Buddha brought a revolution by using the people's language, not the language of the scholars. He used Pali so that every villager could understand. In Pali, *dhyan* is changed into a little different form; it has become *zh'an*. And when Bodhidharma reached China, he talked about *zh'an*. But in Chinese, it took another change; it became *ch'an*. And then from China, it reached Japan; from *ch'an* it became *zen*. Far away it lost the original root. Now in Japanese there is no root for *zen;* the word is foreign to Japanese. For *ch'an* there is no root in Chinese; the word is foreign.

That's why it is a riddle; what is Zen? But if you can come back to the root, things become simple; the puzzle disappears. *Dhyan* means going beyond the mind, going beyond thought process, entering into silence, utter silence where nothing moves, where nothing disturbs, where everything is absent – only a pure emptiness. This space is zen; this space is meditation. There is no riddle about it. But only in this country can the root of zen be found. Zen was born here in this country; it blossomed in Japan. The flowers came in Japan and they were a riddle, because they could not find where the root is, where the tree is. They could only see the flowers and the fragrance. The roots were far away in this country, and it is such an unfortunate thing that *dhyan* flowered to its ultimate in Japan, and in India it disappeared almost completely.

The Indian embassies have been informed by the Indian government that anybody from any country of the world who wants to come to India to learn meditation, should not be given any tourist visa.

The government does not know anything about meditation. Politicians cannot afford to be meditators, because the foundation of meditation is to be non-ambitious, non-desiring, non-achieving. A politician cannot afford to be a meditator. Hence, in Indian universities there is no provision for meditation, which is India's greatest contribution to the world. And people who want to come to India to learn meditation are prevented by Indian embassies all over the world. They are allowed visas to come if they just want to see the Taj Mahal, temples of Khajuraho, go for honeymoon to Kashmir, or for any absurd reason, but not for meditation.

It is one of the unfortunate incidents that has happened in India. India created the greatest meditators in the world, and from India the whole of Asia learned meditation. It still is alive in the monasteries of Japan; but in India there is no support from any source for India's own greatest contribution to human progress. But the reason is clear: the people who are in power don't understand even the ABC of being silent. They know only a tense mind, anxieties and worries, ambitions, cunningness, pulling each other's legs, sabotaging each other's power. Their whole concern is a tremendous ambition for being in power.

Meditation is totally different; not only different, but a diametrically opposite dimension. It is the way of the humble man, it is the way of the simple heart. It is the way of those who want to rejoice in disappearing just like a dewdrop disappears in the ocean.

Even if you can explain thousands of sutras and shastras, unless you see your own nature, yours is the teaching of a mortal.

You may understand the holy scriptures, you may know the *Vedas,* you may know the *Upanishads,* you may know *The Holy Bible,* you may know the holy *Koran,* or the holy *Gita,* but if you don't know yourself, your teaching is just a repetition, a mechanical repetition like a parrot. And perhaps parrots are also more intelligent than your pundits.

I have heard about a bishop who had two parrots, and for years he trained them to recite the official Christian prayer. He made small golden beads for the parrots; they were holding the beads and reciting the prayer, and any guest who used to come was simply amazed. Their recitation was so perfect and they looked almost like saints, with their beads in their hands.

Finally, because he had been praised so much for what he had done in teaching the parrots, the bishop thought he would purchase one more parrot and train him also. So he bought another parrot and put that new parrot between those two sages, reciting the prayer with their beads. As the bishop went in, one parrot said to the other, "George, now drop the beads. Our prayers have been heard; our beloved has reached us."

It was a female parrot. Even parrots seem to be more intelligent....

A man who does not know himself should feel ashamed teaching others just because he knows scriptures. Scholarship has no meaning at all in the authentic world of religion. It is a world of experience, not of explanations. The man who teaches according to the scriptures is:

...a mortal, not a buddha. The true Way is sublime. It can't be expressed in language. Of what use are scriptures? But someone who sees his own nature, finds the Way, even if he can't read a word.... Everything the buddha says is an expression of his no-*mind. But since his body and expressions are basically empty, you can't find a buddha in words.*

...The Way is basically perfect. It does not require perfecting. The Way has no form or sound. It is subtle and hard to perceive. It is like when you drink water. You know how hot or cold it is, but you can't tell others. Of that which only a tathagata knows, men and gods remain unaware. The awareness of mortals falls short.

You have a little awareness – but very little. If your whole being can be taken into account, then nine parts of it are in darkness and in unconsciousness. Only one part out of ten is conscious, just a very superficial layer which can easily be disturbed. Somebody insults you and you forget all about humbleness, you forget all about being nice, you immediately become enraged. Suddenly your barbarousness comes up. Just a little scratch and the animal starts showing its reality from your very being.

Your civilization is so superficial. It is just like your clothes; you can drop them any moment. And you all know that there are moments when you drop all your civilization, all your culture, all your religion, all your great qualities that you talk about; within a second, they disappear. Your consciousness is so small.

The awareness of mortals falls very short. It cannot reach to the heights of a fully awakened human being. That's why a buddha is bound to be misunderstood. Whatever he will do is so far away from you – he is almost on a sunlit peak of the Himalayas and you are in the dark valleys. Even if what he says reaches you, it is no longer the same. You hear only resounding valleys. Something of it reaches you and you interpret according to your own mind.

One night it happened: Gautam Buddha used to say to his disciples every night, after his discourse, "Now it is time; go and do the last necessary thing. Don't forget before you go to sleep." His hint was about the last meditation before you go into sleep. But one night it happened, there was a thief in the congregation and there was a prostitute too. When Buddha said, "Now it time you go and do the last thing before you go to sleep," the prostitute thought, "My God, he knows that I am here, and that it is time for my profession. I should go, hurry up."

The thief said, "I am hiding in dark corners, because nobody knows.... This man, he may recognize that I am a thief, and he has recognized. He is saying to me, 'Now go, and do the last thing, before you go to sleep. It is time.' My God, this man is really strange. I have to run now; it is late and it is time to finish my work; otherwise I won't have any sleep tonight."

Thousands of the sannyasins went to meditation. The prostitute went to her marketplace. The thief started searching for his work. Buddha said one thing, but there were different interpretations according to everybody's own mind.

As long as they are attached to appearances, they are unaware that their no-mind is empty. And by mistakenly clinging to the appearance of things, they lose the Way.

If you know that everything comes from no- mind...

Everything comes from nothingness, and disappears again into nothingness. And you see it happening every day; from a seed a tree arises. You just cut the seed and see – you will not find any tree, you will not find any branches, you will not find any foliage, you will not find any fragrance, any fruits – nothing, just emptiness.

But from a seed, which is nothing but emptiness, a great tree arises with great foliage, with many flowers, with many fruits and with millions of seeds. And from each seed, again millions of seeds. The scientists who study trees, vegetation, say that a single seed can make the whole earth green. It has so much potential, although you cannot see by cutting it – you will not find anything there.

Everything comes out of nothingness and goes back into nothingness. Hence there is no need for attachment, because attachment will bring misery. Soon it will be gone. The flower that has blossomed in the morning, by the evening will be gone.

Don't get attached; otherwise in the evening there will be misery. Then there will be tears, then you will miss the flower. Enjoy while it is. But remember, it has come out of nothing, and it will go back to nothing. And the same is true about everything, even about people.

You love a man, you love a woman; from where have they come? From very small seeds which cannot even be seen by bare eyes. If they are put in front of you, they will not be bigger than the full stop. And you will not recognize that this is you, or that one day you were like this, that this is your old photograph.

One day you will disappear on a funeral pyre – just into nothingness, as smoke. Don't get attached to anything. This attachment takes you away from your real being; you become focused on the thing to which you are attached. Your awareness gets lost in things, in money, in people, in power. And there are a thousand and one things, the whole thick jungle around you, to be lost in.

Remember, non-attachment is the secret of finding yourself, then awareness can turn inwards because you don't have anything outside to catch hold of. It is free, and in this freedom you can know your self-nature.

...don't become attached. Once attached, you are unaware. But once you see your own nature, the entire Canon becomes so much prose.

Then all the scriptures are useless. You have seen the holiest of the holy; the very source of the *Upanishads*, the very source of the *Vedas*, the very source of all so-called holy scriptures. When you have found the source, who bothers about scriptures? They are so much prose, nothing else.

Its thousands of sutras and shastras only amount to a clear no-mind. Understanding comes in mid-sentence.

This is such a beautiful statement. Understanding does not come through words, but through gaps – in the moments of silence.

Understanding comes in mid-sentence. What good are doctrines?

The ultimate Truth is beyond words. Doctrines are words. They are not the Way. The Way is wordless. Words are illusions. They are no different from things that appear in your dreams at night, be they palaces or carriages.... Don't conceive any delight for such things. They are all cradles of rebirth. Keep this in mind when you approach death. Don't cling to appearances, and you will break through all barriers.

This is a great statement to be remembered because everybody is going to pass through the gates of death someday. If you can remember that you are only pure consciousness – not the body, not the mind, not the heart, not your money, not your prestige, not your power, not your house, but just pure consciousness – then you can pass through the barrier of death unscratched. Then death cannot make even a dent in you.

Death has power over you only if you are attached.

You are not afraid of death. The basic psychology is you are afraid of death because it will take you away from all your attachments. If it were possible that you could take your wife and your children and your house and your money and your power and everything that you think belongs to you, with yourself when you are dying, I don't think you would be afraid. You would rejoice; a great adventure – going with the whole caravan. But death cuts everything away from you, leaves you utterly naked – only as a consciousness....

In the *Upanishads* there is an ancient story that I have always loved. A great king named Yayati became one hundred years old. Now it was enough; he had lived tremendously. He had enjoyed all that life could make available. He was one of the greatest kings of his time. But the story is beautiful....

Death came and said to Yayati, "Get ready. It is time for you, and I have come to take you." Yayati saw Death, and he was a great warrior and he had won many wars. Yayati started trembling, and said, "But it is too early." Death said, "Too early! You have been alive for one hundred years. Even your children have become old. Your eldest son is eighty years old. What more do you want?"

Yayati had one hundred sons because he had one hundred wives. He asked Death, "Can you do a favor for me? I know you have to take someone. If I can persuade one of my sons, can you leave me for one hundred years more and take one of my sons?" Death said, "That is perfectly okay if somebody else is ready to go. But I don't think.... If you are not ready, and you are the father and you have lived more and you have enjoyed everything, why should your son be ready?"

Yayati called his one hundred sons. The older sons remained silent. There was great silence, nobody was saying anything. Only one, the youngest son who was only sixteen years of age, stood up and he said, "I am ready." Even Death felt sorry for the boy and said to the young man, "Perhaps you are too innocent. Can't you see your ninety-nine brothers are absolutely silent? Someone is eighty, someone is seventy-five, someone is seventy-eight, someone is seventy, someone is sixty – they have lived – but they still want to live. And you have not lived at all. Even I feel sad to take you. You think again."

The boy said, "No, just seeing the situation makes me completely certain. Don't feel sad or sorry; I am going with absolute awareness. I can see that if my father is not satisfied in one hundred years, what is the point of being here? How can I be satisfied? I am seeing my ninety-nine brothers; nobody is satisfied. So why waste time? At least I can do this favor to my father. In his old age, let him enjoy one hundred years more. But I am finished. Seeing the situation that nobody is satisfied, I can understand one thing completely – that even if I live one hundred years, I will not be satisfied either. So it doesn't matter whether I go today or after ninety years. You just take me."

Death took the boy. And after one hundred years he came back. And Yayati was in the same position. And he said, "These hundred years passed so soon. All my old sons have died, but I have another regiment. I can give you some son. Just have mercy on me."

It went on – the story goes on to say – for one thousand years. Ten times Death came. And nine times he took some son and Yayati lived one hundred years more. The tenth time Yayati said, "Although I am still as unsatisfied as I was when you came for the first time, now – although unwillingly, reluctantly – I will go, because I cannot go on asking for favors. It is too much. And one thing has become certain to me, that if one thousand years cannot help me to be contented, then even ten thousand will not do."

It is the attachment.

You can go on living but as the idea of death strikes you, you will start trembling.

But if you are not attached to anything, death can come this very moment and you will be in a very welcoming mood. You will be absolutely ready to go.

In front of such a man, death is defeated.

Death is defeated only by those who are ready to die any moment, without any reluctance. They become the immortals, they become the buddhas.

A moment's hesitation when death comes and you will be under the spell of devils. Your real body, your real being is pure and impervious. But because of delusions, you are unaware of it. And because of this, you suffer in vain. Wherever you find delight, you find bondage. But once you awaken to your original being and no-mind, you are no longer bound by attachments.

This freedom is the goal of all religious search.

Freedom from attachment is freedom from death.

Freedom from attachment is freedom from the wheel of birth and death.

Freedom from attachment makes you capable of entering into the universal light and becoming one with it. And that is the greatest blessing, the ultimate ecstasy beyond which nothing else exists.

You have come home.

Okay, Maneesha?

Yes, Bhagwan.

GET READY AND CLAIM YOUR INHERITANCE

達磨

108 ___ YO-U-I: READY

7

Beloved Bhagwan,

Anyone who gives up the transcendent for the mundane, in any of its myriad forms, is a mortal. A buddha is someone who finds freedom in good fortune and bad. Such is his power, karma can't hold him. No matter what kind of karma, a buddha transforms it. Heaven and hell are nothing to him.

...If you're not sure, don't act. Once you act, you wander through birth and death and regret having no refuge..... To understand this mind, you have to act without acting. Only then will you see things from a tathagata's perspective.

But when you first embark on the Path, your awareness won't be focused. You're likely to see all sorts of strange, dreamlike scenes. But you shouldn't doubt that all such scenes come from your own mind and nowhere else.

If you see a light brighter than the sun, your remaining attachments will suddenly come to an end, and the nature of reality will be revealed. Such an occurrence serves as the basis for enlightenment. But this is something only you know. You can't explain it to others.

...Or if, while you're walking, standing, sitting or lying in the stillness and darkness of night, everything appears as though in daylight, don't be startled. It's your own mind about to reveal itself.

...If you see your nature, you don't need to read sutras or invoke buddhas. Erudition and knowledge are not only useless, they cloud your awareness. Doctrines are only for pointing to the mind. Once you see your mind, why pay attention to doctrines?

To go from mortal to buddha, you have to put an end to karma, nurture your awareness and accept what life brings.

...Once mortals see their nature, all attachments end. Awareness isn't hidden. But you can only find it right now. It's only now. If you really want to find the Way, don't hold onto anything. Once you put an end to karma and nurture your awareness, any attachments that remain will come to an end. Understanding comes naturally. You don't have to make any effort. But fanatics don't understand what the Buddha meant. And the harder they try, the farther they get from the Sage's meaning. All day long they invoke buddhas and read sutras. But they remain blind to their own divine nature, and they don't escape the Wheel.

A buddha is an idle person. He doesn't run around after fortune and fame. What good are such things in the end?

BODHIDHARMA DOES NOT divide the world into matter and spirit. He is against all divisions. The universe is one organic whole. But there seem to be divisions...then they must be coming from somewhere else, because the world is undivided. They come from your consciousness. If you are not conscious, you are a mortal; if you are conscious, you are immortal. If you are unconscious, you look at the world as mundane, and that which is beyond the world as sacred. But if you are conscious, aware, enlightened, a buddha, then there is nothing mundane and nothing sacred. Then everything is one.

This oneness has to be deeply understood.

Divisions come from our consciousness or unconsciousness; it is our perspective. Just like the blind man standing in the sun is still in darkness...it is not that there is darkness outside of him. It is bright light, a beautiful morning, the birds singing praises and welcoming the sun. And the flowers are opening their buds and releasing their fragrance to the wind. It is a tremendous experience. But for the blind man, there are no colors, no flowers, no sun, no light. If his eyes are cured, suddenly he will be amazed that the world of darkness he used to see before is the same as the world of light which he sees now. The division was because of his blindness, not because there is a division in existence itself.

On this point Bodhidharma has a tremendous contribution to make. Most of the philosophers of the world and founders of religions have always divided the mundane and the sacred, the material and the spiritual, without knowing that the moment you divide existence as material and spiritual you are also dividing man into body and soul. And a man divided within himself is a house divided which can fall any moment. A man divided within himself is always in a constant fight with himself; his whole energy is wasted in fighting with himself. He cannot use his energy in a beautiful flowering. Springs come and go, but he has no energy to bring flowers. He is exhausted.

Perhaps the vested interests of the world have always wanted man to be tired and exhausted. It is supportive to their vested interests, because a man overflowing with energy cannot be prevented from being a rebel.

A man who is tired and exhausted cannot be provoked into any rebellion against any injustice, against any exploitation. He has no energy for it. He is living at the minimum, while he could have lived at the maximum. But a basic conspiracy against man has been practiced down the ages: divide. And that is the fundamental principle of all rulers – divide and rule. Religious preachers, priests, have not been anything other than politicians. Their whole desire is also to divide and rule.

An undivided individual cannot be enslaved. This division is a kind of castration. Just see the beauty of a bull: you cannot force him to carry your cart, you cannot keep him on the road under your control. He has so much power and so much individuality that he will choose his path, he will go this way and that way. And if he comes across a girlfriend, then your life and your cart are both in danger!

But just look at a bullock, carrying your carts, your loads...you have destroyed the beauty, the energy, the individuality, by castrating the bull. It is the same animal, but now without any energy. You have made him impotent, and he was so potent....

Strangely enough, the same has been done with man. All the religions and all the politicians of the world have been castrating man; otherwise man would also have the beauty and the grandeur and the splendor of being a bull, not a bullock. A bullock is a tragedy. A bullock is a condemnation of all those who have destroyed his natural beauty, power, potentiality. But to make a slave of a bull, this was a necessary step.

Why has man tolerated all kinds of exploitations, humiliations, slavery? For a simple reason: he has no energy. Where has his energy gone? He has been taught and conditioned to fight with himself. The conspiracy is really very clever. By fighting with yourself, you are destroying yourself.

Bodhidharma's singular teaching is to know your self-nature, which is undivided, which is neither separate nor profane, which is neither material nor spiritual – which is transcendent, transcendent to all divisions, all dualities. This transcendental in you is your real being. And it has so much energy, so much overflowing power that it brings all kinds of blessings to you without ever being asked. It brings all kinds of beautiful flowers to blossom within your being without being asked. It is simply natural.

Man has been put into an unnatural situation; hence his misery, his suffering, his hell. To be unnatural is to be in hell, and to be in your self-nature is to be in heaven. There is no other hell, there is no other heaven.

These sutras are tremendously significant for all those who want to know their self-nature. Because that is the ultimate wisdom, and out of it, all your actions become beautiful, gracious, good – without any effort on your part, just naturally, as naturally as a roseflower grows out of a rosebush. Goodness, beauty, grace, virtue...everything grows naturally, without any effort, without any action on your part, once you know your self-nature.

This is the greatest knowing in the whole of existence.

Anyone who gives up the transcendent for the mundane, in any of its myriad forms, is a mortal.

To give up the transcendent.... Remember the meaning of the transcendent: that which transcends all dualities. Anyone who forgets the language of oneness with existence unnecessarily becomes a mortal. Then there is death – against life. Then there is body – against spirit. Then everything has its polar opposite. Then there is love as a polar opposite to hate. But remember one fundamental thing: the polar opposites are exchangeable. Love can become hate, hate can become love – and you all know it.

Friendship can turn into enmity, and enmity can become friendship.

You all know – happiness can turn into sadness, and sadness can change into happiness. Although they are polar opposites, they are almost like twins, very close. Just a slight change in circumstances and one disappears...the other was just behind it.

So remember the transcendent – existence belongs to the transcendental. Don't divide it; otherwise you will be continuously tortured by the duality.

A buddha is someone who finds freedom in good fortune and bad.

It does not matter to a man of awareness whether he is successful or unsuccessful, whether he is well known or absolutely unknown, whether he is somebody powerful or just a nobody, a nonentity. To a man of awareness, all these dualities don't matter at all, because awareness is the greatest treasure. When you have it, you don't want anything else. You don't want to become a president of a country, or a prime minister of a country. Those are for children, retarded people, to play the game.

The people who go on running after ambitions are no more intelligent than football players. Their games may have different names, but their reality is the same. And they suffer continuously. Even in their success they suffer, because then they become afraid of whether they are also going to keep this successful position tomorrow. First they were suffering because they were not successful; now they are suffering because people are dragging on their legs, and everybody wants to be in their place.

To be on a powerful throne is to be in a most hilarious position. Everybody is pulling you down and you have to remain glued to the throne, whatever happens. Somebody is pulling your hands, somebody is taking your head, somebody is taking your legs away...whatever happens, dead or alive, you are determined to remain on the throne.

The life of a successful man is not a life of peace. And if this is the situation of success, you can conceive the situation of failure. If this is the situation of times you call good, you can understand the situation of times which are bad.

But for a man of awareness, it is all the same. Success comes and goes, failure comes and goes.

You remain untouched and aloof.

This aloofness, this untouchedness, is your transcendental self-nature. Nothing makes even a scratch on you.

One of the mystics of India, Kabir, sings a song, *Jyon ki tyon dhar dinhi chadariya.* "I have returned to God" or to existence, "the clothing that he had given to me to live in the world – without any change. I have not made it dirty; not even a particle of dust has gathered on it. I have put it back into his hands exactly as fresh as it was when he gave it to me." This is the experience of an awakened man. He lives in the darkest nights in the same silence, in the same peace, as he lives in the brightest day. He never makes the division. He remains always transcendental, he remains always above any divisions. Divisions are left far behind.

Such is his power, actions can't hold him. No matter what kind of action, a buddha transforms it.

This statement has to be taken deep into your heart....

You have heard the story in Greek mythology of King Midas, who had been praying his whole life to God: "Just grant me one wish, that whatever I touch must turn into gold." And it seems God became tired of his continuous nagging...because what are your prayers other than nagging?

And a poor God, and so many nagging people, and he has been nagged for millions of years – it is no wonder if he has disappeared or committed suicide or whatever has happened. Nobody can tolerate that much nagging.

Finally, God granted him the wish – "Whatever you touch will turn into gold. And now leave me at peace!"

But the unconscious man cannot do anything better. Friedrich Nietzsche is right when he says that if all your prayers were fulfilled, you would be in utter hell. Your prayers are coming from your unconsciousness; you don't know what you are asking for. It is good that God is deaf and no prayer is ever answered; otherwise you would repent..."Why have I prayed...?"

And this was the situation with King Midas. He had never thought of all the implications of his whole lifelong prayer. Morning and evening he went on praying only for one thing: "I don't want anything else. Just a simple thing – whatever I touch should be transformed into gold."

But as the prayer was granted he became aware of its implications. He could not eat because whatever he touched turned into gold. He could not drink because by the time his lips touched the water, it would turn into gold. His wife escaped, his children left him, his friends stopped coming to see him. Even his servants remained alert. All his great courtiers forgot to come to his court. He used to sit alone – hungry, thirsty, but it was now too late. It took his whole life to pray to get the wish. Now to get it canceled would take a whole life again!

He started praying but nothing happened. He died from starvation, and he killed a few people by touching them. He certainly made a gold palace by touching his house; all his furniture became gold – but what is the purpose of it? He suffered so badly as perhaps nobody has ever suffered, and he was one of the richest men in the world.

You have heard about "green thumbs" – gardeners have them. Great gardeners have them; whatever they touch turns green. King Midas had golden fingers; whatever he touched turned into gold. But he lost his wife, he lost his friends, he lost his courtiers, he lost everything – although he was the most successful and the richest man.

A man of awareness, a buddha, also has a transforming power: whatever he touches becomes blissful. Misery comes to him and he finds in it something blissful; sadness comes to him and he finds something immensely beautiful and silent in it. Death comes to him but he finds only immortality in it. Whatever he touches is transformed, because now he has the transcendental perspective. And that is the greatest power in the world – not power over anybody, but simply your intrinsic power.

Night becomes as beautiful as day; death becomes as much a celebration as life, because the man of transcendence knows that he is eternal.

Lives come and go, deaths come and go.

He remains untouched, he remains always beyond.

This quality of remaining always beyond is the true enlightenment. Heaven and hell are nothing to him. Hence, once when Bodhidharma was asked, "What do you say about heaven and hell?" he said, "I cannot say anything because it all depends on you."

The man was puzzled: how can heaven and hell depend on a poor man? Bodhidharma said, "There is no hell and there is no heaven. Wherever a man of awareness dwells, there is heaven; and wherever a man of unawareness dwells, there is hell."

You carry your hell in your unconsciousness and you carry your heaven in consciousness. These are not geographical places, these are states of your being. Asleep, you are in hell and suffering from nightmares. Awake, you are in heaven and all suffering has ceased.

Heaven and hell are nothing to him.

I am reminded of a beautiful incident that happened in the life of Edmund Burke, an English philosopher. He had a great friendship with the archbishop of England – and the archbishop of England is equal to the pope. As far as the church of England is concerned, the archbishop is the representative of Jesus Christ.

Edmund Burke and the archbishop were great friends because they had studied together in the university. And the archbishop used to come to listen to Edmund Burke's lectures, whenever he announced lectures. But Edmund Burke never went to the archbishop's sermons – not even once. And naturally, the archbishop was waiting: someday....

Finally, he himself invited him: "This Sunday you have to come. No excuses." And he prepared his life's best sermon. He wanted to impress Edmund Burke...and he constantly looked at him, because he was sitting in the front row. And the archbishop was feeling great fear, because he did not see even a sign on the face of Edmund Burke that he was impressed or moved. Although he was shouting and beating the table and doing every kind of gymnastics that Christian missionaries are trained to do, Edmund Burke remained silent, without saying a word.

The sermon finished, and they both left in the same car. Edmund Burke was still silent...the archbishop was thinking perhaps he would say something now. And they came to his house and he was getting out of the car, and the archbishop could not contain his temptation to ask – "You have not said anything about my sermon. Say *anything*. Even if it was not good, at least say it; otherwise I will continuously think about it, about what your impression was."

Edmund Burke said, "It was neither good nor bad, it was simply stupid. You made such idiotic statements that I would have never thought a man of your intelligence could make."

He said, "What idiotic statements?"

Edmund Burke said, "You said that those who believe in Jesus Christ and do good works will go to heaven. And those who don't believe in Jesus Christ and do evil acts will go to hell. Can't you see the idiocy in it, the stupidity?"

The archbishop said, "I can't see it yet."

Edmund Burke said, "Then I will show it to you: If a man does not believe in Jesus Christ and does good works, where is he going? And if a man believes in Jesus Christ and does evil acts, where is he going? Are good works and evil acts to be decisive? Then the belief in Jesus Christ is superfluous. Or if the belief in Jesus Christ is the criterion, then the question of good acts or evil acts is irrelevant."

The archbishop had never thought about it. Perhaps no religious person ever thinks about it, that a man can be absolutely religious without believing in any religion, that a man's life can be absolutely the life of wisdom and goodness without believing in any God, without believing in any prophet, without believing in any savior. And vice versa: A man may believe in God, in Jesus, and still his life will be nothing but the life of an animal.

The archbishop said, "The question is very difficult and I have never thought about it. You will have to give me seven days. Next Sunday in my sermon, I will answer it. You will have to come once more, because I would like to make my statement before my whole congregation."

Edmund Burke gave him seven days, and those seven days were of great torture to the archbishop. He worked from this way and that way, but he could not find any solution. Either he has to insist that belief in Jesus Christ is the criterion – then virtue and sin, good and evil don't matter. Then the whole morality goes down the drain. If he says morality is decisive, then why bother about Jesus Christ? Then Jesus Christ goes down the drain.

And he was trying to keep both together. He could not sleep for seven days. The whole night the same question was going round and round in his mind. On the seventh day, he reached the church a little early, because he had not found the answer yet and he thought, "It will be better: I should go before the time people start coming – early, in darkness – to pray to Jesus Christ himself: 'You show me the way. I cannot find any way out of the puzzle. Whatever I decide seems to be wrong, and I have never been in such anguish. Help me.'"

But he was so tired, and he had not slept for seven days, so just putting his head at the feet of Jesus Christ's statue, he fell asleep and he dreamt a beautiful dream: He was sitting in a train which was going very fast, and he asked, "Where are we going?" The people said, "You don't know? This train is going to heaven."

He said, "My God, perhaps this is the answer from Jesus Christ – 'look with your own eyes!'" And the train stopped at the station where, in very faded words, hardly visible, was written "heaven" and all over, it looked like a desert, a wasteland.

He could not think that heaven should be like this. He asked again, but people were getting down. They said, "It is heaven." He entered the streets...they were so rotten and so dirty. He saw a few saints, so dry and so dead, sitting under their trees, repeating continuously, "Hallelujah, hallelujah."

He asked them, "Is it truly heaven?" And they said, "What do you think we are doing here? We are great saints and with great austerity we have attained heaven."

He said, "A strange heaven...not a single flower." He asked a saint, "Can I know – is Gautam Buddha in heaven? Is Socrates here? Is Epicurus here?", because all these people did not believe in God, and obviously there was no question of believing in Jesus Christ; they had been born before Jesus Christ. And the saint said, "Never heard of any such people here." But they were the people who were absolutely good, the very essence of goodness.

He rushed to the station and asked, "Is there a train going to hell too?" They said, "It is leaving right now, standing at the platform." So he went on the train towards hell. And as the train entered the station of hell, he could not believe – this should have been heaven! So green, so many flowers and everybody so radiant, so joyous, so much music...as if it were some celebration day.

He enquired, "Is there some celebration going on?" They said, "No, this is our usual everyday life. Celebration is our life." He said, "Can I ask, is Gautam Buddha here? Is Socrates here? Is Epicurus here?"

They said, "They are all here. Just look in the garden by the road – Gautam Buddha is working as a gardener. Since these people came, everything changed. Otherwise, hell used to be just like heaven, but since Gautam Buddha, Socrates, Heraclitus, Epicurus, Mahavira, these godless people came into hell, they transformed the whole situation.

"Now, hell is really heaven. The old names remained, but everything has changed and life is just a continuous dance. Everything has become a blissfulness. They have brought poetry and music and art and they have transformed the whole place."

Seeing the situation – it was so shocking – he woke up. People had started coming; Edmund Burke was already sitting in the first row.

The archbishop must have been a sincere man at least. He said, "I have not been able to find any answer. I prayed to Jesus – I don't know whether this dream is given by Jesus or I have dreamt it myself, but this is the only answer I can give to you."

He simply told his dream, and he said, "Please forgive me for making a stupid statement. I want to correct it: Wherever people are who are authentically good, there is heaven. And wherever people are who are basically evil, there is hell. These are psychological, spiritual spaces."

A buddha transforms everything.

...If you're not sure, don't act.

Bodhidharma is saying in other words, act only out of totality. And this kind of act is possible only if your whole being is totally conscious and your action comes from your whole being, not from a small part of your being – then it cannot be total and cannot be sure. Act totally and act intensely, and act absolutely in consciousness and in spontaneity. Then whatever you do is good.

If you act in uncertainty – with a divided mind, with "either/or," with just a small portion of your mind as conscious and the major part as unconscious – whatever you do it is wrong. It may appear good, but appearances cannot deceive.

For example, you may donate to a poor man, but you are not sure.... To any observer it is a good act; you have helped the poor man. But to a man of the perceptivity of a Bodhidharma or a Gautam Buddha, you have acted out of uncertainty; hence you have not really been compassionate towards his poverty. You are simply bragging about your compassionateness, about your kindness. You are simply fulfilling your ego. Nobody will see it, everybody will see that you are serving the poor. But you can see that you are serving only your own egoistic idea of yourself that you are a great public servant. The whole beautiful act has gone poisonous.

Once you act out of uncertainty *you wander through birth and death and regret having no refuge.... To understand this* no-*mind, you have to act without acting.*

This will look a little illogical, but the philosophy based on meditation takes it as the most logical thing: acting without acting. This is one of the fundamentals of Bodhidharma to be understood. What I call a spontaneous act is the same – that way it does not create in your mind a conflict; what I call a total act is the same.

Whenever you act spontaneously, you are not acting. The action is coming out of your life source on its own accord; it is acting without action. When you *decide* to act, when you bring your mind in, when you bring your past experiences in, the action is *your* action. You have decided to do it. But when you allow existence to respond and your mind is no longer interfering, you are in a state of no-mind.

In utter silence, you allow your self-nature to do whatever is spontaneous; you act without acting.

It is almost like a mirror. When you come before a mirror, do you think the mirror thinks, "Should I reflect this fellow or not?" Do you think the mirror thinks, "This guy looks like a mafia guy with sunglasses – should I reflect him or not?" Somebody is beautiful, somebody is ugly – to the mirror it does not matter; it is not a question of deciding. The mirror simply reflects them as his self-nature – the nature of the mirror is to reflect. There is no question of any decision or any judgment. Seeing a beautiful woman, it does not appreciate her, or seeing a man who looks like a camel, it does not hesitate even for a single moment whether to reflect this fellow or not.

There is a beautiful story about one of the very great mystics, Ashtavakra. The word *ashtavakra* means that he was the ugliest man you can conceive of. On eight points in his body, he was just like a camel; nothing was as it should be. Everything was wrong. His eyes – one would be looking to the left and one would be looking to the right. His legs – one would be going this way, one would be going that way....he was a very strange fellow. How he managed is difficult to conceive.

There was a great spiritual discussion going on in the court of the king, Janak, and all great scholars of the country had gathered there. Ashtavakra's father had also gone – he was a well-known, learned scholar and there was every chance that he might win. And there was a great prize for the winner. But it was getting late and Ashtavakra's mother told him, "You should go and tell your father that it is so late, and the food is getting cold. He can come and take his food, and then he can go back. That discussion is going to continue for days – so many scholars...it is not going to be finished in one day."

So Ashtavakra went into the court of the king, and every single scholar started laughing. They had never seen such an ugly man – everything was wrong. Ashtavakra looked at everybody and said to the king, "I thought that you had gathered the wise people of the land. But these people seem to be shoemakers, because they can't see my being. They can only see my skin, my bones. Are these people shoemakers or butchers? Certainly they are not enlightened; otherwise they would not have laughed. Their laughter is a judgment; they are humiliating me because of this wrong body. But whether the body is wrong or right does not matter; what matters is my consciousness."

King Janak was so much impressed that he dissolved the council of those learned people, and he said, "Now I don't need you. The man I wanted to listen to has come. I wanted a man who knows the ways of awareness, consciousness, of the innermost being. And he is right – you are only learned, but you are not enlightened."

An enlightened man has no judgment. He acts without thinking about it. He acts out of no-mind. Hence his action has a beauty and grace and a truth and a goodness and a divineness in it.

...You have to act without acting. Only then will you see things from a tathagata's perspective.

Unless you come to awareness, spontaneity, total action, action without acting, you cannot know the perspective of an enlightened man, his vision towards things and life.

I have explained to you that a *tathagata* is a man who accepts everything as it is, in its *suchness.* He has no condemnation for anything and he has no appreciation for anything. The camel is perfect as he is, in his suchness, and the lion is perfect as he is, in his suchness. They are simply manifesting their own nature.

A tathagata's perspective means accepting everybody as he is, without any condemnation, without any judgment, respecting everybody as he is, in his suchness. A tathagata never interferes in anybody's life, he never trespasses on your territorial imperative. This is his nonviolence, this is his love, this is his compassion.

But to understand his perspective, you will have to come a little closer to his being. You will have to learn acting without acting, acting without your mind interfering in it, acting with totality. And that is possible only when your whole being is full of light, when you are enlightened, when all darkness has been dispelled from you.

Bodhidharma now gives you a few hints. He has given you the goal, tathagata – now he gives a few hints for the beginners on the path:

But when you first embark on the Path, your awareness won't be focused. It will be wavering. *You're likely to see all sorts of strange, dreamlike scenes. But you shouldn't doubt that all such scenes come from your own mind and nowhere else.*

So don't become attached to any dreamlike scene, howsoever sweet.

Gautam Buddha is reported to have said, "If you meet me on the path, immediately kill me." He is talking about your meditation. If in your meditation you see Gautam Buddha, your mind will try every possible way to convince you that you have arrived – even Gautam Buddha has appeared in your consciousness, now what more do you want? Stop worshiping Gautam Buddha!

And so many so-called saints of the world have only stopped in such dreamlike phenomena. There are Christian saints who have seen Christ and have thought they have arrived, and the Christ is nothing but a projection of their own mind. No Hindu ever sees Christ; the Hindu sees Krishna, the Hindu sees Rama. No Christian ever sees Krishna or Buddha.

These are our conditionings. The mind is carrying the conditioning of Christ or Krishna or Buddha and when you become a little silent, the conditioning comes in front of you. And it is so alive that there is every possibility that you may get deluded. Hence, Bodhidharma is making you aware that anything that happens on the path in your meditation is just a projection of your mind and nothing else. Remove it; whether it is Buddha or Christ or Krishna does not matter. You have to go far; you have to go to a point where nothing appears, where all projections of the mind are left behind.

Then you have reached to the transcendental.

Then you have reached to your self-nature.

But before your self-nature is revealed, one experience Bodhidharma suggests you remember:

If you see a light brighter than the sun, your remaining attachments will suddenly come to an end, and the nature of reality will be revealed. Such an occurrence serves as the basis for enlightenment.

It is not enlightenment, but it serves as a basis. *If you see a light brighter than the sun...* because mind cannot project it. Mind can project only that which it knows. The mind can project the sun, but the mind cannot project a brighter sun which it has never known. *If you see a light brighter than the sun....* Kabir says that in his meditation, it was as if one thousand suns had suddenly risen all around him. The light was so blinding that even to keep looking at it was scary. This is not enlightenment, but this is the beginning of two things: the end of all your attachments – as if they are burned by this light – and the creation of a basis for enlightenment.

But this is something only you know. You can't explain it to others.

And in fact you should not talk about it to others because they will simply laugh. They may make it ridiculous. They cannot accept that you are ready for enlightenment – particularly you, whom they know perfectly well – and they have always thought themselves higher than you, holier than you. You must be cheating; you are trying to deceive but nobody is going to be deceived by you.

It is better not to talk about it, because by talking about it, they can destroy it by their comments, by their criticism, by their ridicule. They can destroy the very basis for enlightenment. It is better to keep it deep in your heart as a secret. It is so valuable that you should not bring it out before others.

...Or if, while you're walking, standing, sitting or lying in the stillness and darkness of night, everything appears as though in daylight, don't be startled. It's your own no-mind about to reveal itself.

To different people enlightenment comes from different doors. It depends on your uniqueness, your individuality.

To some it may start with the happening of a brighter sun, or a thousand suns. To somebody else it may start...you are lying in your bed in the night, in darkness, and suddenly you start seeing things as if it is full daylight. Don't be startled, don't be afraid: it is a good sign. It will create the basis for your enlightenment and it will destroy all your attachments.

...If you see your nature, you don't need to read sutras or invoke buddhas. Erudition and knowledge are not only useless, they cloud your awareness.

They are not only useless, they are also harmful, immensely harmful.

Doctrines are only for pointing to the no- *mind. Once you see your* no-*mind, why pay attention to doctrines?*

There have been many instances of great masters who, when they became enlightened, the first thing they did was to burn their scriptures – their work was finished. Their whole work was somehow to indicate to you your self, your self-nature. And once you have seen your self-nature, all those doctrines are just rubbish.

To go from mortal to buddha...to go from death to deathlessness, to go from divisions to transcendence, *you have to put an end* to all your actions. You have to learn the actionless action.

Nurture your awareness and accept what life brings.

These are points to be remembered by everyone who is walking on the path: *Nurture your awareness*.... How does one nurture one's awareness? Don't miss any opportunity to be aware: walking, walk with awareness.... I can move my hand either without awareness or with awareness – move your hand with full awareness, and it will bring a great grace to your hand, and a great peace and silence will be felt inside.

Eating, eat with awareness. Most of the time people are simply swallowing unconsciously; that's why they eat too much, because their taste is not satisfied.

If they were eating with awareness, then they would not just be swallowing, they would be chewing.

The scientists say that unless you chew every bite forty-eight times, you are loading your digestive system unnecessarily. And your life span depends on your digestive system: if it remains young and alive, you can remain longer in the body. But if you are simply swallowing, you don't know...your digestive system doesn't have teeth, it cannot chew. The chewing has to be done by you in the mouth; beyond the mouth there is no question of chewing. And the unchewed food is a load, is a burden; it hurts your digestive system, it hurts your intestines. It creates all kinds of troubles in your stomach.

Just try one day, to count forty-eight times – and you will remain aware because you have to count. You cannot go on thinking of other things. You have to be focused on your chewing and counting: one, two, three, four, up to forty-eight, and only then are you allowed to swallow.

Nurturing awareness means making everything an opportunity to be aware. So more and more awareness in twenty-four hours...taking a shower, don't just take it unconsciously, mechanically. Because you always take it, you know – you just stand under the shower and you go on thinking of a thousand and one things. Under the shower the only thing is to be aware of the coolness that is coming to you, the freshness that is coming to you. Be fully aware of it.

Nurturing your consciousness means a twenty-four hour, day and night program. It is not tiring; on the contrary, it is very refreshing, rejuvenating.

And the second thing: *And accept what life brings.* That is *tathata* – whatever life brings. Accept it with thankfulness and gratitude, because there was no necessity for life to bring that thing to you.

A cool breeze comes – do you think you have earned it? Do you think you deserve it? Do you think existence owes it to you? A beautiful cloud passes, a beautiful sunset and all the colors on the horizon, a rainbow with all the seven colors...accept everything that life brings to you with gratitude, with joy, with thankfulness. This will slowly, slowly, create in you a deep acceptance of everything. And in that deep acceptance is hidden the transcendence.

...Once mortals see their nature, all attachments end. Awareness isn't hidden. But you can only find it right now. It's only now.

This statement has to be understood. The insistence on *now* is to prevent you from postponing. People, thousands of people have told me during these three decades that I have been working with them, "I will start meditating." *Will* start? If you have understood the meaning of meditation, then *now* is the moment, not postponement.

Postponement simply means you have not understood. Meditation is not yet on the top of your laundry list, it is somewhere at the bottom. First you will earn money, then you have to marry off your daughter, then your son is going to medical college, then you have to build a house, and so on and so forth – the laundry list is infinite. And at the bottom of it – if, God willing you are still alive...most probably you will not be, because the list is too long and your life is too short – you won't have time left to meditate. Death will come before meditation comes.

Hence the emphasis on *now* – because at least one thing is certain: death has not come, not yet. This is the moment you are certain you are alive. But who knows about the next moment? So don't postpone it even for a single moment. If you want to become an enlightened being, then *now* is the moment, then *here* is the place.

If you really want to find the Way, don't hold onto anything.

No prejudices – if you really want to find the way, don't make demands. Don't say that the way has to fulfill these certain demands. You don't know the way. Go with humbleness, not with a demanding ego; otherwise, you will never find the way. Your prejudiced mind will never allow you to go beyond it. And the way goes beyond the mind.

...don't hold onto anything. Once you put an end to all your actions – actions which are decided by your mind and are not spontaneous – *and nurture your awareness, any attachments that remain will come to an end...*by their simply being understood as meaningless.

As your awareness grows, your attachments decrease. A full awareness means no attachments. That does not mean that you can't have friends; that does not mean that you have to renounce the world. That simply means that you don't get glued with people – that is an ugly state. You enjoy, you share, but you never depend on anybody or on anything; you never become a slave.

Dropping attachments is really dropping all slavery and dependence on things and people. It brings to you a great freedom – the only authentic freedom. Political freedoms don't mean much, economic freedoms don't mean much. The only real freedom is spiritual freedom and that comes through dropping all your attachments and creating a great pillar of fire, of awareness.

Understanding comes naturally. You don't have to make any effort. But fanatics don't understand what the Buddha meant. And the harder they try, the farther they get from the Sage's meaning. All day long they invoke buddhas and read sutras. But they remain blind to their own divine nature, and they don't escape the Wheel.

A buddha is an idle person, because he does not do anything on his own part. He is an idle person not because he is lazy, he is an idle person because he is spontaneous. Whenever a situation arises that needs a response, he waits for his consciousness, his self-nature to respond naturally without any effort. He is a man of effortless effort, actionless action. He has simply allowed the existence to function through him.

He is no more.

He is just a hollow bamboo.

A singer can make a flute out of him and can sing songs. The only function of the flute is not to hinder the song. A buddha is just a hollow bamboo; the song comes from existence itself.

A buddha is an idle person. He doesn't run around after fortune and fame. What good are such things in the end?

They simply destroy your life. They destroy all the opportunities to know yourself. They destroy all the opportunities to make your life a great blessing, a great benediction.

These simple sutras of Bodhidharma can bring you the greatest ecstasy that existence is keeping ready for you.

It is just that you are not ready.

Get ready and claim your inheritance.

Okay, Maneesha?

Yes, Bhagwan.

EVERYBODY HAS THE RIGHT TO BE WRONG

達磨

Beloved Bhagwan,

Among Shakyamuni's ten greatest disciples, Ananda was foremost in learning. But he didn't know the Buddha. All he did was study and memorize. Arhats don't know the Buddha. All they know are so many practices for realization, and they become trapped by cause and effect. Such is a mortal's karma: no escape from birth and death. By doing the opposite of what he intended, such people blaspheme the Buddha. Killing them would not be wrong. The sutras say, "Since icchantikas are incapable of belief, killing them would be blameless, while people who believe reach the state of buddhahood."

...People who see that their minds are the buddha don't need to shave their heads. Laymen are buddhas too. Unless they see their nature, people who shave their heads are simply fanatics.

But since married laymen don't give up sex, how can they become buddhas?

I only talk about seeing your nature. I don't talk about sex simply because you don't see your nature. Once you see your nature, sex is basically immaterial. It ends along with your delight in it. Even if some habits remain, they can't harm you. Because your nature is essentially pure. Despite dwelling in a material body of five aggregates, your nature is basically pure. It can't be corrupted.

...Once you stop clinging and let things be, you'll be free, even of birth and death. You'll transform everything. You'll possess spiritual powers that can't be obstructed. And you'll be at peace wherever you are. If you doubt this, you'll never see through anything. You're better off doing nothing. Once you act, you can't avoid the cycle of birth and death. But once you see your nature, you're a buddha, even if you work as a butcher.

But butchers create karma by slaughtering

'animals. How can they be buddhas?

I only talk about seeing your nature. I don't talk about creating karma. Regardless of what we do, our karma has no hold on us.

...In India, the twenty-seven patriarchs only transmitted the imprint of the mind. And the only reason I've come to China is to transmit the instantaneous teaching of the Mahayana: *this mind is the buddha.* I don't talk about precepts, devotions or ascetic practices....

Language and behavior, perception and conception are all functions of the moving mind. All motion is the mind's motion.... The mind neither moves nor functions. Because the essence of its functions is emptiness. And emptiness is essentially motionless.

Hence, the sutras tell us to move without moving, to travel without traveling, to see without seeing, to laugh without laughing, to hear without hearing, to know without knowing, to be happy without being happy, to walk without walking, to stand without standing. And the sutras say, "Go beyond language. Go beyond thought."

...I could go on, but this brief sermon will have to do.

BODHIDHARMA'S TEACHINGS IN these sutras are profoundly interesting and of great importance for all pilgrims of truth. But there are a few false statements. And for the first time, perhaps these false statements are not due to the misunderstanding of the disciples; these false statements have been made by Bodhidharma himself.

Hence, before I go into the sutras, I would like to make clear a few things.

First, the teachings of Gautam Buddha have created two kinds of seekers: one is called *arhata* and the other is called *bodhisattva.*

The arhata is someone who makes every effort to become enlightened and once he is enlightened he completely forgets about those who are still groping in the dark. He has no concern with others. It is enough for him to become enlightened. In fact, according to the arhatas, even the great idea of compassion is nothing but again another kind of attachment – and it has some significance to be understood.

Compassion is also a relationship; howsoever beautiful and great, it is also a concern with others. It is also a desire. Although it is a good desire it makes no difference. According to the arhatas, desire is a bondage whether it is good or bad. The chains can be made of gold or of steel, it doesn't matter; chains are chains. Compassion is a golden chain.

The arhata insists that nobody can help anybody else at all. The very idea of helping others is based on wrong foundations. You can help only yourself.

It may occur to the ordinary mind that the arhata is very selfish. But if you look without any prejudice, perhaps he also has something immensely important to declare to the world: Even helping the other is an interference in his life, in his lifestyle, in his destiny, in his future. Hence, arhatas don't believe in any compassion. Compassion to them is another beautiful desire to keep you tethered to the world of attachments. It is another name – beautiful, but still just a name for a desiring mind.

Why should you be interested that somebody else becomes enlightened? It is none of your business. Everybody has absolute freedom to be himself. The arhata insists on individuality and its absolute freedom. Even for the sake of good, nobody can be allowed to interfere in anybody else's life.

Hence the moment he becomes enlightened, the arhata does not accept disciples, he never preaches, he never helps in any way. He simply lives in his ecstasy. If somebody on his own can drink out of his well he will not prevent him, but he will not send an invitation to you. If you come to him on your own accord and sit by his side and drink his presence, and get on the path, that is your business. If you go astray, he will not stop you.

In a certain way this is the greatest respect ever paid to individual freedom – to the very logical extreme. Even if you are falling into deep darkness, the arhata will silently wait. If his presence can help, it is okay, but he is not going to move his hands to help you, to give you a hand, to pull you out of a ditch. You are free to fall in a ditch and if you can fall in a ditch, you are absolutely capable of getting out of it. The very idea of compassion is foreign to the philosophy of the arhatas.

Gautam Buddha accepted that there are a few people who will become arhatas. And their path will be called *Hinayana*, "the small vehicle," the small boat in which only one person can go to the other shore. He does not bother to create a big ship and collect a crowd in a Noah's Ark and take them to the further shore. He simply goes himself in his small boat, which cannot even contain two. He is born alone in the world, he has lived and died millions of times alone in the world; alone he is going to the universal source.

Buddha accepts and respects the way of the arhata – but he also knows there are people who have immense compassion and when they become enlightened, their first longing is to share their joy, to share their truth. Compassion is their way. They also have some profound truth.

These people are called bodhisattvas. They provoke and invite others to the same experience. And they wait on this shore as long as possible to help all seekers who are ready to move on the path, and who just need a guide; they need a helping hand. The bodhisattva can postpone his going to the further shore out of compassion for blind people groping in darkness.

Buddha had such a comprehensive and vast perception that he accepted both – that this is simply the nature of a few people to be arhatas, and it is also simply the nature of a few other people to be bodhisattvas.

And this is the standpoint of Gautam Buddha, that such is the case, nothing can be done about it – an arhata will be an arhata and a bodhisattva will be a bodhisattva. Their natures have different destinies, although they reach to the same goal finally. But after reaching the goal there is a parting of the ways.

The arhatas don't stay on this shore even for a single moment. They are tired, they have been long enough in this wheel of *samsara,* moving through birth and death millions of times. It has already been too much. They are bored and they don't want to stay even a single minute more. Their boat has arrived, and immediately they start moving towards the further shore. This is their suchness.

And there are bodhisattvas who can tell the boatman, "Wait, there is no hurry. I have lingered on this shore long enough – in misery, in suffering, in anguish, in agony. Now all that has disappeared. I am in absolute bliss, silence and peace, and I don't see that there is anything more on the other shore. So as long as I can manage, I will be here to help people."

Gautam Buddha is certainly one of those people who can see the truth even in contradictions. He accepts both without making anybody feel lower or higher. But bodhisattvas call their path – against the path of the arhatas – *Mahayana,* "the great vehicle," the great ship. The other is just a small boat. Poor fellows, they simply go alone. And there has been a continuous conflict for twenty-five centuries after Gautam Buddha, between these two different approaches.

Bodhidharma belongs to the bodhisattvas. Hence, he is making many statements against arhatas which are not true.

I don't belong either to arhatas or to bodhisattvas. I don't belong to Gautam Buddha's path at all. I have my own vision, my own perceptivity. Hence I have no obligation to agree with Bodhidharma on every point – and particularly on this point; even Gautam Buddha would not have agreed with him. He follows a particular party line.

Secondly, he was an outrageous person, very ferocious. If you have seen his picture…you can use it for making your children afraid. But that is not his true picture; he was a prince, the son of a great South Indian king, Suha Verma – it was a great empire of the Palavas. He must have been a beautiful man. But those pictures don't represent his actual photographs. They depict his strange personality, his outrageousness.

So a few things he can say which you need not agree with. I will make it clear where he is saying wrong things just because he belongs to Mahayana, a particular party, a particular ideology. I have immense respect for both arhatas and bodhisattvas, the same way as Gautam Buddha had.

The first sutra:

Among Shakyamuni's ten greatest disciples… Shakyamuni is one of the names of Gautam Buddha, because he belongs to the clan of the Shakyas; his empire was an ancient empire belonging to the clan of the Shakyas. It was a warrior race, dwelling just on the boundary line of Nepal and India. Because of the Shakya clan, he is called Shakyamuni. *Muni* means one who has attained to ultimate silence.

Among Shakyamuni's ten greatest disciples, Ananda was foremost in learning.

Now, Ananda is a special case, and something has to be understood about him. Ananda was a cousin-brother to Gautam Buddha, and a few years elder to him. And it is part of the Eastern culture that the elder brother is almost like a father, even though he may be a elder cousin-brother.

When Ananda came to Gautam Buddha to be initiated as a disciple, he said, "Listen, Siddhartha" – Siddhartha was Gautam Buddha's name given by his parents. He did not address him as Gautam Buddha, he addressed him, "Listen, Siddhartha" – he was just his younger brother. "I am going to be initiated by you into sannyas, on the path. Once I am your disciple I will no longer be your elder brother. Once I am your disciple, you will be in a position to order me and I will have to obey. Right now I am in a position to order you and you will have to obey. Before the situation changes, I want a few conditions to be remembered."

Gautam Buddha said, "What are the conditions?"

Ananda said, "They are not very great, but to me they mean much. One, promise me while I am still your elder brother that after I become your disciple, you will not tell me to go away from you to preach the message to the masses.

No, I am going to be with you day and night, your whole life. I want to take care of your body, your comfort, your health. You cannot prevent me. This promise you have to give right now, before I am no longer in a position to say anything."

Buddha said, "Granted"…because as a younger brother, there is no other way in the East. You have to accept, respectfully, those who are elder.

Ananda said, "And the second condition is that I can ask any question – relevant, irrelevant, meaningful, meaningless – and you cannot say, 'Wait, someday you will understand.' You will have to answer me immediately; you cannot try to postpone. You cannot find excuses…'Tomorrow I will see.' Whenever I ask the question, immediately you have to give me the answer."

Gautam Buddha said, "Granted."

And Ananda said, "Third, if I bring someone to meet you – even in the middle of the night when you are asleep – you cannot say no. You will have to meet the person, whoever he is."

Gautam Buddha laughed and said, "Granted."

But Ananda said, "Why are you laughing?"

He said, "That is not part of the conditions. Now you get initiated, and then you can ask the question why I have laughed. Whenever you ask the question, I will answer it – but the three conditions are complete."

Ananda became a disciple and lived with Gautam Buddha for forty-two years continuously, day in, day out. Springs came and went, seasons changed, year by year; he was just like a shadow to Gautam Buddha.

But many people came after Ananda and became disciples and became enlightened – and Ananda remained without enlightenment. After twenty years he asked Gautam Buddha, "What is happening? People who have come after me have become enlightened…and I have been so close to you. Nobody has heard you more than I have heard you, nobody has the intimacy that I have with you. Why am I not becoming enlightened?"

Gautam Buddha said, "Now you can understand why I laughed – remember? Twenty years before when you asked, before initiation, for three conditions, I laughed. This was the reason: because your conditions would be a barrier. You cannot forget that you are my elder brother. Even though you have become a disciple, deep down you know that you are my elder brother. That is your subtlest ego – although you have been with me more than anybody else, and you have heard me better than anybody else. You have become so knowledgeable, so learned, you have memorized every sermon that I have given. You have an immense memory but you don't have any experience of your own. You can repeat mechanically everything that I have said in twenty years.

But your subtle ego, that you are my elder brother and you have a special privilege of three conditions, is functioning as a barrier. You will not become enlightened until I die."

And actually, that's how it happened. After forty-two years' initiation, Gautam Buddha died. And amongst ten thousand disciples, Ananda was the first who burst into tears when Buddha said, "Now I want to say goodbye to you all. My body is old and tired, and whatever I wanted to say, I have said. I want now to go into ultimate rest."

Ananda was sitting on his right side and he burst out like a small child, although he was older than Gautam Buddha. And Gautam Buddha said, "Why, Ananda, are you crying and weeping? I am not dying ignorant, I am dying absolutely fulfilled, enlightened – and not an ordinary enlightenment, an enlightenment which has never been excelled before. And I am also dying immensely fulfilled because never before have so many disciples of a single master become enlightened. I am going into ultimate rest, because there is no death for me."

Ananda said, "I am not weeping for you. You misunderstood me. I am weeping for myself – that for forty-two years I have been following you like a shadow, day in, day out, and I have not become enlightened yet. I am still as unconscious as ever. What will happen to me when you are gone? And I don't think that in ages to come I will ever meet anyone of your caliber, nor will I have such an opportunity to be so intimate and so close. You are leaving me in a darkness that seems to have no dawn."

Gautam Buddha laughed again, and even with tears in his eyes, Ananda could not resist asking him, "Why are you laughing? You laugh at strange moments."

Gautam Buddha said, "Within twenty-four hours you will know. Because once I am dead, within twenty-four hours you will become enlightened. Once I am dead, you are no more my elder brother. Once I am dead, your subtle ego will also disappear; it cannot disappear while I am alive."

And actually it happened in the same way: within twenty-four hours, Ananda became enlightened. He did not leave the place, he did not eat or drink or go to sleep. He remained sitting there with his eyes closed, under those two saal trees where Gautam Buddha had lain down and entered into eternal sleep.

Ananda remained in the same place with closed eyes, with an absolute determination that he would open his eyes only if his eyes of the inner opened. If he becomes enlightened, only then will he see the outside world again with his eyes. Otherwise, he will remain within himself.

First he wants to see his own self-nature; then only will he move his eyes or move his body from this place. Otherwise he will die here. With such deter-mination, with such absolute commitment.... The night that had been seen by him as without a dawn, ended quickly, within twenty-four hours. He was enlightened. But he remained an arhata. That was his uniqueness, to be an arhata.

The condemnation by Bodhidharma of Ananda on one point is right, on another point is wrong. He says:

Ananda was foremost in learning, but he did not know the Buddha. That's true.

All he did was study and memorize. That's true.

Arhats don't know the Buddha.

That's wrong.

Arhatas become themselves buddhas; there is no question of their not knowing the Buddha. Yes, as a scholar, as a great learned man, as a man immensely studious and a man of tremendous memory, he has not known what the nature of enlightenment is, what is buddhahood. But it is not because of his being an arhata. The moment he became enlightened, *then* he became an arhata. The arhatahood or bodhisattvahood comes after enlightenment, not before.

Only when you become enlightened do you realize what is your nature. Is there any desire for compassion, or no desire for any compassion? Are you ready to leave this shore immediately, or are you going to stay here to help a few people to become enlightened?

I know this statement that *Arhatas don't know the Buddha* is not the fault of the person who has taken the notes. It is Bodhidharma's statement, because he is a bodhisattva and the conflict between bodhisattvas and arhatas is twenty-five centuries old. They go on condemning each other. They simply cannot understand a person who becomes enlightened and has no compassion.

The bodhisattva cannot understand that enlightenment is possible without compassion and the arhata cannot understand that a man of enlightenment still has a desire to help; he has not yet become desireless. He still wants to interfere into other people's lifestyle. If they don't want to awaken, who are you to awaken them? Then just move silently so that their sleep is not broken...to the arhata that is real compassion. You don't want to interfere in anybody's life; everybody has to live his own life according to his own light, according to his own individuality. And whenever his time comes to become enlightened, he will become enlightened. You cannot force anybody to become enlightened. It is not something that somebody can be persuaded, or somebody can be seduced into.

Neither the arhata can understand the bodhisattva, nor the bodhisattva can understand the arhata. They are such diametrically opposite poles. That's why I say this mistake is not of the note-taker, this mistake comes from Bodhidharma himself; he is not an arhata.

Now, Buddhist countries are divided into sections. For example, Japan belongs to Mahayana, the land of the bodhisattvas, and Sri Lanka belongs to Hinayana, the land of the arhatas. In Sri Lanka there is no respect for Zen at all. If you talk about Bodhidharma in Sri Lanka, they will simply laugh at you – "That man was mad!" And if you talk about arhatas like Ananda in Japan, they will simply say, "That man was utterly selfish; his whole life he was so blindly selfish that he was putting conditions on Gautam Buddha and when he became enlightened, then he simply disappeared, went to the further shore, into eternity – without bothering for a single moment that there are people who need a few guidelines, a few hints; who are borderline cases, just a little push and they will take the quantum leap."

But if Bodhidharma had not been prejudiced, if he had also been capable to understand the position of the totally opposite standpoint, he would have said, "Pundits, learned people, scholars don't know the Buddha." And then it would have been perfectly right. To use the word *arhata* is simply not only wrong, but shows a very fanatic attitude: "Only I am right and everybody else is wrong." I would like to exchange the word *arhatas* for pundits, scholars, learned people – just to help Bodhidharma come to his senses.

Pundits don't know the Buddha. All they know are so many practices for realization, and they become trapped by cause and effect. Such is a mortal's karma: no escape from birth and death. By doing the opposite of what he intended, such people blaspheme the Buddha.

This statement can be true about the pundits, but this statement is absolutely wrong about arhatas. And this shows his fanatic attitude when he says, *Killing them would not be wrong.*

I cannot agree with him. He is saying, "Killing the arhatas would not be wrong." And according to Gautam Buddha even killing an ant is wrong and the arhata is at least something better than an ant.

But this is his fanatic attitude – and it is because of this fanatic, outrageous attitude that his picture has been depicted so ferociously. It is certain he would not have bothered: if there was any need to kill an arhata he would have killed. He was a man of his word; what he says he means. You cannot try to say that it is only symbolic. Bodhidharma does not speak in symbols, he says exactly what he means:

Killing them would not be wrong. The sutras say, "Since icchantikas are are incapable of belief, killing them would be blameless, while people who believe reach the state of buddhahood."

Now, something else has to be understood – this word, *icchantikas.* It means people who are one-dimensional, who know only one aspect of truth.

And opposite to icchantikas are people like Mahavira and the Jaina tirthankaras; they are called *anicchantikas,* people who look from every aspect of the truth. Mahavira was so deeply rooted in the attitude of being multidimensional that he was the first man in the whole history of mankind to bring in the theory of relativity. It took twenty-five centuries for the West.

Only Albert Einstein, through a very different path as a scientist, brought the same message, the same philosophy of the theory of relativity. Mahavira says that whatever you say is only relative. He was so much in his theory of relativity that he never made a single statement about anything – because any single statement will only show one aspect. What about other aspects?

He found that every truth has seven aspects. So you ask him one question and he will answer with seven answers, and those seven answers will be contradicting each other. You will come back from meeting Mahavira more confused than you have ever been – and he was the most clear person who has ever walked on the earth. But his approach was multidimensional.

For example, if you ask Mahavira, "What do you think about God?"…in the first place, he never started his statements without the word "perhaps." Every statement begins with "perhaps," because to be certain is to be a fanatic. "Perhaps" keeps you open: the other can also be right, the opposite can also be right. "Perhaps" does not close the door, it keeps you alert and aware about other possibilities.

You ask about God: the Christians are icchantikas; they will say, "Yes, there is one God and only one God." You ask the Mohammedans, they say there is only one God. These are icchantikas. They believe in a way which can only be called one-dimensional. They don't look at other possibilities – they are afraid to look at other possibilities. That's why they have one God and one prophet – not even two prophets for the Mohammedans, because there is danger: if you take two prophets, they may contradict each other, they may say something, they may not agree with each other. There will be trouble.

It is better to remain with one prophet, one God, one holy scripture. These are people who are afraid of a multidimensional reality.

Against these are people like Mahavira who go to the other extreme: they will not say anything in an absolute way, they will always state everything relatively.

You ask about God and Mahavira has seven statements and you cannot figure out whether God is, or not.

Of those seven statements, the first statement is:

"Perhaps God is – but *perhaps*. I cannot be absolute; neither can you be absolute. There is a possibility." A relative statement – "Perhaps there is a God." This is his first statement.

His second statement: "Perhaps there is no God, because who knows? – there is every possibility that the atheist may be right. Nobody has ever seen him. So all that we can say is, perhaps there is no God."

But after hearing these two statements – "Perhaps there is God, perhaps there is no God…" one is bound to ask, then what am I going to believe? Hence comes his third statement: "Perhaps both are true." But naturally, you are going to ask, "How can both be true?"

Then comes his fourth statement: "Perhaps both are not true." And this way he goes on – seven statements – and you will be so confused…"Perhaps it was not right to ask the question! I was better off before." It is because of this multidimensional, relative approach that Mahavira could not get many followers. There can be very few crazy people who don't care what it means, who simply fall in love with the personality of Mahavira. He is a beautiful man of immense presence and grandeur – so a few crazy people can fall in love with him. They don't care what he says. They only care what he is: "Don't be bothered with what he says; just look at his beauty, his light – his eyes with such grandeur and depth, and his whole life such a song, such an ecstasy. Don't bother with what he says; it is none of our business. The *man* is right. His statements may be right, may not be right. He himself says 'perhaps.'"

But Bodhidharma's statements that: *Since icchantikas are incapable of belief, killing them would be blameless, while people who believe reach the state of buddhahood*…I cannot support this statement.

Icchantikas, the people who believe in absoluteness of truth have a right to exist and live according to their light – just as people who believe in a relative perception of truth have the right to live, and to live according to their own vision. Everybody has the right to live according to his own experience and find his way. Nobody has the right to kill anybody.

But Bodhidharma is in a way very sincere. He is simply saying what he sincerely feels. His sincerity cannot be doubted – his statement can be denied, but his intention cannot be denied. Christians have been killing Mohammedans, Jews; Mohammedans have been killing Hindus; Hindus have been killing Buddhists. Although nobody says "Go and kill those who don't believe in your philosophy," that's what has been happening all over the world. At least Bodhidharma is sincere. He has never killed anybody but he is saying his attitude in clear-cut terms, that his understanding is so valuable to him, so true, that even if a person who does not follow his understanding has to be killed, it is blameless. Although he has never killed anyone...he has a ferocious way of speaking, way of living, but he has a very soft heart.

But religions have been doing the act without saying it. No religion in the world can be said to have behaved lovingly, respectfully, towards others. Every religion thinks they are the only right people; they have the monopoly on truth and everybody else is wrong.

My own approach is that everybody has the right to be right or to be wrong. And if somebody decides to be wrong, still he has to be given every respect and every love. It is his decision, and if he wants to live his decision, it is nobody's business to interfere in his life and in his philosophy.

...People who see that their no-minds are the buddha don't need to shave their heads.

There I can agree with Bodhidharma totally. If you see your nature, then there is no need to do any stupid thing: shaving your head or being naked or standing on your head or doing all kinds of contortions of your body which are good in a circus but not in the search of truth, in the search of your own nature, in the search of God.

Laymen are buddhas too.

There I can agree with Bodhidharma with absoluteness. It is not only for the monks to find the truth. Even a layman – if he finds a little time to be silent and to be meditative and discovers his self nature in his own home, in the marketplace, he will become the buddha. There is no problem that he has to be in a monastery, or that he has to renounce the world. This is my emphasis too, that nobody needs to renounce the world.

The world is not the problem, the problem is your unawareness. Renounce your unawareness, don't be bothered with the world. What can the world do to you? You can live in a palace, the palace cannot prevent your enlightenment. You can live in absolute poverty, poverty cannot help your enlightenment. In poverty or in richness, in a poor man's hut or in a palace, the basic thing is your meditativeness, your awareness. Wherever it happens, you will become enlightened. You don't have to renounce anything.

It is absolutely true:

Laymen are buddhas too. Unless they see their nature, people who shave their heads are simply fanatics.

It is something to be understood that Bodhidharma is himself making statements which are statements of a fanatic – but it is always easy to see a small straw in somebody else's eye, and it is very difficult to see even a camel in your own eye. People never think about their own statements, about their own behavior, about their own life. They are always looking at others – they are very artful, articulate in finding what is wrong with somebody else – and they may be carrying thousands of wrongs themselves and they remain completely unaware. But this is human nature, this is human frailty.

The disciple asks Bodhidharma: *But since married laymen don't give up sex, how can they become buddhas?*

And here I can support Bodhidharma with my total being. What he says is of tremendous importance, because he was saying it fourteen hundred years ago. Sigmund Freud was not born yet; Alfred Adler was still far away in the future; Havelock Ellis or Carl Gustav Jung or Assagioli or Masters and Johnson – people who have been working deeply in the study of man's sexuality had not come into existence yet. But what Bodhidharma says is so luminous, so grand and so great that even this simple statement could have made him a pioneer.

He says: *I only talk about seeing your nature. I don't talk about sex simply because you don't see your nature. Once you see your nature, sex is basically immaterial.*

This is great insight, and from a man who was considered to be one of the greatest saints of Buddhism. The moment you become enlightened, sex is immaterial. It is just the same stuff dreams are made of; it will disappear on its own accord. You don't have to repress it, you don't have to go against it.

It ends along with your delight in it. As you become more and more mature in your meditation, sex becomes less and less interesting. The day you become fully attuned with existence, sex disappears just like a dewdrop in the early morning sun.

And unless sex disappears on its own accord, it is very dangerous to drop it, to force it, because then you will create all kinds of perversions. And all the religions of the world have created perverted human beings: homosexuality, lesbianism, sodomy...and people go on inventing strange, perverted expressions for their sexual energy because their religion condemns sex.

Sex is something natural, biological. Unless you transcend your biology, unless you transcend your body, unless you become attuned with something beyond mind, sex is going to remain there in some form or other. And if it is going to remain there, it is better that it remains natural, biological, because perverted sex is getting into a worse condition. Natural sex can be sublimated, perverted sex becomes more difficult to transform.

I have never heard of any homosexual ever becoming enlightened, I have never heard of any impotent man becoming enlightened. This cannot be just coincidental. In fact, the impotent man should become enlightened sooner than anybody else, because he is a born celibate! All other celibates are just lousy celibates, leaking from here, leaking from there – the impotent person is absolutely certain to be celibate. But the impotent person has never become enlightened.

In fact, it is the sexual energy itself that transforms into your enlightenment. Because the impotent man has no sexual energy, he is in the worst condition; he cannot go higher, he does not have the energy to fly like an eagle across the sun. He cannot become a Gautam Buddha or a Bodhidharma.

Bodhidharma is saying that sex is immaterial; what is important is to know your self-nature, to know your being. And then everything that is needed will happen on its own accord.

Even if some habits remain, they can't harm you.

This is a very significant statement from a man of enlightenment. *Even if some habits remain, they can't harm you.*

For example, if you go on smoking…I don't see that an enlightened man can in any way be disturbed by smoking. Enlightenment that gets disturbed by smoking or drinking tea or coffee will not be of much value. Your small habits – playing cards…I don't see that there is any possibility it can harm your enlightenment.

Bodhidharma here is immensely compassionate and understanding:

Because your nature is essentially pure.

What you do does not make any difference. Once you know your essential pure nature then everything is allowed to you. Then you are capable to decide for yourself what is right and what is wrong. Because of this there have been such problems, so many difficulties in understanding each other. Small differences of habit have become such great barriers to understanding.

Mohammed used to eat in the night. In fact, Mohammedans fast in the day and eat in the night. On their religious days, the whole day they will fast from sunrise to sunset and in the night they will have a good feast. Now, Jainas cannot understand that at all. In the day you can eat, but in the night? And that too, on a religious day?

When Jainas fast they don't eat for days, and even water they drink only during the daytime, not in the night. Naturally, they think that Mohammedans are doing something wrong. But they don't know the situation in which Mohammed lived, in which Mohammedanism was born. It is a desert religion, where the day is so hot that it is easier to fast during the day. It is easier to feast during the night when things become cooler and when the sky becomes full of stars and the desert becomes a beautiful, silent place. In the day, it is just burning hot.

Ramakrishna continued to eat fish. Now, Jainas cannot accept Ramakrishna as enlightened. Can an enlightened man eat fish? But if you understand Bodhidharma's statement, you can forgive Ramakrishna...just an old habit, just living in Bengal where rice and fish are the only food. From his very childhood he has been eating rice and fish, and everybody else is eating it too. Even when he became enlightened, the old habit continued. It becomes immaterial.

In this whole world, situations are different, climates are different. There are cold climates where alcohol may be an essential need. For example, in the Soviet Union it may be impossible even for the enlightened person not to drink vodka. It is so cold, it is freezing even your very blood – a little warmth is needed.

A truly religious man is very understanding – understanding of different people, of different conditions, different geographical situations, different climates, different ages, different patterns, different habits. And small things cannot disturb a great experience like enlightenment.

Despite dwelling in an immaterial body of five aggregates, your nature is basically pure. It can't be corrupted.

Nothing can corrupt your consciousness.

It is intrinsically incorruptible.

...Once you stop clinging and let things be, you'll be free, even of birth and death. You'll transform everything. You'll possess spiritual powers that can't be obstructed. And you'll be at peace wherever you are. If you doubt this, you'll never see through anything. You're better off doing nothing. Once you act, you can't avoid the cycle of birth and death. But once you see your nature, you're a buddha, even if you work as a butcher.

In fact, it has happened: In Japan a butcher became enlightened. He was the butcher of the emperor, and when he became enlightened, even the emperor came to pay his respects. The emperor could not believe, because he had seen the butcher cutting animals just behind his palace...and he asked him, "What about my kitchen? You have become enlightened, obviously you are not going to do your old profession."

The master laughed. He said, "No, I will continue. Now I can butcher animals with more compassion, with more love, with more grace. And anyway they will be butchered by somebody else, who will not be so compassionate as I can be, who will not be so graceful with them as I can be. When they are going to be butchered, what difference does it make?

"And as far as my enlightenment is concerned, it remains uncorrupted in any and every situation. My inner sky cannot be clouded again. I have come to a point from where one cannot fall back. So don't be worried; I will be coming back tomorrow, to my profession." And he remained alive for almost twenty years after his enlightenment. In the morning he would do his profession of killing animals and in the evening he would teach the disciples about enlightenment. And not only did he become enlightened, a few of his disciples also became enlightened.

Bodhidharma is right: if you understand that you are a buddha, if you see your nature, then even if you work as a butcher it is immaterial.

The disciple asked: *But butchers create karma by slaughtering animals. How can they be buddhas?*

I only talk about seeing your nature. I don't talk about creating karma. Regardless of what we do, our karma has no hold on us.

Once you know yourself, nothing has any hold on you. Your freedom is absolutely incorruptible. You cannot do anything that can go against your freedom.

...In India, the twenty-seven patriarchs only transmitted the imprint of the no-mind. And the only reason I have come to China is to transmit the instantaneous teaching of the Mahayana: this no-mind *is the buddha. I don't talk about precepts, devotions or ascetic practices....*

Language and behavior, perception and conception are all functions of the moving mind. All motion is the mind's motion.... The no-mind *neither moves nor functions. Because the essence of its function is emptiness, and emptiness is essentially motionless.*

Hence, the sutras tell us to move without moving, to travel without travelling, to see without seeing, to laugh without laughing, to hear without hearing, to know without knowing, to be happy without being happy, to walk without walking, to stand without standing. And the sutras say, "Go beyond language. Go beyond thought."... I could go on, but this brief sermon will have to do.

This statement seems to be difficult – *walk without walking, hear without hearing, speak without speaking* – but it is not difficult at all, just a little understanding.... If you are speaking spontaneously – unprepared, not knowing what word is going to be uttered by you – you are speaking without speaking. Spontaneous action is without any activity on your part. You are simply allowing existence to sing its own song.

For example, right now I am speaking without speaking. I am simply allowing my whole being to respond to Bodhidharma's sutras, without knowing at all what is going to be my next word. Just as you hear it, I also hear it. Just as you are sitting there, I am also sitting there. This chair is empty. There is a way of speaking when you prepare, when you speak not with your moment-to-moment responsibility, but just repeat something parrot-like which you have rehearsed, which you have been practicing.

All the actions that are enumerated here and many more in your life, you can do in two ways. One is out of awareness, in the present moment – unprepared, spontaneous, allowing existence to possess you, to speak through you or act through you. Then you are absolutely out of the trap of your actions or your words. You are just a watcher. You are not acting, you are simply watching whatever is happening.

This watchfulness, this witnessing is the ultimate secret of creating a religious life, of creating a life of transcendence, a life of spirituality, of enlightenment, of buddhahood.

Okay, Maneesha?

Yes, Bhagwan.

DEAD MEN DON'T BLEED

達磨

148 ___ SHEI-SHI: LIFE-DEATH

9

DEAD MEN DON'T BLEED

Beloved Bhagwan,

Bodhidharma's Wake-Up Sermon

The essence of the Way is detachment. And the goal of those who practice is freedom from appearances. The sutras say, "Detachment is enlightenment because it negates appearances."

...The three realms are greed, anger and delusion. To leave the three realms means to go from greed, anger and delusion back to mortality, meditation and wisdom. The sutras say, "Buddhas have only become buddhas while living with the three poisons and

nourishing themselves on the pure Dharma." The three poisons are greed, anger and delusion....

The Great Vehicle is the greatest of all vehicles. It's the conveyance of bodhisattvas, who use everything without using anything, and who travel all day without travelling. Such is the vehicle of buddhas. The sutras say, "No vehicle is the vehicle of buddhas."

...The sutras say, "The cave of five aggregates is the hall of zen, the opening of the inner eye is the door of the Great Vehicle." What could be clearer?

Not thinking about anything is zen. Once you know this, walking, standing, sitting or lying down, everything you do is zen. To know that the mind is empty is to see the Buddha. The Buddhas of the Ten Directions have no mind. To see no mind is to see the Buddha.

To give up yourself without regret is the greatest charity. To transcend motion and stillness is the highest meditation. Mortals keep moving while arhats stay still. But the highest meditation surpasses that of both mortals and arhats. People who reach such understanding free themselves from all appearances without effort and cure all illnesses without treatment. Such is the power of great zen.

BODHIDHARMA IS MORE clear and transparent than any other enlightened person. But the experience of enlightenment is such that you can still commit mistakes. This is something to be understood. People ordinarily think that the man of enlightenment cannot commit mistakes. That is their expectation, but it is not true to reality.

The same has been the expectation of other religions, that their prophets cannot commit mistakes. Although the *Koran* is full of mistakes, Mohammedans are not ready to accept that their prophet Mohammed can commit any mistake. *The Bible* is so full of mistakes, but still the popes go on declaring for twenty centuries continuously that they are infallible. And their fallibility is so apparent.

Just as an example, Joan of Arc was declared a witch by the pope of that time. And the pope defined a witch – which is not the meaning of the word "witch" –

as someone who has sexual intercourse with the devil. The meaning of the word "witch" is a wise woman. And it has always been the meaning up to the Middle Ages, when the popes started declaring wise women as being in the grip of the devil. It was easy; first they would torture those women to such an extent that it became unbearable. Day after day they were tortured.

Finally the woman had to accept that yes, she is a witch. That was the only way to stop her being tortured. And once she accepted and confessed that she was a witch, she had to go to the court – a special court appointed by the pope – to declare that she has been having intercourse with the devil, which is sheer nonsense, because never before had it been known, and never afterwards – nobody has seen the devil. And these poor women were having intercourse with the devil, and they had to describe the whole ugly thing in every detail. And once they confessed, the court ordered them to be burned alive. Thousands of women in Europe were in danger and thousands had already been burned alive.

Joan of Arc fought for the freedom of her country. She was a young woman of tremendous courage and she won freedom for the country. Hence, there was immense respect for Joan of Arc. And the jealous pope could not allow Joan of Arc to be left alone. It became a competition – who is more respectable, Joan of Arc or the pope. The easiest way was to declare her a witch. He declared her a witch and they tortured the poor young woman until finally she had to accept. There was no way out and she was burned alive.

But this created a very different result than that expected by the pope. He fell more in people's eyes, and Joan of Arc became a martyr. She was loved more, she gained more sympathy. People almost started worshiping her. So after three hundred years another pope realized that it had been a mistake on the part of the previous pope. He had unnecessarily created a martyr; he should have been more careful. It was easy to destroy ordinary women but to destroy a woman like Joan of Arc…he had not been cautious enough.

After three hundred years, another pope declared that Joan of Arc was not a witch, she was a saint, and her bones were dragged out of the grave and worshiped. A great memorial was made, because now she had become "Saint Joan of Arc." You can see, at least one of the popes was fallible – most probably both. But one thing is certain: both cannot be right. And the popes are not enlightened people; they know nothing of enlightenment.

The East has been very concerned for ten thousand years with the phenomenon of enlightenment. It certainly brings you great light, great clarity, great ecstasy and the feeling of immortality. But even though it brings so much, existence is so vast that your enlightenment is just a dewdrop in the ocean of existence. However transparent and clear your understanding may be, there is always a possibility to commit mistakes. And this has been recognized by the East.

Even Gautam Buddha is reported to have said that existence is so vast, so infinite in all dimensions, that even an enlightened man may commit mistakes. This is true religiousness and humbleness.

The idea of infallibility is nothing but ugly ego.

Hence, when I say that Bodhidharma has missed the point, don't misunderstand me. Don't start thinking that Bodhidharma is not enlightened. There is no contradiction. He *is* enlightened – one of the greatest enlightened people on the earth. But enlightenment makes you blossom, come to spring with your whole potentiality becoming actual; it does not mean that you become incapable of committing any mistake.

In fact the enlightened man becomes so humble that if you point out his mistakes he will accept them. He is so detached from his own personality, it does not matter. He has no ego; he is not hurt. And he accepts that there are possibilities where he may become too one-sided, may lean into this multidimensional existence more towards certain dimensions, may become averse to the dimensions which are against his own experiences and feelings. Existence contains all contradictions, and even at the highest point of enlightenment it is very difficult to contain contradictions.

Man, after all, is man, asleep or awake. It is very difficult to conceive contradictions existing together not as contradictions but as complementaries. The easier thing seems to be to choose one side and go against the other. But that does not mean that the enlightenment is not complete; it simply means even an enlightened man can have a partiality. And it is because of the vastness of the universe.

When Gautam Buddha was asked.... He was a contemporary of Mahavira, and the followers of Mahavira were saying about Mahavira that he knows past, present, future; that he knows all that has ever been, that is and that will ever be. They were making him synonymous to the idea of God – omnipotent, omniscient, omnipresent. And it is worth remembering that Gautam Buddha laughed. He said, "I have heard once that Mahavira was begging before a house where nobody has lived for a long time, and there was nobody inside the house. And the people say that he knows everything of the past, of the present, of the future, and he does not know that he is standing before a house and there is nobody in the house!"

And Gautam Buddha joked about Mahavira that once he had heard Mahavira was walking early in the morning.... It was in the hot summer, so he had started to move very early, before the sunrise, and he stepped on the tail of a dog. When the dog started barking, then he became aware that there was a dog. The darkness was there.... This man knows past, present and future and he does not know the tail of a dog is under his foot. And I certainly agree with Gautam Buddha.

Mahavira never claimed this – it was the claim of his disciples. People like Mahavira don't claim anything. The disciples of Gautam Buddha asked, "What is your position about knowing past, present and future?" And the humbleness of Gautam Buddha is so great, he said, "I am not omnipotent or omniscient or omnipresent. I have a clear vision, but compared to the vastness of existence it is a very small phenomenon.

"Yes, I can know about the past if I focus on the past; I can know about the future if I focus on the future; I can know about the present if I focus on the present. But focusing becomes impossible as you become enlightened, because focusing is another name for concentration. That is a quality of the mind, and enlightenment is the quality of no-mind." No-mind cannot focus. It cannot have any boundaries.

So there is a possibility that sometimes an enlightened man may commit subtle mistakes, but that does not go against his enlightenment. I wanted to make it clear to you because in today's sutras he is saying things which are right for a bodhisattva, because he does not know the way of the arhatas, but he is mistaken. He should have rather said, "I don't know the experiences of the arhatas because I am not an arhata." He is bragging about the *Mahayana,* the "Great Vehicle." And he is in some way condemning the *Hinayana,* the "Small Vehicle" of the *arhatas.*

I will not agree with that because I am not a party to any group. It makes my work in one way simple, in one way very difficult – simple because I can see from far away both sides of the coin, which people who are involved cannot see. But on the other hand, it makes my work more difficult because it starts taking a multidimensionality, and I have sometimes to speak against the people I have loved immensely.

But love is not a higher quality than truth.

When it comes to deciding between your love and your truth, truth has to be the decisive factor.

The sutras:

The essence of the Way is detachment.

It is true. All of our miseries are nothing but attachment. Our whole ignorance and darkness is a strange combination of a thousand and one attachments. And we are attached to things which will be taken away by the time of death, or even perhaps before. You may be very much attached to money but you can go bankrupt tomorrow. You may be very much attached to your power and position, your presidency, your prime ministership, but they are like soap bubbles. Today they are here, tomorrow not even a trace will be left.

It happened before the Russian revolution, the prime minister of Russia was Kerensky. During the time of the chaos of revolution when the czar and his whole family were butchered – nineteen persons in all – the revolutionaries were so revengeful that they did not leave even a six-month-old baby. They did not want any trace of the family of the czars left in the world. But Kerensky escaped in time. He died in 1960, and for a half century nobody had any idea what had happened to Kerensky. He was a grocer, running a grocery store in New York, in disguise.

The Russian empire was one of the greatest empires that has ever existed, spreading from one continent to another continent. And the prime minister, who has had great power, one day becomes the owner of a grocery store in New York, and becomes so afraid that he changes his name, he changes his identity. Only when he died was it found in his papers and in his diaries that he was Kerensky, the missing prime minister of the czars.

All our positions, all our powers, our money, our prestige, respectability, they are all soap bubbles. And certainly, *The essence of the Way is detachment.* Don't get attached to the soap bubbles; otherwise you will be continuously in misery and agony. Those soap bubbles don't care that you are attached to them; they go on bursting and disappearing into the air and leaving you behind with a wounded heart, with a failure, with a deep destruction of your ego. They make you sour, bitter, irritated, frustrated. They make your life a hell.

Just to understand that life is made of the same stuff as dreams are made of is the essence of the way. Detachment: live in the world but don't be of the world. Live in the world but don't let the world live within you. Remember that it is all a beautiful dream, because everything is changing and disappearing.

Don't cling to anything.

Clinging is the cause of our being unconscious.

If you start unclinging a tremendous release of energy will happen within you. That energy that was involved in clinging to things will bring a new dawn to your being, a new light, a new understanding, a tremendous unburdening – no possibility of any misery, agony, anguish.

On the contrary, when all these things disappear you find yourself serene, calm and quiet, in a subtle joyfulness. There is a laughter in your being. That's what Bodhidharma says, that a buddha laughs without laughing. Nobody has seen any statue of Buddha laughing – there is no need for him to laugh; his whole being is feeling the laugh.

You have to understand the psychology of laughter. You laugh very easily, but your laughter has a different quality than the laughter of the buddha. You laugh because your life is so miserable that any moment, any incident which looks ridiculous helps you to forget your misery for a moment. All your tensions disappear and there is a laughter. Hence laughter is a great relaxing phenomenon. It is tremendously healthy. Within a second it takes you beyond all your tensions, but only for a moment...and you are back again in your dark cave.

A buddha laughs without laughing because he has no tensions. He does not accumulate the energy in tensions that can explode in laughter. And he knows that life is ridiculous. Here people are doing things which are all laughable. Laughter becomes something ingrained in the very cells of his being; it does not come just to his lips. His clarity makes him see things which perhaps you go on missing seeing.

I have heard...a woman suddenly said to the man who was in bed with her, "Get up, quick! I heard the noise of my husband's car, which is so rotten that you can hear it from half a mile away. He has just braked in the driveway. You just get up!"

The man got up and he said, "But where am I to go?"

She said, "Jump out of the window!" Fortunately it was not a sixty story building – it was just the ground floor – so he jumped out. But he was naked and it was raining. But fortunately a group of joggers was passing by so he joined them, finding no other way; otherwise, standing there naked, he would be caught.

He mixed with the two dozen joggers, and in the darkness of the early morning he managed well. Just one jogger by his side saw that this man looked naked. He could not resist his temptation.

He asked, "Do you always jog naked?"

The man said, "Yes." Then as darkness was disappearing and a little light was coming up, the jogger recognized that the naked man was nobody else but the bishop. And in that small light he saw that he was not just naked, he was wearing a condom.

He said, "Father, do you always wear a condom when jogging?"

The bishop said, "No, not always; only when it is raining."

The more watchful you become, the more you will find life such a comedy. So much is happening all around – so much stupidity, so much ridiculousness. But a buddha does not laugh because twenty-four hours a day, in his clarity and transparent vision, each cell of his being is laughing. There is no need to laugh loudly – silently he is in laughter. That is laughing without laughter.

If you become detached you will be able to see how people are attached to trivia, and how much they are suffering. And you will laugh at yourself because you were also in the same boat before. Detachment is certainly the essence of the way

...And the goal of those who practice is freedom from appearances.

What you see in the world is not the reality, but only an appearance. Deep behind the appearance, the mask, is the reality. To know the reality you have to be free from appearances. And all your attachments prevent you; you become attached to the mask. We rarely grow and become mature. We just go on changing our toys. We remain children; we go on changing our teddy bears.

You must have seen in railway stations, in airports, small children dragging their teddy bears with them, ugly, dirty, but to them they are very essential. Without them they cannot sleep; the teddy bear is their companion. They will become older and they will drop the teddy bear but they will drop it only when they have found another teddy bear. It does not matter what the shape of the teddy bear is – it can be money.

I used to know in my village...and I have never forgotten that man and I don't think I will ever forget him. He was a goldsmith, but very rich, and he had a way of speaking which was very hilarious. He was continuously stuttering and he was attached to a strange idea and he used to brag about it: "Unless I have one hundred rupees in my pocket I don't urinate." He was famous all over the village. What a great idea – one hundred rupees have to be in his pocket, then only can he urinate! He was showing his richness, but a strange way he found; I don't think anybody has ever had that idea, it was so original. But it was hilarious.

In those days there were no notes, so he was carrying one hundred rupees in gold coins – such a weight in his pockets. And people used to ask him, "Where are you going? Have you counted your rupees?" – because if there are ninety nine and suddenly you feel like going to the urinal, you will be stuck. And he would immediately count his money and he would say, "There is no problem. One hundred rupees is a must. Without it I cannot do even such a small thing as pissing – what to say about great things?" That was his teddy bear. He used to sleep with those one hundred rupees.

You may not be aware – because you are not aware – but if you look a little bit, you can find what your teddy bear is.

All appearances in the world are preventing you from knowing the reality of the world and of your own being. What appears is not the reality. Reality is hidden behind appearances, and unless you become attuned with reality, those appearances which are just dream stuff are going to torture you continuously. And everybody is feeling the agony, the misery, but goes on living it because there seems to be no way to drop it.

Bodhidharma is telling you the way, and it is the essential way of all the religions: detachment, freedom from appearances.

The sutras say, "Detachment is enlightenment because it negates appearances." ...The three realms are greed, anger and delusion.

You have to watch these three realms because these are the barriers, the three barriers to your enlightenment.

Bodhidharma is very short, condensed; he does not go in for philosophical discussions, he simply states the fact. And that's his beauty. He has reduced the whole religion and the way out of it into very few words.

Greed is your aggression.

It is the desire always for more.

It never stops; it goes on asking for more. And because it goes on asking for more, you are always miserable. Whatever you may have, you cannot enjoy it because you don't have more. By the time you have more, your greed has gone ahead of you. It is always ahead of you asking for more.

I used to stay in Calcutta in a very rich family and the husband and wife used to come to pick me up from the airport. The husband was always a very cheerful person, but one time I found he was very sad – driving the car, but very sad.

I asked his wife, "What is the matter?" – because he had always been chitchatting and was always cheerful. The wife laughed and the husband looked at her very seriously, very angrily.

The wife said, "You are asking, so I am saying the whole responsibility is yours. I am not to be looked at as if I am committing a sin." And laughingly she said to me, "He is sad because he has lost five lakh rupees."

I said, "But you are laughing and your husband has lost five lakh rupees?"

She said, "I am laughing because in fact he has gained five lakh rupees – but he was expecting ten lakhs, and the trouble is, he cannot understand that he has earned five lakhs out of a business. He's sad because he was counting on ten lakhs. What about the remaining five lakhs? So although he has profited enough, he is not happy."

His misery is that he has lost five lakhs – and he has not lost a single paisa. I asked the man, "What is the matter?"

He said, "In a way she is right, but I am really feeling sad. Ten lakhs were absolutely certain in the business. Even more was possible but only five lakhs turned up, and I cannot forget the five lakhs that I have missed."

Now can you think that a man who is thinking in terms of expectations can be happy, joyous? Your expectations are always more than the reality allows. Hence, there is always a feeling of failure. There is always a sadness lurking somewhere in your being.

Greed is an aggressive attitude towards existence: grab as much as you can and go on grabbing more and more and more. Waste your whole life and your whole intelligence in grabbing more and more and what is the point? Death will not be late, not even for a single minute. It always comes at the right time, and all that you have grabbed and wasted your life for, you will have to leave here.

Bodhidharma has said: One man was so greedy that when his wife was almost dying, his friends told him, "It is time...you should call a physician."

But he said, "It costs too much."

They said, "It is going to be really ugly, inhuman. Your wife is dying and you are thinking about paying some fee to the physician!"

He said, "Wives don't count much. If she dies I can get married again. And death and life are not in the hands of man, they are decided by fate. If she's going to die, she will die whether I call the physician or not. Why waste money? If she is going to live, she will live. Either way, a physician is absolutely unnecessary."

The friends said, "We have never thought that you are so greedy. We have always heard that you are greedy – but so much! Do you think you are going to take all your money with you when you die?"

He said, "Of course. I have a plan." They could not believe him.

They said, "What plan?"

He said, "Before I die I will take all the money in a boat, go deep into the ocean and jump with all my money, into the ocean."

The friends could not believe their ears. They said, "Are you mad or something? Still your money will be left in the ocean and you will have to go alone." At least there would be a satisfaction that nobody else was enjoying his money.

You will find all kinds of greedy people and you will find all sorts of greed within yourself. And when greed is not fulfilled, anger arises, frustration arises. You become angry with the world, you become angry with yourself, you become angry with everybody.

You can see it in all old people. Why are they so irritated? Why is it so difficult to stand them? They are frustrated people; they have wasted their life in grabbing more and more. But the more is never satisfied. Now they are feeling angry at life, so any excuse is enough and they will become angry. Greed is the root cause and when it is not fulfilled, it leaves you with great anger, frustration, irritation, failure.

And in your anger and frustration and failure a third thing arises: delusion. Delusion is a consolation.

Delusion is a way somehow to keep yourself together.

When Pandit Jawaharlal Nehru was the prime minister of India, there were at least ten persons who believed that they were Pandit Jawaharlal Nehru. At least one I knew personally because he lived in the nearby district, and I used to go to that city to lecture in their colleges. I loved that man because he used exactly the same clothes as Jawaharlal Nehru – with the Gandhi cap, with the handwoven khadi, with a Jawahar jacket. And he talked like Jawaharlal.

He was a laughingstock but he never cared. He said to me, "These people are idiots." And he used to send telegrams if he was going to visit a beautiful place which was nearby, Kanhakisli, a beautiful forest with thousands of deer. He would just send a telegram – "Pandit Jawaharlal Nehru is arriving" – to the collector of that district, signed by the secretary of Jawaharlal.

And he deceived people many times. Circuit houses were emptied, cleaned – Pandit Jawaharlal Nehru is coming! And later on they would find that this man is bogus. Finally he was put in a madhouse.

It was not a new phenomenon. In England, when Winston Churchill was alive, there were at least three more Winston Churchills in England, believing absolutely that they were Winston Churchill.

There is on record a case in the life of Kalif Omar. A man was brought to him who was declaring that he had come from God with a new message: "Now the message Mohammed brought is out-of-date. It is time, because almost one thousand years have passed. Everything has changed and God has sent me as his prophet with a new message."

Mohammedans are very fanatic. Omar ordered that this man be tortured for seven days. "Tie him to a pillar, naked, and beat him and don't give him anything to eat. And after seven days I will come and see."

So after seven days he went there. The man was almost dying; so much blood had flowed, because they were beating him continuously, and without giving him food.

Omar said, "What do you think now? Have you changed your mind or not?"

The man laughed and said, "Changed my mind? When I was leaving God, he said to me, 'Remember, my prophets are always tortured.' Your torture has proved perfectly that I am the prophet."

At that very point another man, who had been tied to another pillar for almost one month because he was declaring that he himself was God, shouted to Omar, "Don't listen to that idiot. I have never sent any prophet after Mohammed. Mohammed is my only prophet and this man is a cheat!"

Now what to say about these people? And they are not exceptions. Everybody has some kind of delusion. Everybody is thinking things which he is not. But these delusions are helpful as a lubricating system. It helps your life somehow to move on.

Great consolations – if you cannot become the prime minister, at least you can create a delusion that you are. If you cannot *become* the richest man you can still believe that you *are*. You can make your delusions so solid that nobody can change them.

A madman was brought to a psychiatrist. His madness was very special; his madness was that he had been thinking that he had died. So when his family would tell him to go to the shop, tend the shop, he would say, "You don't understand. Dead people don't go to the shop. They don't tend shops."

They tried hard in every way to persuade him that he was perfectly alive, and he would say, "How can I believe you when I know that I'm dead?"

Finally they brought him to the psychiatrist and the psychiatrist said, "Don't be worried. I will put him right." And he asked the madman, "Do you think dead people bleed?"

The madman said, "No, dead people never bleed."

So the psychiatrist said, "There is a simple experiment to be done." And he took his knife and cut the dead man's finger just a little bit, and blood came running out. The family was very happy that this man, within a minute, had changed the whole situation. But they never knew that delusions are not so easily dispelled.

The madman laughed. The psychiatrist said, "That blood shows that you are not dead."

He said, "No, that blood shows that the proverb that 'dead men don't bleed' is wrong; they do bleed. I am the proof. Now what can you do? The proverb is wrong and I am the proof of its being wrong. Dead men do bleed!"

Delusions settle so deeply in you, and the reason for those delusions is that to live continuously in frustration is a difficult task. You start believing in things which you have not got. You should look into your own mind to see how many things are only delusions.

Bodhidharma says these *three realms are greed, anger and delusion. To leave the three realms means to go from greed, anger and delusion back to morality, meditation and wisdom.* Morality, meditation and wisdom are in fact not three things but only three names.

The exact thing is meditation. On one side it brings morality in your life; on another side it brings wisdom in your life. But you cannot do anything to attain wisdom directly; neither can you do anything to be moral directly. But you can do something for meditation; you can meditate directly, and morality and wisdom both are by-products. Morality will be in your actions and wisdom will be your intelligence, your awareness, your final enlightenment.

The sutras say, "Buddhas have only become buddhas while living with the three poisons and nourishing themselves on the pure Dharma."

Bodhidharma is saying not to be worried about the three poisons of greed, anger and delusion. Even buddhas have lived through the same experience as you all are passing through; but because they started nourishing themselves through meditation and started becoming aware of their self-nature, all these poisons disappeared. They have found the antidote.

Meditation is the antidote to all the poisons of your life.

It is the nourishment of your authentic nature.

The three poisons are greed, anger and delusion. The Great Vehicle is the greatest of all vehicles.

This I call a prejudice. He is continuously insisting and emphasizing that Mahayana, *The Great Vehicle is the greatest of all vehicles. It is the conveyance of bodhisattvas, who use everything without using anything. And who travel all day without travelling. Such is the vehicle of buddhas. The sutras say, "No vehicle is the vehicle of buddhas."*

To an ordinary, logical mind, to anybody who is looking at life with rationality, this will look a very absurd statement. First he says, *The Great Vehicle is the greatest of all vehicles. It is the conveyance of bodhisattvas, who use everything without using anything, and who travel all day without travelling. Such is the vehicle of buddhas.*

And then, *The sutras say, "No vehicle is the vehicle of buddhas."* It is the same as his other statement. Walking without walking, acting without acting, speaking without speaking...so there is no contradiction. He is using the same expression for "vehicle" – the greatest vehicle is a "no-vehicle."

The sutras say, "The cave of five aggregates is the hall of zen."

The five aggregates are the five elements the body is made of: earth, air, fire, water, and the sky. These five are the aggregates – *skandhas* – elements of which your body is made. Just behind these five elements is hidden your treasure, *the hall of Zen.* Just inside the temple made by these five elements, is the fire of your awareness.

This body is a temple, and your consciousness is the god of the temple.

"The opening of the inner eye is the door of the Great Vehicle." What could be clearer?

As you become more and more aware, you start having a third eye. These two eyes look outwards; that third eye looks inwards.

And to see yourself is the greatest experience, because once you have seen your beauty, then all beauties of the outside world fade away.

Once you have seen your purity, then everything outside becomes polluted. Once you have seen your inner splendor, then even a beautiful sunrise, or a grand sunset, or a night sky full of stars, are nothing compared to the splendor of your being. You are the highest peak of evolution, of light, of consciousness.

Not thinking about anything is zen.

Just being silent without any thought is what is meant by meditation.

Once you know this, walking, standing, sitting, or lying down, everything you do is zen.

This is a significant statement. Perhaps there is no other religion that has made your whole life, twenty-four hours a day, a meditative experience. Zen does not believe in meditating one hour in the morning, or one hour in the night. It does not make meditation a separate, particular act. It wants meditation to become a quality of your being.

So whatever you are doing – walking, sitting, standing, lying down, chopping wood, carrying water from the well, it does not matter. Whatever you are doing, you are doing it so silently, so peacefully, without any stirring of thoughts in your mind.

Then your whole life has become meditation. You go to bed silently, you wake up silently, and one day you will realize that you also sleep silently – as thoughts disappear, dreams also disappear. Then the circle is complete.

For Zen, meditation has to be a twenty-four-hour affair. It is not some extra act that you have to do. It is not a Sunday religion – for six days do everything you want to do, but at least on the seventh day, on Sunday, go to the church for one hour and you are a great Christian.

It is absolutely illogical, and absurd. Just going to the church for one hour, and then living your mundane life with greed, with anger, with delusion, is not going to transform you. And no Jesus can save you.

My people in the commune made a small placard for cars. It said, "Jesus saves, Moses invests, Bhagwan spends." I like that. What is the point of saving? Jesus seems to be like a banker. And of course, Moses invests. For Moses, everything is business. And for me, certainly, everything is going to be taken away. Before it is taken away, use it, spend it, enjoy it. Why wait for death to snatch it away? Certainly it is absolutely right. A one-hour religion, or even a Mohammedan who prays five times a day, is not going to help.

Religion has to become something like your heartbeat.

Meditation has to become something like your breathing. Whatever you are doing, you are breathing; it is not a separate action. And only then are you saturated, in every fiber of your being, with meditativeness.

To know that the mind is empty is to see the Buddha. The Buddhas of the Ten Directions have no mind. To see no mind is to see the Buddha.

Now you can see why I have been insisting that the disciple was taking wrong notes. This is the right statement, by Bodhidharma. The buddhas have no-mind. *To see no mind is to see the buddha.*

But it is very strange that these sutras have existed for one thousand years, and nobody has seen the contradiction. Perhaps religious people are so blind, such believers, that they will not see any contradiction, even if it is there – so apparent.

To give up yourself without regret is the greatest charity.

But the Indian constitution will not believe in it. The Indian constitution believes in charity according to the Christian idea. It is a very strange constitution. It is a hodgepodge.

In Hindi we call it *khichri,* humbug. What the people who made the constitution have done...they have collected all the constitutions of the world, and taken beautiful passages from every constitution, without knowing that those beautiful passages were alive in a certain context, in *their* constitution. When you take them out, they become dead.

The Indian constitution is the most dead constitution in the world, because everything has been taken and borrowed from others. It is not a growth, it is simply a combination. Take everything good...somebody's eyes are good, take them out; somebody's ears are really beautiful, take them out; somebody's mustache – pull it out. You can make a man just by taking beautiful things from everywhere – the eyes of Cleopatra, and the nose of Amrapali, the body of Alexander the Great and the mind of Albert Einstein. But remember, although you have taken all the best parts from the best people, you have collected only a corpse – it won't have any life.

What Bodhidharma is saying about charity.... We have been fighting with the Indian government and the Indian courts for almost ten years, that their conception of charity is very poor, their conception is very limited. Give to the poor, make hospitals, make schools...this is charity. There is nothing sublime in their idea of charity.

Bodhidharma's single statement is far more significant. He says: *To give up yourself without regret is the greatest charity.* To give up yourself to whom? To the universe.

Don't be a separate entity. Just drop into the ocean of existence and become one with it. This is the greatest charity. What else can you give? You came empty-handed into the world, and you will go empty-handed out of the world.

Everything that you have is not yours. Your house is nothing but a caravanserai. Your money is not your money; you have exploited for it. Your land is not your land; it was always there before you came and it will remain there after you are gone.

What is yours? You can only give that which is yours, you cannot give that which is not yours. You cannot contribute all the stars to the poor; you cannot contribute the sun to the poor; you cannot contribute the moon to the poor. It does not belong to you in the first place.

All that you can contribute is your own being. Hence, Bodhidharma is absolutely right that there is only one charity and that is to give yourself without regret, in fact with great joy and rejoicing, to existence. Become part of the whole.

To transcend motion and stillness is the highest meditation.

Whether you are sitting silently, or you are walking silently, you have to transcend all form, motion and stillness, action and inaction, day and night, life and death. Transcend all, and you will have the highest fragrance of meditation in you.

Mortals keep moving – and again he comes to his prejudice – *while arhats stay still. But the highest meditation surpasses that of both mortals and arhats.*

He does not know anything about arhatas. Arhatas don't say anything, but they have also transcended motion and stillness. Just because they don't say anything does not mean that they have not transcended. In fact, their transcendence is so great that it cannot be said or conveyed in words. So I will not agree with Bodhidharma. He has to forgive me. With every apology, I want to say to him that his understanding about arhatas is absolutely zero. Instead of arhatas, he should have used the word "ascetics."

Mortals and ascetics don't know this transcending.

People who reach such understanding free themselves from all appearances without effort and cure all illnesses without treatment. Such is the power of great zen.

Such is the power of great meditation. Such is the power of knowing yourself. All illnesses disappear; illnesses of the spirit, all wounds are suddenly cured – wounds of the spirit. And all appearances, delusions, greed and anger are found no more, not even their footprints. Such is the power of knowing oneself in deep meditation.

He is perfectly right about everything, except what he says about arhatas. That has to be changed. In fact I am not against Bodhidharma, I am doing him a great favor. I am taking out his mistakes; I am making him almost infallible. His prejudice against arhatas drags him down from the great sunlit peak which is his home.

If you meet Bodhidharma somewhere, in some life, just remind him that a few corrections are needed. And certainly he cannot make me afraid by his big eyes. I can also make him afraid with my big eyes.

Okay, Maneesha?

Yes, Bhagwan.

NOT TO BE IN THE MIND IS EVERYTHING

達磨

Beloved Bhagwan,

Using the mind to look for reality is delusion. Not using the mind to look for reality is awareness. Freeing oneself from words is liberation. Remaining unblemished by the dust of sensation is guarding the Dharma. Transcending life and death is leaving home. Not suffering another existence is reaching the Way. Not creating delusions is enlightenment. Not engaging in ignorance is wisdom. No affliction is nirvana. And no appearance of the mind is the other shore.

In the light of the impartial Dharma, mortals look no different from sages. The sutras say that the impartial Dharma is something that mortals can't penetrate and sages can't practice. The impartial Dharma is only practiced by great bodhisattvas and buddhas. To look on life as different from death or on motion as different from stillness is to be partial. To be impartial means to look on suffering as no different from nirvana because the nature of both is emptiness. By imagining they're putting an end to suffering and entering nirvana, arhatas end up trapped by nirvana. But bodhisattvas know that suffering is essentially empty. And by remaining in emptiness, they remain in nirvana. Nirvana means no birth and no death. It's beyond birth and death and beyond nirvana. When the mind stops moving, it enters nirvana. Nirvana is an empty mind.

...An uninhabited place is one without greed, anger or delusion.

...Whoever knows that the mind is a fiction and devoid of anything real knows that his own mind neither exists nor doesn't exist. Mortals keep creating the mind, claiming it exists. And arhats keep negating the mind, claiming it doesn't exist. But bodhisattvas and buddhas neither create nor negate the mind. This is what's meant by the mind that neither exists nor

KŌ-MIYŌ: ENLIGHTENMENT ___ 169

doesn't exist. The mind that neither exists nor doesn't exist is called the Middle Way....

When your mind doesn't stir inside, the world doesn't arise outside. When the world and the mind are both transparent, this is true vision. And such understanding is true understanding.

T HESE SUTRAS OF Bodhidharma are pure gold except on one point: wherever he mentions the arhatas he suddenly becomes absolutely blind. His conception about the arhatas is the only flaw that he cannot drop. I will remind you whenever he falls below the ultimate wisdom and becomes attached to his opinion. It is extremely surprising that a man of the caliber of Bodhidharma can behave just like any ignorant person in certain situations. But this reminds us of the frailty of human beings and this can be helpful to you not to become too much attached to your opinions, because every opinion is going to make you blind, blind to the opposite opinion.

A man of pure understanding is available to all the contradictions without any choice. He remains choiceless, just silently aware, knowing that they are contradictions but that ultimately they meet somewhere. Life meets death, day meets night, love meets hate, yes meets no. For the man who is beyond all opinions, for him yes is partial just as no is partial. In fact, when they both meet and merge into each other, when yes is no longer yes, and no is no longer no, when it is absolutely indefinable because where yes and no meet, it is going beyond conceivability – this is the transcendence – going beyond the mind.

But even people like Bodhidharma have certain blind spots. It is something like the scientists say: at least ten percent of people in the world are color blind although they are not aware of it. It is a big percentage; it means out of ten people, one person is going to be color blind. And by color blind they mean that the person cannot see a certain color at all.

Rarely does one come to discover one's color blindness. It happened in George Bernard Shaw's life. For sixty years he was not aware that he was color blind. On his sixtieth birthday a friend sent a gift of a beautiful suit, but he must have forgotten to send a matching tie with the suit. And Bernard Shaw loved the suit and he told his secretary that they should go immediately to find a matching tie, "Because this evening many friends will be coming to celebrate my birthday and I would like to use this suit for the evening."

They went to the shop where the best quality ties were available and he looked at many ties and finally he chose one. The shopkeeper was shocked, his secretary was shocked; they could not believe what he was doing. It looked very ridiculous; the suit was green and he had chosen a yellow tie. Simultaneously the secretary and the shopkeeper both said to him, "It will look very odd. You have chosen a very strange color. With green, this yellow will not look good."

George Bernard Shaw said, "What do you mean? They are the same color." He had no eye for yellow; yellow looked to him like green. He could not see the yellow at all. But it was just coincidental. Perhaps millions of people live and die without knowing that they are color blind. If this certain circumstance had not happened, George Bernard Shaw would have died – sixty years he had lived, forty years more he could have lived, he could have made the whole century – and remained unaware of a certain blind spot in his eyes.

Something similar happens to people. Even though they may be of great awareness, there are points where they are blind, and unless these blind spots disappear, a man's enlightenment cannot be called perfect. It remains imperfect, incomplete. And the surprising thing is, when Bodhidharma talks about great things he is so accurate, so impeccably perfect, but just on a few points he simply forgets everything and falls down into an ordinary state of mind where people become opinionated, prejudiced.

You have to remember him and learn one secret from him, so that this does not happen to you.

The sutra:

Using the mind to look for reality is delusion.

And all philosophers have been doing that and all theologians have been doing that. The great thinkers are doing nothing but playing games with words. *Using the mind to look for reality is delusion.* Mind cannot know reality. It is something like: if you want to hear music with the eyes, you will not be able to, because eyes are not meant to hear. Or if you want to see the light through the ears you will not be able to, because ears are not meant to see the light. Ears are meant for sound, eyes are meant for light. They each have a certain dimension of functioning.

Mind's functioning is to create thoughts, dreams, imaginations, illusions, hallucinations, mirages of all kinds. Its function is not to find the reality.

Not using the mind to look for reality is awareness.

Not using the mind is the way to find reality. Becoming utterly silent, without any thought, just a clean slate, a tabula rasa – in that clarity, in that perceptivity, one comes to know what is real, both within and without, because the reality is one.

It is the mind that divides it into within and without. When the mind is withdrawn, the division is dropped. Then you are the reality; then, even the farthest star is connected with you and even the smallest blade of grass is connected with you. It is all one existence. Suddenly you are no longer separate, you have fallen into the whole. All the walls have disappeared between you and existence.

This experience in the *Upanishads,* the seers have declared as *Aham Brahmasmi* – I am God. It was not out of an ego; it was out of utter humbleness. But what can be done? The moment mind disappears you are one with the whole. It has to be said.

Freeing oneself from words is liberation.

In a small statement there are hidden scriptures. He's a simple man; he does not use learned jargon, big words. He simply states in simple and ordinary words the extraordinary truth and the ultimate experience.

Freeing oneself from words is liberation...not freeing yourself from the world, not freeing yourself from your wife or your husband, not freeing yourself from your money or your house but just freeing yourself from words. And certainly your real world is nothing but words.

What is a wife other than a word? Once she was not your wife; suddenly one day some stupid priest starts chanting mantras that he does not understand – nor do the people who are being married know what is meant by the whole ritual that is going on.

One sannyasin got married a few days ago and she was telling me that she was surprised by the priest. The ritual was going to be one and a half hours long, but her husband gave five rupees to the priest and told him to be quick. The whole ritual went so fast; the priest started chanting so quickly and ended the whole thing within fifteen minutes. And in those fifteen minutes were included all those moments when the photographer said, "Just a moment!" And the priest would stop for the photograph to be taken and when the photograph was taken, he again started the ritual. What is a wife or what is a husband except a game of words?

You come into the world without any possessions and you go out of the world without any possessions. One day the whole thing becomes just like a dream that you had once seen. At the moment of your death you may remember all those things as if they had been seen in a dream. At the time of happening they were so real, but at the time of death everything will become unreal – just words in the mind.

The real renunciation is not of the world. It is meaningless to renounce the world and escape to the Himalayas or to the monasteries. The real thing is to drop the words from your mind so you can become a silent observer, a pure witness. And this is what Bodhidharma calls liberation.

Remaining unblemished by the dust of sensations is guarding the Dharma.

All that is needed of you to be authentically religious, is to be on guard that you are not carried by emotions, sentiments, moods; that you remain above and beyond any strategies of the mind to pull you down. To be aware and alert is all that is needed to be authentically religious.

You don't have to go to any church or to any synagogue or to any temple. You simply have to go within and be alert.

Transcending life and death is leaving home.

I would like to add two words to this sutra, otherwise this sutra can be misleading. I would like to say: *Transcending life and death is leaving this world,* not the home, because your real home is where you are going. This world is not your real home. It is only a so-called home. It is just a consolation to call it home.

I have told you the story of a Sufi mystic. One night in Baghdad, the king heard somebody walking on the roof of his palace. He shouted, "Who is there? And what are you doing there?"

The man was not a thief. Without any fear he said, "Don't shout, that may disturb other people's sleep. It is none of your business. I am looking for my camel. My camel is lost and it is time for you to go to sleep."

The king could not believe what kind of madman could be on the roof of a palace searching for his camel. He called the guards and they searched all over the place but could not find the man. And the next day when he was sitting in his court he heard the same voice again; he recognized it.

The king immediately said, "Bring that man in," because he was arguing with the guard in front of the gate that he wanted to stay in the caravanserai.

And the guard said, "You will be getting into problems unnecessarily. This is the palace of the king; this is not a caravanserai."

The man said, "I know it is a caravanserai and you are just a guard. Don't bother me. Just let me go in. I want to discuss the matter with the king himself. If I can convince him that this is a caravanserai then I will stay. If he can convince me it is not a caravanserai, then of course I will leave. But I won't listen to you; you are just a guard."

And just at that moment the message came from inside, "Don't stop that man. We are in search of him; bring him in."

The Sufi mystic was called in and the king said, "You seem to be a very strange fellow. I recognize your voice. You were the man on the roof searching for your camel and now you are calling my place, my home, a caravanserai."

The man laughed and said, "You seem to be a man of some understanding. It is possible to talk with you. Yes, it was me who was looking for the camel on the roof of the palace. Don't think that I'm insane. If you can look for blissfulness sitting on a golden throne, if you can look for God while continuously conquering and butchering and burning living human beings, what is wrong in searching for a camel on the roof of the palace? You tell me!

"If I am inconsistent you are also not consistent. And what right have you got to call this place your home, because I have been here before and on the same golden throne I have seen another man sitting. He looked just like you – a little older."

The king said, "He was my father. Now he's dead." And the mystic said, "I was here even before that and I found another man. He also looked a little bit like you but very old." The king said, "You are right, he was my grandfather." And the mystic said, "What happened to him?" The king said, "He is dead."

And the mystic said, "When are you going to die? They also believed that this is their home. I have argued with your grandfather. Now the poor fellow is in the grave. I have argued with your father; that poor fellow is also in the grave. Now I am arguing with you and someday I will come back again and I will be arguing with your son and you will be in a grave. So what kind of home is this where people go on changing? It is a caravanserai. It is just an overnight stay, and then one has to go."

The king was shocked but was silent. The whole court was silent. The man was right. And the mystic finally said, "If you really want to know where your home is, go to the graveyard where finally you will have to settle, where your grandfather is, where your father is. That is the real place that you can call your home, but not this palace. Here I am going to stay as if it is a caravanserai."

The king was certainly not an ordinary man. He stood up and told the mystic, "Forgive me, I was wrong. You are right. You can stay as long as you want. I am going in search of my real home. This is not my real home."

This world is only a caravanserai.

In the sutra it says: *Transcending life and death is leaving home.* I would like: *Transcending life and death is leaving* for *home* – leaving the world, leaving for the home, for the real home from where you will not have to go anywhere else again – which will be your eternal, ultimate and absolute refuge.

Not suffering another existence is reaching the Way. Not creating delusions is enlightenment.

Reduced to a single statement: Not to be in the mind is everything – liberation, finding the real home, enlightenment, finding the way.

Not engaging in ignorance is wisdom.

This statement is a little strange because people don't engage in ignorance. Nobody wants to be ignorant; why should they engage in ignorance? Hence I would like to change it, although the meaning will remain the same. The word will not be ignorance, the word will be: *Not engaging in* knowledge *is wisdom.*

Engaging in knowledge is really hiding your ignorance. That is really engaging, indulging in ignorance. But on the surface you are engaged in being more knowledgeable, more erudite, more learned – a scholar, a pundit. And to be so much involved in knowledge is a barrier to wisdom. Wisdom comes to those who are innocent of all knowledge.

The moment you drop all knowledge you have also dropped all ignorance. They exist together as two sides of a coin. And then what remains is pure innocence.

No affliction is nirvana...not to be afflicted – by any suffering, by any anguish, by any anger, by any greed – not to be afflicted is nirvana. You have arrived home. The name of the home is nirvana.

...And no appearance of the mind is the other shore.

When the mind disappears, with the mind this whole world disappears. With the mind, disappears this whole ignorance, this whole knowledgeability, all these nightmares of life. Mind is the creator of this whole drama that you go on seeing. Once mind disappears the other shore appears immediately – coming closer and closer.

The other shore is your real home.

The other shore is your immortality, your eternity.

This shore consists of death, disease, old age and all kinds of miseries. The other shore is the hope, the hope of being liberated, the hope of being saved, the hope of being redeemed from the nightmare in which we are all living. And the secret is simple: not to be a mind, but just to be a pure consciousness, a consciousness without thoughts, a sky without clouds.

In the light of the impartial Dharma mortals look no different from sages. The sutras say that the impartial Dharma is something that mortals can't penetrate and sages can't practice. The impartial Dharma is only practiced by great bodhisattvas and buddhas.

But he's not including the arhatas. And that's his blind spot. Although Bodhidharma has very big eyes, he cannot see one simple thing: the great arhatas belong to the same category as the great bodhisattvas and the buddhas.

To look on life as different from death or on motion as different from stillness is to be partial. To be impartial means to look on suffering as no different from nirvana because the nature of both is emptiness. By imagining they are putting an end to suffering and entering nirvana, arhatas end up trapped by nirvana.

That is absolutely wrong. The arhatas attain to the same height as the bodhisattvas. Their paths are different, but one can reach to the peak of the mountain from different paths. He could have said that the so-called sages and saints end up trapped by nirvana – but not arhatas. Arhatas are buddhas as authentically as bodhisattvas. Their only difference is that arhatas don't care about anybody else – that they have to be helped, that they have to be supported for their enlightenment. Arhatas are simply concerned with their own enlightenment. Bodhisattvas are concerned with others' enlightenment too. That is the only difference. Otherwise their experience is the same, their height is the same, their position has the same ultimateness.

But there are many so-called sages and saints who are neither arhatas or bodhisattvas, who have practiced ascetic disciplines, who have tortured themselves, who have done everything that is within the capacity of man to do, but it is all being done by their mind. That makes all the difference. It has not been a spontaneous and natural growth; they have forced it. They have managed, disciplined, practiced. They always do the right thing, but their right doing is not spontaneous. It is deliberately thought-out. They are continuously weighing pros and cons – what is right and what is wrong. They are always consulting the scriptures – what is right, what is wrong. They don't have their own insight.

I call them so-called saints and sages. They look almost like buddhas, but deep inside there is great darkness. Their own self-nature is not yet realized. They have not attained *samadhi*. They are still wandering in the puzzling mind and its millions of ways. Their great practices, their asceticism, their disciplines, are nothing but their mind projection.

So it can be said that the so-called saints and sages end up trapped by nirvana. Their whole desire is to become enlightened. But that is the problem: you cannot desire to be enlightened. Desire is the barrier. You can become enlightened, but you cannot desire to become enlightened. The moment you desire you are trapped. You are trapped by your own desire.

You cannot make enlightenment an object of your greed.

You cannot make it an object of your ambition.

And that is where the so-called sages and saints come in. They have made enlightenment, liberation, moksha, nirvana, a goal – an achievement. Then it becomes an ego trip. They are trapped, badly trapped.

Nirvana has to flower within you. When you have dropped the mind with all its desire, with all its ambitions, with all its program for achievements, when you have dropped your whole mind full of greed.... Whether the greed concerns money, or the greed concerns enlightenment, it does not make any difference. Mind can go on changing from object to object. But it remains the same mind full of greed. The moment mind is completely dropped, you suddenly find enlightenment is not a goal. It is your self-nature. Suddenly the lotus blossoms open their petals and you are full of fragrance. And this fragrance is not different in the arhatas or in the bodhisattvas. They both are buddhas; they both are enlightened people.

Because I don't belong to any religion, I don't belong to any particular sect – I simply don't belong to anybody, I just belong to myself – I can see clearly where people get trapped in their own ideologies. Even a man like Bodhidharma cannot tolerate the idea that arhatas are the same as bodhisattvas. He belongs to the category of bodhisattvas.

And it is not the case only with him. There have been arhatas who condemn bodhisattvas in the same way. But to me it does not matter whether somebody is of one category or of another category. I can be absolutely impartial. And my being impartial has been my problem because I say things without bothering about who is going to be pleased by my statements, who is going to be displeased by my statements.

It is a very strange world. If I say something that pleases you, you will forget all about it. But if I say something that displeases you, you are not going to forget it, and you are not going to forgive me.

I have said things about Jesus that no Christian has ever said. I have appreciated the man more than any Christian in two thousand years. But when I criticized a few things about Jesus, immediately the whole Christian world turned against me. They were silent when I was saying and appreciating great statements of Jesus. They were happy, but nobody even said a single word. But when I criticized a few things, the whole Christian world, which means almost half the world, immediately turned to destroying my movement.

My books have been banned by the pope. A few Christian associations have published my books on Jesus, but when I criticized Jesus they even burnt my books in which I have praised Jesus.

People are very touchy. If you appreciate something they will not say anything. They will simply enjoy the fact that their mind is being appreciated. It is not a question of Jesus; it is a question of a Christian mind. But when I say something that I see clearly is wrong in Jesus, then it hurts the Christian mind.

For example, I am saying a few things against Bodhidharma, but I am saying many more things in his favor – they will be forgotten. But what I am saying against him...the countries which belong to Mahayana Buddhism will immediately get upset.

My whole life, my whole life's work has been how to influence people and create enemies.

Again: *But bodhisattvas know that suffering is essentially empty. And by remaining in emptiness they remain in nirvana. Nirvana means no birth and no death. It is beyond birth and death and beyond nirvana.*

But this is said only about bodhisattvas, not about arhatas. I would like to make it clear that it refers as much to arhatas as to bodhisattvas.

When the mind stops moving it enters nirvana. Nirvana is an empty mind.

Empty mind can be misinterpreted. I would suggest it is better to call it "no-mind," because mind is never empty. The moment mind is empty, it is no longer there. Empty mind is a contradictory use of words – a contradiction in terms. There is nothing like an empty mind; mind is always thought processes. It is always a traffic of thoughts, emotions, dreams, imaginations.

When the mind is empty, there is no mind. It is better to use the word "no-mind" than to use the word "empty" mind. Empty mind can be misleading. People can start thinking that all that they have to do is to empty the mind.

And you cannot empty the mind even if you go on working for eternity. You have to drop it – wholesale. You cannot go emptying it in installments, because here you will be emptying it, and from all directions, things will go on coming into it.

You cannot empty the mind.

Either you cling to it or you simply drop it.

There is no middle way.

An uninhabited place is one without greed, anger or delusion.

Whoever knows that the mind is a fiction and devoid of anything real knows that his own mind neither exists nor does not exist. Mortals keep creating the mind, claiming it exists. And arhatas keep negating the mind, claiming it does not exist. But bodhisattvas and buddhas neither create nor negate the mind. This is what is meant by the mind that neither exists nor does not exist. The mind that neither exists nor does not exist is called the Middle Way.

He can never forget to condemn the arhatas. It seems to be as if something is constantly hurting him. The situation is again the same: instead of arhatas, he should have said the so-called sages and saints keep negating the mind. But bodhisattvas, arhatas and the buddhas neither create nor negate the mind. They simply go beyond it; they don't fight with it, because to fight with the mind is to give it reality, to recognize its power. There is no need to fight. One has just to be a witness.

Without any fight, just being a witness, mind disappears.

Before the fire of witnessing, there is no possibility of mind remaining within you even for a single second. Create the fire of witnessing, create the flame of awareness. This is done by the arhatas, bodhisattvas and the buddhas without any distinction.

When your mind does not stir inside, the world does not arise outside.

This is a beautiful statement, immensely pregnant. It is saying the world outside is nothing but your projection. When your mind stirs inside, the world is created outside.

Once it happened that a German poet, Heinrich Heine, got lost in the forest. He had gone hunting, but lost his way and lost his companion. And for three days he did not come across any human being. He was utterly tired, hungry and continuously worried about the wild animals.

In the night he used to climb a tree to somehow protect himself from the wild animals. The third night was a full-moon night and he was sitting up in a tree. Three days of hunger and tiredness...he had not slept. And he saw the beautiful moon. He had written so many beautiful poems about the moon, but this day was different because his mind was in a different situation.

Instead of seeing the moon, he saw a loaf of bread moving in the sky. In his diary he wrote, "I could not believe my eyes. I have always seen my beloved's face in the moon. I have never even thought that a loaf of bread...!"

But a man who has been hungry for three days...his mind is projecting one thing, and that is food. The moon disappeared and a loaf of bread was floating in the sky.

What you see is not what is there.

What you see is what your mind projects.

I have told you a story about Mulla Nasruddin. He had a beautiful house in the mountains and he hired one of the ugliest women possible to take care of the house. All his friends asked, "Mulla, there must be some reason – why have you chosen the ugliest woman?" Mulla said, "There is a reason. And when the time comes, I will tell you."

And this created even more temptation to know. And again and again they were asking. It became a continuous temptation for them to enquire about the ugly woman. Mulla used to go to the mountain once in a while to rest, and he would say to his friends, "I am going for three weeks," and he would be back in one week.

And they would ask, "You went for three weeks...?" He said, "Yes, I went for three weeks, but something happened and I had to come back."

And this happened again and again. He would go for six weeks and within two weeks he was back. Finally they said, "You are creating a mystery. You are keeping that ugly woman there, you go there for three weeks, you come back in one week. You never keep your word."

Mulla said, "It is better now that I tell you the truth. The truth is, I have kept that ugly woman for a particular reason. And the reason is that when I go to the mountain house, the woman looks ugly. She is so repulsive, not just ugly. But without another woman, after seven or eight days, she does not look so repulsive. After two weeks, she does not even look ugly. After four weeks, she starts looking even beautiful. That is the time when I leave – now the danger is near. Whenever that woman starts looking beautiful, that is the point to immediately leave the mountains because now there is danger."

Mind has started creating its own reality. Now it does not care at all what is actually fact; now it is creating its own fiction. Because it has not been with a woman for four weeks, there is a certain hunger, biological hunger, and that hunger is creating a loaf of bread.

It is not coincidental that people call beautiful woman "dishes," "delicious dishes." Why is a woman, a beautiful woman, in almost all languages, called a "beautiful dish"?

Perhaps because, just as food is a hunger and biological, so is sex a hunger and biological. Both are different hungers, but both are hungers. The world that you see all around you is mostly a projection of your mind. When the mind disappears completely, you will see a totally different world. With all projections gone, then only the real – the objectively real – remains.

And with the objectively real, there is no attachment. The attachment arises only with your projecting mind.

When your mind does not stir inside, the world does not arise outside. When the world and the mind are both transparent, this is true vision. And such understanding is true understanding.

Bodhidharma is right on all basic points, and should be understood as deeply as possible, because he can help you tremendously on the way – but remember his blind spots.

Avoid those blind spots, because those blind spots make his grandeur a little less than it would have been without them. It makes his wisdom a little tainted, a little damaged. It is no longer impeccable; it is no longer absolute and perfect. Something is missing; he is prejudiced. He has joined a party.

A man of true understanding remains alone; he does not join any party, any organization, any church, any religion. He is available to every form of understanding, but he remains impartial. To me this impartiality is one of the fundamentals of religion.

A Christian is not religious just because he is a Christian. A Hindu is not religious just because he has become part of an organized doctrine. A Jaina is not religious because he has chosen a certain party line.

An authentically religious man is individual.

He is alone, and in his aloneness there is great beauty, great splendor.

I teach you that aloneness. I teach you the beauty, and the grandeur, and the fragrance of aloneness.

In your aloneness you will reach to the heights of Everest. In your aloneness you will be able to touch the farthest star. In your aloneness you will blossom to your total potential.

Never become a believer, never become a follower, never become a part of any organization. Remain authentically true to yourself. Don't betray yourself.

Okay, Maneesha?

Yes, Bhagwan.

MIND IS THE GREATEST ENEMY OF MAN

達磨

184 —— YU-ME: DREAM

MIND IS THE GREATEST ENEMY OF MAN

Beloved Bhagwan,

The sutras say, "Not to let go of wisdom is stupidity." When the mind doesn't exist, understanding and not understanding are both true. When the mind exists, understanding and not understanding are both false.

When you understand, reality depends on you. When you don't understand, you depend on reality. When reality depends on you, that which isn't real becomes real. When you depend on reality, that which is real becomes false. When you depend on reality, everything is false. When reality depends on you, everything is true....

Thus, the sage doesn't use his mind to look for reality, or reality to look for his mind, or his mind to look for his mind, or reality to look for reality. His mind doesn't give rise to reality. And reality doesn't give rise to his mind. And because both his mind and reality are still, he's always in samadhi.

...The sutras say, "Nothing has a nature of its own." Act. Don't question. When you question, you're wrong. When you're deluded, the six senses and five shades are constructs of suffering and mortality. When you wake up, the six senses and five shades are constructs of nirvana and immortality.

Someone who seeks the Way doesn't look beyond himself. He knows that the mind is the Way. But when he finds the mind, he finds nothing. And when he finds the Way, he finds nothing. If you think you can use the mind to find the Way, you're deluded. When you're deluded, buddhahood exists. When you're aware, it doesn't exist. Because awareness is buddhahood.

...Don't hate life and death or love life and death. Keep your every thought free of delusion, and in life you'll witness the beginning of nirvana, and in death you'll experience the assurance of no rebirth.

To see form but not be corrupted by form or to hear sound but not be corrupted by sound is liberation.

Eyes that aren't attached to form are the Gates of Zen. Ears that aren't attached to sound are also the Gates of Zen. In short, those who perceive the existence of phenomena and remain unattached are liberated....

When delusions are absent, the mind is the land of buddhas. When delusions are present, the mind is hell.

THE UNDERSTANDING OF Bodhidharma's teachings will be easier if you understand a few points. First is the hypothesis of reincarnation. All the religions born outside of India believe in only one life. The religions born in India differ on every point, but not on reincarnation. They all insist that you don't have only one life. You have had thousands of lives before and you will go on having lives again and again until you realize your self nature.

Life is only a school and unless you learn enlightenment, you will go on moving into the circle of life and death. This is something very essential.

If there is only one life of seventy years on average, then you don't have much time left for meditation, for exploration of your being – searching for the path. Seventy years is such a small span that one-third of it is wasted in sleep; one-third of it is wasted in educating you to earn your livelihood. And the remaining one-third, you waste in many ways because you don't know what to do with it.

I have seen people playing cards or chess and I have asked them, "Can't you find anything better to do?" And their answer has consistently been the same...they are killing time. Such is the unawareness of man.

You don't have much time.

You cannot afford to kill time.

Moreover time is killing you; you cannot kill time. Each moment, time is bringing your death closer and closer.

If you count all your activities.... Shaving your beard twice a day – how much time you put into it! Listening to the radio or watching the television – how much time you waste on it. An American survey shows that each American wastes seven and a half hours every day watching television. That is one third of his life he is just sitting, glued to his chair, watching all kinds of nonsense.

How much time do you waste smoking cigarettes, cigars? There are people who are chain smokers.... How much time you waste in reading newspapers which never bring any news! All that they bring is simply sick – murders, rapes, suicides, wars. They make you believe that this is the world and this is our life.

you from your responsibility. They convince you that the whole world is like this. Nothing is wrong, everybody is doing it....

They never bring you any news of somebody becoming enlightened. Perhaps that is not news. Somebody is entering deeper realms of meditation – perhaps that is not news. Somebody has become calm and quiet and gone beyond anger, greed, agony. That is not news!

Once Bernard Shaw was asked, "What is news?" He said, "When a dog bites a man, it is not news. When a man bites a dog, it is news."

How much time you are wasting in reading about how many men are biting dogs! If you count carefully, you will be surprised that you don't have, in your seventy years of life, even seven minutes for yourself. This is such an idiotic situation.

And then because there is only one life, there is great speed. Why has the West become so addicted to speed? The idea of one life given by Judaism, Christianity and Islam, has made people speedy. They are always running – on the run – because time is short and there are so many ambitions to be fulfilled. They have to become the richest man, they have to attain great power, they have to become a celebrity. They have to do a thousand and one things and life is so short. The only way is to do everything as quickly as possible.

Most of the housewives in the West don't know what cooking is. The best housewife is the one who knows how to open cans. Everything has to be done quickly and fast. Why bother about cooking?

Nobody is in a state of stillness; they cannot be. That seems to be a waste of time. Sitting silently, doing nothing is the foundation of meditation. In the West, meditation is not possible for the simple reason that one life span is too short. And death comes too quickly. It does not give you enough time.

The Eastern concept takes care of your spiritual growth. The hypothesis of reincarnation, a continuous eternal cycle of birth and re-birth, gives you enough time. You can sit silently for hours; there is no hurry. There is no need to be speedy. There is an eternity available to you – not only seventy years.

The West is very poor. They have only seventy years for each person. The East may look poor from the outside, but its inner arrangement is very rich. Eternity behind – eternity ahead.

Secondly, just one life is not enough to make you bored. Seventy years goes so fast that boredom is not possible. But life after life, running after money. Life after life, running after power. Life after life, running after men or women. As you become aware of this long series of the same stupidities – in which you have succeeded many times, but you have not gained anything....

Each life you have to begin again from A,B,C. Just visualize millions of lives behind you.... You have loved so many women and you have told every woman, "I will love you forever and forever." And you have told every woman, "You are the most beautiful woman in the world." And you have been saying that for millions of lives to millions of women, to millions of men. It is tiring – just the very idea.

It brings a certain maturity to you that now it is time to stop being childish. You have been playing these games so long that it is time to grow up; to do something else that you have never done before.

Meditation fits perfectly well in the Eastern vision of life. That is the only thing you have never done before. You have earned money, you have become rich, you have been in politics, you have become ministers and prime ministers and presidents. You have become great celebrities. You have done everything, because in so many lives there was so much opportunity – so much time.

And once you understand it...that you are still doing the same things, again and again and again. It is good to commit a mistake once, but to go on committing the same mistake again and again proves your stupidity.

And there is a great and urgent need to do something that you have never done before – a search for your own self. You have run after everything in the world and it has not led anywhere. All roads in the world go round and round; they never reach any goal. They don't have any goal.

Visualizing this long perspective, one suddenly becomes sick of the whole action; love affairs, fights, anger, greed, jealousy. And one starts thinking for the first time, "Now I should find a new dimension in which I will not be running after anybody; in which I will be coming back home. I have gone too far away in these millions of lives."

This is the foundation of the Eastern wisdom. It creates a great boredom with life, death and the continuous vicious circle. That is the original meaning of the word, *samsara;* it means the wheel that goes on moving, on and on; it knows no stopping. You can jump out of it, but you are clinging to it.

This is the basic device to bring you to your senses.

You have fooled around enough.

Now stop it, and do something that you have been avoiding for centuries, that you have been postponing for tomorrow.

These are very beautiful sutras. In the East people have never spoken unless they have understood. It is the greatest dishonesty, the greatest crime to speak, either for or against something that you don't know.

In the East, even people who have known – who have come to the ultimate flowering of their being – many of them have not spoken because they were not able to find the right words. They were not articulate, hence, they decided to remain silent. It is better to be silent rather than give wrong ideas to people. Only a very few people have spoken. And they have spoken, only when they were absolutely certain that what they were saying may help millions of people down the ages.

The East has never been interested in the daily newspaper. It has been interested in statements which have the quality of eternity, which will remain valid in every age, in every time. As long as man remains on the earth, the validity of these statements will not be challenged.

A newspaper becomes useless by evening. In the West, there are morning editions and afternoon editions because by the afternoon, the morning edition has become useless. Evening editions, because by the evening the afternoon edition has become useless. Night editions, because by the night the evening edition has become useless.

These sutras will remain as fresh and as young as when they were uttered for the first time – but only for those who can experience what is contained in them. Otherwise, it is so much prose. Once you experience it, the prose starts turning into poetry. The words start turning into silence. The statements prove to be only devices to give you the feel of an eternal dance of existence.

No Western book, and I have gone through all the philosophers and all the theologians – it was a tedious journey – no Western book has anything parallel to the Eastern sutras because they are only mind stuff. The Eastern sutras have a qualitative difference. They have nothing to do with mind. They have something to do with your innermost being and its experiences of blissfulness, ecstasy, the universal joy that pervades this vast existence. Only man is missing it. And man is missing it because of his knowledgeability.

The trees are not missing it because they are innocent. The oceans are not missing it. The mountains are not missing it. The stars are not missing it. They are absolutely innocent, they are not trapped in knowledge.

The first sutra of Bodhidharma says:

"Not to let go of wisdom is stupidity."

Your so-called wisdom is all borrowed. It is not wisdom at all; instead, being wise, you are otherwise. You go on repeating things that you don't understand; things that have not grown up in your own being, things that are absolutely foreign to your own existence, to your own life. You have been collecting, just like small children, sea shells on the beach and thinking that you are creating a great treasure. Yes it is possible to deceive others, and to deceive yourself.

One of my professors has a doctorate on a strange thesis from the University of London – very prestigious. His subject matter was the ways of the growth of consciousness. I was his student. He presented his book to me when it was published, and said, "I would love very much to know your opinion."

I said, "I don't have to read the book. I know you."

He said, "What do you mean?"

I said, "I simply know, that you know nothing about any growth of consciousness. So everything that you have written in this book is borrowed. You deceived yourself, you deceived the professors of London University who have examined it, and now you have published the book, millions will read it and be deceived. Rather than presenting the book on consciousness to me, show some consciousness."

He was very much shocked and he knew what I was saying was right. He was a drunkard. Without drinking alcohol every evening, he could not live.

I said, "Just drop this addiction with unconsciousness, because alcohol is doing nothing but creating more unconsciousness. And you have some nerve to write a thesis on the subject matter of consciousness."

But he was a very learned man; he knew many languages. He had collected materials just sitting in the library and he had managed to write a very beautiful thesis. But I said, "I will not read it because it is simply the work of a clerk. Anybody who has a little intelligence could have taken the information from the many sources which are available and collected it. I will read your book, only when you show me, something as a growing consciousness in you."

I returned the book to him. He said, "I am fortunate that you have not been an examiner of my book. Otherwise, I would have never got the doctorate."

I said, "Between you and me, you will never get it. You can befool the world but not yourself."

People go on collecting knowledge and get mixed up and start thinking that this knowledge is wisdom. Knowledge is not wisdom.

Wisdom comes through your growth of consciousness, and knowledge comes through collecting from the scriptures, from learned people, and making some sort of a system. But you remain the same; you don't go through any transformation.

Hence, the first sutra:

Not to let go of wisdom is stupidity.

Just drop your wisdom and with your wisdom gone, your stupidity will also be gone. If you cling to your knowledge, which you think is wisdom, you will remain stupid forever.

When the mind does not exist understanding and not understanding are both true.

The moment the mind is silent, nonfunctioning, everything is true. It is the mind that distorts everything and makes everything untrue. Knowledge comes through the mind, and wisdom comes when there is no-mind. This is a distinction which has not been made by the great philosophers of the world, except by the mystics of the East.

The dictionaries will say wisdom is knowledge, but actual reality and the experience of it, is not a dictionary. It makes a clear-cut distinction that knowledge and wisdom are not only, not synonymous, they are antagonistic. If your mind is full of knowledge you will remain unwise, stupid.

And if your mind is dropped and you go beyond it, you enter into the world of wisdom – into the world of awakening. In that awakening everything is true. Because you are true, everything is authentic because *you* are authentic.

In the mind you are untrue, you are false. That's why whatever happens through mind turns into falsity, hypocrisy. Mind is the greatest enemy of man.

When the mind exists, understanding and not understanding are both false.

When you understand, reality depends on you.

This is such a pregnant statement that you should try to feel it, not just to hear it: *When you understand, reality depends on you.* And when do you understand? When the mind is put aside and your being encounters reality directly, without the mediator, mind, then reality depends on you. You have risen higher than reality. You have risen to the ultimate reality. Otherwise reality is relative reality.

When you don't understand you depend on reality.

When you don't understand – when you are in the mind – you are a victim of this mundane reality that you see all around. Money deceives you, power deceives you, prestige deceives you, anything...

You are living in so many misunderstandings that if you come to see, you will be surprised at how articulate you are in creating falsehoods. Everything that passes through the mind, is almost as if you have taken a straight staff and put it into the water. You will suddenly see the straight staff is no longer straight. It has become bent at the place where it is in the water because water functions differently. You take it out; it is again straight. You put it back into water; it loses its straightness. The same is the situation with mind. Mind has only one capacity – to falsify things.

Unfortunately we are educated only as minds. And if the world lives in hypocrisy, in misery, in anguish, it is not a wonder. If the world goes on fighting and killing and goes on preparing for a global suicide, it is not a surprise. Mind cannot do anything else. It poisons everything.

The whole message is to get beyond the mind and then everything is crystal clear. Then you don't ask any questions. You simply act out of your clarity, out of your transparent vision. And each of your acts has a beauty – tremendous beauty of its own. It has a grace. And it has a power of blessings to shower over the whole world.

When reality depends on you, that which is not real becomes real.

Right now, it is a weird situation. Everything is real which is not real. And everything that is real, is unreal. Have you ever thought: Is your soul a reality to you? It is not a reality to you. You have only heard about it, but you don't have any experience of it.

But thousands of false things are real. A stone statue in the temple is real to you. Your own consciousness is unreal. Your own buddha nature is unreal. And a statue of marble is real to you. Before the false, you bow down, you worship the false not knowing what you are doing. You are insulting yourself and you are insulting all the buddhas of the past, of the present, of the future.

You are a buddha. You don't have to worship. There is nobody higher than you; there is nobody lower than you. You don't have to worship anybody and you don't have to accept anybody's worship. This whole existence is equally divine.

When you depend on reality, that which is real becomes false. When you depend on reality, everything is false.

Everything that you have known up to now, as real....

I have heard: In a great city, one man had the best palace. People used to come to see it. It was a miracle of architecture. But one night, suddenly, it caught fire. The man had gone to a friend's house. Somebody informed him, "What are you doing? Your palace is burning." He ran; nothing could be more shocking to him. Without his knowing, tears were running from his eyes. His most precious thing, his greatest attachment was being destroyed before his eyes and nothing could be done. The fire had gone too far.

Just then, his youngest son came running to him, telling him, "Father, don't be worried. Yesterday I sold the house. The king was continually saying that it was embarrassing to him that you have a better palace. Finally I decided to sell it – and he was ready to give any price."

Suddenly the tears dried and the man started smiling. Nothing had changed. The house was burning but it was no longer his. So who cares? So it was not the house that was hurting him, it was the ego, *his* house. And then his younger son came and said, "Father, what are you doing here? Although we had agreed to sell the palace, no sale deed has been written yet. And of course the king is not going to pay the money. I have every suspicion that he is behind the fire."

And again the tears started coming. And the situation was the same; nothing had changed. Only the idea had changed; the house became his, then there was great misery. The house was no longer his, all misery disappeared.

And then the king himself came in his chariot and he said, "You need not be worried. I am a man of my word. If I have purchased it, I have purchased it. No sale deed has been written, no money has been advanced, but because yesterday we agreed verbally, that is enough. It is *my* house that is burning. You need not be worried."

And suddenly, instead of tears, the man was smiling.

When reality depends on you, everything is true.

Thus, the sage doesn't use his mind to look for reality, or reality to look for his mind, or his mind to look for his mind, or reality to look for reality.

It is a vicious circle: mind and reality, mind and the world. Mind creates a certain world which is nothing but your projection. And then, that certain projection creates your mind. And this way, this vicious circle goes on supporting the other; your mind supports your projections, your projections support your mind. And you go on living in a hallucination.

Thus, the sage doesn't use his mind to look for reality, or reality to look for his mind, or his mind to look for his mind, or reality to look for reality. His mind doesn't give rise to reality. And reality doesn't give rise to his mind. And because both his mind and reality are still, he's always in samadhi.

This is a beautiful definition of samadhi. When the mind is still and the reality is still – when you are out of the vicious circle – all is silence, profound silence.

The word, *samadhi* has to be understood. It means coming to a state of absolute equilibrium, coming to a state of absolute balance. The word comes from Sanskrit. And Sanskrit is one of the languages in the world which has words with profound meaning. Not just dictionary meaning, but with existential meaning. Other languages have only dictionary meanings.

Sanskrit is the only language in the whole world which was created by enlightened people. It is a created language. It has never been a language of the people. There was no time when the whole country was speaking Sanskrit. All other languages of the world have been used by people at some time or other. Many have become dead languages, like Latin or Hebrew or Pali or Prakrit. Many languages which were once living languages, have become dead ones. But Sanskrit has never been a language of the people.

This is a very strange phenomenon. It has been the language of enlightened people, hence every word has two meanings; one, a dictionary meaning for the scholar and one, the existential meaning for those who are in search of truth.

Sanskrit has two words *vyadi* and *samadhi*. *Vyadi* means "sickness of the soul" and *samadhi* means "health and wholeness of the soul." But these are existential meanings. A man who has not experienced samadhi is spiritually sick. He may be bodily fit, but he is not spiritually fit. It is possible a man may be bodily sick, but he can attain to samadhi. Even at the last moment of your life, you can attain to samadhi. Your spiritual being comes in all its health, wholesomeness. Even if for a single moment you have known samadhí, you have known the greatest secret in existence.

There is no word in any language synonymous to samadhi. Only one word in Japanese comes a little close to it, but it is not synonymous. That word is *satori*. And unfortunately, the Japanese have stopped at satori thinking that it is samadhi.

Satori is only a glimpse of samadhi – a faraway glimpse. For example, you can see the Himalayan peaks from hundreds of miles away, but to see the peak when sitting on it, is a totally different experience. Satori is only a faraway vision of samadhi; a glimpse, beautiful in itself but not equivalent to samadhi.

Samadhi is your very nature in its absolute clarity, in its absolute purity, in its absolute awareness.

Samadhi is your real home.

And the people who don't know samadhi are wandering without a home. They are homeless people, rootless people and their whole life is nothing but a tragedy. Samadhi gives you roots in existence, and it opens the doors of your home. Samadhi is the ultimate actualization of your potential.

And the way to samadhi is simple. Drop the mind – go beyond the mind and you will enter into samadhi. Mind is the only barrier and strangely we are continuously educating the mind to become more and more powerful. Our whole educational systems around the world, are nursing the mind – your enemy, making it stronger, more informative, more knowledgeable.

In a more intelligent world, meditation should become absolutely mandatory in every school, in every college, in every university. And unless a person has some taste of samadhi, he will not be allowed to leave the university. He will not be given the certificates to leave.

And if we can make meditation an intrinsic part of all education systems, then naturally these people are going to be politicians, these people are going to be business men, these people are going to be industrialists, these people are going to be musicians, these people are going to be painters, actors, dancers. But they will all have one thing in common and that will be their experience of meditation. And that will be the common element joining the whole of humanity into one whole.

A man of meditation functions differently. Whatever profession he chooses, it does not matter. He will bring to his profession some quality of sacredness. He may be making shoes, or he may be cleaning the roads, but he will bring to his work some quality, some grace, some beauty, which is not possible without samadhi.

We can fill the whole world with ecstatic people. Just a simple thing has to be accepted.... Whether you are going to be a doctor or an engineer or a scientist, whatever you are going to be, that does not matter. Meditation should be the foundation for every profession, for every dimension of education.

Wars will disappear on their own. You will not have to protest against nuclear weapons. Population will start declining on its own, because a man of meditation functions with awareness. If he sees that the world is overpopulated, he cannot produce children. Nobody has to tell him. Why should he bring his children into a world which is going down every day towards a disaster? Who wants his children to go through a third world war? Who wants his children to die hungry and starving on the streets?

Meditation is the only cure for all sicknesses that man is prone to; a single medicine. And I should remind you that the word meditation and medicine come from the same root. Medicine for the body and meditation for the soul. They both bring health.

...The sutras say, "Nothing has a nature of its own."

This is one of the greatest contributions of Gautam Buddha and his disciples like Bodhidharma. *Nothing has a nature of its own.* It means, your consciousness is a pure space. It does not have any attributes. It is utterly empty, yet full – full of joy, full of light, full of fragrance – but utterly empty.

There is no self nature which makes people different. The moment you are in samadhi, you will see trees are also in samadhi. The mountains are in samadhi. The stars are in samadhi. The whole existence is in samadhi. Only you had gone astray. You have come back, merged and melted into the wholeness of the universe.

"Nothing has a nature of its own." Act. Don't question.

Bodhidharma is not a philosopher and he is not interested in any kind of philosophizing. He is a simple man of action. He says, *Act. Don't question...* because questions lead nowhere. Every answer will create ten more questions.

And you can go on asking, life after life, and you will not be able to find the answer... *Act.*

When you question, you are wrong.

It does not matter what question you are asking. *When you question, you are wrong.* And when you don't question and silently act, samadhi is not far away. Questions come from the mind and whatever answers are given, your mind rejoices in becoming more and more knowledgeable. It becomes more and more powerful. Bodhidharma said, "Please don't ask anything. If you want to know the answer, don't ask the question. Act."

Act, transcend the mind and you will find *you* are the answer. Your very being is the answer.

When you are deluded, the six senses and five shades are constructs of suffering and mortality.

He has great acumen in saying tremendously meaningful things in small sutras. He is saying when you are deluded, when you are in the mind in other words, then the five elements create the world and your six senses.

It is a very strange thing, because it is only just in this century that science has discovered the sixth sense. Otherwise, all old scriptures talk about five senses. It is only Bodhidharma alone, who talks about six senses. And the sixth sense is such, that it is a miracle he came to know about it. It has just been discovered.

It is inside your ear. The ear has always been accepted as one of the five senses, but we didn't know that inside the ear there are two senses. One is the sense of hearing and another is the sense of balance. If you are hit strongly on your ear you will immediately lose balance. When you see a drunkard coming home in the late night, you cannot believe how he manages. He has lost all control and all balance because alcohol affects the sixth sense. Every drug affects the sixth sense and immediately you lose balance.

A drunkard came home late in the night and was trying to open the lock. But his hand was shaking and the lock was shaking; his other hand was shaking and he could not manage to enter the key into the lock. Both were shaking. He said, "My God, what is happening? It must be an earthquake. Everything is shaking."

A policeman watching him from the road felt compassion for him. He was a good man but had fallen into wrong company...just like you. You are all good men fallen into wrong company. Soon you will be walking like a drunkard. The policeman came to him and said, "Can I help you?" He said, "Yes, it would be very kind of you, if you could hold the house for a moment so that I can put my key into the hole. Just hold the house. There seems to be a great earthquake."

It is very strange because that sixth sense is hidden inside the ear. Hence, nobody has ever talked about it because nobody was ever aware of it. It was only in this century, surgeons became aware that in the ear there is also another sense that keeps your body balanced.

But Bodhidharma says six senses and five shades *are constructs of suffering and mortality.* When you are deluded, when you are in the mind, the five elements and the six senses of your body create for you, suffering, death and nothing else.

But: *When you wake up,* that is, when you go beyond the mind, *the six senses and five shades are constructs of nirvana and immortality.*

Everything is the same; the same six senses and the same five aggregates – the elements that constitute the world. Once you are beyond the mind, they create nirvana and immortality.

So Bodhidharma is not against the body and he is not against the world. He is against your sleep. He does not want you to renounce the world. He does not want you to torture the body, because this body and this world will behave absolutely differently. You just have to be awake. So the whole answer is:

Renounce sleeping, renounce the mind which is the citadel of your sleep.

Go into silence, which will release your dormant awareness. And your whole being will become luminous with consciousness.

Then the same body, the same senses and the same world has a totally different significance. It becomes nirvana. It becomes immortality.

Someone who seeks the Way doesn't look beyond himself. He knows that the mind is the Way. But when he finds the mind, he finds nothing. And when he finds the Way, he finds nothing. If you think you can use the mind to find the Way, you are deluded. When you are deluded, buddhahood exists.

This is a very beautiful statement. It is very rare to come across such a statement. *When you are deluded, buddhahood exists* because *when you are aware, it does not exist.*

It is a very strange statement. You would have thought otherwise. You would have thought that when you are deluded, buddhahood does not exist, and when you are aware, it does exist. But Bodhidharma is saying just the opposite. And he is right. *When you are deluded*...when you are wandering in all kinds of illusions in the world, there is a desire in you, deep down. Sometimes you become aware of it; sometimes you forget all about it. The longing to be a buddha, the longing to become aware, the longing for enlightenment....

Even in the deepest sleep, somewhere in the corner of your darkness, a small longing goes on continuing to be alert – to be awakened, to be enlightened because nobody can be satisfied with misery, agony, anguish, forever.

One wants to get out of it. That's why Bodhidharma says: *When you are deluded, buddhahood exists. When you are aware, it does not exist. Because awareness is buddhahood.*

When you are aware, you are a buddha and the longing for buddhahood disappears. And when you are a buddha, you are not aware that you are a buddha. Awareness cannot be aware of itself. Innocence cannot be aware of itself. So the buddhahood exists only for those who are far away from it. Buddhahood disappears for those who have reached home.

A buddha does not know that he is a buddha. Knowledge is always about the other. The mirror can reflect everything in the world except itself. The mirror does not know that he is.

...Don't hate life and death or love life and death. Keep your every thought free of delusion, and in life you will witness the beginning of nirvana, and in death you will experience the assurance of no rebirth.

It fills me with great surprise that the whole Western sphere has never thought about rebirth. Great philosophers from Plato to Kant, to Feuerbach, to Bertrand Russell, to Jean Paul Sartre – a great line of immensely intelligent geniuses, but not a single person has ever thought about rebirth. Their whole idea has remained...just one life. It is too miserly.

Existence is not miserly; it is overflowing with abundance.

Every death is a beginning of a new life, except only rarely, when somebody becomes enlightened. Then his death is the ultimate death. He will not be born again. He will not be engaged in a body again; he will not suffer the agony of another mind again. His consciousness will melt, just like an ice cube melting in the ocean and becoming one with it. He will be all over, but he will not be in any particular place, in a particular form. He will be all over, but formless. He will be the very universe.

Each time a man becomes enlightened, the whole universe gets a little higher in consciousness, because this man's consciousness spreads all over the existence. The more people become enlightened, the more existence will be richer. So it is not only a question of a single person becoming enlightened. In his enlightenment, the whole universe gains immensely. It becomes richer, more beautiful, more joyous, more celebrated.

To see form but not be corrupted by form or to hear sound but not be corrupted by sound is liberation. Eyes that are not attached to form are the Gates of Zen. Ears that aren't attached to sound are also the Gates of Zen. In short, those who perceive the existence of phenomena and remain unattached are liberated...

When delusions are absent, the mind is the land of buddhas. When delusions are present, the mind is hell.

I am reminded of a great Zen master. The emperor of Japan had been wanting to come to see him but the path to his monastery was dangerous, going through wild forests, dangerous mountainous parts. But finally, the emperor decided he had to go. His death was coming near and he couldn't take the risk.... Before death came he must have some understanding that death cannot destroy.

He reached the Zen master who was sitting under a tree. He touched his feet and said, "I have come to ask one question. Is there really a hell or heaven? Because my death is coming close and my only concern is: where am I going; to hell or to heaven?" The master laughed and said, "I have never thought that our emperor is such an idiot."

To say to the emperor, "an idiot"...! For a split second, the emperor forgot and pulled out his sword, and he was going to cut off the head of the Zen master.

The Zen master laughed and said, "This is the gate of hell."

The emperor stopped, put his sword back in the sheath, and the master said, "You have entered into heaven. Now you can go. Just remember: anger, violence, destructiveness. These are the gates of hell. And the hell is in your mind.

"But understanding, compassion, silence, are the doors of heaven. They are beyond your mind. And I have given you the experience of both. Forgive me that I called you an idiot. I had to. It was just a response to your question, because I am not a thinker and I don't answer the way thinkers answer questions. I am a mystic. I simply create the device so that you can have some taste of the answer. Now get lost."

And the emperor touched his feet with tears of gratitude, because no other answer would have been of much help. It would have remained just a hypothesis. But the man was a tremendously insightful master. He created the situation immediately, just by calling him an idiot. And he showed him both: the doors of hell and the doors of heaven. Your mind is hell.

Going beyond your mind is heaven.

Go beyond the mind.

That is the essence of the whole teaching of all the awakened ones.

Okay, Maneesha?

Yes, Bhagwan.

EVERY SUFFERING IS A BUDDHA-SEED

達磨

12

Beloved Bhagwan,

That which follows is witnessed on the Way. It's beyond the ken of arhats and mortals.

When the mind reaches nirvana, you don't see nirvana. Because the mind is nirvana. If you see nirvana somewhere outside the mind, you're deluding yourself.

Every suffering is a buddha-seed. Because suffering impels to seek wisdom. But you can only say that suffering gives rise to buddhahood. You can't say that suffering is buddhahood. Your body and mind are the field. Suffering is the seed, wisdom the sprout and buddhahood the grain.

...When the three poisons are present in your mind, you live in a land of filth. When the three poisons are absent from your mind, you live in a land of purity.

...There's no language that isn't the Dharma. To talk all day without saying anything is the Way. To be silent all day and still say something isn't the Way. Hence, neither does a tathagata's speech depend on silence, nor does his silence depend on speech. Nor does his speech exist apart from his silence. Those who understand both speech and silence are in samadhi. If you speak when you know, your speech is free. If you're silent when you don't know, your silence is tied. Language is essentially free. It has nothing to do with attachment. And attachment has nothing to do with language.

BODHIDHARMA IS A mine of pure gold, except for two points on which he keeps continually insisting. He is a man to be listened to, to be understood, to be absorbed as deeply into your heart as possible. But those two points have to be remembered.

I have been wondering why nobody contemporary to Bodhidharma pointed out those two flaws. The only thing I can think of is that Bodhidharma was too strong an individual, too charismatic, so that in front of him people must have

felt completely silent. His power must have been overwhelming; otherwise, the defects are so clear that it is impossible that nobody would have noticed them.

He himself has reached to his ultimate flowering; he has arrived home. It is no longer his concern that on the path he has gone astray a few times – he always came back. There is an ancient saying in the East that if somebody goes astray in the morning and comes back home in the evening, he should not be considered lost.

And it is very natural for people who are spontaneous to go astray once in a while, because they are not following any ready-made track. They are not like railway trains, continuously moving on the same track. They are more like wild rivers – without any map, without any guide. The river arises far away in the Himalayas and starts its journey into the mountains, into the valleys, into the plains, moving continuously this way and that way. But finally it falls into the ocean. And who cares, when one has arrived at the ocean, that on the way a few steps have been taken which were not necessary, which could have been avoided.

Once a person has reached he almost forgets, in his celebration, the long journey, the long search towards self-realization. Perhaps that is the reason why Bodhidharma cannot see those two simple defects. Except for those two defects, his every word is absolutely sincere and authentic. It is not a word of knowledge; it is an outpouring of innocence. He is not speaking, he is exposing his whole being to you.

But I have to warn you on those two points. One is his continuous antagonism towards the arhatas. And second is... In the beginning I was thinking it must have been the fault of the disciple who was taking the notes, but it is so continuously repeated that there is every possibility it was not the disciple's fault: he was using the word 'mind' in a wrong way.

Because in English there is only one word, the Theosophists and the Christian Scientists have managed a certain device: for the ordinary human mind they use a small m, and for the universal mind, which is equivalent to no-mind, they use a capital M. Certainly the universal mind is not your mind. As far as you are concerned, your mind has disappeared and you have entered into a state of no-mind. On these points I will correct his sutras. I cannot allow such a beautiful statement of the truth to have even a small blemish.

The sutra:
That which follows is witnessed on the Way.

He is saying that the sutras that are going to follow are not his philosophical standpoint; they are his experiences on the way. *That which follows is witnessed on the Way:* I will be saying only that which I have witnessed. It is not my belief, it is not my doctrine, it is not my dogma. It is my absolutely indubitable experience. It has an intrinsic authority. Whoever follows the way will find these same sutras opening their doors, their secrets, their perfume to the traveler, if he is going the right way.

These sutras can be used as a criterion. If nothing like this happens to you, that means you are not on the right path. Then your river has entered into some desert, where it can be lost without reaching the ocean.

He goes on to say, *It is beyond the ken of arhats and mortals.*

I have to correct him. He needed a man like me. It is *not* beyond the ken of the arhats. It is certainly beyond the ken of so-called saints and the mortals, the people who are still living with the idea that this life is all and that with death everything ends...these are the mortals. The so-called saints whose intentions cannot be doubted are sincere people, but they have fallen into wrong ways. They have become followers, imitators. They have ideals in their mind cultivated by the society, by the tradition, and they are trying in every possible way to fulfill those ideals, knowing perfectly well that a buddha is born only once.

Never again will there be another man like Gautam Buddha. There may be many buddhas, but each buddha will have his own statement, his own individuality, his own manifestation. He will not be a true copy of Gautam Buddha. All true copies are, after all, carbon copies. They don't have the beauty of the original. And people go on following precepts given in the scriptures. Those precepts are dead. Just as you will find in the scriptures beautiful roses, dried out – dead. People keep them in *The Holy Bible,* in the holy *Koran,* in the holy *Gita,* but they are not alive anymore.

I had a beautiful garden – I have always had a beautiful garden wherever I have been – and there were two temples nearby, and the worshipers in those temples would simply come into my garden and start picking flowers to worship a god. In India it is absolutely impossible to prevent somebody when he is picking flowers to worship gods. I had to put a notice in front of my garden that except for religious people, everybody was allowed to pick the flowers. Those worshipers were very shocked. As a group they brought what was almost a deputation, saying, "What kind of man are you? Religious people are not prevented from picking flowers anywhere else, because those flowers are going to be offered to a god."

I said to them, "Those flowers in this garden are already offered to God, and I will not allow flowers of God, which are alive and dancing in the wind and in the sun, to be destroyed by you idiots. These flowers are living gods and you are going to destroy their life for your dead gods. That's why I have made it clear on the notice: except for religious people, anybody can pick the flowers. If somebody wants to give a flower to his girlfriend or to her boyfriend, they are perfectly welcome. These flowers are divine, and perhaps they may also transform their love into a divine affair. But one thing is certain; at least they are going to offer the flowers to someone who is alive. You are going to offer them to dead statues, stones. This cannot be tolerated."

The so-called saints pick up precepts, disciplines, from the scriptures. They are like dead flowers, thousands of years old, dried up. They don't have any fragrance anymore.

It is something very significant to remember, that every discipline is a device given by a living master. Every precept is a certain strategy given by a living master; without the master all those devices, precepts, commandments become dead. Then you can go on following them with absolute sincerity, but they will bring only torture and suffering to you and nothing else. Following the dead, you are going to become slowly, slowly dead. Your so-called saints are almost dead, dried up. They have lost touch with life. They have created a thousand and one barriers between themselves and existence and those barriers they call discipline, austerity, religious practice.

I can consider that these sutras are beyond the ken of these people – the so-called saints and the ordinary mortals who are not aware of their immortality. But they are not beyond the ken of arhats. Arhats are absolutely on the same heights as any bodhisattva. Bodhisattvas have nothing more than the arhats have. They have followed different paths, from different directions, but they have reached to the same peak. The peak is always only one; the paths leading you to it can be thousands.

When the mind reaches nirvana...

That is his second fallacy, because the mind never reaches nirvana. In fact, mind cannot even conceive the idea of nirvana. Nirvana... the very word means cessation of mind, it is annihilation of the mind. The actual meaning of the word nirvana will help you to understand: literally it means "blowing out a candle." Mind is just a small candle with a small flame of awareness, but even that small flame can do immense harm.

I will tell you of one incident in Rabindranath Tagore's life. His father was a great landlord. Their estate consisted of hundreds of towns and thousands of miles, and there was a beautiful river flowing through their estate. Rabindranath often used to go on his small houseboat and live for months on the beautiful river, surrounded by thick forest, in absolute silence and aloneness. One full-moon night, it happened: he was reading a very significant contribution to the philosophy of aesthetics, by Croce.

Croce is perhaps the most significant philosopher who has thought about beauty. His whole life's work was concerned with finding the meaning of beauty – not truth, not good. His sole concern was with what is beautiful. He thought if we can find what is beautiful we have found what is true, because truth cannot be ugly, and we have found what is good, because the beautiful cannot be evil. A beautiful conception...and with this foundation he worked his whole life to find out from different angles what beauty is.

Rabindranath himself was a worshiper of beauty. He lived a very beautiful and aesthetic life. He not only created beautiful poetry, but his life itself was a beautiful poem. He was a very graceful man.

On that full-moon night with a small candle inside his houseboat he was reading Croce. In the middle of night, tired from Croce's very complicated arguments, he closed the book and blew out the candle. He was going to his bed to sleep, but a miracle happened. As the small flame of the candle disappeared, from every window and door of the small houseboat, the moon came dancing in. The moon filled the house with its splendor.

Rabindranath remained silent for a moment...it was such a sacred experience. He went out of the house, and the moon was immensely beautiful in that silent night amongst those silent trees, with a river flowing so slowly that there was no noise. He wrote in his diary the next morning, "The beauty was all around me, but a small candle had been preventing it. Because of the light of the candle, the light of the moon could not enter."

This is exactly the meaning of nirvana. Your small flame of the ego, your small flame of the mind and its consciousness, is preventing the whole universe from rushing into you; hence the word nirvana – blow out the candle and let the whole universe penetrate you from every nook and corner. You will not be a loser. You will find, for the first time, your inexhaustible treasure of beauty, of goodness, of truth – of all that is valuable. Hence, mind cannot be said to reach nirvana; only no-mind is equivalent to nirvana.

No-mind need not reach to nirvana.

No-mind *is* nirvana.

Bodhidharma says – I'm correcting him – *When the* no-*mind reaches nirvana, you don't see nirvana*...because you are not separate from nirvana. You can only see something which is separate from you. You are one with it; hence there is no possibility of seeing it. *Because the* no-*mind is nirvana. If you see nirvana somewhere outside the no-mind, you are deluding yourself.* In short, the mind is the world and the no-mind is freedom from the world. The mind is misery and no-mind is the end of misery and the beginning of ecstasy.

Every suffering is a buddha-seed. This is a very important assertion on the part of Bodhidharma. *Every suffering is a buddha-seed. Because suffering impels to seek wisdom. But you can only say that suffering gives rise to buddhahood. You can't say that suffering is buddhahood.*

Bertrand Russell, in his autobiography, has a very profound statement. He says, "If misery in the world ends, all the religions will end of their own accord. It is misery that is keeping religions alive." He is speaking from a very different angle. He was an atheist; he wanted all religions to disappear.

I am not an atheist. I also want all the religions to disappear but for a different reason. He wants religions to disappear because he thinks religions have been detrimental to the evolution of man. I want religions to disappear so that religiousness can have the whole space that is being occupied by religions. Religions have been detrimental to the progress of religiousness, and to me, religiousness is the highest flower of evolution.

Bodhidharma is right when he says that even suffering has to be gratefully accepted, because it is the very seed of buddha. If there was no suffering, you would never search for the truth. It is suffering that goes on impelling you to go beyond it. It is anguish and agony that finally compels you to seek and search for the path that goes beyond suffering and agony, to find a way that reaches to blissfulness and to eternal joy.

Bodhidharma is saying: Don't be antagonistic to suffering; even feel grateful to suffering. That is a great idea. Feel grateful to pain, suffering, old age, death, because all these are creating the situation for you to search for truth. Otherwise you would fall asleep; otherwise you would be so comfortable, you would become a vegetable. There would be no need.... Suffering creates the need for a search.

Your body and mind are the field. Suffering is the seed, wisdom the sprout and buddhahood the grain.

In this synthesis he is giving credit to your body, to your mind, to suffering. He is taking into account your whole life. He is not denying anything its contribution. He is being very impartial.

Your body and the mind are the field. Suffering is the seed, wisdom the sprout and buddhahood the grain.

This is the way of a man who looks at life as an organic unity. The so-called religions which have lost contact with their living founders, are against the body. They torture the body, rather than being grateful to the body because it is the very field, it is the very temple in which the buddha has to be discovered. Even suffering, agony, is not to be condemned by a man like Bodhidharma. He says that too has a part to play. It keeps you awake. It keeps you constantly alert, provokes you and challenges you to find a way that can lead you beyond it.

...When the three poisons are present in your mind, you live in a land of filth. When the three poisons are absent from your mind, you live in a land of purity.

So in fact, heaven and hell are not separate from each other; they happen in the same life. Only the structure has to change. Where there were the three poisons of greed, anger and delusion, you created a hell within yourself. The moment you drop those poisons of greed, anger and delusion which really constitute your mind – the moment you have dropped the mind, your very being becomes heaven itself.

The idea that is prevalent in the world is that those who are good will enter one day after death into heaven, and those who are bad will one day enter hell after death. That idea is absolutely wrong. The good have already entered heaven – there is no need to wait for death. Heaven is not somewhere else. It is just your own transformation. The same energy that is anger becomes compassion, the same energy that is greed becomes sharing, the same energy that is delusion becomes awareness. The energy is the same, just its direction changes.

To change the direction of your energies, to create a new symphony out of your energies, is the whole art of religion. Anybody who preaches anything else as religion is himself blind and taking other blind people into a dark night. They are all going to fall into a well somewhere or other.

Man has been given everything by nature. If it is put right, man becomes a buddha. If that energy is in discord and you cannot create an orchestra out of that energy, your life becomes a hell. You are the space where both heaven and hell are possible. Just a little awareness and you can change the hell into heaven. Just a little change, a slightly different arrangement...but it is the same energy; nothing has to be added to you, nothing has to be deleted from you.

This is one of the greatest insights possible. It makes man the master of his own life. If he is living in hell, he should take the responsibility upon his own shoulders. He should not say, "It is God's will." He should not say, "It is my fate, my destiny, my kismet." He should say, "It is my unconsciousness, it is me."

The moment you take the responsibility on your own shoulders, the possibility is you will start changing – because nobody else is putting you in hell. You don't have to wait for anybody to change you, to save you. You can simply start watching your energies and you can see how they create hell, how they create misery. You can see also how in some moments you are silent, in some moments you are happy, in some moments joy grips you. Watch what those energies are doing. They are the same energies – you don't have anything else. One has just to understand how one's energies function.

If someone wants to live in hell that is his choice, that is his birthright. Nobody has the right to disturb him. Let him live in hell. And if he wants to change, he has every possibility to change himself. There is no need to wait for a savior, for a Jesus Christ or a Krishna. You have to become your own saviors. That is the fundamental teaching of Bodhidharma.

...There is no language that is not the Dharma. Here Bodhidharma is taking a very strange but significant turn. I have never come across any other mystic who has said what he is going to say in this sutra.

...There is no language that is not the Dharma. To talk all day without saying anything is the Way. To be silent all day and still say something is not the Way.

Sometimes his penetration into human reality is so great and so surprising. He is saying that there is a possibility of a man who may talk the whole day, knowing well that nothing can be said about truth. Then why is he talking? Perhaps through talking he can create a situation for silence – just as after every storm there is great silence.

When the master speaks and stops for a moment, suddenly there is a great silence. He speaks not to say the truth, because the truth cannot be said. He speaks to engage your mind and then suddenly, when he sees that you are engaged, he gives just a small gap. And in that gap the transmission of the lamp happens. That's what the language of Bodhidharma is: the transmission of the lamp. In those moments between two words, something miraculous just takes a jump from the being of the master and enters into the silence of your being.

Hence it is possible that a Gautam Buddha may have spoken for forty-two years continuously – morning, afternoon, evening – and still he has not said the truth, but he transmitted the lamp. He used the language in such a way that it created small gaps of silence. And those gaps are his real sermons.

Bodhidharma says there are people who take the vow of being silent...and I have known many so-called saints who don't speak, but their silence is so ridiculous because they find other ways. I have seen some carrying small boards with the whole alphabet. They cannot speak but their chief disciple is sitting by their side and they go on putting on the alphabet board: Y-e-s, yes. And that dodo disciple who is sitting by his side, he says, "Yes." It is ridiculous. If you want to say yes, why go such a roundabout way, unnecessarily creating a circus? And there have been people who have dictated whole books, just on the board. It would have been easier to learn typing, because this is a very primitive way of typing. It takes such a long time.

I have seen people who will not use any board but they will make gestures with their hands, and those gestures you cannot understand. Their trained disciple knows what they mean when they show the fist, what they mean when they show the five fingers, what they mean when they show the two fingers. These people are not saints, these are showmen. And their silence is absolutely nonsense. But all kinds of stupidities go on being perpetuated in the name of religion.

A man came to see me when I was in Bombay. He was a very well-known saint; he lived in the Himalayas and he had come specially to see me. Usually I avoid saints, sages…that kind of idiot I don't want. But when I was informed that he had come from the faraway Himalayas to Bombay just to see me, I said, "He has taken so much trouble; I should also suffer a little." So I called him in. He came with his disciple; he wanted to know about meditation.

I said, "From tomorrow morning I am going to have a meditation session, every day in the morning for seven days. You have come at the right time, because meditation is not something to be explained, it is something to be experienced. So, from tomorrow morning at eight o'clock, for seven days you meditate with me. And then, if you have any questions I will give you an individual appointment and you can ask all your questions."

He said, "It will be difficult tomorrow for me to come."

I said, "What is the problem? You have come to see me."

He said, "For me there is no problem. The problem is that the man, my disciple, has to go somewhere, to meet someone – his relatives live nearby in Kalyan."

So I said, "I don't understand. Let him go to hell, you come to meditation."

He said, "You don't understand my problem. I cannot touch money. He keeps the money to pay the taxi driver. I always have him with me; otherwise how can I manage to come here?"

I said, "It is strange. It is your money – he is the keeper. You are famous for not touching money and this poor fellow will fall into hell. He is touching *your* money! It is not even his! What kind of karma is he committing? Touching one's own money is bad and touching somebody else's money – that must be worse." I said, "Think of this poor man also. If it is your money, whether you touch it or not…or you can purchase rubber gloves. Make it simple so you can touch the money but still you are not touching it."

But that will not make somebody a saint. If somebody is wearing rubber gloves and having all kinds of money with him, you will not call him a saint. This seemed to be very cunning man...but having another person is not very different either.

So there are people who are silent, but inside they are boiling. They want to speak and they find ways of speaking by making gestures, which is a very difficult thing because they become absolutely dependent, almost slaves, on the person who interprets for them. And it is up to him how he interprets. They cannot even prevent, they cannot even say, "You are not right." They have to accept whatsoever the interpretation is.

One man, Adi Irani, was the secretary of Meher Baba for almost his whole life. And whenever I used to go to Ahmednagar, Adi Irani, if he was in the city, used to come to see me. He has written all Meher Baba's books; Meher Baba simply made signs. First he used to use the board, then he dropped the board because people started criticizing him. "It is the same thing as typing, just a slower process, a bullock cart process in a rocket age. What nonsense is this?"

So Meher Baba dropped the board and he trained Adi Irani. He would make gestures with his hands; nobody knew what he was doing. Only Adi Irani knew and he wrote the books. I asked Adi Irani, "Are you certain that whatever you are writing is really what he wants to say?"

He said, "I cannot speak a lie – at least to you. I don't know. I figure it must be right because he has never objected."

Now this seems to be hilarious. He did not know whether he was interpreting him exactly or he was just managing himself....and because Meher Baba had never objected, that was the only reason that Adi Irani thought he must be right.

I said, "Do you really understand exactly?...because by symbols small things can be explained: you are hungry, you can just show your stomach; you are thirsty, you can just show by your hands that you need water. But great philosophical treatises? I can't conceive how you can make symbols for them – and how many symbols will be needed? With only your ten fingers..." And Adi Irani has written almost fifty books, and not small ones – five hundred pages, one thousand pages.

I told Adi Irani, "It is all your imagination. You are a good writer, but those books are your writings, not Meher Baba's. But he is silent because you are writing well and people are accepting those writings in his name." Meher Baba had a worldwide following, but he was absolutely dependent; he could not move anywhere without Adi Irani because wherever he went alone he would be thought mad. Nobody would understand what he was trying to say.

But if you want to speak, what is wrong with speaking with your lips and your tongue? And how is it right speaking with your fingers? Just as your lips and your tongue are part of the body, your fingers are also part of the same body, and they are not meant to speak. Why not use the right natural vehicle?

Symbols are dangerous. When Japanese sannyasins started coming here, I was in great trouble because they are the only people in the whole world who have a different symbology. It is strange how they have developed it. All over the world in every country, in every race, from very primitive people to the very sophisticated ones, when you want to say "Yes," you make the sign with your head moving up and down – yes. Japanese when they make this sign mean no. I was asking something and the poor fellow was saying yes, but I understood no, because his yes means.... That is his yes. In the beginning I used to ask a Japanese, "Do you want to become a sannyasin?" and he was saying yes and I would say, "If you don't want...then why have you come?"

They have developed in a very strange way. Somebody has to look into it, because they are the only people.... Then I had an Japanese interpreter to tell me what signs they were making because it was a continual misunderstanding. When they nodded yes, I understood no, when they said no, I understood yes.

Bodhidharma is saying: *To be silent all day and still say something is not the Way.* If you are silent it does not mean you cannot speak. You can remain silent and still you can speak, just as you can remain silent and still you can walk. You can remain silent and still you can eat. Silence is something inner, a calmness, a quietness, a peace. In fact, the man who is silent inside can speak better than anybody else, because his mind is no longer a disturbance. He can speak more emphatically, more directly. He can reach to your very heart because his words are coming from a depth, and that which comes from a depth has the capacity to reach to a similar depth if you are open to it. But silence is not something that is against speaking.

Silence is a far greater experience than speaking or language. And when you are silent even while speaking, then your words have a beauty and a tremendous authority in them, because they are coming from a pure heart – from a silent land, from the very lotus paradise of Gautam Buddha.

Hence, neither does a tathagata's speech depend on silence, nor does his silence depend on speech. Tathagata is another name for Gautam Buddha, or for anyone who has awakened to the suchness of things.

Hence, neither does a tathagata's speech depend on silence, nor does his silence depend on speech. Nor does his speech exist apart from his silence. Those who understand both speech and silence are in samadhi.! Let me repeat it:

Those who understand both speech and silence are in samadhi...because samadhi is the balance between speech and silence. It is just the exact middle, where silence and speech meet, where silence and sound meet. That exact middle is beyond both. It is neither just silence, empty of noise, nor is it just speech, full of chattering and noise. It is beyond both. It is a silence with a song, but the song is soundless. It is a silence with music, but a music which is not produced on any instruments, a music which is simply your very nature.

The ancient seers of this land have called it *omkar,* the sound of *om*...not that you repeat *om, om,* you simply hear it. You are utterly silent, surrounded with a sound which is similar to om. That's why om has not been made a part of the Sanskrit alphabet. It is not a word; it is a symbol. Perhaps that is the only alphabet in the world which has a symbol in it which is not part of the alphabet. But every *Upanishad* begins with om and every *Upanishad* ends with om. And you may have observed that it is not just the om, but also a repetition three times of the Sanskrit word for silence: *shanti. Om shanti, shanti, shanti....*

It is a silence which has sound which cannot be produced on any instrument, and cannot be exactly spoken. So we have made a symbol for it. It is beyond language, beyond alphabet, beyond speaking, beyond silence. Om has been called the very stuff of which the existence is made...the music of the universe.

If you speak when you know, your speech is free. If you are silent when you don't know, your silence is tied...and dead and empty and meaningless.

Language is essentially free. It has nothing to do with attachment. And attachment has nothing to do with language.

It all depends on your mind or no-mind. If mind uses language, it creates false realities – illusion. If no-mind uses language, it creates devices to also help others to enter into the same space. What you make of it all depends on you, whether you are functioning as a mind or as a no-mind. If you speak through the mind, you miss the point. If you allow existence to speak through you, without any interference by the mind, language is pure expression of truth.

In short, the whole thing can be summarized into a single statement:

Mind is your prison. No-mind is your freedom.

Mind is your ignorance, no-mind is your enlightenment.

Move from mind to no-mind. This is the whole path, this is the whole religion.

Okay, Maneesha?

Yes, Bhagwan.

達磨

13

MIND IS THE BONDAGE

Beloved Bhagwan,

Without the mind there's no buddha means that the buddha comes from the mind....

Whoever wants to see a buddha sees the mind before he sees the buddha...once you've seen the buddha, you forget about the mind.

If you don't forget about the mind, the mind will confuse you....

Mortality and buddhahood are like water and ice. To be afflicted by the three poisons is mortality. To be purified by the three releases is buddhahood.

That which freezes into ice in winter melts into water in summer.

Eliminate ice, and there's no more water.

Get rid of mortality, and there's no more buddhahood. Clearly, the nature of ice is the nature of water....

Mortals liberate buddhas and buddhas liberate mortals. This is what's meant by impartiality. Mortals liberate buddhas because affliction creates awareness. And buddhas liberate mortals because awareness negates affliction. There can't help but be affliction. And there can't help but be awareness. If not for affliction, there would be nothing to create awareness. And if not for awareness, there would be nothing to negate affliction. When you're deluded, buddhas liberate mortals. When you're aware, mortals liberate buddhas. Buddhas don't become buddhas on their own. They're liberated by mortals. Buddhas regard delusion as their father and greed as their mother. Delusion and greed are different names for mortality....

When you're deluded, you're on this shore. When you're aware, you're on the other shore. But once you know your mind is empty and you see no appearances, you're beyond delusion and awareness. And once you're beyond delusion and awareness, the other shore doesn't exist. The tathagata isn't on this shore or the other shore. And he isn't in midstream. Arhats are in midstream, and mortals are on this shore. On the other shore is buddhahood.

BODHIDHARMA HAS INSIGHTS which are unparalleled. There have been many disciples of Gautam Buddha who have attained to enlightenment, but nobody has shown such great insightfulness. Either they have remained silent or they have spoken, but neither their silence nor their speaking has reached to the heights and to the depths of consciousness.

Perhaps the reason is that Bodhidharma is unafraid of what he is saying. He knows no fear. He has no concern with what people will think about his statements. He does not take into account anybody else when he is speaking. It is almost as if he is speaking to himself.

For nine years he was sitting before a wall and when people would come, they would have to sit behind him. They could ask questions but Bodhidharma would answer only to the wall. He was not at all concerned about who was asking the question; he was more concerned with his own insight.

Just last night I received the last book of J. Krishnamurti, in which he is not speaking to anybody – he is speaking just to himself. The words are recorded but there was no audience, and perhaps in this book he comes closer to truth than in any of his other books. The audience is a limitation.

This has been my experience too. If I am speaking to my own people, then there is no limitation; then I don't feel that I have to say something, or not to say something. Then I simply speak as if I am speaking to myself. When I am speaking to people who don't know me, who don't understand me – moreover they misunderstand me – there is a great limitation. Then I am not at freedom to speak. Their very faces, their eyes, their gestures prevent me from saying something that may hurt them.

Just a few days ago, seventy people from the *Times of India* group of papers came to have an exclusive interview with me. The owners were also present – Samir Jain, Nandita Jain and their mother Indu Jain were also present. But the strangest thing that I immediately felt as I entered the auditorium...so ugly, so inhuman and so uncultured: when I was giving my greetings with folded hands to everybody, those seventy people, including Indu Jain, could not even respond. That is, in India, a simple thing. Even a stranger on the street folds his hands. It need not be known to you who he is, but you respond because a folded-hands greeting has a spiritual meaning.

Shaking hands has no spiritual meaning; shaking hands has a very mundane meaning. You have to shake with your right hand. It was a device created by the West to show that you are not keeping any weapon in your right hand. It was not a greeting – it was a search. It was being alert that the man is not an enemy, that he cannot do any harm because his right hand is empty. The reason for shaking hands and its psychology is totally different; in a way very mean, political.

But greeting somebody with folded hands has a spiritual meaning: first, that I bow down to your godliness. Whether you are a stranger, friend or enemy, it does not matter; still you are a temple of god, of a living god. Those folded hands are showing respect for the living god. These things are immaterial – whether you are a friend or a stranger or an enemy.

And secondly, the folded hands show that I am not halfhearted in my greeting. I am total. Both hands, my left hemisphere, my right hemisphere both, are greeting you together. I am greeting you as one organic unity.

But I was surprised that the *Times of India* press people – who are well educated, who own the biggest newspapers, magazines, weeklies, fortnightlies who are all journalists – they could not respond to me. They sat there like stone statues, even Indu Jain.

The only man who responded to me was Samir Jain, who is now in charge of the *Times of India* publications, and his sister, Nandita Jain. But she could not come to the full greeting. She was hesitating, so she came halfway. She could not come to the full greeting, but she could not remain a wooden statue. She looked to both sides. Even her mother, Indu Jain, who in private touches my feet, but in public...she remained just a wooden statue. So she looked at her mother and she looked at her brother and she chose the middle way. She just came halfway.

To speak to such people is almost worse than speaking to a wall. I took the initiative of greeting them and they were not even human enough to respond to the greeting, and particularly in the East, such ugliness is unforgivable. And they have been insisting on the interview. I was reluctant – reluctant for the simple reason that they would ask stupid questions, then they would distort what I say. But when I saw that they had come with the whole staff of the *Times of India* press, I agreed.

But I really agreed for Samir Jain. He is a young man, he has been to the ashram before, he has meditated. He wanted to become a sannyasin but his father was absolutely against it, so much against it that if he became a sannyasin, his father would disown him. Now they are some of the richest people of the country. He has not the guts to say to the father, "It is perfectly okay, you can disown me," but he has a sympathetic heart – and he was the only man who raised his hands.

Now to talk to such people becomes impossible, unless you completely forget them, and whether they exist or not. And that's what I had to do. I did not look at them at all, I just looked at my people and talked to my people. And I made a condition to them that they could not distort any statement; they had to publish my whole statement as I have given it. But they don't even have the guts to publish their own questions and my answers, because my answers expose the dirty politics and the dirty journalism that follows politics.

Bodhidharma speaks as if he's speaking to himself. Then he can open his heart totally, without any limitation. He is absolutely unconcerned about who is going to listen to him, who is going to read him. Perhaps this is the reason why he reaches tremendously deep insights into human nature. You will see statements that have never been made before, but Bodhidharma has made them so clearly that they cannot be refuted either.

These sutras have been in existence for at least one thousand years, but no Buddhist scholar has commented on them. The book was kept hidden in the Buddhist pagodas, temples. It has just been discovered a few years ago by some Western scholars, and they could not believe that Buddhists have not been allowing the world to know what such a tremendously significant book contains.I can understand the fear of the Buddhists. They have translated thousands of books into English and into German and into other international languages, but Bodhidharma has been neglected completely.

It is a strange world. Here, to be sincere and truthful is the most dangerous thing.

Just a few days ago, here in Poona, the Shankaracharya of Jyotirmath, Swami Svarupanand, declared in a press conference that "Bhagwan is unparalleled, the most dangerous man in the whole history of mankind."

I don't go out of my house. I am not a terrorist. I am not interested in any power politics. I don't have any nuclear weapons. On what grounds is this man saying that I am unparalleled the most dangerous man in the whole history of mankind? What danger is there?

The danger is that I don't care about anybody when it comes to asserting the truth.

It is not that I am dangerous.

It is the truth that is dangerous.

Just console people with lies. Go on giving them hope so they can manage to drag themselves towards their graves; just go on giving them opium so they don't feel the pain, the agony, the stupidity of their lives.

And that's what all the religions have been doing. Whenever somebody has said the truth, he immediately becomes a dangerous man. Otherwise Jesus was not a dangerous man; he was only thirty-three when he was crucified – a young man, uneducated, doing no harm to anybody, but stating the truth. The rabbis of Israel could not tolerate that man. He was disturbing all their fabrication of lies. They crucified that young man. Socrates never harmed anybody, but his great crime was to speak the truth. He was poisoned and killed.

Bodhidharma was also poisoned. Although the people who poisoned him thought that he was killed, he was not. He was made of a different kind of matter. He simply went into a coma and in the night disappeared, leaving one of his shoes in the tomb and the other shoe hanging on his staff.

After three years, when people completely believed that he was dead, he was seen by a high government official passing the boundaries of China and entering into the Himalayas. The official could not believe his eyes. He had heard that Bodhidharma had been poisoned and killed. He asked Bodhidharma, who said, "I was in a coma and I waited for the night. When the coma disappeared a little and I was able to get up, I escaped from the tomb. I have left one of my shoes there in the tomb as proof that I have been there and another shoe I am taking, hanging on my staff to prove that I am Bodhidharma – my identity card."

The official immediately rushed to the mountain where Bodhidharma had been poisoned and he told the disciples. They showed the tomb and the official said, "I would like it to be opened because I have seen the man with his sandal hanging on his staff, and he has told me that he left the other sandal as a signature in the tomb. I would like to open the tomb and see whether that man was really Bodhidharma or somebody else who was playing a trick on me." The tomb was opened and only one shoe was there, nothing else.

What was the need to poison Bodhidharma? One cannot conceive how human beings have behaved with such people...they are making every effort to awaken you, and you respond by killing them. Who is insane? Is Socrates insane? Is Jesus insane? Is Mansoor insane? Is Sarmad insane? Is Bodhidharma insane? Or the people who have killed them...?

Here are a few sutras for this morning, of great importance for those who want to understand the truth and who are ready to drop all kinds of lies.

Without the mind there is no buddha means that the buddha comes from the mind...

But the buddha is not the mind. The mind is the bondage of a buddha, and as he goes beyond the mind and enters into the state of no-mind, he becomes the buddha. But he comes from the mind – and you all have the mind, so you have fulfilled at least half the journey already!

The other half is to get out of the mind and declare your buddhahood. You need not shout it, you need not even whisper it. It will declare itself in your presence, in your words, in your silence, in the depth of your eyes, in the grace and beauty of your individuality, in the fragrance that will surround you...you will be like a cool breeze.

The word *tathagata* used for Gautam Buddha has two meanings. One meaning I have explained to you: it means the man who trusts existence and its suchness. Whatever happens, good or bad, misery or blissfulness, he remains unperturbed. He says it is the suchness of things. There is no need to be disturbed by suffering and there is no need to be disturbed by blissfulness. All these are natural phenomena. You have to remain aloof. That is one meaning of *tathagata*.

There is another meaning also, and that other meaning is significant in understanding these sutras. *Tathagata* means a man who comes like a breeze and goes like a breeze. Literally it means, "thus came, thus gone" – he does not wait for your invitation. Suddenly he comes, and he does not wait for you to prevent him; suddenly he is gone, but he has left behind an experience of coolness and calmness and tranquillity.

That calmness, coolness, serenity, silence, declare more loudly than anything else to the whole existence that a buddha has arrived, that now all the priests are in danger, that all the politicians are trembling inside. All those who are living on lies are scared to death. Truth has such power. It never harms anybody but it makes the whole fabrication of lies around the world tremble. A single man of truth is enough.

I am reminded of a Jewish story. In the Old Testament it is said God became very angry – the Jewish god is a very angry God. He became angry about two cities, Gomorrah and Sodom, because they were practicing perverted sexual things, and he was ready to destroy them. In the Old Testament he actually did destroy them. It reminds one of Hiroshima and Nagasaki...total destruction, and the cities were almost exactly of the same size as Nagasaki and Hiroshima. They were great cities in those days, with populations almost equal to Hiroshima and Nagasaki. And God destroyed them completely because they were becoming perverted.

But in Judaism there is a small stream of authentic mystics – that is the only beautiful thing that Judaism has contributed to the world. They are called Hassids. They are not accepted by orthodox Judaism, they are condemned, but they are people of truth. They cannot conceive of a God who can get angry, so they have written their own story. They don't care what the Old Testament says.

Their story is that one Hassid mystic, hearing that God is going to destroy Sodom and Gomorrah, approached God and said, "Before you destroy them, you have to answer a few of my questions. First, if there are two hundred people who are not perverted in those two cities – who are good, who are pure of soul, who are sincere, who are people of realization – are you still going to destroy those cities and those good people?"

God was taken aback. He could not say that he could destroy two hundred self-realized people. He said, "I was not aware of it; it is very kind of you to inform me. I will not destroy them. Those two hundred people are going to save two hundred thousand people."

The Hassid said, "The second question: if there are not two hundred people, but only twenty, are you going to destroy them? Do you consider quantity more significant than quality?"

And God was again defeated. Certainly quality is of higher value than quantity. What does it matter whether there are two hundred self-realized people or twenty? God said, "I accept your argument. Even if there are twenty people...if you can prove there are twenty people, those cities will be saved."

The Hassid laughed and said, "My last argument: If there are not twenty people but only one self-realized man, who lives six months in Sodom and six months in Gomorrah, are you going to destroy the cities? Do you still think quantity means much – or quality?"

God became very fed up with the man; he was a real Jew. He was bringing him down, haggling, and now he had brought him down to one man from two hundred. He said, "Okay, but then you will have to present that one man!"

The Hassid said, "I am that man!" Jews don't allow this beautiful story. They say it is fiction, but to me their idea of God being angry and destroying Gomorrah and Sodom is a fiction. To me, the Hassid story seems to be more authentic.

Just one man of truth is enough to save the world. But the world does not want to be saved. God need not kill that one man, the world kills that man. The people whom he was going to save are the people who destroy him.

Without the mind there's no buddha means that the buddha comes from the mind...but he is not the mind. It is just like a lotus flower. It comes from mud, but it is not mud. Can you think of two things as different as mud and a lotus flower? But the lotus flower comes from the mud and rises above the waters...the lotus flower is such a transformation, but without the mud there will be no lotus flowers.

Without lotus flowers, mud can exist...this is something to be understood. The higher is very fragile, the lower is very solid. The lower is like a rock and the higher is like a rose flower. The higher you move, the more fragile you become. These people, Socrates or Jesus or Bodhidharma, could be poisoned. These were the lotus flowers. But the muddy minds became very angry. Seeing the lotus flowers coming out of them, their anger is understandable. The lotus flower is such a beauty – there is no other flower in the world compared to the beauty of the lotus; hence Buddha has called his paradise "a lotus paradise." To make it the ultimate in beauty, he has used the word "lotus."

But this is the strangest thing about the world – that the mud can exist without any lotuses, but no lotus can exist without the mud. Minds can exist in millions without there being a single buddha, but a buddha cannot exist if all the minds are absent. Minds function like the mud. He has to transcend the mud and the water, and rise above to meet the sun, to see the sun. So remember: the buddha comes from the mind, but he is not the mind.

Whoever wants to see a buddha sees the mind...because the buddha is invisible. It is not a flower that blossoms for the outward eyes. It is a flower that blossoms only for the inner eye. Unless your inner eye is open, you will not recognize the buddha.

The no-mind is needed before one can see the buddha.

A tremendously beautiful story is that when Buddha became enlightened, his first thought was to go back to his kingdom; his father must be old if he was not dead. If he was still alive, then Buddha owed something to him; he was his only son and he had given him immense suffering. Buddha had been going to be his support in his old age, and he was going to be his successor – and then he escaped. So his first thought was to reach the kingdom and to impart his own ecstasy, his own blissfulness, to his father.

But he was not aware of the fact that his father would not be able to recognize him as a buddha. His inner eye was not open. He thought only through the mind; he did not know any approach through the no-mind. So when he faced the old man, the old man was really angry. And you could not complain about his anger.

The father said, "You deceived me in my old age. Where have you been for twelve years? What have you been doing? What is all this nonsense...? An emperor's son carrying a begging bowl! You are born to be one of the greatest emperors in the world. Perhaps, as the astrologers said when you were born, you have the capacity to become a world conqueror, and you have chosen this stupid life."

Buddha stood silently, not saying a single word. He first wanted to let the man release his anger. But the old man recognized, after half an hour had passed, that while he had been shouting and he had been abusing and he had been condemning, his son was simply standing there with such silence, absolutely unperturbed. He looked closely.

Buddha said, "This is a right gesture, look closely. I am not the man who left you; that man died long ago. Yes, I am in the same continuity but before it was the mud; now I am the lotus. So don't take revenge against the lotus because you are angry with the mud. Just let me wash your tears," because the old man was full of tears, "and clean your eyes. Just cool down and just have another look – I am not the same man who left the palace. A great transformation has happened; I left the palace as a mortal, I am coming back to the palace as an immortal. I left the palace as an ordinary human being, I am coming back to the palace divine.

Just have a little look."

The father looked at him – certainly there had been a great change. For a few moments there was utter silence – the father simply went on looking at him. Something transpired between the father and the son, and the father said, "Forgive me. In my anger, with my tears, with my old eyes, I could not recognize the transformation. Now my only desire is that you initiate me on the same path which transforms mud into a lotus. You have certainly become a lotus. I have never seen you so beautiful, so graceful." Nothing had been said, and the father was being initiated.

The moment you know, you don't have to declare it. It declares itself. But only those who have a certain sensitivity, a certain music in their heart, a certain poetry in their being, will be able to recognize you. Those who are simply accountants, bankers, running after money, running after power, will be absolutely blind when it comes to recognizing a buddha.

...once you have seen the buddha, you forget about the mind.

Once you have seen the lotus flower you forget all about the mud.

If you don't forget about the mind, the mind will confuse you....

It will not allow you to recognize the great transmutation, the great transformation that has happened – perhaps in your son, perhaps in your friend, perhaps in a stranger. You need a certain sympathetic attitude and an opening of the heart to allow the transformed man to leave his imprint within you.

And your recognition is going to be a seed of transformation within you: then you cannot remain in the mind anymore; then you cannot remain contented with your muddy world; then you would like to become another lotus. You have heard the challenge and you have seen the reality that you contain the lotus, but you have been unaware of it, it has remained dormant.

Everybody is a buddha, but only in the seed, hidden in the mud. Recognizing a lotus flower is recognizing your own future, your own possibilities, your own grandeur.

Mortality and buddhahood are like water and ice.

There is not much difference between the mortals and the immortals. The difference is just like water and ice.

To be afflicted by the three poisons is mortality. To be purified by the three releases is buddhahood.

The three poisons, Bodhidharma says, are greed, anger, delusion. With these three poisons you remain a mortal. Once you are purified of these three poisons, you have become an immortal. You have attained to the eternity. Now there is no death for you.

That which freezes into ice in winter melts into water in summer.

There is no qualitative difference between water and ice or vapor. The difference is only of temperature. Every human being – the greatest criminal, even an Adolf Hitler – has the potential to be a buddha. However unconscious you may be, however deep may be your sleep, you can be awakened.

Awakening is not a difference of quality. It is a difference only of degree. The sleeping man is less awake and the awake man is less asleep. Remember, the difference between people is only of degree – and that is not much of a difference. A slight understanding and the difference can be dissolved.

Get rid of mortality, and there is no more buddhahood.

This is how Bodhidharma is special. He says, *get rid of mortality, and there is no more buddhahood.* It is only in the eyes of the mortals that buddhas appear so high. When their mortality is finished, their own buddhahood is attained. And the essential quality of awareness is that it is there, but you are not aware of it.

You cannot be aware of awareness.

You cannot be conscious of consciousness.

You cannot be a knower when you really know. Then you are one with it. The buddhahood happens only to you because you are a mortal and Buddha looks so far away. You are only in the mud, just a seed, and the lotus looks so far away, so different. You cannot conceive any connection between you and the lotus. But when you become a lotus yourself, all differences disappear. And the lotus is not aware of its beauty, is not aware of its fragrance; it is simply its nature.

Except for Bodhidharma, nobody else has been able to make these kinds of statements for the simple reason that they are so strange, they look so illogical, irrational. But existence is illogical. It is irrational. If you are only thinking in the mind, then it is one thing, but if you are experiencing the process of mud transforming into a lotus flower, you will understand Bodhidharma without any difficulty. You will rejoice in his strange statements.

Mortals...again, a very strange statement: *mortals liberate buddhas and buddhas liberate mortals.*

I can understand why Buddhists have been hiding these sutras for one thousand years, because the very idea is outrageous that *mortals liberate buddhas and buddhas liberate mortals.* But Bodhidharma is right.

Every buddha comes from the mortals and seeing the agony, the suffering, the misery, the continuous meaninglessness of mortals is the cause of his liberation. If there were no mortals, there would be no buddhas.

When I came back from the university, naturally my parents were anxious that I should get married. They were afraid that I was not the sort and my father was very alert that once I say no to something, then there is no way to make it yes. So he asked his friends, "Just find out what's on his mind, if it is possible that he would say yes. Only then, I will ask him. Once he has said no to me, it is finished."

So his friends started asking me. One of his friends was the best physician of that area. He called me to have a dinner with him and along the way he mentioned, "What do you think about marriage?"

I said, "Uncle, I am unmarried; I don't have any experience. You have been married thrice. You have three times more experience than anybody else. You tell me, what do you think?"

He looked very miserable and he said, "My experience – I am a fool! I should have stopped when my first wife died. But fools are fools. I married again thinking that not every woman is going to be the same. But within a few days...the woman was different but the problems were the same. And God has been so kind to me, even the second wife died. But my stupidity is such, I married again and now I am suffering. And you are asking me, 'What do you think about marriage'!"

I said, "That's enough. Just tell my father your experience. You have liberated me from marriage."

He said, "What do you mean by that? I have done just the opposite of what your father asked me. I was going to convince you."

I said, "You have convinced me! Just tell my father the whole thing that happened...I will get married only if you say yes."

He said, "I cannot. No, I will not drag you into the same hell in which I have lived. I cannot say yes."

"Then," I said, "tell my father that you have convinced me that I should not get married."

He said, "You have put me in such trouble. Your father is depending on me."

He reported to my father. My father said, "You should have been a little more cautious. Instead of convincing him about marriage, you have spoiled the whole thing."

He said, "What can I do? He managed in such a way that I forgot completely what the purpose of the dinner was."

Mortals liberate buddhas...just look around at mortals and you cannot resist being a buddha – the sooner the better! And *buddhas liberate mortals*. That is just repaying the debt. When they become buddhas they start hammering the mortals. That's what I have been doing my whole life: first mortals liberated me, now I am trying to liberate mortals.

The statement is very strange. Perhaps Buddhist scholars could not find how to explain it, so they thought it better to keep it in oblivion, not to bring it out. Otherwise it is perfectly okay that buddhas liberate mortals, but mortals liberating buddhas? The learned, the scholarly, cannot understand it.

This is what is meant by impartiality.

Mortals liberating buddhas, buddhas liberating mortals – this is called impartiality. Now everything is balanced. Nobody owes anything to anybody else; neither the buddhas are obliging you, nor are you obliging buddhas. You have come to a state where both have paid their debts to each other.

Mortals liberate buddhas because affliction creates awareness.

Seeing the mortals and their afflictions...if you are intelligent enough you will not follow their path. So many are following that path and everybody is falling in a ditch. And everybody is suffering.

When my father failed with the physician, he approached another friend of his. He thought that would be the last resort, because he was a supreme court advocate and it was known that he had never lost any case. So my father told him, "If you can win this case, then we will accept that you are really a great advocate of the supreme court."

The judge said, "This is nothing. Just with my left hand I can do it. I will be coming tomorrow to your home."

My father told him, "Come prepared!"

He said, "Don't be worried. I know your son. And do you think he can defeat me in arguments?"

My father said, "I don't think he can defeat you in arguments, but he has strange ways. The physician who is known to be the wisest man in the area...he managed to manipulate him. Now he is in his favor."

The advocate was very egoistic and he had reason to be an egoist. He said, "Don't you be worried."

But my father said, "Still, you do the homework. Don't come unprepared. I warn you. You may lose the case. My boy is strange."

The advocate said, "You calm down and don't be worried. Tomorrow I will settle everything."

So the next day he came. I welcomed him and I asked him, "I know what you have come for. And I think my father must have told you, 'Be prepared, do the homework.'"

He looked at me and said, "How do you know?"

I said, "That's what he told the physician, so I know he must have told the same things to you. And you are his last resort. So if you are defeated, then the whole question of marriage is finished."

But he said, "Who said I am going to be defeated?"

I said, "I am not saying that, I just want to make it clear that if I get defeated, I will be married – but if you get defeated, are you ready to divorce your wife?"

He said, "My God, your father was right. I have never thought about it…that it could be a question. Certainly you are right. I should also put something at stake. But listen, I have children, and you know my wife. She even beats me. I cannot even utter the word 'divorce' before her."

So I said, "You have not come with preparedness. And I don't need any judge. I trust you, although you will be a party in argument and you will also be the judge."

He said, "I don't want to argue at all!"

I said, "What you are going to answer to my father?"

He said, "That's what I am thinking."

The argument never started. And I used to go to his house every day, knocking on the door, and he would simply say, "I don't want to quarrel with you. I am already tortured too much."

And one day his wife came out and she said, "Why is he so afraid of you?"

I said, "Because of you."

He started hiding in the bathroom and he would not come out. His wife said, "This is strange. He is never afraid of anybody. He hides, he says to me that he is not at home. What is the matter? What is cooking?"

I said, "Nothing is cooking. He is afraid of being defeated. And you are my great support."

She said, "I don't understand. What is going on? What is the problem? In what way am I the support?"

I said, "You ask him. He is thinking of divorcing you."

And he immediately came out of the bathroom. He said, "Don't lie! I am never going to divorce her. I love her. I will love her my whole life."

I said, "It is up to you. But what about the argument?"

He said, "Finished. I don't want to see you at all. You have made me so shaky that even in the court, the moment I remember you I feel afraid. Don't disturb my family life."

I said, "You were going to disturb *my* whole life!"

Mortals liberate buddhas because affliction creates awareness. And buddhas liberate mortals because awareness negates affliction.

All the buddhas come from the mortals. They are just more watchful than you are. They look all around – the whole scene is tragic, pathetic. That creates great awareness. And buddhas liberate mortals because awareness negates affliction.

All the buddhas come from the mortals. They are just more watchful than you are. They look all around – the whole scene is tragic, pathetic. That creates great awareness in them. And when they have come to the highest peak of their awareness, they make every effort to help you to be aware so that you can also get out of these afflictions.

It is not only that man is in misery. The woman is in more misery. It seems there is a strange conspiracy going on where everybody is creating misery for everybody else. Many times I have been asked why I have not married. I said, "Because of the married people. I have known so many and they warned me."

And now my whole work is somehow to get you out of your trap, to make you more alert, more aware, whether you are a husband or a wife. With your awareness your misery will disappear. Just as light dispels darkness, awareness dispels misery.

There can't help but be affliction because people are unconscious. *And there can't help but be awareness.* Once in a while somebody is going to be alert enough to see all around. And the person who becomes aware, feels to share with people who are unaware.

If not for affliction there would be nothing to create awareness. And if not for awareness, there would be nothing to negate affliction. When you are deluded, buddhas liberate mortals. When you are aware, mortals liberate buddhas. Buddhas don't become buddhas on their own.

This is the greatness of Bodhidharma. He can say it exactly, however hard it hits. He is saying, *buddhas don't become buddhas on their own.* Without this whole world of misery around them, they would never become buddhas. They should be grateful to all these people who are miserable because these are the people who impel them not to get trapped, as they themselves are trapped.

Buddhas regard delusion as their father and greed as their mother.

Only a Bodhidharma can say such things, seeing the greed of people and the anguish and the anxiety that greed creates, seeing the delusions of people. Everybody is thinking of himself, not of exactly what he is. Everybody is multiplying his personality, his ego, his knowledge. He is pretending things that he knows nothing of.

One of my professors, I found, never read anything after he had left the university thirty years before. Everything that he said was out of date. Psychology was his subject – and psychology is a very fast-growing subject; in thirty years, everything that was right has gone down the drain. But he was still quoting books which he read in his post-graduation courses.

He had a difficulty with me, because I was reading the latest and I would quote from the latest researches. He was a poor soul, he could not even say, "Forgive me, I am not aware of these researches." To keep his ego, he would say, "Yes, I have seen those papers." But if he had seen those papers or those books, which had just come out, then he should not have been teaching outdated theories about human mind and consciousness.

I reported to the vice-chancellor. I said, "It should be made compulsory for every professor to spend at least two hours in the library every day."

He said, "In no university is anything like that in existence. And all the professors will protest against it. Why are you saying that?"

I said, "All your professors were taught twenty years, thirty years ago and all that they know is no longer relevant. I have been checking in the library, who the professors are who take the books from the library. And this particular professor I am mentioning has never taken a single book from the library. He has never come to the library." And the library of the university was very rich, very up-to-date, because the man who founded the university was a man of tremendous learning and he loved books above anything else.

So I told the vice-chancellor, "Call this professor in front of me and I will show you why I am demanding this. And if you don't listen to me, then I am going to the students' union to talk to all the students, to boycott all those professors who don't go to the library for at least two hours."

He knew me – that I can manage this, so he said, "Don't go that far. Bring that professor here."

I said, "I will not bring him. You call him. I am sitting here."

He called the professor, the professor came in. And I just invented two fictitious names of psychologists and two fictitious names of books which have never been written and will never be written. And I asked the professor, "Have you read these books?"

He said, "My God, how have you found out? They are on my desk in my room. I have been reading them; they are the latest contribution."

And I told the vice-chancellor, "Both these names are fictitious, both these books are fictitious; they don't exist. Now tell this man to bring those two books into your office. They are lying on his table."

Then he became afraid. From where was he going to get those two books which are fictitious? And he had said they were lying on his table, he was reading them, and they were great.

I said, "This is the situation: these are the people who are teaching and their students will become professors tomorrow. And they will continue fifty-year-old, rotten experiments which have failed and have been replaced by new ideologies."

The vice-chancellor said, "I concede to you." And he made it a compulsory rule that every professor had to go to the library, study the latest journals, books, magazines and be up-to-date.

Professors were angry, they were all angry at me. But I said, "Anger is not going to help. I am checking every day in the library, who is coming and who is not coming. For those who are not coming, I will bring a procession of protest of all the students to their department. Then don't tell me, 'You are creating chaos.' You are the cause of it!"

The librarian was surprised. All the professors were coming, reading, taking books home. But the day I left the university, I was informed, the rule was removed. After seven or eight years, I went to that university to deliver a lecture. I went to the library. The same librarian was still there and the library was empty. There was nobody. I asked him, "What happened?"

"Those professors no longer come," he said. "The day you left the university, the rule was removed; it was just out of fear that you might create trouble. Even the vice-chancellor had started coming to the library. Now nobody comes."

People go on creating delusions, magnifying them, exaggerating them. Bodhidharma says greed is the father of the buddhas and delusion is the mother.

Delusion and greed are different names for mortality....

When you are deluded, you are on this shore. When you are aware, you are on the other shore.

These are only symbolic ways of saying you are here...deluded, you are in misery; aware, you are in blissfulness.

But once you know your mind is empty and you see no appearances, you are beyond delusion and awareness.

Each statement is difficult for scholars to explain. Only a buddha can explain these statements. He is saying, when you are in the know that your mind is empty – in other words, when you encounter your no-mind and you see no appearances – you are beyond delusion and awareness.

I have never come across any statement that says that you are beyond awareness. But he is absolutely rational, logical and existentially true because when you don't have the disease, I don't think you will go on carrying the medicine with you. The moment you are healthier, your disease has gone, you donate your medicine that remains to the Lions Club. What are you going to do with it? The Lions need it to show to the world that they are a great charitable institution. It is useless to you, you were going to throw it; why not enjoy donating it to the Lions Club? A good gain – you donate something useless to the Lions Club. And the Lions Club gives it to the poor people, and without spending anything the Lions Club becomes a charitable institution.

The same is the situation with misery and awareness. The moment there is no delusion, what is the need of awareness? That does not mean you fall asleep. That simply means awareness becomes your very nature; you are no longer aware of it.

And once you are beyond delusion and awareness, the other shore does not exist. What is the need of the other shore? The other shore was only a symbolic concept. This shore is the world, the other shore is the paradise. When the world and the attachment with the world is gone, who cares about paradise? You are already in it, wherever you are. A Sufi saying is, "Wherever the enlightened person is, there is paradise." The paradise is something within your being.

The tathagata is not on this shore or the other shore. And he is not in mid-stream.

These are the only possibilities – either on this shore, or on the other shore, or in mid-stream.

The tathagata is nowhere. One who has understood himself can be said to be either everywhere, or nowhere; both are equivalent.

But in the last sutra he remembers again his antagonism to the arhatas: *And mortals are on this shore.* On the other shore are arhatas and the mortals. The *Arhats are in mid-stream* going to the other shore – which does not exist. They are still carrying a counter-delusion. *And the mortals are on this shore. On the other shore is buddhahood.*

But the moment you are on the other shore, the other shore disappears. You are simply a light unto yourself.

But about arhatas, he cannot forget. He puts them in mid-stream, neither on this shore nor on that shore. Arhatas are also on the other shore, just as bodhisattvas are, as buddhas are. The moment they reach the other shore, both the shores disappear simultaneously. Suddenly they are awake and they find themselves part of the whole, a great shower of blessings coming over them.

If Bodhidharma could have forgotten his antagonism with arhatas and used instead of "mind," "no-mind," his sutras would have been perfect, without any flaw. But even with these two flaws, they are great. And anybody who understands can make you aware of these two flaws.

Don't carry any antagonism. And use, as far as possible, the closest word to reality. Mind is not the closest word to meditation; no-mind is.

Arhatas may have angered him because they become enlightened and they never care about anybody. They don't even speak. It is very difficult to get anything out of the arhatas. But my own feeling is, everybody has to be his own self, his own individuality, his own uniqueness. Arhatas have their own uniqueness. After becoming enlightened, they become utterly silent.

This is the antagonism of Bodhidharma, that they should be more compassionate. They should help others to become enlightened. And if you see the arguments from both sides, you will see that both are right in their own way. Arhatas say, "It is interference into somebody's life. If he wants to remain unenlightened, it is his right." Arhatas say, "This is our compassion that we don't interfere into anybody's life."

Bodhisattvas say, "This is our compassion that we make every effort to make others enlightened. This is our compassion."

I think both have beautiful arguments, and there is nothing wrong in either of the arguments. Existence is multidimensional, it has so many aspects.

A man of ultimate understanding will not see any contradiction anywhere. In his understanding and clarity, all contradictions become complementary to each other.

Okay, Maneesha?

Yes, Bhagwan.

TO FACE A BUDDHA IS DANGEROUS

達磨

Beloved Bhagwan,

Buddhas have three bodies: a transformation body, a reward body and a real body. The transformation body is also called the incarnation body. The transformation body appears when mortals do good deeds, the reward body when they cultivate wisdom and the real body when they become aware of the sublime.... But actually, there's not even one buddha-body, much less three. This talk of three bodies is simply based on human understanding, which can be shallow, moderate or deep.

People of shallow understanding imagine they're piling up blessings and mistake the transformation body as the buddha. People of moderate understanding imagine they're putting an end to suffering and mistake the reward body as the buddha. And people of deep understanding imagine they're experiencing buddhahood and mistake the real body as the buddha. But people of the deepest understanding look within, distracted by nothing. Since a clear mind is the buddha, they attain the understanding of a buddha without using the mind....

Individuals create karma. Karma doesn't create individuals.... Only someone who's perfect creates no karma in this life and receives no reward. The sutras say, "Who creates no karma obtains the Dharma".... When you create karma, you're reborn along with your karma. When you don't create karma, you vanish along with your karma....

Someone who understands the teaching of sages is a sage. Someone who understands the teaching of mortals is a mortal. A mortal who can give up the teaching of mortals and follow the teaching of sages becomes a sage. But the fools of this world prefer to look for sages far away. They don't believe that the wisdom of their own mind is the sage. The sutras say, "Among men of no understanding, don't preach this sutra."

...The sutras say, "When you see that all appearances are not appearances, you see the tathagata." The myriad doors to the truth all come from the mind. When appearances of the mind are as transparent as space, they're gone....

When mortals are alive they worry about death. When they're full, they worry about hunger. Theirs is the Great Uncertainty. But sages don't consider the past. And they don't worry about the future. Nor do they cling to the present. From moment to moment they follow the Way.

BODHIDHARMA, FOR THE first time in these sutras, looks at the people who are not enlightened and who are bound to misunderstand him. Hence, he talks about the possibility of the ordinary, unenlightened mind, and how it looks at things. He himself talks about it, so that he can make it clear that all these so-called understandings of the mind – either shallow or deep, or even very deep – all are wrong.

This is very rare, because Bodhidharma never thought about the people who would be his audience. He only thought about the truth. And he talked about it without any consideration of those who were listening to it, or reading it. This is part of his compassion; this is the part that makes the arhatas and the bodhisattvas separate.

Arhatas never, never think about anybody else. If they speak, they are just speaking to themselves. Most probably they remain silent. They have a profound respect for others, but they know that to tell them about the ultimate is to disturb their ordinariness. It is an interference in their mundane minds – although it is for their own benefit. But they are not asking for it, and unless they invite the truth, the truth is not going to knock on their doors.

The truth is almost like the sun in the morning. It rises...it does not knock on your doors saying, "I am here and the night is over and you can wake." It does not go to every nest of the birds, to tell them, "Now it is time to sing, I have come," nor does it go to every flower to open its petals and release its fragrance. It simply comes. Those who are receptive will receive it. Those who are not receptive will not receive it. Those who are awake will know that the morning has arrived, but those who are fast asleep will not know, even in their dreams, that the night is over. But the sun does not interfere.

The understanding of the arhatas is that compassion means not to interfere, not to trespass, even though it is for the benefit of those against whom you are trespassing. Trespassing in itself is against the dignity of individuals and it is a humiliation. To say to someone, "You are asleep," means you are putting yourself on a higher pedestal. You are saying, "I am awake and you are asleep," you are saying "I am holier than thou, higher than thou; I have arrived to the ultimate peak of my consciousness and you are still wandering in the world of darkness, groping everywhere, stumbling, falling and finding no way out."

Even to advise anyone is to take a certain position: "I know and you do not know." The arhatas' standpoint is that it is against compassion, it is against reverence for life; hence they remain silent. If anybody feels their presence on his own accord and comes close to them to drink the living waters of their experience, they are available – just like the river passing by. You can quench your thirst, but it is absolutely up to you; the river will not do anything on its own part. It is a beautiful approach. But the approach of the bodhisattvas, to whom Bodhidharma belongs, has its own beauty.

The bodhisattvas make every effort to awaken people, knowing perfectly well that out of a million people, perhaps one may understand them and the remaining will either be indifferent, or most probably will misunderstand. Bodhisattvas know perfectly well that speaking the truth is a very shortcut way to create enemies in the world, because the whole world is full of lies. All the vested interests are based on lies. The so-called religions, the so-called nations – all are fabrications of cunning minds.

An authentically religious man belongs to no religion and belongs to no nation and to no race and to no color. He belongs to the whole humanity. All the nations are his. He does not believe in political boundaries created by the cunning and dirty politicians. And he does not believe in the discriminations created by the priests, by the popes, by the archbishops, by the shankaracharyas, by the rabbis. He believes that every human being has a divine nature, and every human being has the potential to grow into a beautiful lotus flower – a lotus flower that belongs to eternity, a fragrance that comes but never goes.

Knowing all this, the bodhisattva still makes every effort; it does not matter even if he is crucified. Jesus is a bodhisattva, so is Socrates a bodhisattva, so is Al-Hillaj Mansoor. Even if it means crucifixion, it does not matter if it can help somebody, somewhere, to get out of his sleep. A bodhisattva is ready to accept all condemnation from the whole world, but he cannot remain silent and unsharing. That is impossible for him.

As far as I am concerned, both are absolutely right. There is no contradiction.

They are both representing two sides of the same phenomenon. Their expression of compassion is different, but it *is* the expression of compassion. Both are expressing it in their own unique ways.

The sutra: *Buddhas have three bodies: a transformation body, a reward body and a real body. The transformation body is also called the incarnation body. The transformation body appears when mortals do good deeds, the reward body when they cultivate wisdom and the real body when they become aware of the sublime.... But actually, there's not even one buddha-body, much less three. This talk of three bodies is simply based on human understanding, which can be shallow, moderate or deep.*

People of shallow understanding imagine they're piling up blessings and mistake the transformation body as the buddha. People of moderate understanding imagine they're putting an end to suffering and mistake the reward body as the buddha. And people of deep understanding imagine they're experiencing buddhahood and mistake the real body as the buddha.

It needs some explanation. It is possible you may pass a Gautam Buddha without recognizing him because the recognition of a buddha, of an awakened being, needs some insight on your part. It depends on you, your understanding. If you don't have any understanding of the awakened one, you may pass by his side and you may not even feel anything. You are closed. The sun is there but your doors and windows are closed. The sun is there but you are standing with closed eyes.

The first recognition comes from people who are trying to do good according to their small understanding. Whatever they feel – helpful to humanity, helpful to the animals – they are trying to do something to beautify existence. They don't want to be just a burden on the earth. They want to contribute something; they want to leave the world a little better than they found it when they came into existence.

These people will see buddha's first body, the transformation body. They will see buddha surrounded with an aura of light. You have seen pictures of Jesus, of Krishna, of Buddha with a surrounding aura. That is an actual phenomenon and now it has a scientific basis to support it.

In the Soviet Union, a great scientist and philosopher, Kirlian, developed a special camera and specially sensitive films, so sensitive that they can see things which your eyes cannot see. His first experience was of tremendous wonder because his photographs showed auras around everybody, not only around human beings but around animals and around trees, around a roseflower. The roseflower was there in the picture and just by the side, a small light-aura.

He was surprised to know that the more silent, peaceful a man was, the bigger was the aura. And the more angry, anxiety-ridden, sad, miserable, full of anguish a man was, the smaller was the aura. And before a man was going to die, six months before, the aura completely disappeared; then his photographs came without any aura, just like ordinary photographs.

This aura has been seen by sensitive people, just as Kirlian's sensitive films photograph it. The sensitive disciples of Jesus will see something which others will not be able to see. The sensitive disciples of Gautam Buddha who have lived in deep love with him, who have been showered by his blessings, who are completely drowned in his being, will be able to see something which an ordinary spectator will not be able to see. The more they become receptive, the more they become sensitive, the more Buddha's reality becomes apparent to them.

The first experience is of the transformation body: a thin light body, just four inches bigger than your body…just around your body a four-inch aura of light, very soft light. This is the body that transmigrates. That's why, before death – as Kirlian discovered – six months before, this body starts disappearing, it starts becoming condensed inside the being of man. It takes six months for it to come back to the center and become just a point of light instead of a big aura. And this small point of light transmigrates while your whole body remains here.

Scientists have been trying to prove that there is no soul on the grounds that when they weigh a living man just a moment before he dies, and when they weigh him a moment after, his weight is the same – absolutely the same. Naturally their conclusion is that nothing has gone out and; hence, that there is no soul. If something goes out and, then the weight will be less. But now it can be told to the scientists that light has no weight; that's why if a point of light transmigrates it won't make any difference on your weighing scales.

Light is absolutely weightless and the transmigration body is nothing but pure light. This is experienced by people even of shallow understanding. Those who don't understand much, but still have a little consciousness – just a shallow consciousness – even they can see this light.

But the people of moderate understanding can see a deeper body, hidden behind this thin layer of light, a thicker layer of light known in the Buddhist scriptures as the reward body. It arises only when one has been meditating so much that one is earning immense reward. In this world the greatest treasure and the greatest reward is to learn to be silent, to be utterly silent. This is a silence body. But it is possible to be seen only by those who have come very close to Gautam Buddha.

I have always divided people into three categories. The first is the student who comes to the awakened one. The student is capable of seeing the first body, the transformation body.

The second is the disciple, who is not there with the buddha or any awakened human being out of curiosity – who is not there just to accumulate knowledge – but who himself wants to come to the same space, to the same blissfulness, to the same benediction. The disciple has taken a quantum leap from the student. The student is interested in collecting more and more information; the disciple is interested not in information but in transformation. He wants to change into a different being, a being which is beyond the mind. He is capable of seeing the second body, the reward body.

The reward body is really existence recognizing your meditation, your silence, and showering flowers on you. Existence is immensely happy when someone becomes enlightened, because the enlightenment of one person is really the triggering of enlightenment for many people. It can become a long chain, which can go for centuries. For example, what was triggered by Gautam Buddha's enlightenment is still triggering people into enlightenment. Twenty-five centuries have passed, but the chain has continued. It is a chain reaction.

There are very few religions in the world which are still alive. Zen is still alive. There are still people who can be called contemporaries of Gautam Buddha; they are connected so deeply that you cannot separate them, by time or by space.

In Mohammedanism, only a small school of Sufis is a living part; the whole of the rest of that religion has died. But Sufism is still continuing a chain reaction. Still there are people who are awakened.

In Judaism, the whole religion except for a small school of the Hassids is dead. Those Hassids have been carrying the torch for centuries. They are still creating more and more enlightened people.

Strangely, Hinduism and Christianity are completely dead religions. They don't have even a small stream of living masters. And they are very important religions. Hinduism is the oldest religion of the world and Christianity is the biggest religion of the world, but both are completely dead. They are just an ugly weight on humanity. Nothing blossoms in their gardens; no flower comes to release its fragrance. They are lamps without any flame in them.

It is said of Diogenes, a man of the same caliber as Bodhidharma.... If they had met, it would have been a great meeting. Diogenes was in Greece. He lived naked; he had such a beautiful body that to hide it behind clothes would have been a crime. It is perfectly good to hide an ugly body behind clothes but a beautiful body needs to be available for anybody who wants to see the beauty, the proportion. Diogenes was one of the most beautiful men. Even when Alexander the Great met him, he felt a little embarrassed – although he was a world conqueror, compared to Diogenes he was utterly poor.

Diogenes had nothing, but his richness was radiating from his naked body. Diogenes used to carry a lamp, even in the daytime. He was thought to be a little crazy – obviously. In a world of insane people, anybody who is sane is bound to be thought a little crazy. And he was doing something which you will also feel looks a little crazy. Whomever he would meet on the way, he would take up his lamp and look at his face. And when asked, "What are you doing, Diogenes? It is full daylight; you don't need to keep your lamp burning," he would say, "no, I have to keep it burning. I am searching for an authentic man."

When he was dying, his lamp by his side, somebody asked, "Diogenes, your whole life you have been searching for an authentic man. What happened? Did you meet any authentic man or not?"

He said, "Thank God, although I never met any authentic man I have saved my lamp."

Because the world is so cunning, so full of thieves, even to save one's lamp is to be fortunate. This Diogenes was an awakened man. In fact, he was not looking in your eyes when he raised his lamp, he was showing his eyes, so that you could see clearly into his eyes, and *there* was an authentic man. And if you had looked into his eyes, you would have changed totally into a new being.

A disciple looks into the eyes of the master. He looks into the very depth of his eyes. A disciple is not interested in what the master is saying, he is interested in what the master *is*.

Then he comes to know the second body of the master; his treasure, his reward body. The whole existence has been showering millions of rewards on the master. But there is still a third step. The man of the deepest understanding comes to know the third body, the deepest body.

The student comes to know the first body, the disciple comes to know the second body and the devotee comes to know the third body, the real body, the buddha's real being. Again there is a quantum leap – from disciple to devotee. Disciple comes very close, very, very close, but even closeness is a distance. The devotee simply melts and merges into the master. He is not close, he becomes one. And in this oneness he comes to know the real body of the awakened being.

But Bodhidharma says: these three bodies and the experiences of these three bodies are of the normal mind. Actually, there is not even one buddha-body. A man of enlightenment is utterly nobody – or no body. That's what the meaning of nobody is. He is pure emptiness. He is just pure sky without any limitations. This infinitude is known only when one becomes a buddha.

The devotee merges with the buddha, but in a subtle way he still carries his idea, "I am a devotee, a lover. I have surrendered everything." A very subtle "I" – almost on the verge of disappearing, but it is there. He has not yet experienced the emptiness of the master.

There is a story about a great Zen master, Lin Chi. The day one of his disciples was going to become enlightened...he had come a long way and the master had been watching his progress, and he knew that as the sun set that day, before that time, the disciple was going to become enlightened. He had come so close, it was just like a moth flying closer and closer to the flame of a candle. One could say that it was not going to take much time. The moth has come so close that soon it will be falling into the flame and disappear for ever.

Lin Chi called his disciple and told him, "Listen, I have been beating you for years." That is part of Zen tradition. That is the only tradition where the master is allowed to beat the disciple...for strange reasons, or for no reason at all. Only he knows why he is beating him: sometimes he brings a wrong answer to a question, then the master slaps him.

But sometimes disciples are simply amazed. They have not even spoken a word and the master starts slapping them and they say, "This is too much because we have not said anything." The master says, "That does not matter. We know what you were going to say, we could read it on your face. We knew the way you entered the room...so why waste time? First, you will have to say things and then we will have to beat. Make it short. Get a good beating and go away. Find out the right answer."

And it is a well-known fact that when the disciple finds the right answer he has nothing to say, because the right answer cannot be said. Only wrong answers can be said.

So Lin Chi had been beating the disciple on and off, and suddenly he called him. He was sitting outside in the garden meditating on the koan for which he had been getting beatings. The disciple said, "Why has he called me? because I don't have anything to say." And before entering the door of the master's room he said clearly, "I don't have anything to say, so don't start slapping me. And I have not come of my own accord; you have called me."

Lin Chi said, "That's true. You have not come, I have called you, but I will slap all the same for a totally different reason today. Just come close."

The disciple said, "This is going too far. I have been told that when you don't have anything to say, you cannot be slapped. You are breaking even that rule."

The master said, "Don't waste time. Just come close. I am going to slap you because after today I will not be able to slap you again. This day you are going to become enlightened, so this is the last chance. Let me have a good…. Tomorrow you can slap me – you will have the right – but today is my last chance." And he slapped him.

This is a beautiful tradition. It shows great love. A master beating the disciple for no reason at all, just because he is going to become enlightened today and from tomorrow he will not be able to beat him…! The disciple became enlightened that day and the next day when he came to see the master, the master closed the doors. He said, "You can say anything you want to say from outside the room, because I am an old man. You must understand that slapping me is not right, so from now on doors will remain closed for you. You can say anything you want to say a little loudly from outside."

The moment a devotee forgets even that he *is,* that no idea of *I am* arises in him, then he comes to know that the buddha has no body at all. That buddha is a nobody; he is simply pure silence, emptiness, a total zero.

But actually, there's not even one buddha-body much less three. This talk of three bodies is simply based on human understanding, which can be shallow, moderate or deep.

People of shallow understanding imagine they're piling up blessings and mistake the transformation body as the buddha. People of moderate understanding imagine they're putting an end to suffering and mistake the reward body as the buddha. And people of deep understanding imagine they're experiencing buddhahood and mistake the real body as the buddha. But people of the deepest understanding look within, distracted by nothing. Since a clear mind or better, no-mind, *is the buddha, they attain the understanding of a buddha without using the mind….*

Individuals create karma.

Before we enter into this sutra, you have to understand this word *karma.* It means action. But action can be of two types: either it can be a reaction or it can be a response.

Somebody insults you. You become angry – he has pushed your button. In fact he is the master, you are behaving like a slave. He has managed to create anger in you. He is in control. If he wants to change the situation he can say, "I am sorry," and things will be different. You are just a victim; you don't have any control of the situation. When somebody insults you, you are immediately reacting out of your past experiences.

This reaction is really karma.

It is a binding force; it creates chains for you.

But a response is a totally different thing from reaction. A response is not produced by the other person. He insults you, he abuses you – you listen to him, he is making certain statements about you. A man of understanding, a man of awareness, a man of meditation will simply listen to it. He is making some statements…good or bad, that is not the concern of the moment. First you listen to him without immediately going into a reaction. You allow your awareness like a mirror to reflect whatever he is saying, or whatever he is doing. And out of your mirror-like, immediate, in the present, not-from-past-experience awareness, some response comes.

He was telling you that you are greedy, he was telling you that you are ugly, he was telling you that you are dirty. And if you silently listen, there is nothing to be angry about. Either he is right or he is wrong. If he is right, you have to be grateful to him. You have to tell him, "Thank you, you have a great compassion. You have made me aware of things of which I was not aware. Please, always remember, whenever you see something in me, tell me. Don't feel that I will be offended. I will always remain grateful."

Or if you find that he is wrong, you can simply say, "I have heard your statements but they are not true. And about something which is not true, why should I react? You will have to reconsider. Reconsider your statements and then we will see. But as far as I can see, there is nothing true in them and I need not be offended by lies." There are only two alternatives.

George Gurdjieff's father died and at that time he was only nine years old. The father was poor but a very integrated man, a man of tremendous awareness. He called Gurdjieff and said, "Listen. You are too young to understand what I am saying, but remember it. Soon you will be able to understand it, and if you can start acting accordingly, start acting so that you don't forget. I don't have anything else to give to you; no money, no house, no land." He was a nomad. "I am handing you over to my friends, but remember, this is the only treasure that I can give you as an inheritance. And listen carefully; these are the last words of your father – his whole life's experience."

A nine-year-old boy…he came close to listen to the old father and the father said, "It is a very simple thing: If somebody insults you, listen silently, carefully, in detail to what he is saying – what are the implications. And then tell the person, 'I am grateful that you have taken so much interest in me. After twenty-four hours I will come and reply to you. I cannot help it, because my dying father has made it a condition to me that only after twenty-four hours consideration am I allowed to answer.'"

And in his own old age, Gurdjieff said to his disciples, "This simple principle helped me tremendously, because after twenty-four hours who remains angry? And after considering twenty-four hours, either one finds he is right – and if he is right there is no need to bother, it is better to change yourself – or he is wrong. Then too there is no need to be bothered. It is his problem, not your problem."

A man who is fully awakened remains undefiled by whatsoever he does, because it is a response. It is a pure reflection from a mirror, with no judgment. It does not come from the past, it comes from the present consciousness. But anything that comes from your past experiences is going to create a chain for you.

In the East, for ten thousand years we have been thinking about it, experimenting with it. It is the only thing that the whole East and its genius has remained involved with: how a man can come to a stage where his actions don't make any bondage for him, don't create another birth for him – how a consciousness can be created where one can act without acting, and where nothing contaminates his being.

Individuals create karma. Karma doesn't create individuals....

So it is in your hands. You are not a by-product of your actions. You are far bigger than your actions; good or bad, you are always bigger. And it is in your hands to change everything.

The East has paid tremendous respect to the individual and has given him the greatest power over his own destiny ever given anywhere in the world. In the East there is no savior. You are the savior. Nobody else can do that for you.

It would be really ugly if somebody else could save you. Then even your being, saved or redeemed, is a kind of slavery.

And if somebody else can redeem you, somebody else can push you back into the wheel of birth and death, because you are just a puppet. All the religions that believe in saviors reduce man into a puppet. They take away the freedom and the dignity and the pride of individual beings.

Bodhidharma is saying: *individuals create karma.* You can create hell for yourself, you can create heaven, or you can go beyond both. This going beyond both, does not exist in Judaism, in Mohammedanism, in Christianity. That is the special contribution of the Eastern mystics. Hell and heaven exist as hypotheses in Christianity, in Mohammedanism, in Judaism. But *moksha,* being beyond heaven and hell...because hell is misery and heaven is happiness, but happiness too becomes boring after a time. No Western religious leader has ever thought about it, that happiness after a time becomes boring. How long can you tolerate happiness? Just as pain, after a long time, becomes a companion...without it you feel something is missing.

I have known a man who had suffered from headache, migraines, for almost ten years. I used to go into the mountains and he was also a professor in the same university where I was a professor. Once he asked me, "Can I come along with you?" I never liked anybody else to go with me, because I was going out of the city just to avoid all the idiots – and this idiot was not only an idiot, he had a migraine! I said, "My God," but I said, "Okay. It looks very unkind to say no to you. Just sit, but don't talk about migraine because I have an allergy."

He said, "What kind of allergy?"

I said, "If anybody talks to me of his disease, I become sick with the same disease."

He said, "I have never heard that such an allergy exists."

I said, "It is not a question of hearing, I am the example – it is not a bookish question. Just don't talk about migraine!"

So I took him to the mountains. It was the season of the mangoes, and the mountain was full of the sweetness of the mangoes. I have the habit of climbing trees from my very childhood. I had fallen from the trees so many times that my father used to tell me, "Now it is time you stop." I used to say, "I have fallen so many times that I am almost an expert in falling. You don't be worried. I am not a beginner. I fall with a certain method, that's why I am surviving."

So I took him to a mango tree which had very ripe mangoes and many parrots – parrots love mangoes – and I told him, "You come along with me, up the tree."

He said, "What?"

I said, "You come along."

He said, "I have never been climbing up a tree."

I said, "Try, it will be an adventure for you."

And he fell down from the tree. I had to rush, come back down the tree. He looked very amazed. He said, "It is strange. I had the migraine and by falling from the tree, it has disappeared."

I said, "Sometimes it happens, but don't make it a practice. And don't tell anybody, because it may not happen to somebody else. It is just coincidence." But the migraine disappeared.

And after seven days he met me and he said, "I miss my migraine."

I said, "First, you were continuously complaining about migraine, and now you miss it?"

He said, "I never knew that I would miss it. Now I have nothing to talk about; migraine was my whole philosophy. And because of the migraine I was getting everybody else's sympathy. Now nobody sympathizes with me!"

I said, "Then the only thing is, we can go to the mountains again, climb the tree and fall. Perhaps – I can't be certain because there is no science in it – perhaps the migraine will come back."

He said, "I will have to think about it because it was really very difficult. The suffering was bad."

But next day he told me, "I am ready because without migraine I cannot live. I feel so empty because I had lived ten years with migraine."

And you will not be surprised if you watch your own behavior!

There are people who are smoking and they know they are burning their lungs. They know they are destroying their health…but it makes no difference. In a few countries the governments have even decided that the factories which produce cigarettes should also write on the packets that it is dangerous to health. First the cigarette companies were against any such law being passed, because this may destroy their whole business. Who is going to purchase cigarettes when it is written on the package that it is against your health? "The medical opinion is that it is dangerous for your health," or something like that.

But governments passed the law and the people who had been smoking are still smoking, and the number of smokers goes on increasing. It does not make any difference. The law has been absolutely meaningless. Man becomes accustomed to anything. Then it is very difficult, even if it is dangerous, even if it is killing him, even if it is proved that it is going to give you cancer… You would rather have cancer than change your habits.

But Bodhidharma is saying: You are the master of your destiny. You can change every act, you can change every habit. You can change what you think has become your second nature and you can create a totally new individuality, fresh and young, with more awareness, with more understanding, with more blissfulness, with a great ecstasy.

Only someone who is perfect creates no karma in this life and receives no reward.

Who is perfect? The only person who is perfect is one whose consciousness has dispelled all unconsciousness from his being. Right now only one-tenth of your consciousness is conscious and nine-tenths is unconscious.

The perfect man is one whose whole being, all ten parts, are absolutely conscious and full of light. There is no darkness in his heart. In the very depths and silences of his heart there is nothing but peace, silence, light, joy. Such a man is perfect and such a man can do anything. Nothing is binding on him. He creates no karma, he creates no chains, he creates no new life. He has come to the very end of the road.

A perfect man, an awakened man, is not born again. What happens to his consciousness? It becomes part of the universe, just like a dewdrop slipping from a lotus leaf into the ocean. Either the dewdrop becomes the ocean, or the ocean becomes the dewdrop. You can say it either way. But this is the goal of all religiousness, the dropping of the dewdrop into the ocean.

The sutras say, "Who creates no karma obtains the Dharma."

One who is fully conscious knows his self-nature. That is the meaning of dharma.

When you create karma, you are reborn along with your karma. When you don't create karma, you vanish along with your karma....

Someone who understands the teaching of the sages is a sage. Someone who understands the teaching of mortals is a mortal.

You may be a student of a great philosopher, but he is not an immortal. He is as afraid of death as you are, or perhaps more, because he is thinking more about life, death, birth. The more he thinks, the more he creates a paranoia.

Sigmund Freud was thinking more about death just because he was thinking about sex. Sex is one side of life, the beginning. And death is the other side of life, the end. A person who thinks about sex cannot avoid thinking about death. He has to. Sex and death are so deeply connected.

You will be surprised that there are, in South Africa, a species of spiders: the male makes love only one time in his life because the next chance never arises. While he is making love, the female spider starts eating him. He has long legs and the female starts eating through his legs. And he is in such an ecstasy, he is not in his consciousness. By the time his orgasm is finished, he is also finished. Every spider knows that this is happening every day – but what to do? Sooner or later every spider finds himself trapped into the same thing. Sex and death have come very close in that species. It is not that close in human beings, but it is not very far either. Sex is the beginning of death.

Sigmund Freud was so afraid of death that he prohibited anybody from creating any discussion about death in front of him. And he had hundreds of disciples. Perhaps in this whole century he was one of the greatest teachers. He created the great profession of psychoanalysis, and those who learned psychoanalysis from him brag about the fact that they are disciples of the original master, the founder of psychoanalysis itself.

But they don't know that Sigmund Freud was so much afraid of death that even at the mention of it, three times in his life, he fainted. He became unconscious just because somebody mentioned the word, 'death.' Even the word reminded him of his own death. He never used to pass through any cemetery; even if he had to go around a few miles to avoid a cemetery he would go, but he would never go to a cemetery. He never went to the cemetery to say the last goodbye to a friend who had died, never! He went only once, but then he never came back!

Bodhidharma is saying: *Someone who understands the teaching of mortals is a mortal. A mortal who can give up the teaching of mortals and follow the teaching of sages becomes a sage.*

Drop the teachings of those who don't know that there is life beyond death. Then they don't know anything at all. All their knowledge is simply verbal, just so much prose. In fact, it is just rubbish and crap.

If you want to be a disciple, at least choose someone who knows something beyond death. And the person who knows something beyond death is bound to be the person who knows something beyond mind, because they are the same experiences.

But the fools of this world prefer to look for sages far away.

It is a very significant statement. *The fools of this world prefer to look for sages far away.* There are people who worship Gautam Buddha, twenty-five centuries far away. There is no fear; Buddha cannot do anything to you.

To face a living buddha is dangerous.

He can overwhelm you.

But worshiping a Buddha who has been dead for twenty-five centuries.... You can carry the Buddha statue wherever you want and you can do with the statue whatever you want; the statue cannot do anything to you. But a living buddha is dangerous. To be in contact with him is to be constantly risking, because he is taking you towards the goal where you will disappear. You will *be,* but just pure consciousness, not an ego.

The *Upanishads* say that the authentic master is a death. He kills the disciple as an ego. He makes the disciple just a nothingness.

The fools love very much to worship Jesus, but the contemporaries of Jesus crucified him. It is a very strange world. There is not even a mention of the name of Jesus in his contemporary literature. Except for his own disciples, nobody had even taken note of him. It is strange...such a man, whom the contemporaries could not tolerate alive – when he was only thirty-three they crucified him – but they have not even mentioned his name. Yet after two thousand years, half the world is Christian...strange! And if Jesus Christ comes today, the same Christians will crucify him again.

I have heard that in a New York church, on a Sunday morning, the bishop came a little early to see if all the arrangements were okay or not, because only on Sunday do Christians become religious. It is a Sunday religion. As the bishop entered he found a young man looking exactly like Jesus Christ. His heart sank. He felt he was going to die. "My God, why has he come here? He has not learned any lesson. When he came, what people did to him – and again he is back! But it is better to enquire who he is. Perhaps he is just a hippy who looks like Jesus." So he went close to him and asked, "Who are you?"

Jesus looked at him and he said, "This is a strange question. You represent me on the earth and you don't recognize me? I am Jesus Christ."

The bishop immediately phoned the Vatican to the pope saying, "What do you think I should do? Jesus Christ is here in the church."

The pope said, "I am tortured so much with a thousand and one worries, and you bring another. Can't you figure out what to do? The first thing is, inform the police. And the second thing is, look busy."

If Jesus Christ comes back, he is not going to be treated differently from how he was treated before. That's why he is not coming back; otherwise he promised, "I will be coming back soon." Two thousand years and the soon has not ended. Any intelligent man will not come back; it was enough. One experience is enough.

Contemporaries have always misbehaved with the people of awareness, with the people who have enlightenment. And the same people have always worshiped the dead saints, dead sages, dead prophets, dead messiahs.

There were at least five attempts made on the life of Gautam Buddha while he was alive. Now there are more statues of Gàutam Buddha in the world than of anybody else. And the same people tried five times to kill him.

But the fools of this world prefer to look for sages far away.

Because to be close is dangerous, they can change you. And nobody wants to be changed.

They don't believe that the wisdom of their own no-*mind is the sage.*

And the reality is, you don't have to look far away in time or in space. You have just to look inwards, and this very moment you can find the awakened one. This very moment you can find the buddha...not twenty five centuries back; there is no need to go that far. And there is no way to go backwards. God has forgotten, when he made the world, to put in a reverse gear. You can simply go forward, just go forward.

Even Henry Ford forgot to put the reverse gear in the first car that he made as a model. If God can forget, poor Henry Ford has to be allowed! And when he got into his car, then he realized that this was a very difficult problem. If you have gone five feet past your house, then you have to go around the whole city to get home, to come back. It was Henry Ford's genius, to create a reverse gear. God has not learned, even now. But he must be meeting with Henry Ford there, to put in a reverse gear so you can go to see Jesus Christ, or Gautam Buddha, or Mahavira, or Krishna.

But my feeling is that even if there is a reverse gear available, nobody is going to use it for the simple reason that to face such colossal individuals needs guts, needs courage. And the greatest courage in the world is to go through the transformation from being a mortal to being an immortal god.

The sutras say, "Among men of no understanding, don't preach this sutra."

But where can you preach it? If people have understanding, they don't need the sutra. Only the people who don't understand need the sutra. So I cannot agree with this sutra which says, *"Among men of no understanding, don't preach this sutra."*

Be compassionate, preach to everybody. If they can understand, good. If they cannot understand, perhaps some seed may fall into their heart without their knowing. And then someday spring comes; it may sprout. Perhaps they may not hear you, but somebody again repeating the same thing...they may feel that they have heard it before, there must be something in it.

No, one has to go on repeating continuously to people of no understanding, because if they are people of no understanding there is dormant in them the possibility of understanding. You just go on hitting. They need just a little more hitting, a little more repetition of the message to reach to their heart. They have thick skulls.

But don't listen to any sutra which teaches you unkindness, which teaches you to be uncompassionate.

...The sutras say, "When you see that all appearances are not appearances, you see the tathagata."

The moment mind disappears with all its illusions and dreams and thoughts and imaginations, you see within yourself the awakening, which you can call the buddha, you can call the Christ. These are simply names. But one thing is certain: the moment your mind disappears, something divine appears in you and starts growing into a huge tree with great foliage, with great flowers, with great fruit.

The myriad doors to the truth all come from the mind. When appearances of the mind are as transparent as space, they are gone....

When mortals are alive they worry about death. When they are full, they worry about hunger. Theirs is the Great Uncertainty. But sages don't consider the past.

Because the past is no more...

And they don't worry about the future.
Because the future is not yet...
Nor do they cling to the present.
Because the present is fleeing every moment...what is the point of clinging? Clinging will bring you misery. So they don't think of the past...it is gone. They don't cling to the present...it is going. And they don't think of the future...it has not come yet. There is no point in thinking about it. It may come, it may not come.
From moment to moment they follow the Way.
Just in this single sentence is hidden the whole secret of religion...*moment to moment they follow the Way.* In full awareness and spontaneity, moment to moment, they go on living joyously, peacefully, silently. Slowly, slowly, as their silence deepens, as their understanding deepens, as their awareness reaches to the highest climax, each moment becomes a paradise. Then they don't think of a paradise somewhere in the clouds.
Then the paradise is here.
Then the paradise is now.

Okay, Maneesha?

Yes, Bhagwan.

BREAKTHROUGH...TO BUDDHAHOOD

達磨

15

**BREAKTHROUGH...
TO BUDDHAHOOD**

Beloved Bhagwan,

Bodhidharma's Breakthrough Sermon

If someone is determined to reach enlightenment, what is the most essential method he can practice?

The most essential method, which includes all other methods, is beholding the mind.

But how can one method include all others?

The mind is the root from which all things grow. If you can understand the mind, everything else is included.

It's like with a tree. All of its fruit and flowers, its branches and leaves, depend on its root. If you nourish its root, a tree multiplies. If you cut its root, it dies. Those who understand the mind reach enlightenment with minimal effort. Those who don't

understand the mind practice in vain. Everything good and bad comes from your own mind. To find something beyond the mind is impossible.

But how can beholding the mind be called understanding?

When a great bodhisattva delves deeply into perfect wisdom, he realizes...the activity of his mind has two aspects: pure and impure...the pure mind delighting in good deeds, the impure mind thinking of evil. Those who aren't affected by impurity are sages. They transcend suffering and experience the bliss of nirvana. All others, trapped by the impure mind and entangled by their own karma, are mortals. They drift through the three realms and suffer countless afflictions. And all because their impure mind obscures their real self.

The *Sutra of the Ten Stages* says, "In the body of mortals is the indestructible buddha-nature. Like the sun, its light fills endless space. But once veiled by the dark clouds of the five shades, it's like a light inside a jar, hidden from view." And the *Nirvana Sutra* says, "All mortals have the buddha-nature. But it's covered by darkness from which they can't escape. Our buddha-nature is awareness: to be aware and to make others aware. To realize awareness is liberation." Everything good has awareness for its root. From this root of awareness grow the tree of all virtues and the fruit of nirvana.

THE SUTRAS THIS morning belong to a special sermon by Bodhidharma called the "Breakthrough Sermon." I would like you to understand the word "breakthrough."

You know another word which is close to "breakthrough," and that is "breakdown." Mind has both the possibilities. Under tension, anxiety, anguish it can break down, but breakdown is not a breakthrough. Breakdown brings you below the mind; it is insanity. Breakthrough comes out of watching the mind in deep silence, in great awareness. Then you go beyond the mind and to go beyond the mind is to attain authentic sanity.

Mind is just in the middle. You are nothing but a mess. If you can go beyond it, intelligence grows in you; if you go below it, any intelligence that you had disappears.

But in either case, either in breakthrough or in breakdown, you are out of the mind. That's why there is a certain similarity between the enlightened person and the madman. The madman has gone through a breakdown but he is out of the mind. The enlightened person has gone beyond the mind; it is a breakthrough. He is also out of the mind but because he has gone beyond mind, he attains to ultimate sanity, to great intelligence, to a clarity, mind cannot even conceive of.

But the similarity is that both are out of the mind and the mind can interpret both either as enlightened or as insane. Hence a strange thing has been happening in the East and in the West. There are many enlightened people in the West inside insane asylums because Western psychology does not believe in any breakthrough. For anyone who goes out of the mind, only one interpretation is available: that he has gone mad.

In the East there are many madmen who are worshiped as enlightened because the East interprets going out of the mind always as a breakthrough. I have come across a few madmen who were not enlightened but they were worshiped like God. In a place near Jabalpur there was one man who was half paralyzed and utterly mad, but thousands of people used to gather around him. He had nothing to say and there was no light in his eyes and there was no joy in his being.

I used to go and simply sit there and watch the man and what people were doing. He was living almost by drinking only tea. It was difficult for him to drink tea because half his body was paralyzed, so only half of his mouth was able to move; the other half was not able to move. So even while drinking tea, his saliva was dripping into the tea. It was an ugly scene. And the followers would take away the cup of the tea when he had just taken a few sips out of it and they would distribute it to people as *prasad,* as a gift from God.

I watched this whole nonsense...and the man was not able to even utter a single word. Anywhere else in the world he would have been in a mad asylum, but in India even the breakdown is misunderstood as a breakthrough. And in the West even the breakthrough is understood as a breakdown.

A tremendous synthesis is needed between Western psychology and Eastern understanding of the mind. These are totally and diametrically opposite dimensions. Breakdown brings you back to the stage of the animals, and breakthrough brings you to your ultimate flowering, your buddhahood. And their happening is so different, so qualitatively different, that they can be easily distinguished. Breakthrough happens only to a meditator. Breakdown happens to anybody whose mind becomes too tense, unbearably tense, so that he loses all control of the mind mechanism, and falls down.

The name of the sermon is immensely significant. The East has been aware for centuries that the madman and the enlightened man have a certain similarity. They both are out of the mind, but at that point the similarity ends. One has gone beyond, towards the stars; the other has gone down towards darker spaces.

Breakthrough is the very science of meditation.

The sutra:

If someone is determined to reach enlightenment, what is the most essential method he can practice?

The most essential method, which includes all other methods, is beholding the mind.

To be aware of the mind is being a witness of the mind. As the witnessing grows stronger, you already start feeling yourself beyond the mind. Slowly, slowly the distance grows. Your witness reaches to a sunlit peak and the mind is left in the dark valleys, far away. You can still hear the echoes, but they don't affect you at all. You are beyond their reach.

The disciple asked: *But how can one method include all others?*

And Bodhidharma says: *The mind is the root from which all things grow,* from madness to enlightenment. *If you can understand the mind, everything else is included. It's like with a tree. All of its fruit and flowers, its branches and leaves depend on its root. If you nourish its root, a tree multiplies. If you cut its root, it dies. Those who understand the mind reach enlightenment with minimal effort. Those who don't understand the mind practice in vain. Everything good and bad comes from your own mind. To find something beyond the mind is impossible...*except yourself, the enlightenment – that is my addition to the sutra.

Now there are a few important things that Bodhidharma is saying. The first is: *If you can understand the mind, everything else is included.* But the word "understanding" can be misunderstood, because the Western psychology is now the predominant psychology all over the world. West or East, the only psychology prevalent today is Western psychology. And the Western psychology tries to understand the mind by analysis. That is a futile effort.

It is like peeling an onion. One layer is taken off and you find another layer, more fresh, waiting for you. You take that layer off and another layer is there. People have been under psychoanalysis for fifteen years continuously; still their psychoanalysis is not complete. The psychoanalysts themselves recognize that they have not yet been able to psychoanalyze a single man perfectly, totally – until nothing is left to be psychoanalyzed. But still, even the psychoanalysts do not have the insight to understand that perhaps they are doing something absurd.

Mind can never be totally analyzed because while you are analyzing it, it goes on creating new things. It does not remain static. You go on analyzing every week twice or thrice, but the remaining time the mind is creating more ideas, more imaginations, more dreams. You can never come to an end – it is simply impossible. And if you cannot come to an end, the rock bottom, your understanding of the mind is very superficial.

The East does not believe in analysis. It believes in awareness. In two ways the difference is of tremendous importance. First, for analysis you have to depend on somebody else; it creates a dependence, almost a kind of addiction. Once people have been in psychoanalysis, it is very difficult to get them out of it, because at least twice a week while in psychoanalysis they feel a little light, unburdened, a little relaxed. The mind will gather the tensions again because the roots have not been cut; you have been only pruning the leaves.

And just when you prune a leaf watch what happens: three leaves will come in place of the one you have cut. The tree takes the challenge. You cannot destroy the tree; it is also a living being. It shows its effort to survive. You cannot destroy it by cutting its leaves; hence if you want a tree to have a thick foliage, you have to prune it. By pruning it, the foliage becomes thicker, not thinner.

So first, in psychoanalysis you have to depend on somebody else. And you become addicted, just like with any drug. Yes, let me call the psychoanalysis prevalent in the West and borrowed by the East a very subtle drug. And to come out of it is almost impossible. You get tired with one psychoanalyst, then you move to another psychoanalyst. It is just like getting immune to one drug, then you move to another drug which is stronger and more dangerous. Soon you will become immune to that drug too. It won't affect you. Then you will have to move ahead again.

I have been in monasteries in Ladakh where they had been taming cobras, because there is a certain school in India which tries awareness through drugs. It is perfectly scientific. Its approach is scientific, but very dangerous. One can go wrong any moment, on any step. It has to be done under a master. One starts by taking small doses of a certain drug and getting immune to it; then a stronger drug, then an even stronger drug; and finally a moment comes when no drug affects the man.

At that point only the poison of a cobra can affect him a little bit. He is not being killed by the cobra. You will be surprised to know – a man who is bitten by a cobra does not survive, but these ascetics I have seen in Ladakh...and they are in many places, in Assam, in Nagaland. The cobra has to bite them on their tongue so the poison immediately reaches to their bloodstream, and you will be immensely amazed that the cobra dies from biting them! Those people have become so full of poison that the poor cobra....

This is the fire test. When a man can kill the cobra and not be killed by the cobra, he has become immune to all kinds of poisons in the world.

But the basic method in that school is also awareness. You have to keep alert and aware; that's why no drug affects you. That's the whole process of a strange school – but the man attains to great awareness.

Psychoanalysis is a very mild drug. You become accustomed, immune to one psychoanalyst. You go to somebody who is stronger, who goes deeper into your mind and finds stuff that the first one has not been able to find. This goes on and on. Psychoanalysts have been around for almost a century, but in one hundred years, they have not been able to bring a man to the understanding of his mind. Psychoanalysis has failed utterly.

Awareness has a beauty: it does not depend on anybody else; it is just the arising of a new force that has been dormant in you. And you don't analyze the mind. That is an absolutely futile exercise. You simply watch the mind without any analysis, any judgment, any appreciation, any condemnation, any evaluation – you simply watch, as if you have nothing to do with it. You are separate and you are watching the mind.

But this separation creates the miracle, because the mind is a parasite; it lives on your blood, it lives on your energy. Because you are identified with the mind, it lives. You are nourishing its roots. So the whole process of psychoanalysis is simply stupid. You are not cutting the roots; you are nourishing the roots and you are simply cutting the leaves. The foliage will become thicker and thicker.

It is no wonder that psychoanalysts go mad four times more than any other profession, and four times more psychoanalysts commit suicide than any other professions in the world. If this is the situation with psychoanalysts, what to think about their patients? The patients have fallen into wrong hands. But psychoanalysis is in fashion and it is one of the most highly paid professions in the West.

It has been joked about around the world that the Jews missed Jesus; it was their own boy who created the greatest profession in the world – of the priests and the monks, Catholics and Protestants. They have never been able to forgive themselves. Now Catholics are the richest religious organization. The Jews cannot forgive themselves that they unnecessarily crucified their own boy who was creating a great profession.

But they have taken revenge through Karl Marx, by creating another religion, communism. Karl Marx was a Jew. If half the world is Christian, then the other half of the world is communist. They are even. And they are even better off, because through Sigmund Freud, another Jew, they have created a highly paid profession in the world. But neither Christianity nor communism has been of any help; nor has psychoanalysis been of any help. They all have exploited men in different ways.

Communism has taken away the whole dignity of man, his pride, his individuality, his freedom.... Christianity has destroyed the very possibility that you have a reality of your own. You are just a puppet in the hands of God. The strings are in his hand. If he wants you to dance, you dance; if he wants you to cry, you cry. You are not a master of your own destiny.

And then finally psychoanalysis comes, and this also has not been able to give man back his dignity. Now patients in millions, around the world are in the hands of the psychoanalysts. And they depend on them as their father-figure and those father-figures themselves suffer from the same sickness, from the same schizophrenia, from the same split personality.

The Eastern method given by the mystics in the first place gives dignity to man, gives him pride and makes him aware: you have a hidden source of awareness – just wake it up and become aware of the mind. You don't have to do anything: just becoming aware of the mind, you are separate. And the moment you are separate, you are no longer nourishing the roots of the mind. The mind will soon wither away, without any analysis; what is the need of analyzing it?

That's why Bodhidharma is saying: Awareness, beholding the mind, is the most essential method to have a breakthrough. And once you have gone just a step beyond the mind, you have entered the world of nirvana, you have entered the world of light and eternal life. You have attained to spiritual integrity, freedom, and tremendous ecstasy which the mind cannot even dream about.

Those who understand the mind reach enlightenment with minimal effort. Those who don't understand the mind practice in vain.

And psychoanalysts should be included with those who don't understand the mind, and are practicing on themselves and on others something absolutely in vain. It is sheer wastage of time and life and energy. Psychoanalysis has to understand the mystical ways of the East, and then it will go through a transformation and it will be of tremendous help to people.

But the trouble is the profession will be gone, and thousands of psychoanalysts who are earning so much money will not be ready for the whole profession to finish. This is a problem. It is such a deep problem that some way has to be found. Otherwise, even if somebody understands the fact intellectually, he will not be ready to do anything, because that will destroy his own vested interest.

It is like the doctors: they help the patient to be cured, but deep down they want the patient to take as long a time to be cured as possible. They don't want to kill him because that would not help their profession, but they would like him to hang between life and death as long as possible, because the longer he is hanging between life and death, the longer they are earning money. If he is cured, their earning is finished. If he dies, their earning is finished. So they neither want him to live nor do they want him to die. They want...and this is very unconscious, maybe no doctor is clearly aware of it.

I have heard.... A young man came home from the medical college after attaining all his degrees. His father was a doctor and he had sent his son also to become a doctor. On his first day in the practice he saw an old woman whom he used to see coming to his father when he was a child. He could not believe that she was not yet cured.

He said to the father, "Now I am here, and you are old and must be tired. You rest. I will take care of the patients."

And after three days he told his old father, "You will be surprised: the woman that you could not cure in thirty years, I have cured in three days!"

The father hit his head with his hand. He said, "You idiot! That woman has been providing money for your education! And you have cured her. She is so rich that she could have been able to provide for your other two brothers who are in college. And she is strong enough; she will not die, but we have to keep her just in the middle."

The boy could not understand. The old man said, "First learn the basic rule: if a poor man comes to you, cure him quickly. And if a rich man comes to you, then take your time; go slowly."

To avoid this situation in China, they have practiced for thousands of years a very different system. And I think that system should be the system for the future man too. In China the doctor is not paid for curing the patient, he is paid if his patient remains healthy. Every doctor has his patients and the patients pay him if they remain healthy. If they fall sick, then the payment to the doctor stops. Then he has to cure them at his own expense.

This looks strange, but in the Soviet Union also they have started the same process – they are experimenting on a small scale. But the process is tremendously significant. Everybody should be given to a certain doctor; a certain area should be given to him. If the people are healthy in that area, they have to pay the doctor; they pay for their health. But if they fall sick, then the doctor has to cure them from his own pocket. Naturally he will cure them quickly and he will not want anybody to be sick. Obviously China has been a healthier country than any other country in the world. They have changed the whole pattern.

The psychoanalyst should be paid only if the person who is his patient is becoming independent, alert, getting beyond the mind. But if he falls into the mind or below the mind, then the psychologist has to cure him from his own pocket. That will change the whole situation.

Awareness is your own power.

And to depend on your own power brings a great freedom and a great authority and a great integrity. The mind is cut from the roots; soon it withers away. And the space that mind was occupying is no longer occupied by anything; it is now pure space. That is your real, authentic being.

Just in the last line I cannot agree with Bodhidharma. I don't know – and there is no way to know – whether it is his own line or added by his disciples when they were writing the notes. But it does not matter. What matters is that I should make you aware that the last line is wrong when he says: *To find something beyond the mind is impossible.* No, it is not. That is the only possibility for human growth. That is the only possibility for enlightenment: going beyond the mind.

So I want to add: *To find something beyond the mind is impossible*...except yourself, except enlightenment, which are different names of the same thing.

To find yourself is enlightenment.

Except for enlightenment, certainly you will not find anything beyond the mind. But without this addition the statement remains dangerous and can corrupt people's minds. They can stop with the mind, thinking that there is nothing beyond it. And in fact, everything is beyond it. What is in your mind? Just soap bubbles, signatures on the water, or at the most, sand castles which just a little breeze may be able to demolish.

Your mind is nothing but a fiction. But when you are living in the fiction it looks happier. Watch it from the outside, and the fiction disappears.

But the disciple asks: *But how can beholding the mind be called understanding?*

When a great bodhisattva delves deeply into perfect wisdom, he realizes...the activity of his mind has two aspects: pure and impure....

There is no need to be a great bodhisattva to know this simple fact. You can look into your mind and you will find this distinction: that you have activities which are pure, and activities which are not pure. You have love, you have hate; you have peace, you have tensions; you have compassion, you have cruelty; you have creativity and you have destruction. No need to be a great bodhisattva; everybody who has a mind can know without any effort that it has two aspects: pure and impure.

...The pure mind delighting in good deeds, the impure mind thinking of evil. Those who aren't affected by impurity are sages.

Again I would like just a little addition, otherwise there is going to be misunderstanding. The sutra says: *Those who aren't affected by impurity are sages.* Do they get affected by purity? In fact, the definition of a sage is one who is not affected by anything, pure or impure, because one who can be affected by purity cannot avoid being affected by impurity. They are not so different. So I would like to say: Those who are not affected by purity or impurity are sages.

They transcend suffering and experience the bliss of nirvana. All others, trapped by the impure mind and entangled by their own karma, are mortals. They drift through the three realms and suffer countless afflictions. And all because their mind obscures their real self.

The mind is just like a dark cloud around your self. It does not in fact damage your self, but because of the dark cloud you cannot see the sun. The sun is not affected by dark clouds. It is still shining in its grandeur, but the dark clouds can cover it so much that even the day starts looking like night.

The Sutra of the Ten Stages says, "In the body of mortals is the indestructible buddha-nature. Like the sun, its light fills endless space. But once veiled by the dark clouds of the five shades, it's like a light inside a jar, hidden from view." And the Nirvana Sutra says, "All mortals have the buddha-nature. But it's covered by darkness from which they can't escape. Our buddha-nature is awareness: to be aware and to make others aware. To realize awareness is liberation."

...Liberation from the mind, liberation from all afflictions, liberation from purity and impurity, liberation from good and evil, liberation from God and devil, liberation from all dualities and entering into oneness with existence.

Everything good has awareness for its root. From this root of awareness grow the tree of all virtues and the fruit of nirvana.

This is a significant sutra. The moralists, the puritans of the world have been teaching people, "Do good works, charity, service to the poor, learn to be kind, be virtuous, be celibate, stop being possessive; all good qualities you have to practice."

But Bodhidharma is saying what I have been saying my whole life: that these are not possible to be practiced; they are by-products. You can only create more awareness in yourself, and all these things will come up on their own accord. And then they have a beauty of their own. If practiced they are only hypocrisies – they don't go very deep. They are just masks, but they don't change your original face.

This is where morality and authentic religion differ completely. Morality teaches you superficial things: be good to others, be nice to others, be a gentleman, be non-violent, be compassionate and avoid all that is thought to be evil – cruelty, anger, greed. You can manage, millions are managing. And they are respected deeply, by all kinds of fools that the world is full of. But their morality is not even skin-deep. Just scratch them a little, and suddenly you will see they have forgotten all their practices and their real barbarous nature comes out.

I have heard about a Christian saint who was continuously repeating in his sermons, "When somebody slaps you on one cheek, remember Jesus Christ and what he has said: 'Give him the other cheek also.'" It is a beautiful teaching, but only if it comes from your innermost core. If it comes out of your awareness, it has a different significance. If you practice it, then it is not of much value.

One day it happened: A mischievous fellow, just to see whether the saint himself gives the other cheek or not, stood up and he said, "Now let us see: you have been telling us again and again to give the other cheek." He was a wrestler so the saint got very afraid, and the wrestler came and gave him a good slap on one cheek. But the saint had to keep his word; his congregation was there and everybody was watching what would happen.

He gave him his other cheek thinking, "I have never done any harm to this fellow. He should feel ashamed and guilty." But the wrestler was really a mischievous fellow. He gave an even bigger slap on the other cheek. But then he was suddenly surprised and the whole congregation was surprised: the saint jumped on the wrestler and started beating him this way and that way. He was not expecting it. Although he was a wrestler he forgot; it was so unexpected. He simply could manage to say, "What are you doing?"

The saint said, "What am I doing? Jesus has only said: 'Give the other cheek.' I don't have a third cheek. Now I am free from that discipline and I will show you what it means." It is very easy to practice, but a practice has a very thin layer which can be scratched.

One sannyasin asked me a few days ago...she was going after the evening discourse, on her bicycle to the place where she is staying. And a Poona-ite came on his motorbike, stopped the poor girl and squeezed one of her breasts. This they call in Poona, "Hindu culture."

The girl was asking me, "According to Jesus Christ, should I have given him my other breast too?"

Even I have not thought about it, that it is not only a question of cheeks. She has asked a really profound question, "What do you say, what should I do in such a situation?"

But basically the teaching of Christ is only a morality. You don't have to give your other cheek, and you don't have to give your other breast. You should have slapped that man as hard as possible, because these so-called Hindu chauvinists...and this city has a strange ego. They think it is a very cultural city; it is a dead city, it is a cemetery. But certainly in a cemetery nothing happens. How this ghost managed to come on the motorbike I don't know, but ghosts are interested in women's breasts because their whole life, when they were alive, they were interested in women's breasts. So even when they are dead, the old habit continues.

There is no need...it is not *my* teaching to give the other cheek, because what will you do when he hits the other cheek? You don't have a third one!

Her question reminded me about a conference of psychoanalysts. A very old psychoanalyst, who has been a disciple of Sigmund Freud, was reading a paper before the conference. And just in the front row was a beautiful woman who was a psychoanalyst. Another psychoanalyst, who was very famous, was playing with her breasts. And it was such a constant disturbance to the poor fellow who was reading the paper. He was hiding his eyes, but even – he was also after all a man, the same kind of man.... So once in a while he was looking at what was going on. And he could not believe what kind of woman this was...that old ugly fellow was playing with her breasts and she was listening to the paper as if nothing was happening. And so much was happening to the man who was reading the paper, who had no breasts and nobody was doing anything to him!

But the question: what kind of woman was this? The man was simply ugly although he was a famous psychoanalyst. But fame does not change people; fame simply makes them more hypocritical, fame simply makes them do things in the dark, from the back door. Their front door is kept very clean and very pure, with pictures of all the great saints.

Somehow he managed to finish. It was very difficult to finish the paper – because his priority was to ask the woman – and as he finished the paper he stepped down from the podium and went directly to the woman. As he went there, the old man pulled his hands away. He said to the woman, "The whole time I was reading the paper, I have been seeing this man playing with your breasts, and you did not object."

The woman said, "I am a psychoanalyst. It is his problem. Although he is old, he is not grown up; he is childish, immature. It is his problem; nothing to be worried about."

The reader thought it strange but that gave him an idea that it was his problem too. Why should he be disturbed? Perhaps he wanted to be in that old man's place....

Your so-called moralists, your so-called preachers, your so-called psychoanalysts, your so-called philosophers are just so superficial. And they are carrying the whole load of problems inside them, because they have not cut the roots and they have taken the whole situation from the wrong end.

Bodhidharma is very clear when he says: *Everything good has awareness for its root. From this root of awareness grow the tree of all virtues and the fruit of nirvana.* He far transcends moralists, puritans, so-called good people, do-gooders. He has touched the very rock bottom of the problem.

Unless awareness arises in you, all your morality is bogus, all your culture is simply a thin layer which can be destroyed by anybody. But once your morality has come out of your awareness, not out of a certain discipline, then it is a totally different matter. Then you will respond in every situation out of your awareness. And whatever you will do will be good.

Awareness cannot do anything that is bad. That is the ultimate beauty of awareness, that anything that comes out of it is simply beautiful, is simply right, and without any effort and without any practice.

So rather than cutting the leaves and the branches, cut the root. And to cut the root there is no other method than a single method: the method of being alert, of being aware, of being conscious. Be more conscious, and everything that will happen through you is going to beautify this existence, make it more divine, make it more mature. Your awareness will not only bring flowers to you; it will bring fragrance to millions of people.

Awareness is the golden key to the gate of God.

Okay, Maneesha?

Yes, Bhagwan.

THE COURAGE TO SAY "I DON'T KNOW"

達磨

Beloved Bhagwan,

You say that our true buddha-nature and all virtues have awareness for their root. But what is the root of ignorance?

The ignorant mind, with its infinite afflictions, passions and evils, is rooted in the three poisons: greed, anger and delusion. These three poisoned states of mind themselves include countless evils, like trees that have a single trunk but countless branches and leaves. Yet each poison produces so many more millions of evils that the example of a tree is hardly a fitting comparison.

The three poisons are present in our six sense organs as six kinds of consciousness, or thieves. They're called thieves because they pass in and out of the gates of the senses, covet limitless possessions, engage in evil and mask their true identity....

But if someone cuts off their source, rivers dry up. And if someone who seeks liberation can turn the three poisons into the three sets of precepts and the six thieves into the six paramitas, he rids himself of affliction once and for all.

But the three realms and the six states of existence are infinitely vast. How can we escape their endless afflictions if all we do is behold the mind?

The karma of the three realms comes from the mind alone. If your mind isn't within the three realms, it's beyond them.

And how does the karma of these six differ?

Mortals who don't understand true practice and blindly perform good deeds are born into the three states.... Those who blindly perform the ten good deeds and foolishly seek happiness are born as gods in the realm of desire. Those who blindly observe the five precepts and foolishly indulge in love and hate are born as men in the realm of anger. And those who blindly cling to the phenomenal world, believe in

false doctrines and hope for blessings are born as demons in the realm of delusion.

...If you can just concentrate your mind and transcend its falsehood and evil, the suffering of existence will automatically disappear. And once free from suffering, you're truly free.

THE SUTRAS FOR this evening... Bodhidharma is facing the ultimate question which nobody has ever been able to answer. The ultimate question is ultimate because it cannot be answered. Every philosophy, theology, mysticism, finally comes to the ultimate question, and there is no answer for it.

But even a man like Bodhidharma, a man of tremendous courage, intelligence, awareness, still has not the ultimate courage to say that there is no answer to this question. He tries – just as millions of philosophers, thinkers, mystics, have always tried but have always failed.

He also tries as if there *is* an answer and he knows it, but whatever he says is not the answer and the question remains untouched. What he says is exactly what is written in the scriptures of the Buddhists. Here he is no longer responding to the question immediately, out of his own awareness; otherwise he would have simply laughed and recognized that there is no answer for it.

I could have simply said, "I don't know." But to say, "I don't know" needs the greatest courage in the world. Even Bodhidharma does not have that ultimate courage. But I have got it! I will not in any way try to camouflage – through philosophical jargon, or theological hypotheses – to hide the fact that there is no answer and create an illusion of an answer.

Whatever Bodhidharma says here is only an illusion. He is trying his best to rationalize it, to support it from the scriptures. Perhaps he may have been able to pacify the disciples, but he cannot pacify me!

First I will read the disciples' question. Their question is more important than the answer of Bodhidharma. Their question at least has a sincerity, an authenticity. Bodhidharma's answer is just to hide the fact that ultimate questions remain questions. This is the whole reason why we call the essential religion "mysticism." If everything can be answered, then there is no question of any mystery.

Existence is a mystery because you can go on answering, but finally you cannot answer the ultimate question. And it is not far away; it soon comes up. You can answer all superficial things, but as you go deeper the ultimate question is coming closer. And the moment the ultimate question comes, I have not yet come across a single man in the whole history of mankind who has had the courage to say, "I don't know."

The question: *You say that our true buddha-nature and all virtues have awareness for their roots. But what is the root of ignorance?*

From where does the ignorance come in? In other words, in other symbols which will be more easily understood....

The religions that believe in God can go on answering questions up to the point where it is asked, "Who created existence?" They have a ready-made answer: God created it. Now comes the ultimate question: "Who created God?" Because if everything needs a creator, then God must need a creator. And if God needs no creator, then why bother about God? Then why can't you accept existence itself – without a creator? If you have to accept somewhere or other, then it is better to stop with existence as the ultimate, because at least we know it – we are part of it.

God is just a hypothesis. Existence is reality. But all the religions have moved from reality to the hypothesis, and then they are faced with a problem which nobody has been able to answer. And nobody will ever be able to answer it, because any answer is going to lead into an infinite regress.

If you say that God Number One was created by God Number Two, the question remains the same: "Who created God Number Two?" You can go on and on and on. But whatever the number, the question will still remain relevant, "Who created this God?" And this is the same question from which we have started, "Who created the universe?"

So God has not been of any help. The hypothesis has not done any service. God is simply a futile hypothesis. It is just a pretension of an answer, but it is not a true answer because the question remains the same. A true answer means the question should disappear. That is the criterion.

In Buddhism there is no god. In the place of god is the ultimate awareness, the buddhahood, the buddha-nature. This is only a different language.

Now the disciples are asking: We can understand that *the buddha-nature and all virtues have awareness for their root.* But from where has the ignorance come in? Why in the beginning the ignorance? Why not the awareness from the very beginning? This is the same question, only a different theological framework. And any answer to it – without any exception, without knowing about it – I can say is going to be wrong.

We have simply to accept the mystery that we are born in ignorance and the possibility is intrinsic in us to dispel this ignorance and become aware. We are born in misery, but with an intrinsic potential to overcome it, to transcend it, to become blissful, to become ecstatic. We are born in death, but with the possibility of going beyond death into immortality.

But if you ask from where the death comes in, from where the ignorance comes in, from where the misery comes in, you are asking an ultimate question. There is no answer for it. It simply is the case. It is better to use Buddha's expression, "suchness." Such is the case.

But Bodhidharma could not say that. He started answering. The only right answer would have been, "I don't know." And Bodhidharma would have done a tremendous service to humanity. He missed! Whatever he is saying is very childish. It has to be very childish, because it is not possible that a man like Bodhidharma will not be aware of the fact that he does not know the answer. Nobody knows the answer. Nobody can know the answer because nobody can *be* before the beginning.

Just think of it for a single moment: you cannot *be* before the beginning. If you are before the beginning, then it is not the beginning. You are already there, so the beginning must have been before you were there. And unless somebody can be before the beginning, there is no witness who can say, "God created the world."

Who can say from where ignorance came? All that we can say is that existence is drowned in ignorance and slowly, slowly, a few courageous beings are moving into awareness, rising above the darkness of life and attaining to the light which is eternal.

In another reference, Gautam Buddha makes it clear...although he also never recognizes at any point that it is a mystery and he doesn't know.

I want you to understand that it remains a mystery and it will always remain a mystery. By its very nature there is no way to know the beginning.

But in a different context, Buddha has come very close. He says, "Ignorance has no beginning, but an end. And consciousness has a beginning, but no end." This way he completes the circle. I will repeat it, so that you can deeply feel it: Ignorance has no beginning, but an end. And because ignorance ends, awareness has a beginning, but it has no end. It goes on and on forever.

With this, Buddha is recognizing the fact that it is better not to ask about the beginning of ignorance and not to ask about the end of awareness. These two things will remain forever mysterious. And these are the most important things in existence.

If the question was asked of me, I would simply say, "I don't know," because that is the most sincere answer. It simply means that it is a mystery.

But Bodhidharma starts trying to answer the question, and you can see it does not even touch the question at all. *The ignorant mind*...now the question is from where the ignorance comes, and he has already accepted it, without answering:

The ignorant mind, with its infinite afflictions, passions and evils, is rooted in the three poisons: greed, anger and delusion.

Is this the answer? He is saying the ignorant mind is rooted in certain things: delusion, anger, greed. But was this the answer? Was the disciple asking it? Was he asking for this kind of explanation?

The question was, "What is the root of ignorance?" And if you answer that for example greed, anger and delusion are at the root of ignorance, you are simply postponing the answer. Again the question will arise, "From where comes the greed? From where comes the anger and from where the delusion?" And then you fall into a vicious circle. Then you start saying, "They come from ignorance. It is because man is ignorant; that is why he is greedy, that is why he is angry, that is why he is deluded." And when we ask from where this ignorance comes, "It comes from anger, from greed and delusion." Whom you are trying to befool?

But for centuries these kind of answers have befooled people. Perhaps nobody questioned these irrelevant answers – either because they were so much impressed, so much overwhelmed by the individuality of a man like Bodhidharma, or perhaps they could not figure out that Bodhidharma is simply creating more smoke around the question, so they cannot see their question clearly. He is throwing dust into their eyes. It is not an answer.

But this is not only the case with Bodhidharma. This is the case with everyone...with Gautam Buddha, with Mahavira, with Confucius, with Lao Tzu, with Zarathustra, with Jesus, with Moses...with everyone without exception. Whenever they come close to the ultimate question, they start talking nonsense. And these are very sensible people, very intelligent people.

But the ultimate question can be answered not by intelligence but by innocence, can be answered only by an innocent person, a person who does not care for any respectability, for any wisdom, for any enlightenment, who can risk everything for his sincerity.

These people were not able to risk their wisdom. They could not say, "I don't know." But that is the only authentic answer, because that gives you the sense that you have come to the ultimate: now begins the mystery – and it is unsolvable. There is no way to reduce it into knowledge. It is not an unknown which can be made known by efforts, by intelligence, by practice, by discipline, by any method, by any ritual.

The mystery can be lived, but cannot be known. It remains always, unknowable. It remains always, a mystery.

One man, a great contemporary, G.E. Moore, has written a book, *Principia Ethica*. And perhaps he is the only man in the whole of history, who has thought so deeply just to define the word "good." Because without defining good, there can be no ethics and no morality. If you cannot define what is good, then how you can decide what is moral, what is immoral; what is right, what is wrong.

He took a fundamental question, without knowing that it is the ultimate question and he got into trouble. And he was one of the most intelligent people of our contemporary world. He looks at it from every direction enquiring for almost for two hundred and fifty pages, just on a single question, "What is good?" And he was utterly defeated in defining such a simple word as good. Everybody knows what is good, everybody knows what is bad, everybody knows what is beautiful and everybody knows what is ugly. But when it comes to definition – you will be in the same trouble.

He was thinking that everybody knows what is good...there must be some way to find the secret and define it. But finally, after two hundred and fifty pages of very concentrated thinking, of the keenest logic and rational analysis he comes to the conclusion that good is indefinable. These two hundred pages have been just going round and round and reaching nowhere. Good is indefinable.

Croce has done the same work on "beauty"...one thousand pages. He has gone far deeper than G.E. Moore has gone into "good." And after one thousand pages, comes the last statement: that beauty is indefinable.

Everybody knows that the most difficult problem is that it is very difficult to find a man who does not know what beauty is and what ugliness is. But don't insist on a definition. Even the greatest minds have failed.

This is accepting failure, when they say beauty is indefinable. G.E. Moore became so frustrated that he said, "Don't blame me that I have not been able to define what is good. Even simpler questions – this is a very complex question – are indefinable. For example, what is yellow...?"

That is what G.E. Moore asks, "Can you define what yellow is?" You all know what yellow is. There is no doubt about it. You can all indicate towards a marigold flower...this is yellow. But he is not asking for indications; he is asking, "How have you come to know that this is yellow? What is the definition? What is the criterion that this marigold flower fulfills? Why it is not red? Why is it yellow? You must have certain definitions. Why is something red and something blue and something green and something yellow...on what grounds?"

And then he says, "If yellow cannot be defined and although everybody knows what it is, nobody says, then perhaps all our knowledge is just very superficial."

Perhaps we have never enquired deeply into anything; we have never gone to the very rock-bottom. Otherwise my own understanding is everything is indefinable, because everything is mysterious. It is not only a question of beauty, or good, of ignorance, or awareness – everything, the whole existence consists only of indefinables. To recognize this is to recognize our ultimate ignorance. And to be able to recognize our ultimate ignorance, you need an absolutely selfless, egoless innocence, because that has been missing.

Bodhidharma is doing the same as everybody else has done. And it is not a new thing – for centuries philosophers have been indulging in simple questions.

You all know two plus two is four. But you have never gone deep into enquiry, whether it is so, or just hearsay. You have heard people saying two plus two is four, so you are repeating it generation after generation.

Bertrand Russell, one of the greatest mathematicians of our age, and perhaps of all ages, has written a book, *Principia Mathematica*. It takes him two hundred and fifty pages to go into the question, whether or not two plus two is four. You cannot even conceive what he will be writing in two hundred and fifty pages.... Two plus two is simply four and forget all about it. Two hundred and fifty pages...such a dense, logical argumentation that his book is one of the most unreadable books in the world.

Just a few crazy people like me, who don't care whether it is readable or unreadable.... I have seen in many university libraries that the book has not even been opened. Many pages are joined – nobody has cut them, because even to read two pages is enough! It is one thousand pages in all and one-fourth has gone only in discussing whether or not two plus two is four.

And the conclusion? The conclusion is that it is only a belief. It cannot be said with certainty, that two plus two makes four. It is a utilitarian concept. It is good, workable, but Bertrand Russell has not been left unchallenged – even on that. Another mathematician, Godel, challenged it. Because Godel says there is no possibility of two plus two being four. There is no possibility at all. And Godel has the same quality of genius as Bertrand Russell. He is not in any way a smaller genius – perhaps a greater genius. His argument is very clear and Bertrand Russell has not been able to answer it.

Godel argues that you can put two chairs and two chairs together and naturally, there are four chairs. but two in itself is just an abstract symbol. Two chairs is another matter. Two is just a concept. It is as hypothetical as God, or the devil. Have you seen two anywhere? Have you met with two and said hello? Have you ever seen two with two meeting and hugging each other?

And Godel's criticism is that two things in existence are never exactly the same; something is always different. You cannot find two people the same; you cannot find even two leaves in the whole forest exactly the same. Then how can two leaves which are not equal, together with two other leaves which are also not equal, be four? They can be three, they can be five, they can be anything, but not four!

And I understand Godel is right. Of course my understanding comes from a totally different dimension. To me, Godel is more appealing because that makes existence mysterious. You cannot even count on such simple answers as two and two are four. Everything is pragmatic. But as far as reality is concerned, it remains unknowable.

So you have to remember this. I will go through the answers of Bodhidharma, but it is not the answer. It may be useful to go into it: it may help you to understand something else but it is not the answer to the question.

But it is not Bodhidharma's fault. There is no answer. His only fault is that he is not recognizing that he doesn't know. And I cannot forgive him for that because I love him and I respect him and I wanted him to be sincere. Had he said, "I don't know," he would have risen far above the thousands of other mystics and buddhas and bodhisattvas and arhatas. He would have become absolutely unique, but he could not manage.

The ignorant mind, with its infinite afflictions, passions and evils, is rooted in the three poisons: greed, anger and delusion. These three poisoned states of mind themselves include countless evils, like trees that have a single trunk but countless branches and leaves. Yet each poison produces so many more millions of evils that the example of a tree is hardly a fitting comparison.

The three poisons are present in our six sense organs as six kinds of consciousness, or thieves. They're called thieves because they pass in and out of the gates of the senses, covet limitless possessions, engage in evil and mask their true identity....

But if someone cuts off their source, rivers dry up. And if someone who seeks liberation can turn the three poisons into the three sets of precepts and the six thieves into the six paramitas, he rids himself of affliction once and for all.

All this is okay. But can you see it as an answer to the question? It is true, that if you can change your greed, your anger, your delusion – the poisons – with awareness, they transform into nectar. The same that was your disease, becomes your health. The same that was your bondage, becomes your freedom. All that is needed is to bring awareness into the darkness of your being.

This is true. We have already discussed it many, many times in different ways. But it is not the answer to the question: "From where does the ignorance come?"

This is also true, that if you cut the root then the tree withers away. And the root of your bondage, of your blindness, of your darkness, is your mind. If you cut the root of the mind – and the root of the mind is identity with yourself... when you are angry you say, "I am angry." That is the root. If you are *really* aware when you are angry, you will not say, "I am angry." You will say, "I am seeing anger passing through my mind." If you can say that, you are a seer, you are a witness. The root is cut.

One Indian sannyasin, who traveled far and wide in the world, was Ramateertha. He had a very strange habit of never using "I." Instead of using I, he would use the third person for himself. For example, "Ramateertha is thirsty." He would never say, "I am thirsty." He would say, "Rama is thirsty."

With those who knew him, there was no difficulty. But he was continuously traveling all over the world. For many years he was in America and people could not understand when he would say, "Rama has a headache." They would ask, "Where is Rama?" Or, "Rama is thirsty," or "Rama is feeling sick."

In a strange land, he was moving with strange people and they were continuously saying, "This is a strange way of speaking. Why can't you simply say that you are thirsty? Why make it unnecessarily complicated?" But he was practicing a certain method of cutting the root. By not saying, "I am thirsty, I have a headache, I am feeling sick, I am feeling sleepy," he was trying to avoid the "I" and trying to be just a watcher. "Rama has hunger; Rama is thirsty" or "Rama is suffering from a headache." He is just a witness reporting to you that this is what is happening to Rama...if you can do something, do it.

He was trying to pull himself away from whatever was happening in his body, in his mind, in his heart. He was trying to clarify himself completely from all identities. He wanted just to be a witness.

To be a witness is to cut the very root, and you will be liberated. This is perfectly right. But this is not the answer to the question.

I will go on insisting on the fact that Bodhidharma is creating unnecessary verbiage...so much prose. Perhaps the disciples forgot about the question, but I cannot forget and neither can I forgive. Everything that he is saying is right in other contexts, so he is not saying anything wrong. But whatever he is saying, although it is right, is not at all relevant. And just being right is not the question. The answer has to be relevant to the question.

He goes on creating more and more.... *But the three realms and the six states of existence are infinitely vast.* What relation has it to the source of ignorance, from where it comes?

How can we escape their endless afflictions if all we do is behold the mind? The disciples are asking another question. They have been deceived. They think they have received the answer to their first question. They have not received the answer, because there is no answer.

Now they are asking another question:

But the three realms and the six states of existence are infinitely vast. How can we escape their endless afflictions if all we do is behold the mind?

They are caught by Bodhidharma. He has deceived them. He has brought them to a question that can be answered.

I am reminded of a doctor who was treating a very rich woman...just for a common cold, but it was not going away. The doctor was tired because every day she was standing in his clinic with the complaint that the cold has not gone – and in fact, there is no treatment for the common cold.

Those who know say, "If you take medicine, it goes in seven days. If you don't take medicine, it goes in one week."

But the doctor was tired. Every day the rich lady in her limousine...and as he would hear the limousine being parked in front of his door, he would say, "My God, she is back again. That common cold is going to kill me."

Finally he became so fed up that he said, "Listen, there is only one cure. I have not told you because it is a little difficult." The woman said, "No problem. I am ready to do anything, but I want to get rid of this cold."

So he said, "You do one thing: just behind your palace where you live is a big lake. So get up in the middle of the night, when it is absolutely cold and freezing, drop all your clothes and take a jump into the lake."

The woman listened breathlessly to what kind of treatment it was. "...and then stand on the shore, naked. Don't dry the water on your body. Let the breeze take it away."

And the woman said, "My God, this is treatment for a common cold? This will give me double pneumonia!"

The doctor said, "That is right. I have a treatment for double pneumonia, but I don't have a treatment for the common cold. So first create double pneumonia; then everything is within control. When you come back, come with double pneumonia and I will treat it. But for the common cold, I just don't have any other treatment. This is the only treatment. When somebody wants to be treated, then I have to give him this as a last resort. If you can manage to create pneumonia, or double pneumonia…no fear. I have experimented perfectly and have found a valid treatment for them. I guarantee it; you just do what I have told you."

That is what philosophers have been doing. Whenever you ask them the ultimate question that cannot be answered, they start going into pneumonia, double pneumonia. And ordinary people get puzzled with their words. They either think their question has been answered, or perhaps they have forgotten the question by the time the long sermon ends.

They are asking another question. Now there is no problem; they are asking, "There are so many afflictions and existence is so vast, and one has so many lives and so many evil acts…just by beholding the mind, how can one get free of all that?"

Just a simple cure, so simple: watch your mind and everything is finished. It is unbelievable. People want something complicated, because the problem is complicated.…

In millions of your lives in the past you must have done uncountable evil acts, you must have dreamed uncountable evil dreams. If you have not committed crimes, you may have thought to commit them. That makes no difference – whether you actually murder somebody or you simply think of murdering somebody, in both cases your mind is functioning in an evil way. It is vibrating in an evil way, and the mind carries those vibrations for millions of lives. Now so many past evil actions have been accumulated, how can they be dropped just by beholding the mind?

But this is not the ultimate question. This is a very simple question…because you may have dreamed your whole life. In the night you may have dreamed that you lived a hundred-year life. And the time scale between waking and dreaming is different: if you fall asleep in a single second, you can dream a long dream of years' duration. And when you wake up and look at your watch, you are puzzled: just one minute has passed. In one minute, how could you manage a long, long dream? Years and years have passed in the dream.

In dreams the time scale is different. When you wake up, the time scale is different. We don't yet know exactly what the time scale is in dreams; otherwise, we might be able to create watches which you can wear when you are asleep which will give you exactly the right time. They will not be in minutes and hours; they will be years, and perhaps light-years because you can dream that you have been on the moon, you can dream that you have been on the farthest star.

It takes four years to reach to the nearest star and four years to come back – and that is about the nearest star! There are stars which will take four million years, five million years to reach, and then five million years to come back. You can manage in a single night; in a single dream, you can reach to the farthest star and you can come back too. You have to come back. You cannot remain there. It is not possible that you can wake up in your room and not find yourself there because you are gone....

I have heard: Two friends were talking with each other about the dream they had last night. One man said, "Boy, what a beautiful dream...such big fish! In my whole life I have not been able to catch so many big fish. It was such a joy...the whole night, I was going in and in, inside the lake, and finding bigger and bigger fish."

The other said, "This is nothing. You cannot even conceive what happened last night in my dream." His friend said, "What happened?"

And the man said, "I am thinking if I should say it or not – because you will not believe it. Even when I am awake, I myself cannot believe it but it happened. Suddenly I found that in my bed, on one side is Sophia Loren. I said, 'My God, how did she get in?' and I turned to look at the other side and I found Marilyn Monroe. I said, 'What is happening? Have I died and reached heaven?'"

By this time the other fellow had become very angry. He said, "You idiot, why did you not call me? When two women came...what were you doing with two women? One is enough for you. You could have chosen. It was your dream of course, so the first choice was for you. But the other woman belonged to me. What kind of friendship is this?"

And the other man said, "I went to your house but they said you had gone fishing."

In a small dream you can do everything...possible, impossible, everything! The time scale is different. In the morning when you wake up, do you ask how it was possible that just by waking up, all the dreams have disappeared – so many dreams, such beautiful dreams...?

The same is the situation when a man becomes enlightened. All the millions of lives simply evaporate like dreams. It is not a question of fighting with each and every evil act separately – that you have to fight on, doing good, balancing the evil – then it will take millions of lives again before the time you can become awakened.

And meanwhile, in these millions of lives when you are trying to undo your past, you will still be continuing to do something or other and that will go on accumulating. You cannot get out of this trap. The only way to get out of this trap is to wake up.

Nothing else is needed. You don't have to change your anger, you don't have to change your greed, you don't have to change anything. You have simply to be alert and aware. And all the projections of greed, all the projections of anger, all the projections of delusion, will evaporate – just the way, every morning, your dreams evaporate. They are made of the same stuff as dreams are made of.

So it seems a simple method and inconceivable to the rational mind that it can solve anything. Just by watching your mind everything will be transformed and you will discover your buddhahood, your ultimate beauty and joy, your ultimate existence, your greatest ecstasy. How is it possible? That's what the disciples are asking.

Bodhidharma says: *The karma of the three realms comes from the mind alone. If your mind isn't within the three realms,* it is no-mind, *it is beyond them.*

The moment you are aware, the mind becomes silent. And all the actions, good or bad, are created only by the mind. They are just like a film that you are seeing on the screen of the mind. Once you wake up, the film disappears. Suddenly there is a blank screen...utterly silent, nothing moving, absolute stillness.

Mortals who don't understand true practice and blindly perform good deeds are born into the three states.... Those who blindly perform the ten good deeds and foolishly seek happiness are born as gods in the realm of desire. Those who blindly observe the five precepts and foolishly indulge in love and hate are born as man in the realm of anger. And those who blindly cling to the phenomenal world, believe in false doctrines and hope for blessings are born as demons in the realm of delusion.

...If you can just concentrate your mind and transcend its falsehood and evil, the suffering of existence will automatically disappear. And once free of suffering, you are truly free.

The words he is using are theological, but what he is saying is that those who are living in greed want more and more pleasure. They can project a life of heaven, they can be born in heaven as gods, but this will be only a mind projection. It will be only a belief.

I used to live with a professor and when one day I talked about projection, he was not ready to believe that everything is a projection. He had a younger brother and I had been watching the younger brother, because we had lived almost three months together in the same house. The younger brother had become very much attached to me and I was interested in him because I could see he had a tremendous capacity to be hypnotized.

Thirty-three percent of people are very capable of being hypnotized. It is a very strange percentage – thirty-three percent, because only thirty-three percent of people are talented, too. And only thirty-three percent of people are ever interested in any kind of inner search. And only thirty-three percent of people are open, available, to be hypnotized. There must be some inner connection between all these things. Perhaps the quality of being hypnotized may be the criterion for a man's possibility of going inwards. Because in hypnosis one goes inwards with the help of others; in meditation, one goes inwards on his own. But the way is the same.

So to prove to this man – who was a professor of logic and never believed in anything unless some evidence was produced – I hypnotized his younger brother. And I was surprised that even in the first sitting, he went so deep that there was no need to have more sittings. I was thinking at least nine sittings and then the experiment could be done. But he went so deep in the first sitting that I told him, "Tomorrow, exactly at twelve o'clock – and tomorrow is Sunday so I will be at home, your brother will be at home, you will be at home – don't go anywhere. Exactly at twelve o'clock you have to kiss the same pillow you are lying on right now. I am marking the place with a cross; exactly on that cross you have to kiss."

I repeated it again and again and again. And when I became certain that it had become an imprint in his unconscious mind, before waking him up I made a cross on the corner of his pillow with red ink.

It took almost half an hour to bring him back, he had gone so deep. After waking up, he became normal except for one thing; again and again he used to look at the pillow and particularly at the cross. And then he would also feel embarrassed at what he was doing, because there was no reason to look at the pillow and at the cross. His conscious mind was not aware at all, but his unconscious mind was now projecting something of which he was not aware.

The next day, near about eleven-thirty, he became very restless. Something from the unconscious was going on, telling him to do something which of course he was thinking was insane...to kiss. And I was present, his brother was present and I had told his brother that he had to just sit and watch what happened.

At eleven-fifty, I took the pillow, put it in my suitcase and locked it. And you could see what was happening to that young boy...tears flowing from his eyes. And I asked, "What is the matter? Why you are crying?"

He said, "I don't know, but don't put my pillow in your suitcase. I beg you."

I said, "But what is wrong? I will give it back to you, by the evening when you go to sleep."

He said, "No, I need it right now."

"What is the need?"

"I don't know any need. That is why I am crying, because I cannot give any explanation, but I need the the pillow immediately."

So I gave him the key. He rushed – because it was getting close to twelve – he opened the suitcase, took out the pillow and started kissing that cross almost like mad. Just like any lover who has found his beloved after many years.

I asked him, his brother asked him, "What are you doing?"

He said, "I don't know, but I feel such a relief. Such a burden has been removed from my heart. But I don't know what...who has made this cross, why I have such tremendous compulsion that if I don't kiss the cross I may die. I had to do it exactly at twelve. That was coming from inside me and I don't know anything about it."

His brother said, "I accept the evidence."

When you become infatuated with a woman, do you think your woman is just a cross on the pillow? A biological infatuation? A projection from the unconscious, very deep rooted – not by anybody, but by nature itself.

Your hormones, your chemistry, your biology, they are all functioning in a certain conspiracy against your awareness. They are making you restless, they are making you irresistibly attracted towards somebody and it is beyond your power to prevent yourself from this attraction or infatuation. You will be pulled like a puppet.

It is not coincidental that all languages say, people fall in love. People certainly fall in love – fall into unconsciousness, fall into biological hypnosis, fall into the instinctual nature. They are no longer conscious human beings. That's why this kind of infatuation and love affair finishes very soon. Once you have got the woman, once you have kissed the pillow...finished! A great burden, a great relief, but it was a pillow.

So it was a simple phenomenon, but the woman you have kissed...and you cannot kiss without a preface. It needs some introduction – going to the movies, to the disco, all kind of things as preliminary necessities. Promising all kinds of promises, bringing roses and ice cream – this is the preface. And after all this preface, when you kiss a woman, she is not just a pillow. Now she will cling to you. Now you cannot escape. Now you want to escape but your own preface has created the prison. Now you cannot go against your word.

All the seekers of human consciousness absolutely agree on the point that all your misery or your happiness, your sadness or your joy, is nothing but your projection. It is coming deep from your unconscious mind and the other person is functioning only like a screen.

Once it is fulfilled, you are finished. And suddenly, the same woman you suddenly, the same woman you were ready to die for...you are ready to kill her.

Strange...such a great change. Love turns into hate so easily. And yet you are not aware that love and hate both are your projections. When one is finished, the other remains there.

It is true that once you are free from suffering, you are truly free. All that Bodhidharma is saying is right. But he has not answered the question.

I want to say to you that nobody has answered the question. And the reason is because life is a mystery.

You can go only so far, and then all your mind has to be left behind and you enter into existence where no question is relevant, no answer ever comes to you.

But you can enjoy the experience immensely. I am all for experience, not for knowledge.

I feel sad and sorry for Bodhidharma, because he has failed me. If he had said, "I don't know" he would have raised himself as the highest and the greatest mystic the world has ever known.

But I want to say to you: I don't know. And I want to emphasize that you should also remember, whenever there is an ultimate question, don't try to deceive others or yourself. Simply accept your innocence. Say with humbleness, "I don't know."

It is not a question of ignorance. It is a question of your awareness that life is a mystery, a miracle. You can taste it but you cannot express anything about the taste. You cannot define it. And this is the greatness of existence. This is where all scientists have failed, this is where all philosophers have failed. This is the only place where mystics have succeeded.

Bodhidharma is a mystic and if he meets me... and somewhere there is a possibility in this eternal life, this unending existence, someday, somewhere I am going to catch hold of him. And he will recognize me because I am wearing the same sandals that he was carrying on his staff – the exact type. My sandals come from the Zen monasteries of Japan. It is particularly Zen – Zen people have everything of their own. Even if they use cups and saucers from the market, first they break them, then they glue them back together. Then they make them unique, then there is no other piece like that – then it becomes Zen, original, and without any other copy anywhere. Just one of a kind.

This sandal that you see has been used by Zen people since Bodhidharma, for almost fourteen centuries. The first sandal was sent to me by a Zen master from Japan as a present.

So he will immediately recognize me. I have just to show him my sandals. And I have to ask him why he missed a great opportunity...when he could have become the greatest mystic in the world. And he had every capacity. He has the genius for it.

Okay, Maneesha?

Yes, Bhagwan.

TAKE THE RISK WHOLESALE

達磨

294 ___ TOBU: JUMP

TAKE THE RISK WHOLESALE

Beloved Bhagwan,

But the Buddha said, "Only after undergoing innumerable hardships for three asankhya kalpas did I achieve enlightenment." Why do you now say that simply beholding the mind and overcoming the three poisons is liberation?

The words of the Buddha are true. But the three asankhya kalpas refer to the three poisoned states of mind. What we call *asankhya* in Sanskrit, you call countless. Within these three poisoned states of mind are countless evil thoughts. And every thought lasts a kalpa. Such an infinity is what the Buddha meant by the three asankhya kalpas....

But the great bodhisattvas have only achieved enlightenment by observing the three sets of precepts and by practicing the six paramitas. Now you tell disciples merely to behold the mind. How can anyone

anyone reach enlightenment without cultivating the rules of discipline?

The three sets of precepts are for overcoming the three poisoned states of mind. When you overcome these poisons, you create three sets of limitless virtue. A set gathers things together – in this case, countless good thoughts throughout your mind. And the six paramitas are for purifying the six senses. What we call *paramitas,* you call *means to the other shore.* By purifying your six senses of the dust of sensation, the paramitas ferry you across the River of Affliction to the Shore of Enlightenment.

According to the sutras, the three sets of precepts are, "I vow to put an end to all evils. I vow to cultivate all virtues. And I vow to liberate all beings." But now you say they're only for controlling the three poisoned states of mind. Isn't this contrary to the meaning of the scriptures?

The sutras of the Buddha are true. But long ago, when that great bodhisattva was cultivating the seed of enlightenment, it was to counter the three poisons that he made his three vows. Practicing moral prohibitions to counter the poison of greed, he vowed to put an end to all evils. Practicing meditation to counter the poison of anger, he vowed to cultivate all virtues. And practicing wisdom to counter the poison of delusion, he vowed to liberate all beings. Because he persevered in these three pure practices of morality, meditation and wisdom, he was able to overcome the three poisons and reach enlightenment. By overcoming the three poisons, he wiped out everything sinful and thus put an end to evil. By observing the three sets of precepts, he did nothing but good and thus cultivated virtue. And by putting an end to evil and cultivating virtue, he consummated all practices, benefited himself as well as others and rescued mortals everywhere. Thus, he liberated beings.

BODHIDHARMA IS NOW really facing a question for which he has no answer. The case was the same in last night's sutra and it continues because the disciples are asking more and more about the ultimate, which simply baffles all knowledge. It is a peace, a silence...there is no answer.

But it is really difficult to accept that you are enlightened and you don't know the answers to the ultimate questions. Then what has your enlightenment done for you if it has not solved the mystery? Then what kind of wisdom have you received?

This has to be clarified for you. It is sad that Bodhidharma did not clarify it for his disciples; on the contrary he continued to answer questions which cannot by their very nature be answered.

But this is a problem that every master has to face. When the questions are trivial the master is perfectly at ease to answer, but as the disciples become more and more keen in their enquiry and they start touching the ultimate, the master comes to a difficult situation. So as not to let the disciples feel that the master does not know, he goes on answering – but those answers are not true answers. They are in themselves perfectly right for some other questions, but not for the questions that have been posed before him.

The question is very important. But even the greatest masters like Bodhidharma belong to a particular line of philosophy, a particular set of doctrines; hence they have to keep on repeating the ideological system they have accepted.

It is totally different with me. I don't belong to any ideology. I don't have to console anybody. I am not concerned with who gets annoyed and irritated. My sole concern is that when you ask a question, you need a sincere answer – not according to ideology but according to my own experience.

The disciple asks: *But the Buddha said, "Only after undergoing innumerable hardships for three asankhya kalpas did I achieve enlightenment." Why do you now say that simply beholding the mind and overcoming the three poisons is liberation?*

The truth is a little complicated. First I will explain my position, if I were to answer the question. Then it will be easier for you to understand the difference, when a person answers because of a certain ideological school that he belongs to, and when a person answers just out of his own experience and response.

The Buddha has certainly said: *"Only after undergoing innumerable hardships for three asankhya kalpas did I achieve enlightenment."* But as far as I can see, this is not a true statement of Gautam Buddha himself. It is what the Mahayana school of Buddhism maintains is the answer. Now Buddha is not there to refute it, and everything that he has said has been written after his death. And it has been written by common consent: a great gathering was called of all the old disciples who had been listening to him from the very beginning, and they assembled what everybody remembered.

There was dissension, there was conflict, there was contradiction, and the whole gathering divided into thirty-two groups and they separated from each other. And all thirty-two groups have their own scriptures, their own reports of what Buddha said. Mahayana is only one school, the biggest, which has the greatest following. And certainly the reason why it has the biggest following is that it says that Buddha, once awakened, remains on this shore to liberate people.

In fact, they have even invented a story: When Buddha reached the doors of *moksha,* the ultimate resting place for liberated beings, the doors were opened and there was great music and celebration because it rarely, very rarely happens that a man comes to such great enlightenment. Thousands of years pass and the door remains closed. Naturally there was great jubilation among the other buddhas who had entered moksha during the millions of years that had passed. They were welcoming a new guest.

But Buddha refused to enter the gate. He turned his back towards the gate and told the gatekeeper, "Please close the gate. I will stand outside the gate until the last human being has become enlightened. It may take millions and millions of years – it does not matter. I'm at peace. I'm in absolute ecstasy. I can wait. But this will be a little selfish to enter the gate and forget all about those who are still groping in the darkness."

Every effort was made to persuade him that this is not the way…nobody has done this before. He said, "That simply means nobody has entered moksha with a compassionate heart. For compassion towards my human brothers and sisters, I can renounce moksha itself. It does not matter to me. It cannot give me more than I have already got. I will stand here before the door and when the last human being has passed in, then I will pass through."

This is a fictitious story of the Mahayana school. Because of this idea of compassion for other human beings, naturally Mahayana attracted more people who are not able to become awakened on their own. They need help. They need a compassionate, awakened person. And the Mahayana school preaches that every enlightened person in Mahayana will be doing every possible thing that he can do to make more and more people liberated. Because he has now a dual duty: people have to be liberated and secondly, if people are not liberated, Gautam Buddha has to stand at the gate for millions of years. So compassion for the people – they have to make every effort to liberate them, and gratitude to Gautam Buddha and his strange stand, that he is boycotting moksha, the the ultimate state of silence and peace and rest just to make sure that nobody is left behind.

The other school is Hinayana; it has not attracted so many people. The very word means "the small boat." Mahayana means "the big ship"...an ocean liner, so thousands of people can go to the other shore together. But in a small boat, only one man can go. And the people who created Hinayana are the arhatas. They are enlightened and their standpoint is that even to make an effort to liberate people is interfering with their individual freedom. It is not compassion, it is not love: love gives freedom.

Compassion does not force a certain way of life on people, and liberation is a certain way of life. Although it is for their good, still you are forcing them, insisting on it, that they follow the path, that they don't waste time. You are not allowing them total freedom to be themselves. When they feel like moving on the path, they will move. And if they don't feel to, it is nobody's concern. It is their absolute right to remain in the world and not to go to moksha.

The arhatas interpret compassion in a very refined way, with a very total, different perspective.

It is very difficult to choose who is right. Both seem to be right.... But Hinayana naturally could not gather as many disciples. Who would be interested in the people in the Hinayana school, who are not even interested in your liberation? They will not speak, they will not support, they will not give you a hand to pull you out of the ditch. They will simply wait. If you are capable of falling in the ditch you are certainly capable of getting out of it. If you are capable of falling into wrong paths, you are perfectly capable of feeling the misery, the suffering of the wrong path; you can change your path. Nobody else can do it for you.

So this is the Mahayana interpretation, that Buddha took millions of ages to become enlightened. For the arhatas the situation is totally different. They say it is not a question of millions of years and arduous effort. It was all a dream. Whether you dream for three million years, or three days, or three minutes, it makes no difference. The moment you wake up, all the dreams will be found to be simply hot air. There is no such tension then.

Even your disciplines – what you are practicing to obtain liberation – are really a kind of greed. And greed cannot destroy greed. It is ambition, and ambition cannot destroy the ego. Perhaps it is the greatest ambition – to be liberated, to be enlightened.

But wherever there is desire and ambition, you are in bondage. And all your practices and all your disciplines are but practicing in a dream. It is almost as if you are weak, but in your dream you do great gymnastics and you feel that you have become a world champion. But in the morning when you wake up, the same mouse is sleeping in the bed. What happened to all your gymnastics that you have been dreaming about?

You can dream about being a great sage, you can dream of being a great thief, you can dream of murdering many people, you can dream of serving many people but in the morning you will feel there is no distinction between all those dreams. They are all dreams made of the same stuff. They are all fictions. The good is as much a fiction as bad. The spiritual discipline is as much a fiction as murdering somebody. So those who don't believe in the Mahayana doctrine say you can become enlightened, here and now. That was really the position of Bodhidharma. And that is creating the problem now. He cannot say Buddha is wrong; that is impossible. He loves Gautam Buddha, he is a disciple of Gautam Buddha, so he cannot say Gautam Buddha is wrong. He has to say the words of the Buddha are true.

But his own position is that whatever you have been doing in your unconsciousness is meaningless. When you wake up it all disappears within seconds. And you can wake up at any moment. Just a certain right device and you will be awakened.

You can wake up in the middle of the night. The dreams cannot prevent you from waking up; neither can your sleep prevent you from waking up. It is just your own will not to wake up. That's why the sleep continues and the dream continues. If the will to wake up arises in you, then enlightenment is instantaneous.

Now this is Bodhidharma's own position. But he is in a difficulty because he belongs to the Mahayana school and he was teaching in China, to the Mahayana schools to which China belongs. Those disciples who were asking were quoting Buddha according to Mahayana sutras. Now nobody knows whether Buddha said them or they were inventions of a certain school, because in the Hinayana school those sutras are not found. And these are only two schools...the main ones. There are thirty other schools which are very small streams, but they also have something, a grandeur of their own, and they all differ.

But on one point they all agree: that Buddha cannot be wrong. They cannot say that Buddha is wrong. So they have to go round about saying that Buddha is right. Still, what they are saying is also right, although it is contradictory. The disciple is asking: "Why do you now say that simply beholding the mind and overcoming the three poisons is liberation? You are making it too simple."

Buddha himself is saying that he has been undergoing *innumerable hardships for three asankhya kalpas* – that is, innumerable ages – and then he achieved enlightenment. It was not instantaneous. It had a long history of millions of years behind it...of doing good, of avoiding evil, of practicing meditation, of practicing other disciplines. It took three innumerable ages for him to become a buddha.

If this was the situation of a Gautam Buddha, who seems to be the greatest human being who has lived on the earth, then what will be the situation for an ordinary man? Perhaps instead of three...thirteen asankhya kalpas, or thirty! But you are saying that just by watching your mind, just at this very moment, you can become enlightened.

How did these two different attitudes arise? If you don't understand the background, you will not be able to understand the difficulty of Bodhidharma. Buddha left his palace when he was twenty-nine years of age. He went to every great teacher who was famous in his day and he was such a sincere seeker that he risked everything. Whatever those teachers said, he did it more perfectly than they had ever expected from anyone. In fact, they themselves were not so perfect.

And Buddha said, "I have done it, but nothing has happened. I am still as ignorant as I was before. Yes, I have learned a certain skill. I can do a certain distortion of the body, by yoga. But that does not make me aware of my being; it does not deliver me the good, the truth."

His sincerity was indubitable. Even his teachers felt ashamed. They had never come across such a student. The teacher, the ordinary teacher, always likes mediocre students because compared to them, he is a great teacher. And whenever – sometimes it happens – a great student, who towers higher than the teacher himself, comes to him, then the teacher feels angry, irritated, because the student continuously brings questions which the teacher cannot answer. Whatever he answers, the student is always able to refute it.

One of my teachers got tired of me because for eight months continuously, I would not let him move a single inch. We were stuck on a single point. He would bring all kinds of arguments and he was looking into books.... I was also working hard to refute him and all the other students enjoyed it – because the teacher was so much engaged with me, he had completely forgotten to give homework, or to teach anything else. There was no time, because the first lesson had not yet been learned so he could not move to the second.

The examination was coming near and then he became really mad at me. He started shouting at me. I said, "Listen, you are an old man. If you shout so much, you may have a heart attack. And I hope it is not heart failure...just a small attack. But don't think that by shouting, you can shut me up. And if you think it is a match in shouting, I can also shout. And you are an old man – I will really enjoy shouting. So calm down."

He understood the point, but he left the class and went to the principal and said, "Now it is absolutely certain that either I remain in the school, in the college, or this student remains. You can choose." The principal said, "But what is the matter? Has he done anything wrong to you?"

He said, "He has not been allowing me to teach the students and the examination is coming close. All the students are going to fail, except for him. And he has a strange stamina. I have been working hard. I have never worked so hard, reading late into the night, finding new arguments, and the next day he simply refutes them. He is working harder than me. Of course he is young and it is very humiliating to get defeated every day. I resign. I will not come to the college again if you don't expel him." And he left for his home.

The principal called me. He knew me. I had brought so many trophies and so many cups from all over the country, from all the universities, for debating, for eloquence competitions... He was very happy that I had made his college famous nationwide.

He said, "I'm in a difficulty. Why are you irritating that old man? He is our oldest professor, well educated; he has two Ph.D.'s, has been conferred D.Litt. recently by the university. He is a well-known scholar and we cannot lose him."

I said, "You can keep him, but you are being unfair and unjust because I have not done anything harmful to him. He is the professor of logic and if a professor of logic cannot argue with a student, then who is going to argue? The whole subject of logic is argument and sharpening of arguments, and I'm really doing my work as every student should do. The students are behaving like dodos; they don't bother about the subject. They have other interests – somebody has a girlfriend, somebody has an interest in the movies – there are a thousand and one things in the world. And they study only at the end of the year.

"And now, because questions have become stereotyped, the same questions are being repeated every year. Just read four years' question papers and that is enough – prepare for twenty questions and you are going to find five questions from those twenty in your examination. There is no need to bother about the whole course because professors are lazy. Even to find a new question is difficult for them, so they just look at four or five year-old examinations questions and find questions – maybe they rephrase them. That is their whole work.

"And in the market now examination keys – which are a very profitable business – have appeared. Some retired professor knows perfectly well what is going to come up in the examination. He takes ten years of questions in his book and gives the answers to each point. You just purchase a key book. There is no need to go into the originals because that is a difficult task.

"And if you give the answers, nobody bothers whether you know it or whether you have crammed it. Those keys are made by retired professors in such a way that the answer is very small and can be crammed, so no intelligence is needed.

"I was trying…because I have not come to the college just to sit there. I am not interested in degrees – my interest is to sharpen my intelligence."

The principal said, "I can understand you, but still I will have to expel you. It is unjust and I am feeling guilty because I cannot let that professor leave. Without him, our whole logic department will collapse. He is the most senior professor and he's a very stubborn man. If he has said that he will not come unless you are expelled, he will not come. But knowing the injustice…you have not been doing anything harmful, you just don't have a teacher of a real caliber and genius.

"He is a mediocre man. He can write Ph.D. theses and he can be awarded a D.Litt. for his services, but he is not a genius. That I know. So I will expel you because he will insist on seeing that your name is there on the notice board and that you are expelled. But I will make arrangements for you in another college. I will phone the principal."

I said, "I don't want to create any trouble for your institution, or for you, or for the old professor. I have no antagonism towards him – I just feel a great pity. You make arrangements, but it is not going to be easy because this situation which has been happening for eight months, has become the talk of all the colleges in the university. Every principal knows…."

He tried. He phoned one principal who was very close to him and the principal said, "Just forgive me. You are sending a trouble to us because you cannot manage it."

He tried a few other colleges, because the city I was in was one of the most significant cities as far as education was concerned; there were twenty colleges in all. He called a few other principals, and everybody said, "You can send anybody else, but we have heard about that student. And you are the oldest college and you have the best professors. If they are ready to resign because of him, what will happen to our professors who are not so senior, who are not so experienced?"

The principal was in a dilemma. And I was sitting there listening to all this phone talk. I told him, "You will not be able to manage. I will manage myself. You just give me expulsion orders and I will manage."

And I arranged with one principal to enter his college on the condition that I would never come to the college. I would pay the fee but I would never come to the college. I would go to the library but not to the classes. I would not attend the classes, so no problem would arise. And the principal would see to it that I got the right attendance necessary for appearing at the examination. I said, "That's a great arrangement. In fact, I have always wanted it."

For two years I never went to a single class for a single day. But those two years were of great importance. I settled into the library as deeply as possible. Before the library would open, I was there and only when the librarian pushed me out because it was being closed did I reluctantly leave.

The same is the situation with Bodhidharma, who belongs to the particular school of Mahayana. Because China – the whole of China – does not have any other school except Mahayana. And to tell the Mahayana people that you can become enlightened just like a click of the fingers...it is not possible for them to believe, because Buddha himself said he had to do hard work for three asankhyas – innumerable ages – before he became enlightened. But Bodhidharma knew from his own experience that he had become enlightened without any austerity, without any discipline, without going through fasting, without doing prayers, rituals. He became enlightened just by becoming aware of his mind.

But to say that Gautam Buddha is wrong.... He would be surrounded by the whole country which believed that Gautam Buddha cannot be wrong. And in actual fact, for six years after leaving his palace, Gautam Buddha did everything, and all the teachers finally felt that he was a far greater soul than they themselves were. And they said to him, "Forgive us. All that we knew, we have told you. More than that is beyond our capacity. But we will suggest a greater teacher to you."

For six years he went from one teacher to another teacher, and finally, the greatest teacher of those days said to him, "You are wasting your time. No teacher can help you. It is time enough that you should be on your own.... Just watch your mind. I don't have any other teaching for you."

Tired of those six years of continuous discipline.... It was a full moon night. He had been was refused by the teacher and told, "Just watch your mind. There is no discipline for you; those disciplines are for mediocre minds. They are compromises, according to everybody's capacity – a certain ritual to console him that he is doing some work for enlightenment. Nothing will satisfy you unless enlightenment happens."

So he went away. A full moon night – he had left the teacher just a few days before. And he was sitting under the tree by the side of Niranjana in Bihar. In India even trees are worshiped – and I don't see anything wrong in it, because a tree is also a living being and they are very nice people. They don't do any harm to anybody. A woman had been a worshiper of that Bodhi tree. And she had told the God of the tree that if she became pregnant – because for years she had not been getting pregnant – if she became pregnant she would bring sweets, fruits and flowers as a present to the god of the tree.

And on the full moon night, she came. She had become pregnant and when she became absolutely certain and the physicians had said, "You are pregnant," she brought delicious food, sweets, flowers. Her name was Sujata. It is a significant name in the history of Gautam Buddha.

And he was hungry, because he had been fasting for months – very hungry. But he was a beautiful man, a prince, and because of the hunger he had become almost pale. And in the full moon night, he looked as if he were the god of the tree who had come out.

The woman could not believe it – she was a villager, and she really thought that the god of the tree had come out to receive her presents. She fell to his feet and offered him all that she had brought.

This was the first time in those six years that he had taken a full meal. And that too, in the night. It is not allowed for ascetics to eat at night, but now he was no longer an ascetic.

When the teacher had said, "All that you have to do is to watch," he dropped all disciplines, all asceticism. He had renounced his kingdom; now he renounced his renunciation too. For the first time he was perfectly relaxed. He ate well, and after six years he slept for the first time without any tension. There was no ambition. There was no desire. There was nowhere to go, nothing to be searched.

In this relaxed state, even in his sleep he became aware that he was watching his mind; just a small flame of awareness was there. Although the body was asleep, the mind was asleep, something beyond was alert.

And in the morning when he opened his eyes, the last star was disappearing.

And the actual fact was that as the last star was disappearing, he also disappeared as an ego, as a personality. The enlightenment was sudden. Suddenly he saw his authentic being.

Now the problem arose: Mahayanists say that this sudden experience happened because of those six years of continuous austerity – this is gradual enlightenment.

And there are people, a certain school, who believe in sudden enlightenment. They say it had nothing to do with those six years. If he had stopped at five years, the experience would have happened. And if somebody had told him the very first day, and if he had had the intelligence to understand it, it would have happened the very first day he left the palace.

Those six years are not a cause for the effect of enlightenment. Enlightenment cannot have a cause. Their reasoning is very clear. Bodhidharma has said in the sutras that enlightenment has no cause. Then the question of millions of ages and arduous effort is meaningless.

Enlightenment is always sudden.

If it is not sudden, it is not because the nature of enlightenment is gradual. It is because your mind leaves you gradually. You are not ready to take the risk wholesale. You take the risk retail, inch by inch, part by part – the American way, in installments. A little bit you lose today, a little bit tomorrow, a little bit.... It takes time because you are not ready to drop the mind in its totality, in this very moment. You say, "I will do it slowly…tomorrow, then the day after tomorrow. What is the hurry?"

So there are these two schools: the gradual school of enlightenment which appeals to many people because they don't have the guts to drop the mind immediately; and the sudden school of enlightenment which belongs only to people who have the heart of a lion, who can simply risk everything.

I remember a story about a Japanese actor. He was very famous in America and he earned millions of dollars. He wanted to return home, he had earned enough. But before returning home, he thought it would be better to go around the world. Then he would not have to leave his home again. Then he wanted to rest. But first he wanted to see every beautiful place around the world.

He reached Paris. His guide took him to many places and then he said, "Would you like to see a casino?" The actor said, "Certainly, I want to see everything. In Paris, not to see a casino is missing much." Casinos are gambling places and France has the best casinos.

And as he entered the casino and he saw people putting up hundreds of dollars, thousands of dollars…and he got interested in the game. He risked all his millions of dollars that he had earned in America – just on one stake, not gradually.

Even the owner of the casino was afraid. "What to do with this man? If he wins, my whole casino is gone. A strange fellow!" He had been in the business for so long but he had never seen a man putting millions of dollars at risk, at stake.

But there was no way to refuse; it was not possible to refuse. You have to accept the stake and fortunately for the casino owner, the Japanese lost. He lost every single dollar that he had earned and was hoping to live a retired life on. He had nothing.

He went into his hotel and went to sleep. In the morning he saw in a newspaper that a Japanese had committed suicide by jumping from a forty-story building, and naturally it was thought that it must be the same Japanese who had lost millions of dollars in the casino. So they mentioned that it seemed that it was the same Japanese who had lost millions of dollars the previous night and had not even a single dollar left for himself.

He read the news and he laughed and the owner of the hotel read the news and he said, "He was in my hotel. How did he reach the other hotel? He was a famous name." The Japanese rushed to his room and he was laughing so madly. The owner asked, "Why are you laughing?"

He said, "I am laughing because I am alive and this newspaper said I have committed suicide by jumping from a hotel. Some other Japanese has committed suicide." And it was a very logical conclusion by the journalist that it must be the same famous Japanese actor from America. The body was so distorted, so broken in pieces that there was no way to find out who the man was.

The owner of the hotel asked him, "It is strange. You lost all your life's earnings and still you slept well?" He said, "It does not matter. I enjoyed the thrill for a moment – this way or that. And I enjoyed the owner of the casino trembling. As far as money is concerned, I can go back and earn again. That is not a problem. It was not stolen money, I earned it."

The owner said to him, "But you could have played the way all gamblers play – small sums. You could have played the whole night. Why did you stake everything?"

And I was reading in his autobiography that he said, "I belong to the sudden enlightenment school. I don't believe in gradual installments. If you have to do something, do it totally and intensely. If you don't want to do it, then don't unnecessarily befool yourself by doing it partially."

Bodhidharma is authentically a man of sudden enlightenment. But he was initiated by the woman, Pragyatara. She was a Mahayanist and she sent him to China to help the growing religion there. The religion had grown like wildfire – just in six hundred years. It reached China at the time of Jesus Christ, five hundred years after Gautam Buddha. And after six hundred years, there were thirty thousand Buddhist temples and two million Buddhist monks in China, and that is not including the laymen.

Millions and millions of people, because they were really hungry.... Confucius had made them so hungry for religion because in Confucius' mind there was no soul, no religion. It is because of Confucius that China turned to communism because Confucius' mind was very close to that of Karl Marx; there was not much difference. Both believed that there is no God, there is no soul, and all religions are useless. Both believed that consciousness is just a by-product of five elements getting together, and death is the end. So there is no question of good actions or bad actions.

Confucius had been such a dominant figure, such an influential figure that the whole soul of the Chinese people was hungry. There was an appetite which the Buddhist monks fulfilled. There was a gap so there was no conflict, no quarrel. The Buddhists were accepted without any struggle against anybody.

And Pragyatara sent Bodhidharma because up to then, no enlightened men had gone to China. Many scholars had gone – thousand of scholars – who were trying to translate Buddhist scriptures into Chinese. But they were only scholars, and Pragyatara thought China needed to see an enlightened man. It deserved it. In just six hundred years, great work had been done – almost the whole country had gone from Confucius to Gautam Buddha. Pragyatara told Bodhidharma, "You have to go," and he went there. But his own enlightenment was sudden and in China the school that had spread to the people was Mahayana, which believed in gradual enlightenment.

This is the dilemma. The students are raising the question: Buddha says one thing and you are saying just the opposite. *Why do you now say that simply beholding the mind and overcoming the three poisons is liberation?* You are making it too simple, saying that one can do it now. Then what about Gautam Buddha's struggle for three innumerable kalpas...?

But perhaps even Bodhidharma is not aware about the distinction that I have made, that just before his enlightenment Gautam Buddha dropped all disciplines. That would have been the right answer: Gautam Buddha may have struggled for three or thirty innumerable kalpas – it was just a dream, and when the dream is broken it always happens in a single moment. Just a single moment before, you were asleep; after a single moment, you are awake. And when you are awake all dreams which were appearing so real, disappear.

This would have been the right answer, but it would not have fitted with the Mahayana school. That's why he goes on creating theological smoke around the question again.

The words of the Buddha are true. But the three asankhya kalpas refer to the three poisoned states of mind.

That is not true. He actually refers to innumerable lives in which he has struggled to achieve buddhahood and finally, in the last life, he has achieved it. Now Bodhidharma is trying to somehow make a plausible answer.

What we call asankhya in Sanskrit, you call countless. Within these three poisoned states of mind are countless evil thoughts.

Now this is all nonsense, because it is again not relevant to the question.

And every thought lasts a kalpa.

That is even worse than nonsense; it is absurd! – and you know it. A thought does not last even for an hour. Just try for any thought to remain in your mind for one hour continuously and you will be surprised – it goes on slipping out of the mind.

Mind is in a constant traffic. You cannot stand in the middle of the traffic, your thoughts are moving faster than anything. And one kalpa is a very long time. A thought does not remain even for a few seconds. Your mind is continuously a flux; it is just like a river.

Heraclitus says, "You cannot step in the same river twice because it going so fast. By the time you step twice, it is other water. It is the same river just for the name's sake, but the water that you have stepped in for the first time is no longer there."

I go a little further than Heraclitus. I say, You cannot step even once in the same river, because when your feet touch the upper part of the water, the lower part is rushing by. As your feet go a little deeper, the lower part and the upper part is rushing by. By the time you reach the bottom, everything has changed from the time when you first touched the surface of the water. You have not stepped in the same water, because every second new water is coming in and the old water is going out. Heraclitus is not aware that even stepping once in the same water is impossible. Twice is too much.

The same is the situation with the human mind: it is just a flux. Hundreds of thoughts queuing and going – relevant, irrelevant, consistent, inconsistent. But he is trying to make some sense of Buddha's statement.

Such an infinity is what the Buddha meant by the three asankhya kalpas.

No, he actually meant what the words say. Bodhidharma is imposing his own idea on it, just to dilute it, just to bring it closer to his sudden enlightenment idea.

In his place I would have said, "Gautam Buddha is wrong. What he is saying about the three innumerable ages must have been said before he became enlightened. It is not a statement made after his enlightenment. If he had ever said anything like that, it must have been before his enlightenment."

Even before his enlightenment he had five followers. Seeing him – a king and a perfect ascetic – five brahmin seekers had become his followers. They left because he accepted the food from Sujata, at night.

And the word *sujata,* has great implications. It means "well born," born into a very high family. Now anybody who is really born into a high family will not have that name. Sujata must have been a sudra, an untouchable woman. This is how the human mind and human psychology functions. If she cannot belong to a high caste, at least she can have a beautiful name which means that she is well born. Her name indicates that she certainly belongs to a very low strata of the society.

Seeing that Buddha was accepting food from a sudra woman – he was not even asking, "To what class do you belong?" and in the night he was eating joyously – all the five disciples left him immediately. "He is a fraud, a fake. We have been deceived. He is not an ascetic at all."

Buddha may have said something like that to those five disciples, but he was not enlightened then. And one has to remember that any statement which has been made by Buddha before enlightenment should not be taken into account at all. It means nothing. Only that which he said after enlightenment has significance.

Bodhidharma could have explained it very easily, but he is not as courageous as he has been believed for centuries to be. He cannot say the words of the Buddha are not true. He is trying to polish them and somehow dilute them and bring them closer to his own understanding.

But the great bodhisattvas have only achieved enlightenment by observing the three sets of precepts and by practicing the six paramitas. Now you tell disciples merely to behold the mind. How can anyone reach enlightenment without cultivating the rules of discipline?

He is really putting the disciples in a dilemma – and these are their last questions. Bodhidharma says that no discipline is needed, no austerity is needed. All that is needed is an awareness of your mind. And I agree with him absolutely. That's what brings enlightenment.

A man who is unconscious can discipline himself. He can shave just like the

Buddha...he can shave his head, he can eat only once in twenty-four hours, he can have only three sets of clothes – not more than that – but he will not become enlightened by this. If this were so, then all poor people who don't have even three sets of clothes, who sometimes have to go to bed without eating anything, would have become enlightened.

I have known people who have gone to sleep tying a brick on their stomach so they don't feel that their stomach is empty. Such poverty exists in many parts of this country. Would these people have become buddhas? – no. Enlightenment has nothing to do with poverty, fasting, discipline, religious rituals.

There is only a single way to enlightenment and that is creating more and more awareness about your acts, about your thoughts, about your emotions.

Bodhidharma could have said that exactly, but this is the trouble when you belong to an organization, when you belong to a certain philosophy, when you belong to a certain system of belief, when you are not a master of yourself, when you worship somebody else as a master...then this kind of dilemma is bound to happen. You have lost your individuality in a way. You have to support Gautam Buddha even if it goes against your own understanding.

Bodhidharma says: *The three sets of precepts are for overcoming the three poisoned states of mind. When you overcome these poisons, you create three sets of limitless virtue. A set gathers things together – in this case, countless good thoughts throughout your mind. And the six paramitas are for purifying the six senses. What we call paramitas, you call means to the other shore. By purifying your six senses of the dust of sensation, the paramitas ferry you across the River of Affliction to the Shore of Enlightenment.*

Can't you see that the answer has not even a far-off relationship to the question? It is not even a distant cousin.

Bodhidharma could not manage...to simply say the truth would have been the right thing: "Whether it goes against Buddha, or Krishna, or Christ does not matter – I have to be my own truth. If it goes against somebody else's truth, that is his problem, it is not my problem."

Truth has beauty when it arises in you, but if you are somehow trying to fix it into a certain system created by somebody else, you start distorting the truth. And to me that is one of the greatest crimes.

The question was simply significant, but the answer is not. The answer is right in some other context but this place is not the place for this answer. He should have said that for all those three innumerable kalpas and the disciplines and austerities, Buddha lived in dreams.

But perhaps he could not say this to the Buddhists of China, because he was sent from India to make Buddhism more solid and if he started speaking in this way, how was he going to make Buddhism more solid? He started compromising. And the moment somebody starts compromising, he loses touch with the truth.

Truth is an uncompromising experience.

According to the sutras, the three sets of precepts are – the disciples are asking again – *"I vow to put an end to all evils. I vow to cultivate all virtues. And I vow to liberate all beings." But now you say they are only for controlling the three poisoned states of mind. Isn't this contrary to the meaning of the scriptures?*

It is, but Bodhidharma is not capable of saying so. In fact it is said that Gautam Buddha made these three vows: to put an end to all evil, to cultivate all virtues and to liberate all beings – but this was before he became enlightened. Hence, it has no value at all.

After his enlightenment, he knew that all these vows were made in a state of dreaming. And what you decide in a dream, you are not supposed to follow when you wake up. You may have been flying in the dream – just like any bird across the sky – but when you wake up, you know it was a dream and you don't insist that you really flew like a bird.

These three vows were certainly made by Buddha, but they were made before his enlightenment. It is true nobody has asked Buddha, "What happened to your vows?" But Bodhidharma is being asked. He should have made it clear that they were made in dreams and dreams don't matter at all. What matters is the awakened consciousness – and then Buddha did not make any vows.

But instead of that, he goes on saying:

The sutras of the Buddha are true.

But you can see, even as he says *the sutras of the Buddha are true,* he has lost the authority and the strength that comes from sincerity, that comes from your own experience of truth. He has become mild.

But long ago, when that great bodhisattva was cultivating the seed of enlightenment, it was to counter the three poisons that he made his three vows.

He goes on again and again, bringing those three poisons to his help.

Practicing moral prohibitions to counter the poison of greed, he vowed to put an end to all evils. Practicing meditation to counter the poison of anger, he vowed to cultivate all virtues. And practicing wisdom to counter the poison of delusion, he vowed to liberate all beings. Because he persevered in these three pure practices of morality, meditation and wisdom, he was able to overcome the three poisons and reach enlightenment. By overcoming the three poisons, he wiped out everything sinful and thus put an end to evil. By observing the three sets of precepts, he did nothing but good and thus cultivated virtue. And by putting an end to evil and cultivating virtue, he consummated all practices, benefited himself as well as others and rescued mortals everywhere. Thus, he liberated beings.

He is not being authentic. He is simply trying somehow to manage the answer. The answer is not a spontaneous response. It is clever, intellectual. It may have satisfied his disciples; it cannot satisfy me.

I am nobody's disciple. I don't belong to any belief system. I love people from all over the world and I never compare them. They are all unique: a Zarathustra is a Zarathustra, a Mahavira is a Mahavira, a Buddha is a Buddha, a Jesus is a Jesus, a Moses is a Moses...they are so unique that you should not make one of them a criterion that everybody else has to fit with.

Bodhidharma himself belongs to the same category, but because of his compromise, he falls down. He could not maintain his uniqueness. He remains a disciple of Gautam Buddha – and how can a disciple say that the words of the master are not right?

It is a unique opportunity for you to listen to a man who has no master, and who has a tremendous respect for truth – whether it comes from Zarathustra, or Lao Tzu, or Buddha, or Moses, or Jesus, or Mohammed. If it is truth which rings bells in my heart, I am in absolute support of it. But if it is not true, I know my heart. The bells don't ring and I immediately know something is wrong.

Bodhidharma is trying to pacify, console. He is no longer interested in truth. He is more interested in spreading the message of Buddha, and that's where he loses his uniqueness; otherwise he is as unique a person as Gautam Buddha himself.

I cannot conceive of what happened to him why he could not say directly, "These words are not true. They are not true because they don't resonate with my being." But this is what happens when you are toeing the line of a certain party – political, religious, social. Then you have to be in agreement with everything, without choice.

The Buddhists were very happy with Bodhidharma because he established the discipline of Buddha in China, gave it a very solid foundation, and spread the message – not only to China, but from China to Taiwan, to Korea, to Japan.

He did a great job, but he fell down from the heights. He could have remained there if he had said the truth exactly and explained to the people, in a very simple way, "These are statements made by Buddha before his enlightenment, and anything he said before enlightenment is immaterial. To me, Buddha's statements after his enlightenment are pure gold."

I don't think Bodhidharma would have hurt the feelings of people. Perhaps he would have created a precedent for other enlightened people: You need not agree with everything. You have certainly an obligation to accept the truth from whichever direction it comes, but you don't have any obligation to agree with any untruth, any fiction created by the priests who know nothing of the truth.

He did the job for which he was sent, but he lost something beautiful in his own being. To me that is more important than the whole of China becoming Buddhist. A single individual in crystal-clear truthfulness is more important than millions of people fast asleep.

Okay, Maneesha?

Yes, Bhagwan.

WAKEFULNESS IS AWARENESS

達磨

Beloved Bhagwan,

You should realize that the practice you cultivate doesn't exist apart from your mind. If your mind is pure, all buddha lands are pure. The sutras say, "If their minds are impure, beings are impure. If their minds are pure, beings are pure." And, "To reach a buddha land, purify your mind. As your mind becomes pure, buddha lands become pure." Thus, by overcoming the three poisoned states of mind, the three sets of precepts are automatically fulfilled.

But the sutras say the six paramitas are charity, morality, patience, devotion, meditation and wisdom. Now you say the paramitas refer to the purification of the senses. What do you mean by this? And why are they called ferries?

In cultivating the paramitas, purification of the six senses means overcoming the six thieves. Casting out the thief of the eye by abandoning the visual world is charity. Keeping out the thief of the ear by not listening to sounds is morality. Humbling the thief of the nose by equating all smells as neutral is patience. Controlling the thief of the mouth by conquering desires to taste, praise and explain is devotion. Quelling the thief of the body by remaining unmoved by sensations of touch is meditation. And taming the thief of the mind by not yielding to delusions but practicing wakefulness is wisdom. These six paramitas are transports. Like boats or rafts, they transport beings to the other shore. Hence, they're called ferries.

But when Shakyamuni was a bodhisattva, he consumed three bowls of milk and six ladles of gruel prior to attaining enlightenment. If he had to drink milk before he could taste the fruit of buddhahood, how can merely beholding the mind result in liberation?

What you say is true. This is how he attained

enlightenment. He had to drink milk before he could become a buddha. But there are two kinds of milk. That which Shakyamuni drank wasn't ordinary impure milk but pure dharmamilk. The three bowls were the three sets of precepts. And the six ladles were the six paramitas. When Shakyamuni attained enlightenment, it was because he drank this pure dharmamilk that he tasted the fruit of buddhahood. To say that the Tathagata drank the worldly concoction of impure, rank-smelling cow's milk is the height of slander. That which is truly-so, the indestructible, passionless dharma-self, remains forever free of the world's afflictions. Why would it need impure milk to satisfy its hunger or thirst?

The sutras say, "This ox doesn't live in the highlands or the lowlands. It doesn't eat grain or chaff. And it doesn't graze with cows. The body of this ox is the color of burnished gold." The ox refers to Vairocana. Due to his great compassion for all beings, he produces from within his pure dharmabody the sublime dharmamilk of the three sets of precepts and six paramitas to nourish all those who seek liberation. The pure milk of such a truly pure ox not only enabled the Tathagata to achieve buddhahood, it enables any being who drinks it to attain unexcelled, complete enlightenment.

I FEEL GREATLY sorry for poor Bodhidharma. He has got into trouble – and this trouble was bound to arise because he belongs not only to a tradition of Buddhism, but to a sect of Buddhism, called Mahayana, "the great vehicle." Anybody who belongs to any tradition, any sect, any doctrine, is bound to be in the same trouble as Bodhidharma. Whatever he is saying is becoming more and more stupid and nonsensical for the simple reason that he cannot say anything against the tradition.

He had been sent from India specially to make Buddhism more solidly grounded. That was the order of his own master, the enlightened woman Pragyatara, who had said, "I am sending you to China not to disturb people but to establish Mahayana in the great land of China, because if the whole country is converted to Buddhism, one-fifth of humanity is converted." One person out of five people in the world is Chinese.

That reminds me of a man who was reading a newspaper in which he read that out of five people, four people are of different countries, different races, different religions but one is certainly Chinese. He called his wife who was working in the kitchen and told her, "Have you ever realized that out of five people in the world, one is Chinese?"

She said, "My God! It is good you told us because we already have four children. Now is the time for birth control, otherwise the fifth will be Chinese."

China has been one of the largest lands up to now. But by the end of this century India will go ahead; it will become more populated than China. Otherwise, for the whole of history, China has been the most populated land in the world.

And if Buddhism was spreading like wildfire, it was time to give it a solid foundation. Bodhidharma had been specially sent as a messenger because although during the six hundred years before Bodhidharma, thousands of Buddhist scholars had gone to China at the invitation of emperors to translate all Buddhist scriptures into Chinese, not a single one had been enlightened.

So Bodhidharma was sent specially to give people a certain taste of what enlightenment is. They had heard the word, they were enchanted with the idea, a great longing had arisen in millions of people to attain to enlightenment, but they had not even seen an enlightened person. His presence, his silence, his compassion...they were absolutely unaware; it was only theoretical.

By sending Bodhidharma Pragyatara had a certain specific purpose in her mind: to give China its first enlightened master. The trouble was that he could not say anything against Mahayana that would disturb all the new initiates into Buddhism. He could not say anything against Gautam Buddha, because nobody was going to listen to him.

They were so much impressed with Gautam Buddha and his life and his teachings that in just six hundred years, they created thirty thousand temples and monasteries. Two million people were initiated as Buddhist monks and almost the whole country became Buddhist. They may not all have been monks but they were laymen; they had started the journey hoping that one day they would also become monks. Five percent of the whole population of China had become monks.

It was a tremendous time of upheaval, change, transformation.

And Bodhidharma, I think, had not realized the responsibility that he was taking upon his shoulders.

As far as superficial questions were concerned, he was perfectly right and perfectly in tune with his own experience. But when the ultimate questions started arising – which are bound to arise sooner or later – if he had declared, "I do not know" at the first ultimate question, when he was asked "From where does ignorance come?"...if he had accepted his innocence, if he had announced, "I know how awareness can be created, but I don't know from where ignorance comes. Perhaps ignorance is forever there."

Ignorance never comes; it is just like darkness. Have you ever seen darkness coming or going? You always see light coming in and the darkness is not there. You always see light going out and the darkness is there. Darkness is always there – no coming, no going. It is the light that comes and goes. Darkness is simply the absence of light.

This would have been the perfect answer to the people: that darkness has always been there. There is no source for it because it is non-existential. Only something that exists can have some source. Light has source. In the same way, awareness has a source, consciousness has a source, but unconsciousness is simply nothing but darkness.

And if he had stopped there he would have done a tremendous job of protecting himself from falling into all kinds of nonsense. But he could not say "I do not know," because people had been expecting him for three years. The whole country had been waiting, Emperor Wu included, with great longing and desire for Bodhidharma, the first enlightened person to enter China. All their thirst would be quenched; all their questions would be answered. And his answers were not scriptural; his answers were from his own experience.

So he hesitated to say, "I don't know. I'm utterly innocent. At the most I can say darkness has always been there, ignorance has been always there. There is no root to it. It is rootless, causeless, because it is non-existential." That would have been my answer.

He could have told them, "I have come here to teach you how to get out of ignorance. I don't know how you have entered into ignorance. That is your business."

But rather than doing that, he went into long, theological descriptions. And that allowed the disciples to ask more and more about things which he was perfectly capable of answering but then those answers were going to be against Mahayana, or even against Gautam Buddha.

So he is in a very difficult dilemma. He knows what is right and he also knows what is traditionally right. And he proved not as strong as I have always thought.

He could not prove himself to be a true revolutionary. He could not go against the tradition. I will show you how he becomes mixed up and how he starts talking nonsense. He has to – just to console the traditional people, just to keep in line with the orthodox theology.

This question also belongs to the same category. And he falls into such idiotic answers that it becomes almost hilarious. Once in a while he is true, but only once in a while. Most of the time what he is talking about is irrelevant and I for one absolutely disagree with his answers.

The sutra: *You should realize that the practice you cultivate does not exist apart from your mind.*

This is true. Whatever you practice, you have to practice through the mind. Hence enlightenment cannot be attained through practice. Because if enlightenment could be attained through practice, that means it is a by-product of the mind, just like any dream, any hallucination, any illusion, any thought. And just as thoughts disappear, your enlightenment may disappear at any moment.

I had one German sannyasin, Gunakar, who has become enlightened so many times that now he has stopped completely, dropped the whole idea. When he became enlightened for the first time – he has a beautiful castle in Germany, in a very beautiful, scenic place – he declared his enlightenment to all the presidents and prime ministers and to all the ambassadors and to all the members of UNO. He wrote a letter...he informed me also....

I said, "Gunakar" – he had just gone from here a week or two weeks before and I had not seen any sign that he was going to become enlightened so soon. I informed him, "Just come back; first I have to see...."

So he came back, and as he came back, slowly, slowly as he came closer to Poona, enlightenment disappeared. He became aware that this was stupid..."I don't know anything." But in Germany it was perfectly good, because nobody understands what enlightenment is. When he declared, "I am enlightened," people thought, "Perhaps...nobody has ever heard what this enlightenment is. He may be." And naturally, nobody contradicted it. But he became afraid, and when he came in front of me he said, "Just forgive me. I have become absolutely unenlightened again."

I said, "Remember that whenever this desire arises in you, before acting and starting to write letters to all world governments and ambassadors and presidents that if they want any advice, you have become enlightened; first, you have to come here."

Two years he remained silent and one day I received his letter again. He said, "Bhagwan, this time it has really happened and I am coming."

I said, "Okay, come."

And as he came to me he said, "Just forgive me. This is very strange. When I come here I become unenlightened and when I go back to Germany the desire arises, and nobody is there who can even say that I am not enlightened. Why wait? Declare! And the desire becomes so persistent...."

It happened many times. The last time I heard he had joined a commune and he was washing dishes there. Somebody who was going to see me soon asked Gunakar, "What are you doing? Have you ever heard of any enlightened man washing dishes in a restaurant?" It was the commune restaurant.

He said, "Forget all about enlightenment. Let me just do my dishes and if you are going to Bhagwan, just tell him that I am not going to become enlightened – at least not in Germany! If I have to become enlightened, I will become enlightened when I am close to him. I am feeling immensely joyful just washing the dishes and that enlightenment was such a torture..." because he started just imitating me.

He closed himself up in his castle on the mountain. He would not come out of his room. He would not meet with anybody. He had a secretary and naturally he got unnecessarily tortured. He could not come out, otherwise he would lose his enlightenment. He could not meet people, only the secretary, and the secretary informed them that he was in samadhi. "He cannot see anybody. Don't disturb him."

He said, "I have suffered enough because of this enlightenment. Now I am enjoying life more as a dishwasher in the restaurant of the commune. At least I can go out, I can go to a movie, I can go to the disco, I can sing and dance. That enlightenment was a very difficult thing, just remaining closed in one room...."

Enlightenment cannot come from the mind. Enlightenment can come only when the mind disappears. In fact, enlightenment is the light and mind is the ignorance. Enlightenment is the wisdom; mind is the darkness.

If your mind is pure, all buddha lands are pure.

I would like to correct it. I would like to say, if your no-mind – which means beyond purity and beyond impurity – is the buddha land.... It is not the pure mind which is the buddha land. Even the purest mind is still mind. And purity and impurity are a duality. And buddha land has to be beyond the dual. It cannot be one part of duality. It has to be beyond both.

There was in India a poet, Surdas, who has been worshiped by Hindus as a great saint. Surdas saw a beautiful woman – he had gone to beg, not aware of who was inside the house. He knocked on the door and a beautiful woman opened the door. And suddenly a desire, a fancy for her arose in his being. It was natural; it was not wrong. If you can enjoy a beautiful flower, why can't you enjoy a beautiful face? But religions are very much against all pleasures. It seems all religions have been founded by masochists. Torture yourself! The more you torture yourself, the more you become spiritual.

Surdas became very much guilty – and he had done nothing; just the face was so beautiful that it was natural a great appreciation arose in him. But it was against the religious precepts. He destroyed both his eyes and he became blind. And because of this blindness, he has been worshiped for centuries as a great saint.

But do you think by destroying his eyes, he would have stopped dreaming? Just the opposite – then he would dream more and more of that beautiful face. The face that was beautiful would become more beautiful, more fancy, in his dreams. And this is the meaning of charity?

Charity simply means an unconditional sharing. It has nothing to do with the eyes and nothing to do with the visual world and its abandonment. It simply means you have something; you should enjoy to share it. Don't be a miser. Don't hold on to it because this whole life is going to end one day and you will not be able to take anything with you. So while you are alive, why not share as much as you can? Things which can be taken away any moment...it is better that you share them. And it is a great joy to share. The man who learns the art of sharing is the richest man in the world. He may be poor, but his inner being has a quality of richness that even emperors may feel jealous of.

I have always loved a small Sufi story: A poor man, very poor, a woodcutter, lived in the forest in a small hut. The hut was so small that he and his wife could sleep...only that much space was in the hut.

In the middle of one dark night, it was raining hard and somebody knocked on the door. The wife was sleeping close to the door. The husband said to the wife, "Open the door. The rain is too much and the man must have lost his way. It is a dark night and the forest is dangerous and full of wild animals. Open the door immediately!"

She said, "But there is no space." The man laughed and said, "This is not a palace of a king, where you will always find a shortage of space. This is a poor man's hut. Two can sleep well; three can sit. We will create space. Just open the door."

And the door was opened. The man came in and he was very grateful and they all sat and started talking and gossiping and telling stories to each other. The night had to be passed somehow because they could not sleep; there was no space. And just then, another knock....

The man, the new guest, was now sitting by the side of the door. The owner of the hut said, "Friend, open the door. Somebody else is lost." And the man said, "You seem to be a very strange fellow. There is no space."

He said, "This was my wife's argument too. If I had listened to her argument, you would have been in the forest, eaten by the wild animals. And you seem to be a strange man that you cannot understand that we are sitting just because of you. We are tired after a long day. I am a woodcutter – the whole day I cut the wood and then sell it in the market and then we can hardly get food once a day. Open the door. This is not your hut. If three persons can sit comfortably, four persons can sit a little closer, with a little less comfort. But we will create the space."

Naturally he had to open the door, although reluctantly. And a man entered and he was very grateful. Now they were sitting very close; there was not even a single inch of space left. And then suddenly, a strange knock, which did not seem to be a man's! There was silence from all three; the wife and the two guests were afraid that he would say open the door.

And he said it. "Open the door. I know who is knocking. It is my donkey. In this wide world he is my only friend. I carry my wood on that donkey. He remains outside, but it is raining too much. Open the door."

And now it was the fourth guest to be allowed in, and everybody resisted and they said, "This is too much. Where is the donkey going to stand?"

This man said, "You don't understand. It is a poor man's hut, it is always spacious. Right now we are sitting; when the donkey comes in we will all be standing and we will keep the donkey in the middle so he feels warm and cozy and loved."

They said, "It was better to get lost in the jungle, rather than to be caught in your hut."

But nothing could be done. When the owner said to open the door, the door was opened.

And the donkey came in. The water was dripping from all over his body and the owner took him into the middle and told all the others to stand around. He said, "You don't understand. My donkey is of a very philosophical mind. You can say anything, he is never disturbed. He always listens silently."

I have loved this story which says that the emperor's palaces are always short of space – although they are so big....

The house of the president of India has one hundred rooms with attached bathrooms, one hundred acres of garden. This used to be the viceroy's house and still they have separate guesthouses.

What are these hundred rooms doing there? One wonders....

I have once been there because one of the presidents, Zakir Hussein, was interested in me. He was a vice-chancellor of Aligarh University and when he was the vice-chancellor, I spoke there. He was presiding, and he loved what I had said. When he became president and he came to know that I was in Delhi, he invited me to come and he took me around. I asked him, "What purpose are these one hundred rooms serving?"

He said, "They are just useless. In fact to maintain them, one hundred servants are needed. For the maintenance of this big garden of one hundred acres, one hundred rooms – and in front you see two big buildings. They are guesthouses and each guesthouse must have at least twenty-five rooms, not less than that."

I said, "This is absolute wastage. In how many rooms do you sleep?"

He said, "In how many rooms? I sleep in my bed. I'm not a monster that I will spread myself into many rooms...head in one room, and the body in another and the legs in another."

"But then," I said, "these hundred rooms which are simply empty, fully furnished with everything available that a man needs, should be put to some use."

But this is the situation around the world. The emperors have big palaces and still there is no space. They are always making new palaces, new guesthouses.

And the poor man in this story said, "It is a poor man's hut, there is no shortage of space. We will manage." And they managed. The night passed beautifully, although they had to stand up.

But it is beautiful to share whatever you have. Even if you don't have anything, you can find something in your nothing, also to share.

Charity is sharing. What Bodhidharma is saying is simply nonsense.

Keeping out the thief of the ear by not listening to the sounds is morality.

Have you ever heard of such a definition? Not hearing the sounds, not hearing the music is morality! Then killing a man, or raping a woman is not immoral? Listening to music is immoral, listening to the birds in the trees in the early morning is immoral. My feeling is that because he got entangled with the ultimate question and lied, he has lost his grip and he is now trying to make all kinds of definitions which are absolutely meaningless and absurd.

Humbling the thief of the nose by equating all smells as neutral is patience.

He is really original! I have read thousands of books on morality, on virtues like patience, but I have never come across the statement that it is a question of the nose, not of you. If you can equate all smells as neutral – a roseflower and cow dung smell the same – you are patient!

To hell with such patience – this is simply insanity, insensitivity.

A man of intelligence will become more sensitive. The poet sees the greens of the trees differently from how you see them. He sees them more green. He sees not just green trees, he sees different shades of green. His sensitivity for color is very acute, sharp.

The musician hears sounds even in silence, his ears are so attuned. And the same with the other senses.

But Bodhidharma is really making a laughingstock of himself: *Controlling the thief of the mouth by conquering desires to taste, praise and explain is devotion*.

If you can eat the most delicious food and the holy cow dung without it making any difference, this is devotion! My whole life I have been trying to define devotion, but Bodhidharma knows better!

Quelling the thief of the body by remaining unmoved by sensations of touch is meditation.

If somebody touches you and you don't feel it, you are in meditation? If somebody touches you and you don't feel it, you are simply dead. It is not meditation.

But he has done a great job. And the people who were listening to him, must have wondered…. "From India an enlightened man has come. We have also heard" – those Chinese had also heard much about meditation – "but this is really original!"

They have also their own Lao Tzu, and Chuang Tzu and Lieh Tzu – contemporaries of Gautam Buddha, of the same caliber, who know what meditation is. And he is trying to make a definition, an almost unbelievable one. He has just lost his nerve.

When the ultimate question was asked, that was the point from where he started falling. And he forgot everything. Now he is trying to make up, in any way he can…patching up this hole, patching up that hole, and new holes are coming up and he is running hither and thither and he cannot make any sense of what he is doing.

And taming the thief of the mind by not yielding to delusions but practicing wakefulness is wisdom.

Only this one seems to be a little sensible – just a little, not much, because wakefulness cannot be practiced. He himself has said before that it is a spontaneous phenomenon, you cannot practice it. Anything practiced will be practiced by your mind. Who is going to practice it?

You have your body; you can practice yoga. You have your mind; you can practice meditation, wakefulness. But anything that comes from the body will go with the body, and anything that comes from the mind will go with the mind. They will not be able to go with you when death takes away everything.

Something has to happen in you which is not part of the body, not part of the mind – something which has no roots in body-mind structure. And wakefulness is awareness, witnessing from far away all the activities of the mind and the body. Then wakefulness will go with you. Even when the body and mind are taken away by death, wakefulness cannot be taken away by anyone.

So that's why I say just a little bit – at least he is not making too much of an idiot of himself.

These six paramitas, that which takes you beyond, *are transports. Like boats or rafts, they transport beings to the other shore. Hence, they're called ferries.*

But when Shakyamuni was a bodhisattva, he consumed three bowls of milk… Now this is going to be the last imaginable madness. The disciple is asking:

But when Shakyamuni was a bodhisattva, he consumed three bowls of milk and six ladles of gruel prior to attaining enlightenment. If he had to drink milk before he could taste the fruit of buddhahood, how can merely beholding the mind result in liberation?

Because Bodhidharma is getting eccentric the disciples are also starting asking questions which ordinarily they would not have asked. But now everything is okay. It is true that Buddha consumed three bowls of milk but that does not mean that because of those three bowls of milk he became enlightened, that one has to do something before enlightenment. It does not mean that it is a condition.

But that's what the disciples are asking: *If he had to drink milk before he could taste the fruit of buddhahood, how can merely beholding the mind result in liberation?* First one has to drink three bowls of milk – and you are telling us just to watch the mind and you will become liberated. What about those three bowls of milk?

And this is not only with Bodhidharma, this is the case with all religious scriptures, commentaries. They come to points where you are simply shocked that these people…. Can't they see a simple thing, that it was just incidental? He was hungry and somebody offered the milk. But what the disciples are asking can be forgiven. They are disciples, ignorant. But the answer is really great! The disciples are nothing before the answer.

The answer is: *What you say is true. This is how he attained enlightenment. He had to drink milk before he could become a buddha. But there are two kinds of milk.* This is something that you cannot go beyond. I used to think there is a limit to stupidity, but there is none. He says:

But there are two kinds of milk. That which Shakyamuni drank wasn't ordinary impure milk but pure dharmamilk.

Not just ordinary milk – religious milk! And what is religious milk? Nobody has ever heard about it. People have heard about powdered milk, and all other kinds, but dharmamilk? How can milk be religious?

The three bowls were the three sets of precepts. And the six ladles were the six paramitas. When Shakyamuni attained enlightenment, it was because he drank this pure dharmamilk that he tasted the fruit of buddhahood. To say that the Tathagata drank the worldly concoction of impure, rank-smelling cow's milk is the height of slander. That which is truly-so, the indestructible, passionless dharma-self, remains forever free of the world's afflictions. Why would it need impure milk to satisfy its hunger or thirst?

On the one hand, we have seen Bodhidharma saying again and again, in many sutras, that your intrinsic being is always pure, there is no way to make it impure. And now, to become aware of your self-nature – that's what buddhahood is – you need a very special kind of milk, dharmamilk. He gives the whole description for how this dharmamilk is created.

The sutras say, "This ox doesn't live in the highlands or the lowlands."

The first thing to remember is that it is not a cow because a cow is a woman, female, and you cannot expect dharmamilk from a female. Dharmamilk comes only through males. You should send this sutra to Morarji Desai; it supports his ideology. He is drinking the dharmamilk every day…milking and drinking and milking and drinking his own milk. I think he has attained more virtue than any buddha!

This ox is not a mistake, because before this, he has used the word cow. When he is condemning the milk he is saying, *To say that the Tathagata drank the worldly concoction of impure, rank-smelling cow's milk…* So he knows perfectly well the difference between cows and oxen.

The sutras say, *"This ox does not live in the highlands or the lowlands. It doesn't eat grain or chaff. And it doesn't graze with cows* – because even to graze with cows, there is a possibility the dharmamilk may get impure.

The body of this ox is the color of burnished gold." The ox refers to Vairocana. Due to his great compassion for all beings, he produces from within his pure dharmabody the sublime dharmamilk of the three sets of precepts and six paramitas to nourish all those who seek liberation. The pure milk of such a truly pure ox not only enabled the Tathagata to achieve buddhahood, it enables any being who drinks it to attain unexcelled, complete enlightenment.

This is really very discouraging. Where are you going to find this dharma-ox?

That reminds me of a Hindu monk, very famous. I was traveling with him to participate in a Hindu conference and we stayed in the same house. He used to drink only milk; that was his only great spirituality. Otherwise, I could not see – three days I had been with him – I could not see any intelligence. The only thing was that he used only milk – and that milk had to be from a white cow, an absolutely white cow.

When I heard this I asked him, "I should not interfere in your great discipline, but I cannot resist the temptation because I have never seen even a black cow giving black milk. Milk is always white, so why do you worry? If a cow has a dot, just a small dot...black or brown or anything...is that canceled?"

In the morning, many cows were brought for the saint to see and to look all around to see whether they were absolutely white or not. And when he accepted some cow, that it was absolutely white, then a man had to take a bath with his clothes on and with those wet clothes on he had to milk the cow, in front of the saint, so no impurity or anything wrong goes into the milk.

In three days I got so tired of his idiotness. I had not heard about Bodhidharma then; otherwise I would have told him, "What you are doing is absolutely right. Only one thing is wrong; you drink the milk of the cows. You should drink the milk of the ox, a white ox." But even white ox milk will not be white. It will be yellow. But to attain enlightenment one can do any austerity – and this is a great discipline!

Bodhidharma has simply made himself an utter fool, when in fact things were simple to explain. But it is not just with this religion – with every religion the same problem arises again and again.

The Jaina tirthankara, Mahavira, became enlightened sitting in a certain pose which is very strange because you are rarely found in that pose. In yoga that posture is called, "cow-milking posture." In India, machines are not used; men sit on a tripod and milk the cows by hand. But what was Mahavira doing? – because he was certainly not milking a cow so why should he sit in the milking-a-cow posture?

That can be done only for one reason...and I will not tell you the reason. You can ask Morarji Desai; tell him, "You are doing perfectly. Just remember, sit in the right cow-milking pose. Collect the milk and drink, and enlightenment is sure."

Now, after Mahavira Jaina monks had been thinking one could not become enlightened because to sit in that posture is very difficult. You cannot sit long enough – and it is a very strange posture. To meditate one needs to sit in such a way that one is relaxed, at ease. Mahavira's is a very tense posture.

But what is accidental, people start thinking of as if it is the cause – as if that posture is a necessity for enlightenment. Nothing is a necessity for enlightenment because enlightenment is not caused by anything that you can do. Enlightenment happens only when you are absent, so utterly silent that it is not your doing.

You cannot brag, "This is my enlightenment. I have done it." When enlightenment happens, you can simply say, "I was not. And because I was not, I was so silent, so absent – just a pure nothing, only a receptivity – it happened." It came from the beyond just as sunrays come to the flowers and they open their petals. Something from the beyond comes into you and your lotus opens its petals and releases all its inexhaustible fragrance. But there is no cause.

Cause and effect are scientific terms. They don't have any significance in the mystery of your inner life. There is nothing caused, nothing effected. The buddhahood, the enlightenment, the awakening, the liberation is already there. It is not to be created, hence no cause is needed. It has only to be looked at. You have just to turn your eyes inwards and see it. It is a discovery. It has been there for millennia so you can do it at any moment – just a small thing which is not a cause – you just open your eyes inward. And that's what I call meditation.

Mind opens outside; meditation opens inside. Mind is a door that leads you outside in the world; meditation is the door that leads you to your interiority – to the very innermost shrine of your being. And suddenly, you are enlightened. Enlightenment is always sudden; it is never gradual.

And Bodhidharma knew it. His own enlightenment was a sudden experience. But just so as not to contradict the tradition, not to annoy the people, not to make enemies, he compromised. I categorically condemn this compromise.

A man of his genius should not have compromised on any ground. Even if all Buddhism in China disappears, nothing is lost.

But Bodhidharma compromising has destroyed his own integrity, his own sincerity, his own authority. He has become a pygmy when actually he was a giant.

Okay, Maneesha?

Yes, Bhagwan.

19

— **RELISH THE MYSTERY**
IN THE DEPTHS OF YOUR HEART

達磨

Beloved Bhagwan,

Throughout the sutras, the Buddha tells mortals they can achieve enlightenment by performing such meritorious works as building monasteries, casting statues, burning incense, scattering flowers, lighting eternal lamps, practicing all six periods of the day and night, walking around stupas, observing fasts and worshiping. But if beholding the mind includes all other practices, then such works as these would appear redundant.

The sutras of the Buddha contain countless metaphors. Because mortals have shallow minds and don't understand anything deep, the Buddha used the tangible to represent the sublime. People who seek blessings by concentrating on external works instead of internal cultivation are attempting the impossible.

What you call a monastery, we call a *sangharama,* a place of purity. But whoever denies entry to the three poisons and keeps the gates of his senses pure, his body and mind still, inside and outside clean, builds a monastery.

Casting statues refers to all practices cultivated by those who seek enlightenment....

And burning incense doesn't mean ordinary material incense but the incense of the intangible Dharma, which drives away filth, ignorance and evil deeds with its perfume....

When the Buddha was in the world, he told his disciples to light such precious incense with the fire of awareness as an offering to the buddhas of the ten directions. But people today don't understand the Tathagata's real meaning. They use an ordinary flame to light material incense of sandalwood or frankincense hoping for some future blessing that never comes.

For scattering flowers the same holds true. This refers to speaking the Dharma, or to scattering flowers of virtue, in order to benefit others and glorify the real self....

If you think the Tathagata meant for people to harm plants by cutting off their bloom, you're wrong. Those who observe the precepts don't injure any of the myriad life forms of heaven and earth. If you hurt something by mistake, you suffer for it.

But those who intentionally break the precepts by injuring the living for the sake of future blessings suffer even more. How could they let would-be blessings turn into sorrows?

The eternal lamp represents perfect awareness.

...Long ago, there was a Buddha named Dipamkara, or *Lamplighter*. This was the meaning of his name.... The light released by a buddha from one curl between his brows can illuminate countless worlds. An oil lamp is no help....

Practicing all six periods of the day and night means among the six senses is what's meant by all six periods.

As for walking around stupas, the stupa is your body and mind. When your awareness circles your body and mind without stop, this is called walking around a stupa....

The same holds true for observing a fast.... To fast means...to regulate your body and mind so that they're not distracted or disturbed.

Also, once you stop eating the food of delusion, if you touch it again, you break your fast. And once you break it, you reap no blessing from it.

The world is full of deluded people who don't see this.

They indulge their body and mind in all manner of evil. They give free rein to their passions and have no shame. And when they stop eating ordinary food, they call it fasting. How absurd!

It's the same with worshiping. You have to understand the meaning and adapt to conditions. Meaning includes action and non-action....

Worship means reverence and humility. It means revering your real self and humbling delusions. If you can wipe out evil desires and harbor good thoughts, even if nothing shows, it's worship....

Those who fail to cultivate the inner meaning and concentrate instead on the outward expression never stop indulging in ignorance, hatred and evil while exhausting themselves to no avail. They can deceive others with postures, remain shameless before sages and vain before mortals, but they'll never escape the Wheel, much less achieve any merit.

AM DEEPLY hurt to have to say that Bodhidharma has gone senile. He was going so great up to the point when the question was asked, "From where does ignorance come?" But he lost the track. It often happens...if you lie once, you have to lie one thousand and one times more; each lie needs another lie to protect it – and still it remains unprotected. Instead of one lie, now you have to protect two lies, but lies cannot be protected by truth – so you bring in a third And this is an endless series.

That's what has happened to Bodhidharma because he simply could not say, "I don't know." Now he's in a dilemma: whatever is asked, he has to give some answer – whether he knows or not. And there are things which cannot be known by their very nature. So it should not have been a calamity at all to accept that this is an ultimate question and ultimate questions cannot be answered – either by Bodhidharma or by anybody else, past, present, or future.

The ultimate will remain always a mystery. You cannot demystify it by giving an answer. The moment you face the ultimate, you simply have to be like a child, an innocent. Enjoy the wonder of it, relish the mystery of it in the depths of your heart. Let it reach into the silences of your being. Let it penetrate you and transform you. It is not a question to ask about, or to expect any answer to.

But Bodhidharma took only one single wrong step, and now he is going on down the drain. Each day he has to go on creating unnecessary lies. Once in a while he says something true, but now the amount of truth goes on lessening and the lies are becoming more and more, their quantity goes on increasing.

I had never thought that a man like Bodhidharma was not courageous enough to simply say, "Forgive me, I don't know," to the ultimate question. If he had said that and stopped there, he would have risen above millions of mystics in height, in depth, in magnificence.

But I can understand the problem: he did not want to disappoint his disciples, he did not want to disappoint the Chinese people. He did not want to tell them that there are fundamental questions which even an enlightened person cannot answer. So he goes on fabricating fictions. He cannot say that the Buddha is wrong, so he has to produce strange answers which don't fit at all with what Buddha said – and they don't fit absolutely with what Bodhidharma himself said earlier. His whole teaching was to be aware of the mind and to go beyond the mind, and that was absolutely perfect. Nothing was to be added to it.

Now he's answering questions reluctantly, but he cannot stop. It needs tremendous courage to ignore your disciples' questions and to simply say that this is not a question because it is ultimate. He has been trying in every way to satisfy the disciples and to satisfy the Chinese people that an enlightened man knows everything.

The reality is not so. The more you become enlightened, the less you know. At the ultimate peak of enlightenment, you simply know yourself…and nothing else. But at that peak, you yourself are the whole universe.

I will tell you where he's still right – because he knows what is the truth – but he is compromising. He is not a rebel, he is a pacifying person. He does not want to say a single word to disturb the newly-converted Buddhists in China. It would have been alright if he had remained in India and never gone to China. Here he would have been his real self; there was no need even to consider others. The moment you start considering others, you fall from the height.

As far as I am concerned, my absolute commitment is towards the truth. Even if I irritate and annoy the whole world, I will not say anything just to console them, and I will not say anything that goes against my experience of truth. People have been asking me, "Why is the whole world against you?" The world is not against me. I am against the world because I have chosen truth. And I will say only that which is absolutely my experience. I will not compromise in any way, for any reason whatsoever.

But Bodhidharma started compromising. He may have been worshiped by people because he consoled them, but in my eyes he has lost his grandeur; he has lost his beauty and intelligence. He has come just too low to be understood.

This is the question of a disciple:

Throughout the sutras, the Buddha tells mortals they can achieve enlightenment by performing such meritorious works as building monasteries, casting statues, burning incense, scattering flowers, lighting eternal lamps, practicing all six periods of the day and night, walking around stupas… Stupas are the graves of ancient enlightened people. ...*observing fasts and worshiping.*

In fact, this whole sutra is an invention of the Mahayana school of Buddhism. Buddha never said anything like that, and if he said it he was wrong. That should have been Bodhidharma's simple approach, because even at the time of his death Buddha's last words were, "Don't make my statues."

And you have heard Bodhidharma in the beginning saying, "Buddhas cannot worship buddhas." There is no need, and it is really humiliating. You have the same quality of consciousness within you, you just have not discovered it. Somebody else has discovered it, but as far as *having* it is concerned, you both have it in the same way.

Bodhidharma mentioned the name of Dipamkara. He was an ancient buddha long before Gautam Buddha, and in Dipamkara's time Gautam Buddha was an ordinary man. Just out of curiosity he had gone to see Dipamkara. He was given the name Dipamkara because his presence was so infectious that those who innocently came close to him immediately caught something invisible, as if a flame had jumped from Dipamkara into their heart, which was utterly dark, and now there was light. Hence the name, Dipamkara Buddha, was given to him – a man who lights the unlit lamps of others just by his presence.

Gautam Buddha was not enlightened at that time but he had gone just out of curiosity, like a small child, to see what was happening, why so many people were going there. His curiosity was innocent. He had not gone to attain knowledge or enlightenment, or anything. There was no greed in it, there was no ambition in it. It was simply the wonder. He had heard that people who went to Dipamkara...just sitting silently with him something had transpired, and they returned home totally different people. Their actions changed, their lifestyles changed. They became more loving, more compassionate, greed disappeared, ambition disappeared, anger disappeared. They became individuals so beautiful and so fragrant that Buddha wanted to see this man...this man was a wonder. He did nothing, yet....

The master never does anything. His whole work is somehow to bring you close...as close as when you bring one candle which is burning with a flame close to another candle which is unlit. There is a certain point when the unlit candle will catch fire from the flame of the lit candle. The lit candle will not lose anything, but the unlit will gain a tremendous treasure. Unlit it was dead, and when the flame started, life came to it. Now it can also dispel darkness in the same way as the first flame was doing.

Dipamkara was such a man; in fact every great master is such a man. Whatever happens around him is not done by him. Whatever is done is just to bring you close, to make himself available to you and a mystery to you, so that without your knowing you are pulled like a magnet pulls things…and at a certain distance, suddenly you become aflame. The old dies, and the new man is born.

This sutra is absolutely wrong. It is not a statement of Gautam Buddha, because a man of his understanding cannot tell people that *they can achieve enlightenment by performing such meritorious works as building monasteries, casting statues, burning incense*…. Can you see any connection with enlightenment and burning incense? You can burn mountains of incense…there is no logical relationship with your becoming enlightened. You may get burned, that's the only thing. Making monasteries…and you are not a monk! – you are making monasteries for other fools to become monks. How can that become your enlightenment? How many monasteries did Gautam Buddha make before he became enlightened? How much incense did he burn? How many flowers did he scatter? How many eternal lamps did he burn?

No! This statement is not at all Gautam Buddha's. It is the invention of the Mahayana School, a certain creed and doctrine. And there was a historical reason why such things were created. Buddha was a very straightforward man. He said whatsoever was right – whatever the consequences. For example, he said, "All the pundits and the scholars and the brahmins are idiots – and they are parasites. For centuries they have been sucking the blood of the people." He called the *Vedas* "just rubbish." And the *Vedas* were so much respected by the Hindus that anybody calling them rubbish must have had great courage. He did not accept any Hindu *avatara,* any Hindu incarnation, as having any value.

For example, Parasurama is one of the Hindu incarnations of God. He was the son of a man who was thought to be a great seer, but he was suspicious…as all husbands are suspicious about their wives, and all wives are automatically suspicious of their husbands. That is their only relationship. Finally the father became so convinced of his suspicion – which may have had grounds or may not have had grounds, he could not be certain on this point – that he ordered his son, Parasurama, to cut off his mother's head and bring it to him. And Parasurama went, without asking why. It was not a small thing! He cut off his mother's head and brought it to his father.

Then the father told him, "I have been suspecting her, but now I have certain evidence that she has been in love with a man who is a great warrior." Parasurama and his family belonged to the caste of the brahmins. Parasurama said, "Don't you be worried. I will not leave a single man of the warrior caste alive." The story may be exaggerated, but it shows the quality of the man. It shows that he killed all the warriors of the whole world many, many times. And from where were these new warriors coming? The Hindu society accepts a very strange thing, and nobody ever considers.... They go on claiming they have a great culture, but they never look at its foundation; their culture is just a phony name.

The Hindu society accepted that if a woman came to a brahmin seer and asked that she be given a child, then it was obligatory for the brahmin seer to make love to her and make her pregnant. He could not reject her. So Parasurama went on cutting off the heads of the warriors; the widows were left, and they were going to the seers.... It was a good business, a great conspiracy!

The whole country was in a state of prostitution, and Parasurama was killing. Such violence cannot be accepted as a quality of God. And it seems illogical... If his mother was in love with a warrior, he could just have killed him – we can make a few concessions, because he was thought by the Hindus to be an incarnation of God. But to kill all the warriors of the world, not even of this country, does not seem to have any logic behind it. And it was not certain that what the father was saying... Parasurama should have asked for evidence, for proof. His father may have been just a jealous man.

Now Buddha could not accept Parasurama as a reincarnation of God, and if Parasurama is a reincarnation of God then who will be the reincarnation of the devil? Buddha could not accept Rama as and incarnation of God because Rama killed a sudra, a young man, by pouring hot liquid lead into his ears because he had been listening while hiding behind a tree when a few brahmins were reciting the *Vedas*. The sudras were not allowed to read; they were not allowed even to listen! What kind of culture has this country created, where one-fourth of the people are not even allowed to listen to its religious scriptures?

And because this young man, just out of curiosity hiding behind a tree, listened.... He could not have understood it though, because it was in Sanskrit, and Sanskrit has never been the language of the people. It has always been the language of the priests – only of the priests. So even if he had listened, he would not have understood anything. And do you think it is a crime? Is it worth destroying a young man, by pouring hot boiling lead into his ears, because he committed a sin by listening to the *Vedas*? And the man died....

Buddha could not accept Rama, and he could not accept Krishna, a man who was so mad that he collected sixteen thousand women...any woman that he fancied was taken away from her family. She may be a virgin, she may be married, she may have children, she may have a husband, she may have to look after her old father-in-law, her old mother-in-law. Sixteen thousand women were just simply taken away by his soldiers. They were treated as if they were cattle – and I don't know if he even remembered the names of those sixteen thousand women. But he was powerful, and he had a great army and he was a great king. Buddha could not accept such nonsense, such a corrupted man, as a reincarnation of God.

Buddha was very straightforward. He said, "All the statues, all the temples, all the *Vedas* are creations of a cunning priesthood to exploit people." How can he tell his own people that they can attain enlightenment by *building monasteries, casting statues, burning incense, scattering flowers, lighting eternal lamps, practicing all six periods of the day and night, walking around stupas, observing fasts and worshiping?*

Buddha was against worship, he was against statues. His last words before his death were, "Again I remind you: don't make statues of me, don't create temples in my name, don't start worshiping me because worshiping is not going to lead you anywhere. I have shown you the path of meditation – meditate. And if even in your meditation I appear, don't hesitate. Immediately cut off my head." A man who can say this...do you think this sutra can possibly come from him?

Bodhidharma could have simply said, "These are not the words of Buddha." But he did not say it. That's where he falls low in my eyes.

He did not say it because in China the Buddhists were trying to make as many monasteries, as many temples, as many statues as possible. One temple exists in China with ten thousand statues of Buddha. The whole mountain has been carved as a temple. This is the biggest temple in the world, where there are ten thousand statues of Buddha, and to say anything about this not being right would go against the very Buddhists who have been working to convert the Chinese. And they had been giving the certainty to the Chinese that they would become enlightened if they fed the monks, if they worshiped the Buddha, if they gave donations to the monasteries.

Bodhidharma must have hesitated a moment, but finally he fell into the trap of being part of an organized religion. Organized religion always insists on these stupid things which don't lead you anywhere, but they help the organized religion to exploit you; otherwise, who is going to feed one million Catholic nuns and monks? Who is going to take care of all the expenses of thousands of Catholic monasteries? It has to be continuously emphasized by the sermons of the priests every Sunday, people have to be reminded to donate, reminded that, "Donation will bring you salvation." Salvation is the Christian word for enlightenment.

The disciples can see it, so they are asking:

But if beholding the mind includes all other practices, then such works as these would appear redundant.

If a single method of beholding the mind creates enlightenment, then what is the need of all these things? These are all things that come out of the mind; they will strengthen the mind. But all that you have to do is to weaken the mind, go beyond it...so beyond that it cannot take any energy from you and it dies out of hunger and starvation.

And when you don't have any mind, but just a pure silence of no-mind, you have attained enlightenment.

The disciples are perfectly right to ask the question, "You yourself have been saying, 'Just behold the mind and that's enough.' Then what is the need of all these rituals?" Now he is caught in a catch-22.... If he says, "These words are not from Buddha," he goes against Mahayana Buddhism and he belongs to that sect.

That's why I insist: Don't belong to any sect, to any creed, to any religion; otherwise, you cannot be absolutely committed to truth. Any other commitment side by side with the commitment to truth is dangerous. Then you would like somehow to also console that other commitment.

And if a man like Bodhidharma could not manage to say the truth, because he could see that if he says it – and he was the first enlightened man to enter China – if he says it, the whole edifice that thousands of Buddhist monks had created in six hundred years, the whole atmosphere that you can become enlightened by worshiping Buddha, by burning incense, by offering flowers, by making temples, statues, monasteries would simply flop, because none of them was enlightened. The whole of China was waiting to hear what is actually the truth from an enlightened man. But because he also belonged to a certain business firm, he decided in favor of the business rather than in favor of the truth.

I have always told a small story.... A small school, a Christian school, but the only one in the vicinity and little kids.... The teacher was telling them for almost one hour, "Jesus Christ is the greatest man who has walked on the earth." And then she asked the students, "Who is the greatest man that has walked on the earth?"

One American boy student said, "Abraham Lincoln." She said, "Not bad, but not quite right."

An English girl stood up and said, "Winston Churchill." The woman could not believe that she had wasted one hour insisting on a single point. She said, "Not bad, but not quite right yet."

And then a little boy who never used to speak stood up raising his hand. The teacher said, "You never do that. For the first time you are raising your hand!" And she was afraid that certainly his answer was not going to be right. But the boy said, "Jesus Christ." She was shocked by the previous two answers, but this answer was even more shocking because the boy was Jewish.

After the class she caught hold of the boy, took him aside and said, "Hymie, aren't you a Jew?"

He said, "Yes, I am."

"Then do you really think Jesus Christ is the greatest man who has walked on the earth?"

He laughed and said, "Business is business. In the deepest part of my heart I know Moses is the man, not Jesus Christ. He's just a pygmy. But business is business...." because there was a big trophy to be given to the person who answered the question right, and Hymie was carrying the big trophy, bigger than himself.

But you can forgive a small child. And he was very logical; he must have thought, "What does it matter if I say once in a class, just to win the game, 'Jesus Christ' I know the rules for who is going to win, so why unnecessarily bring in Moses and get defeated? In the deepest part of my heart I know Moses is the greatest man who has ever walked on the earth."

But even people who are enlightened, when it comes to deciding between their commitment to an organized religion and their commitment to truth, decide for their commitment to the organization. This is really sad. The answer Bodhidharma gives is simply irrelevant. It's just trying to make something that can prove that the sutra is spoken by Buddha.

I absolutely deny that such a statement was spoken by Buddha. It goes against his very life, his very teaching, his very way.

Bodhidharma says, *The sutras of the Buddha contain countless metaphors.*

Now can you see the trick? Now he cannot say it is wrong and he cannot say it is right. He finds a middle way and says that Buddha is speaking in metaphors.

Because mortals have shallow minds...

And to whom is he speaking – to the mortals or the immortals? If Buddha's audience had shallow minds, does Bodhidharma think that his audience is of higher status? Buddha had perhaps the most intelligent audience any man ever had. Bodhidharma is talking to the recently converted Buddhists.

The Buddha used the tangible to represent the sublime.

This is tricky, and unforgivable.

People who seek blessings by concentrating on external works instead of internal cultivation are attempting the impossible.

But he knows the truth, so once in a while it comes up in spite of his effort to suppress it and to go with the crowd and the mass mind. This is true when he says ...*concentrating on external works instead of internal cultivation is attempting the impossible.*

What you call a monastery, we call a sangharama, a place of purity.

That is absolutely wrong. *Sangharama* is exactly a monastery; it is not different from a monastery, it is not a metaphor. And even for these last two thousand years, thousands of monasteries have existed in China. It is just since the communist revolution thirty years ago that many monasteries have been destroyed; otherwise millions of monks were living on the people's blood. But they are coming back again....

It was Mao Tse-tung's very adamant, stubborn, fascist and communist mind that turned the monasteries into hospitals, into schools and forced the monks to go to the fields and work. Mao stopped begging – and Buddhism has lived only on begging. In fact begging had been a discipline, a practice, because it makes you humble. But Mao made it illegal to beg and forced the monks to work for their food, for their clothes, for their shelter.

Now Mao is dead and his enemies in the communist party – who he had not allowed...many of them were forced into jail, many have been killed – have come into power. Now the opposite party inside the communist party itself has come into power and it wants to win the heart of the people. Monasteries are coming back again because two thousand years of Buddhism cannot be erased so easily. Now Buddhist monks can again be seen with their begging bowls. Those hospitals have been removed, those schools have been removed, and monks are no longer forced to work in the fields, or in the factories, or wherever they can be of any use....

But whoever denies entry to the three poisons and keeps the gates of his senses pure, his body and mind still, inside and outside clean, builds a monastery.

Now this is a very farfetched idea. And if Bodhidharma can explain it to very new candidates of Buddhism, why cannot Buddha himself have said that he was speaking in metaphors? He could have explained it himself, and he was far better as far as speaking was concerned, far more articulate; he could have explained that these are just metaphors. But nowhere does he mention them as metaphors. It is very arduous for Bodhidharma to turn everything into a metaphor, but we will see that with everything he goes on with the idea that they are metaphors.

Casting statues refers to all practices cultivated by those who seek enlightenment.

I cannot understand how this can be a metaphor. *Casting statues refers to all practices cultivated by those who seek enlightenment.* What relationship, even a farfetched one...? A metaphor should be representative; it should explain something, it should be helpful to understand. This is not at all concerned with casting statues and practicing for enlightenment! Could not Buddha himself say, "Practice for enlightenment"?

And burning incense does not mean ordinary material incense – as if there is somewhere available some spiritual incense – *but the incense of the intangible dharma....* Where are you going to get it? That's why I said it hurts me to say that Bodhidharma seems to have gone senile, although he was only seventy-five. *...which drives away filth, ignorance and evil deeds with its perfume.*

Great! But where to get it? that spiritual incense *which drives away filth, ignorance and evil deeds with its perfume....* Nobody has ever seen such a thing; otherwise life would have been so simple. There is no need to bother people with meditation, with any discipline, with any awareness. Just burn the spiritual incense and everything is driven out and you are purified by the perfume!

I alone will not be enlightened because I am allergic to perfume, whether it is tangible or intangible. But there is not much harm if one man is not enlightened, it can be tolerated if the whole world will be enlightened! I am perfectly ready....

Bodhidharma is not even aware for how long he can deceive people, but he has deceived them for one thousand years...that's how long these sutras have been in existence. They have certainly been preserved, because they were in the hands of the Mahayana Buddhists, who were not willing for them to be translated. And I can understand now why they were not willing for them to be translated: they will destroy the great image of Bodhidharma. They themselves may have understood that what he is talking about is absolutely outlandish.

When the Buddha was in the world, he told his disciples to light such precious incense with the fire of awareness as an offering to the buddhas of the ten directions.

It may be precious, but where is it available? And then he makes awareness like a fire just to burn the incense, and the incense will do everything...you will become enlightened. So now your sole search is to find that dharma-incense, that spiritual incense!

Perhaps you can find it in Poona...it is a very spiritual city – so spiritual that only spirits roam around, no living human beings.

But people today don't understand the Tathagata's real meaning.

Only Bodhidharma understands the Tathagata's real meaning. Perhaps the Tathagata himself did not understand his own real meaning!

They use an ordinary flame to light material incense of sandalwood or frankincense hoping for some future blessing that never comes.

He's going round about, and round about...he could have simply said, "This statement is not Buddha's, and this statement is absolutely nonsense." And that would have been absolutely correct.

For scattering flowers the same holds true. This refers to speaking the Dharma, or to scattering flowers of virtue.

How do you scatter flowers of virtue? Even if one accepts this stupid explanation, how do you scatter the flowers of virtue? You go on giving to people saying, "This is truth, this is love, this is compassion," and your hand is empty.

Two madmen from a madhouse were sitting in the park. Every day for one hour they were allowed to go out in the garden. One man, who was keeping his fist closed, asked the other, "If you tell me what I am keeping in my fist, I will give you one rupee."

The other man said, "Really? Will you keep your word?" The first man took out one rupee from his pocket and said, "This is the rupee. Just tell me what is in my hand?" And the other man looked and said, "It's seems it is an elephant."

The first man said, "You cannot get the rupee. It seems you have looked. You are being tricky." He did not give the one rupee because he also believed he was keeping an elephant in his fist!

How can you scatter *flowers of virtue, in order to benefit others and glorify the real self? If you think the Tathagata meant for people to harm plants by cutting off their bloom, you are wrong.*

That seems to be right, but he's mixing everything in such a way that it loses all significance. Certainly Buddha would not like you to pluck flowers; that is killing. The flower on the rosebush has a life, a beauty. The moment you pluck it, it is dead. Leave it there.

Mukta is my gardener. She is not allowed even to cut any leaf or to cut any flowers. In the beginning she used to move with gardener's scissors hidden behind her back! But right now I can see, whenever I go to Buddha Hall – otherwise I don't get out – I can see flowers are there, I can see the garden has become a jungle so she must have dropped those gardener's scissors. Let every tree grow in its own way; at least in my garden! Don't kill any tree, don't destroy any living flower.

So I can understand that Buddha would not have allowed the cutting off of their blooms, but rather I would say that the whole sutra was inserted by the Mahayana School. But why did the Mahayana School have to insert such things...?

There is something very fundamental to be understood here. When Gautam Buddha worked in this country, twenty-five centuries ago, he almost converted the whole land. He was a man of such charisma. He was not just a learned man; he has known existence, he has been part of it. His impact was tremendous – perhaps nobody else has ever made such an impact.

But the moment he died, the brahmins, the priests, came out of their caves where they had been hiding because they could not face Gautam Buddha – whoever went to face him became a disciple. But they were waiting for their chance: one day he was going to die. He has destroyed their whole profession. Now no bells were ringing in the temples, people were not going to worship, people were not calling brahmins for their rituals...and brahmins are the most clever priesthood in the whole world.

People get caught...each person when he is born is immediately under their control: first some ritual, then his birth chart has to be made, then his naming ceremony has to be performed. And in all these, the priest is exploiting the people. Then shaving the head....and this goes on and on. Even if you go to some other city you have to consult the brahmin for the right constellation of the stars, whether to go north or to south, or to east or to west, what will be the most appropriate and beneficial time?

Then comes marriage – then again the priest is there. And then after the marriage, children start coming from the new marriage – and the priest is there. And then the man becomes old.... From the cradle to the grave, the priest keeps his hold.

Even after the man has died there are rituals to be performed! And in a poor country, those rituals cost so much that people have to sell their houses, their lands, their possessions – on which they were dependent for their livelihood – because their father has died. Then they have to give a great feast for brahmins.

And even the forefathers who have died... It must have been a long line, an unending line in fact, millions of people in a queue behind one another...for that they have a special time. One month completely they devoted to the forefathers because the number is so big, so one month of continuous rituals – fire worship, mantra chanting – for the peace of all those who have died in the family...you don't know even their names!

And millions must have died. Scientists calculate that wherever you are sitting, at least eight persons' graves are underneath you. Don't be afraid, they are dead!

But so many people have died; even thousands of years after the man has died, the priest is still exploiting you.

Buddha has created a tremendous revolution in this sense, in that he destroyed the whole integrity of the priesthood. But the moment he died, the priests came back.

People were also missing them. Life had become very simple. A child was born – no priest was chanting for a blissful, long life for him. Somebody died and the priest was not there chanting and blessing him for the great journey he has gone on. People were also missing all these rituals. So when Buddha died, slowly, slowly brahmins came back, and they started driving out the Buddhists from the land.

Just fifty years ago in India there was hardly a single Buddhist. In these last fifty years, one man has done a great service – although he himself was not a religious man, he was a politician. But by accident he had to do something; it was political tactics.

Babasaheb Ambedkar was a sudra, but caught the eye of a very rich man who, seeing he was so intelligent, sent him to study in England. He became one of the greatest experts of law in the world and he helped make the constitution of India. He was continuously fighting for the sudras to whom he belonged, and that is one-fourth of the Hindu society. He wanted a separate vote for the sudras – and he was absolutely right.

I don't see why they should belong to the Hindu fold which has tortured them for ten thousand years, forced them to do every sort of ugly work and paid them almost nothing. They are not even allowed to live in the cities, they have to live outside the city. Just before freedom, they were not allowed to move in many streets of the town. In many places they were forced to announce loudly, "I am a sudra and I am passing through here. Those who can hear me, please move out of the way..." because even their shadows falling on you, defile you.

But finding no way, because Mahatma Gandhi was insistent that sudras should not leave the Hindu fold.... That was also a political strategy, because if one-fourth of the Hindus leave the fold, then Hindus will become a minority in their own country. There are Mohammedans, there are Christians, there are Jainas; now if a new big chunk would go out of the Hindu fold, the country of the Hindus would become almost the country of other religions. And if they all got together, Hindus would never be in power.

I don't consider Mahatma Gandhi a religious man either; he belonged to the same category as Doctor Ambedkar. Gandhi went on a fast to death so that Ambedkar had to take back his stand. He had to withdraw the idea that sudras should be given a separate vote. And Gandhi was clever...he started calling sudras *harijans*. Cunning people always play with words. Words don't make any difference – whether you call them sudras, untouchables, or harijans...harijans means, "children of God."

I had a long discussion with Mahatma Gandhi's son, Ramdas. I said, "Don't you see the cunningness? The children of God have been suffering for ten thousand years and those who are not children of God are exploiting them, torturing them, oppressing them, raping their women, completely burning their towns with all living people inside. If these are the children of God, it is better not to be a child of God. That is dangerous."

Gandhi changed the name just to give it a beautiful meaning, but everything inside remained the same. And he went on a fast unto death unless Ambedkar takes his statement back.

If I had been in the place of Ambedkar, I would have told Mahatma Gandhi, "It is your business to live or to die. It is your business if you want to fast – you are free to. Fast unto death or even beyond!"

But Ambedkar was pressurized from all over the country, because if Gandhi died the whole blame would come on Ambedkar. And I would have told Gandhi, "This is a very violent method, and you have been talking about nonviolence. Is this nonviolence?"

It happened...I was in Raipur teaching in the Sanskrit college there. A very beautiful young girl was asked by a gangster if she would be married to him. He was a dangerous man, a criminal. He had been to jail many times, he had committed many crimes, and he was almost the same age as the girl's father. But he took a fancy to her, and seeing the success of Gandhi fasting to death and how he managed everything...because Gandhi *had* managed Ambedkar.

After Gandhi had been fasting for twenty-one days, and his health had started to fall fast, the doctor said, "Do something; otherwise the old man will be gone." Ambedkar was much pressurized by all the Indian national leaders who said to him, "Go to Mahatma Gandhi. Ask for his forgiveness, offer him a glass of orange juice to break his fast...and renounce your movement; otherwise you will be remembered always as the one who killed the greatest man of this country, the great religious man." And Ambedkar had to do it, although unwillingly.

I would not have done it! I would have accepted the blame, I would have accepted history's condemnation. Who cares when you are dead what is written in history about you? At least you don't know what is written, and you don't read. Let them write anything....

But I would have insisted that this was not a nonviolent method. It was absolutely violent but in a very subtle way. I threaten to kill you – this is violence. And I threaten to kill myself if you don't accept me – is this logical? The standpoint that Gandhi was taking was absolutely illogical, but he supported it by threatening. It is blackmail to say, "I will kill myself."

Ambedkar managed another way. He started converting the sudras to Buddhism. That's why now there are a few lakhs of Buddhists, but they are not in any way religious. It was just a political manoeuver.

This man in Raipur went to the girl's house with a bed, and declared that if the girl was not married to him, he was going to fast to death. It became the talk of the whole city; photographers and journalists were there, and the whole day the crowd was there. The father became afraid, and pressure was put on him, "Why take the responsibility of his death?" But the father said, "This is absolutely ugly. This man is my age and he's a criminal. I cannot give my daughter to him."

I knew the father and the girl – the girl was my student in the college. The girl suggested to her father to consult me as to what could be done. I had not known him before. He came to me and he told the whole story. I said, "It is very simple. You just find some old, rotten prostitute."

He said, "What?"

I said, "Just listen to the whole point: find a very rotten, old bitch, and put another bed in front of the house. The bitch should declare, 'I'm going to fast to death unless this man marries me.' Other than this nothing will work."

That gangster man escaped in the middle of the night. He was never seen again, he never asked again! This is the Gandhian methodology, a very religious thing.

The Buddhists were burned, driven out of the country, and the whole country was absolutely cleaned of all the impact that Buddha had left. Even in the temple that had been raised in memory of his enlightenment in Bodhgaya, there was not even one Buddhist to take care of the temple. A brahmin has been taking care of it for two thousand years, the same family, generation after generation.

Now they have become the owners of the temple. They don't believe in Buddha. They are against Buddha, but the temple is very precious, because from all over the world people come to the temple. Much money comes to the temple, so the priest is not concerned. He is earning lots of money and he is not willing to hand over the temple, because for two thousand years it has been in his possession. No law can take it away from him.

So when the Buddhists reached China and Tibet they had learned a lesson, that if you go against the people and their traditions.... Perhaps when a charismatic person is alive you may seem to be winning the game, but when the charismatic person is gone...what has happened in India, will happen in Tibet, will happen in China, will happen in Sri Lanka, will happen in Japan.

So they compromised. That was the reason for inserting all these wrong sutras. The Buddhist scriptures in Tibet have different sutras, to console and to convince the Buddhist population of Tibet; Chinese Mahayana sutras have differences, in Sri Lanka they have differences. This is the historical reason why these absolutely absurd sutras, which cannot be Buddha's, have entered into the scriptures. They have been knowingly put in, because without them there was no question of survival.

But as far as I am concerned, and as far as Bodhidharma should have been concerned, truth is the ultimate value, not survival. And survival by creating lies, by distorting the truth...what is the point? Even if Buddhism disappears from the whole world, it does not matter. But the purity of Buddha's statements should have been preserved.

Whenever a seeker wants to search, he has not to get lost in a forest of unnecessary disciplines, rituals. Bodhidharma should have made it clear. I *know* the risk. I understand that he must have felt very guilty, because after these sutras, he left China for the Himalayas. He must have felt tremendously hurt that what he was doing was against his own understanding. But still I can not forgive him. I cannot forgive anyone who goes against truth.

Those who observe the precepts don't injure any of the myriad life forms of heaven and earth. If you hurt something by mistake, you suffer for it. But those who intentionally break the precepts by injuring the living for the sake of future blessings suffer even more. How could they let would-be blessings turn into sorrows?

The eternal lamp represents perfect awareness.

Only in this statement does the metaphor seem to be correct. It can be interpreted as perfect awareness, the eternal lamp. But he has not been able to relate other metaphors to his interpretations.

...Long ago, there was a buddha named Dipamkara, or Lamplighter. This was the meaning of his name.... The light released by a buddha from one curl between his brows can illuminate countless worlds. An oil lamp is no help....

Practicing all six periods of the day and night means among the six senses constantly cultivating enlightenment and persevering in every form of awareness. Never relaxing control over the six senses is what's meant by all six periods.

But these are contradictory to his own statements. Control is not needed because it is through the mind. Practice is not needed because it is through the mind. One has to live a life of let-go – that was his basic teaching.

One has to be spontaneous.

One has to live moment to moment, neither thinking of the past, nor thinking of the future, nor clinging to the present.

He has given such beautiful sutras, and at the end he spoils his own work completely.

As for walking around stupas, the stupa is your body and mind. When your awareness circles your body and mind without stop, this is called walking around a stupa....

He is just trying to manage somehow, even though the whole thing is so stupid. Stupas actually exist and Buddhists of Mahayana school go on pilgrimages to the stupas and go around them. But your body and mind is not a stupa. A stupa is for when you are dead; then a grave has to be created for you. The Buddhist grave is called a stupa. It is made in a certain round way.

But your body and mind are alive. And how can your consciousness go around body and mind? He is not even taking into consideration that all his interpretations can be questioned. They were not questioned because they consoled the people. They wanted something tangible and if it was a metaphor – no harm; he is not denying Gautam Buddha.

The same holds true for observing a fast.

Even a man of very small intelligence can see the stupidity....

To fast means...to regulate your body and mind.

I cannot conceive how a fast can mean *to regulate your body and mind so that they are not distracted or disturbed.* Fast simply means fast, and nothing else.

Also, once you stop eating the food of delusion, if you touch it again, you break your fast.

Now he has forgotten what he was saying. In fact, because that saying is not coming from his inner-most being – it is just his mental gymnastics – he has forgotten that he has defined body and mind as 'stupa' and that he has defined fasting as, 'regulating your body, disciplining your body.'

Now from where comes this idea: *once you stop eating the food of delusion?* It was not in the very definition of the metaphor. Food was not brought in.

If you *stop eating the food of delusion...* And is there any food that is not of delusion? Buddha also eats the same bread as you eat and Buddha also drinks the same water as you drink.

...if you touch it again... Not even eating, but just touching and it is delusion! What harm is there in touching a delusion? A delusion does not exist, you cannot touch it. But *if you touch it again, you break your fast.* He has forgotten the metaphor that he explained before. Now, even if you touch the delusion food,

you have broken your fast.

And once you break it, you reap no blessing from it. The world is full of deluded people who don't see this. They indulge their body and mind in all manner of evil. They give free rein to their passions and have no shame. And when they stop eating ordinary food, they call it fasting. How absurd!

I agree only with the last: How absurd!

It's the same with worshiping. You have to understand the meaning and adapt to conditions. Meaning includes action and non-action....

He is just trying to deceive people – bringing in words which have no relation at all.

Worship means reverence and humility.

That is true. It means revering your real self and humbling delusions. But if you know your real self, where will you find the delusions? Both cannot exist together. Either you are awake – then the dreams are no more there – or the dreams are there and you are not awake. The man who knows his real self has no delusions. But he has got into a mess and he is trying hard to get out of it, but he is getting deeper and deeper into it.

If you can wipe out evil desires and harbor good thoughts, even if nothing shows, it is worship....

Early in his sutras he said that one has to go beyond good and evil. Now good becomes worship.

Those who fail to cultivate the inner meaning and concentrate instead on the outward expression never stop indulging in ignorance, hatred and evil while exhausting themselves to no avail. They can deceive others with postures, remain shameless before sages and vain before mortals, but they'll never escape the Wheel, much less achieve any merit.

It is a strange compilation of sutras. He goes really deep, like a sharp sword cutting all that is wrong, to the point when he is asked the ultimate question, 'From where does ignorance arise?' He cannot answer it and he is not humble enough to accept that he doesn't know. He gets into such a mess that after that every question remains unanswered; he pretends to answer it, but the answer is not even related to the question.

If this can happen to a man like Bodhidharma... You have to be aware. My insistence that you don't belong to any religion, don't belong to any doctrine, don't belong to any scripture, is for the simple reason that your whole and total commitment should be to truth and not for anything else. Your commitment should not be divided, otherwise you will have to make a compromise, which will make anybody who understands feel that you have gone either insane, or senile, or mad. But one thing is certain: you have lost the path.

Bodhidharma himself may not, in his innermost core, have lost his enlightenment – enlightenment cannot be lost – but he has defiled it. His enlightenment is not anymore so clean, so bright, not any more a pillar of light. And just for the simple business of an organized religion....

Humanity will never be religious unless all organized religions disappear and religion becomes an individual commitment towards existence, so no question of compromise arises.

Let me say to you: Religion is rebellious, and the man of religion is a rebel. He is rebellious against all orthodoxy, against all traditions, against all organizations, against all ideologies. His only love is for truth, and his whole love is for truth. Only such a man finds it. Others only wander into ignorance, into dreams, into sleep – and they suffer.

Okay, Maneesha?

Yes, Bhagwan.

達磨

Beloved Bhagwan,

But the Bathhouse Sutra says, "By contributing to the bathing of monks, people receive limitless blessings." This would appear to be an instance of external practice achieving merit. How does this relate to beholding the mind?

Here, the bathing of monks doesn't refer to the washing of anything tangible. When the Lord preached the Bathhouse Sutra, he wanted his disciples to remember the dharma of washing. So he used an everyday concern to convey his real meaning.

...The bathhouse is the body. When you light the fire of wisdom, you warm the pure water of the precepts and bathe the true buddha-nature within you. By upholding these seven practices, you add to your virtue. The monks of that age were perceptive. They understood the Buddha's meaning. They followed his teaching, perfected their virtue and tasted the fruit of

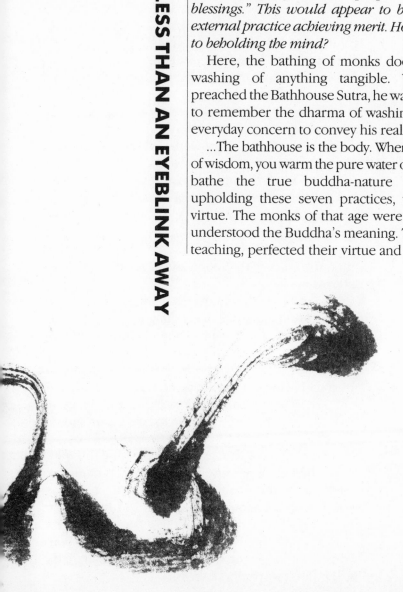

buddhahood. But people nowadays can't fathom these things.

...Our true buddha-nature has no shape. And the dust of affliction has no form. How can people use ordinary water to wash an intangible body? It won't work. When will they wake up? To clean such a body, you have to behold it. Once impurities and filth arise from desire, they multiply until they cover you inside and out. But if you try to wash this body of yours, you'll have to scrub until it's nearly gone before it's clean. From this you should realize that washing something external isn't what the Buddha meant.

The sutras say that someone who wholeheartedly invokes the Buddha is sure to be reborn in the Western Paradise. Since this door leads to buddhahood, why seek liberation in beholding the mind?

...Buddha means awareness, the awareness of body and mind that prevents evil from arising in either. And to invoke means to call to mind, to call constantly to mind the rules of discipline and to follow them with all your might.

...To invoke the Buddha's name, you have to understand the dharma of invoking. If it's not present in your mind, your mouth chants an empty name. As long as you're troubled by the three poisons or by thoughts of yourself, your deluded mind will keep you from seeing the Buddha.... If you cling to appearances while searching for meaning, you won't find a thing. Thus, sages of the past cultivated introspection and not speech.

This mind is the source of all virtues. And this mind is the chief of all powers. The eternal bliss of nirvana comes from the mind at rest. Rebirth in the three realms also comes from the mind. The mind is the door to every world. And the mind is the ford to the other shore. Those who know where the door is don't worry about reaching it. Those who know where the ford is don't worry about crossing it.

The people I meet nowadays are superficial. They think of merit as something that has form. They squander their wealth and butcher creatures of land and sea.... They see something tangible and instantly become attached. If you talk to them about formlessness, they sit there dumb and confused. Greedy for the small mercies of this world, they remain blind to the great suffering to come. Such disciples wear themselves out in vain. Turning from the true to the false, they talk about nothing but future blessings.

If you can simply concentrate you mind's inner light and behold its outer illumination, you'll dispel the three poisons and drive away the six thieves once and for all. And without effort you'll gain possession of an infinite number of virtues, perfections and doors to the truth. Seeing through the mundane and witnessing the sublime is less than an eye-blink away. Realization is now. Why worry about gray hair? But the true door is hidden and can't be revealed. I have only touched upon beholding the mind.

THANK GOD THAT this is the last Bodhidharma sutra. I was worried about where he is going after the bathhouse! It has been a tremendous journey to the mountaintop and back to your home. Bodhidharma has been taking you on the whole merry-go-round.

I started with Bodhidharma – the name Bodhidharma means "the self-nature of awareness" – but unfortunately I have to end the journey with Buddhudharma. Buddhudharma means "the nature of unawareness, of stupidity."

He got himself into this mess, but it has been of tremendous insight to us. Watching him you can avoid the same mess.

Whatever he said earlier showed his insight into the deepest potential of man, but what he is saying now is just absolutely irrelevant. Once in a while he remembers who he is but it seems he goes on forgetting; or perhaps he is too much attached to his special doctrine of Mahayana and much worried about disturbing the newly initiated Buddhists.

In this situation, he must have suffered a lot. I can see – perhaps nobody may have noted it – but I can see his suffering. His suffering is that he is saying things very unwillingly and this is the problem with all those who accept any doctrine, any scripture, any church. They are in constant trouble. If they listen to their own inner voice, it says something; if they listen to the tradition, it says something else.

There have been very few people in the world who are ready to antagonize everybody. If Bodhidharma had said whatever his experience was, perhaps he would have lost all his prestige, respectability and his great name in the annals of Buddhism. But to me, it would not have been a loss. To me, he would have risen higher than anyone else, just because his single commitment was concentratedly and consistently one...and that is his own experienced truth. Nothing else can change it.

You laughed listening to the very name of the sutra, *The Bathhouse Sutra,* because you don't know that there have been two rebellious religions against Hinduism in India – Jainism and Buddhism. The Jaina monk never takes a bath; he does not even brush his teeth. He stinks and it is thought to be a great discipline that you are not at all concerned with your body which is ephemeral, which is going to die anyway. Why go on cleaning it and wasting your time? It will become unclean again tomorrow.

Buddhism is almost a parallel religion to Jainism. They agree on all the essential points, but Buddha seems to be more sensible than Mahavira. He wanted his monks to take a bath every day so that they would remain clean, so that their bodies would not be condemned but respected as a temple of their divine nature. But there were so many monks: to feed them, to give them use of your bathhouses, to give them clothes, to give them medicines when they were sick, was becoming more and more of a burden to the society.

Just a few years ago in Thailand, the situation became so bad that almost one-fourth of the population of the country were monks. The government had to pass a law saying unless you had the permission of the government, you could not become a monk.

This is the first time in history that any government had taken such a step but it was absolutely necessary in a poor country. If out of four persons, one person does not work, does not create and yet needs all kinds of things which are absolutely necessary, he is going to become a burden.

It is an ugly situation where half the population is starving, where half of the country sleeps only with one daily meal, where people not only eat fruits but dig out the roots of trees, boil them and eat them, hoping that they must have nourishing power. Because they are nourishing the whole tree – they are nourishing the flowers and the fruits – naturally the roots must have great nourishment.

Gautam Buddha has to talk about such trivia because if it is not talked about, then people start taking decisions on their own. And Buddha wanted his disciples to be integrated individuals – clean, pure, alert in every possible way both outwardly and inwardly. His concern and compassion were so great that there are thirty-three thousand rules for a Buddhist monk. It is mind-boggling; thirty-three thousand rules! Even to remember them is difficult.

But Buddha has taken care of every detail: when to wake up, when to go to beg for your food, not to take all your food from one house but from five houses so nobody is burdened. Five houses can give you small bits and that will be enough for you. On one house, you might be a little heavy...and not to stay in one city more than three days so you don't create any kind of burden for anybody. Eat only one time a day because millions of people eat only once a day. You should not ask for two meals.

Don't have more than three pieces of clothing; two to use, one for emergency situations. For example: you suddenly find yourself coming back to the place where all the other monks are staying and it starts raining. Both your pieces of clothing, upper and lower, are wet. At least you still have one cloth to cover yourself – this third is for an emergency. Two are for your essential needs but you should not have more than three.

These details were essential though they look like trivia. You think, "What nonsense is this? A Gautam Buddha should talk about spirituality, about growth and awareness and freedom and he is talking about these small matters." But he had to for the simple reason because he accepted the idea of renouncing the world. Once people renounce the world they are bound to become burdens...and on poor societies.

So when Buddha says that one who gives his bathhouse to be used by a monk earns great virtue, he is simply trying to persuade people that they should not think of it as a burden, but as a blessing.

When a monk accepts the food you offer he is not obliged to you, Buddha says. You are obliged to him. Just his receiving your food, on your part gives great virtue. Perhaps you have given your own food, perhaps you have given your children's food, but you have sacrificed something and you have respected a man who has no possessions, no money.

Buddha has said that the mother is blessed who gives birth to a child who is going to renounce the world. The father is blessed who has a child who is going to renounce the world. They are renouncing the world just to develop their potential to its ultimate. Help them. If you cannot raise your consciousness, at least you can help in some small way those who are making the tremendous effort of raising their consciousness to its ultimate illumination.

Hence, whether it is trivia or not, it would have been perfectly good if Bodhidharma had accepted the sutra as it was. And what I have said, he should have said. But he himself is feeling embarrassed, so he starts trying again, saying it is a metaphor for something invisible, and that makes his whole approach fallacious. I will read the sutra and then I will read his fictitious explanations. The sutra is absolutely clear; it needs no clarification.

But the Bathhouse Sutra says, "By contributing to the bathing of monks, people receive limitless blessings." This would appear to be an instance of external practice achieving merit. How does this relate to beholding the mind?

The disciple is asking Bodhidharma: You say beholding the mind is enough, but Buddha is talking about such small things. In your beholding the mind is there any place for such things?

The simple answer would have been: I am talking about the essential and Buddha is talking about both the essential and the nonessential. He is taking care not only of what the monk has to do. The monk has to behold his mind; that is his only essential practice – awareness, vipassana, watching, witnessing. But also, the poor monk needs food; he needs some shelter in rain, he needs some clothes.

Buddha has a very comprehensive view. It was not just a question of a single monk but when millions of people were becoming monks, then certain rules had to be made; otherwise it would have created chaos in the whole society.

A monk is not supposed to say what he wants to eat. Whatever is made by the family for itself, he should take only that. He should not say to which family he is going to beg tomorrow, because his information may make the family feel that then they have to make some delicious food, some costly food because the monk is coming to their home. This may be an unnecessary burden and the monk may become a parasite.

To avoid all this, Buddha had to talk about such small things that people ordinarily don't like, and in those days very few people had their own bathhouses. Even today after twenty-five centuries, except in a few big cities, ninety percent of the Indian population has no bathroom in their house. They go outside the village, either to the bank of a river, or to the bank of a lake. That is their bathroom, that is their toilet.

It is thought to be a great luxury to have a bathroom attached to your bedroom; only a very few people in India can afford it, the country is so poor. And not only poverty has prevented it; even people who had enough money in the days of Buddha had no idea of having a bathroom attached to their bedroom.

You will be surprised to know that just a hundred years ago there was a case in the Supreme Court of America, because a man attached a bathroom to his bedroom. It was thought to be against Christianity; it was thought to be such a dirty thing. The man had learned about it from Europe and he thought he was bringing a gift to America. It certainly is a gift!

But the Christian associations filed a case against him in the Supreme Court saying that he was trying to corrupt people's minds. "This is an idea implanted in his mind by the devil," they said. "Who has ever heard of a bathroom attached to your bedroom?"

And you will be surprised that the Supreme Court ordered the man to move the bathroom to the back of the house where it belonged. They were called outhouses. They were not attached to the main house – just in the backyard, far away. Dirty places!

But in Buddha's time, there were rich people who had attached bathrooms and the most surprising, almost unbelievable thing is that in Harappa and Mohanjodaro, two most ancient cities discovered in Pakistan…. They are seven thousand years old. Some natural calamity, or perhaps some man-made calamity, destroyed those beautiful cities not only once, but seven times, because seven times those cities were built. People have been excavating for almost half a century. They could not believe what kind of calamity had continuously happened: one layer of the city is covered with mud, then another layer of the city is again covered with mud.

As they went on digging, first they thought the first layer, the superficial layer was the city, but somebody tried to dig a little deeper to see what is underneath that. They were surprised to find that after a few feet of layers of mud, there was another city. Then they tried again and again and finally they have found seven layers of great cities – cities which had streets as broad as San Francisco or New York. And certainly cities don't have those broad streets if they don't have big vehicles to move on them.

Varanasi is thought to be the ancientmost city in India. Not even the smallest car can enter in the old part of Varanasi. What to say of a car? – even sunlight never reaches there because on both sides are huge buildings. Just when the sun comes exactly in the middle of the sky, for a few minutes there is sunlight; otherwise the whole day there is no sun. A great civilization must have been there.

I remembered them because all the houses in Mohanjodaro and Harappa – both the cities – had bathrooms attached to their bedrooms, had swimming pools as big as we have them now. And they had a system, a very strange system which they had invented, for hot and cold running water in every house. It is simply amazing! It seems they had reached to the same height of civilization, perhaps better, because even in the beginning part of the twentieth centurey the Supreme Court of America refused to let that man have a bathroom in his own house.

The future is going to be different because there are architects.... I have seen a few designs sent to me from a friend who is thinking about a very strange thing which will be fought in courts by every religion all over the world. The idea is not to have an attached bathroom but to have the room inside the bathroom. They have made such beautiful designs that the bathroom does not look out of place; it enhances the beauty of the room.

But certainly it is going to be contested by every religion...that this is going too far. Somehow we have accepted bathrooms attached to the rooms. Now these insane architects are trying to enforce an idea...and I think that idea is going to work out. Their designs are just superb. Why have an attached bathroom? The bathroom can be made so beautiful that you can attach yourroom to the bathroom. And in fact both can be in the same place – there is no need for any partition. It is *your* bathroom, it is *your* bedroom. And things can be made so beautiful and so clean, there is no question of....

But it was a problem. Very few rich families had bathrooms and the problem was bigger because the Buddhist monks could not take a bath in the river. They didn't have enough clothes, they didn't have any underwear. They had only three pieces of clothing, one to wrap around underneath, another to wrap around on top – just plain pieces of cloth.

To avoid tailoring – because that is a luxury – they were just using plain pieces of cloth; one they wrap around their waist, another they wrap around their chest, and that's all. It was difficult for them. Either they had to be naked – which was not allowed by Gautam Buddha – or they had to enter the river with their clothes on and then their clothes would get wet.

So you have to see the whole situation...why Gautam Buddha has to talk about such trivia. It is giving an incentive to the people who have their own bathrooms to allow the monks to have a bath and then people would receive limitless blessings. There is no metaphor in it. It means exactly what it says.

The disciple is absolutely right to ask: "This would appear to be an instance of external practice achieving merit, because the man who is allowing you use of his bathroom is achieving merit. He is not doing anything – just allowing you to use his bathroom."

And Bodhidharma says, "There is nothing and no need and no possibility either, of attaining any merit from any outside practice. The only meritorious thing is beholding the mind."

He could have simply said, "This is only an incentive for people; otherwise why should they allow anybody?" In fact, nobody likes his bathroom to be used by anybody else, and particularly not by strangers. It is not a public place. Everybody wants his bathroom to be private, his own, and the richer people are…. They certainly would not like the idea of strange monks wandering with dirty clothes, dirty feet because they have no shoes, perspiring in hot summer, collecting dust on the roads which were not coal tar, asphalt, or cement – they were just dusty roads for bullock carts. Rich men would not like this.

And you don't have any idea of the rich men of those days. They used to have in their bathtubs, not ordinary water, but rosewater. It is a strange story of a strange humanity: one part is dying for food and another part of the same race of human beings takes such a costly bath – thousands of roseflowers have to be used for one bath. These people would not like vagabonds, monks, beggars – they were all beggars in their eyes – unless they had some incentive that they would get great blessings in the other world. Buddha is simply talking in business terms and he is perfectly right.

But the problem with Bodhidharma is that he cannot accept things simply as they are. He says:

Here, the bathing of monks doesn't refer to the washing of anything tangible.

How do you wash anything intangible? A thing that is not tangible is not visible either. Only tangible things have to be washed. Your body can be given a shower but not your soul. Your clothes can be cleaned but not your being. But that does not mean that you have to use dirty clothes, that you have to remain dirty in your body.

Buddha was very aesthetic in comparison to Mahavira, his contemporary, and that's why he has more grace than Mahavira. Mahavira has a very strong personality but he's not graceful…a personality of a wrestler, but not the individuality of a lotus flower.

It is not accidental that Gautam Buddha has become synonymous with the lotus flower. It is so fragile and so beautiful and so graceful that no other flower on the earth even comes close to it. He wanted his monks to be sensitive, aesthetic, clean, and naturally the only way was to tell the people that if you help these poor monks with food, with a bath, with medicine, with clothes you will be getting great merit in the other world. This was simply a pragmatic affair.

When the Lord preached the Bathhouse Sutra, he wanted his disciples to remember the Dharma of washing. So he used an everyday concern to convey his real meaning....

The bathhouse is the body.

Now this is nonsense and he himself in the beginning sutras has said Buddha never teaches nonsense. He is contradicting almost everything that he has said with tremendous clarity in the beginning sutras. But now he himself has got into trouble.

The bathhouse is the body. When you light the fire of wisdom, you warm the pure water of the precepts and bathe the true buddha-nature within you.

Could not Buddha have said something other than the *Bathhouse Sutra*? He could have talked about the *Buddha-nature Sutra.* Do you think Buddha was less intelligent than Bodhidharma...that he did not know that it is better to say exactly what he means? And there is no difficulty in saying it. A Bodhidharma can say it – why can't Buddha say it?

By upholding these seven practices, you add to your virtue. The monks of that age were perceptive.

If this is true, that the monks of that age – that means Gautam Buddha's time –were perceptive, then certainly the *Bathhouse Sutra* does not need to be called *Bathhouse Sutra* at all. It should be called the *Buddha-nature Sutra,* or any other beautiful word. Why bring bathhouse into it? And if Bodhidharma can make it clear to less perceptive people – and Buddha's disciples were more perceptive – it is strange that he had to use such strange metaphors. Bodhidharma is making the whole thing up.

They understood the Buddha's meaning. If they understood the Buddha's meaning then why was he hiding it behind the bathhouse?

They followed his teaching, perfected their virtue and tasted the fruit of buddhahood.

If these disciples of Buddha had even experienced buddhahood, what was the need to speak to them in metaphors? Buddha could have been direct – metaphors are needed for children. So what he is saying is right, but it goes against him, not in favor of him.

But people nowadays can't fathom these things....

But the *Bathhouse Sutra* is not written for Bodhidharma's time. Bodhidharma came eleven hundred years after the *Bathhouse Sutra* was spoken by Buddha. Do you think Buddha was talking to the people of Bodhidharma's time? This is something to be understood because it is a constantly repeated thing: that people of older times were more perceptive, more sensitive, more intelligent than the people of today. Even today it is being said.

In Babylon a brick has been excavated and on the brick there is an inscription which says, "People of the old days were very intelligent" – and the brick is six thousand years old. Gautam Buddha and Mahavira both repeat many times that people of the old days were very intelligent, but I don't know when those old days were.

In the Hindu *Vedas,* which are supposed to be the oldest scriptures in the world, one man from this very city, Lokmanya Balgangadhar Tilak has proved, and proved with great argument and evidence – and such evidence that it has not been refuted by anybody for almost half a century – that the first Veda out of the four, *Rig Veda,* is ninety thousand years old. But even in *Rig Veda,* it is the same: that in the old days, people were very perceptive, very intelligent. I don't know when these old days were. It simply seems to condemn the people of the present day. This idea has been continuously used.

Is man's consciousness evolving or not? According to all these people, it seems that it is going downwards, not upwards. In fact the further back in history you go, the more primitive people you will find with more primitive practices. Cannibalism was a prevalent practice. The few cannibals that are left are in the thick forests of Africa, but they are the ancientmost people.

If you want to see the ancientmost people, you can go to Africa, but be careful! I have heard that when the first Christian missionary went there to convert the cannibals and to tell them, "God loves you all and Jesus will come to save you," they enjoyed his sermon very much. They took him on their shoulders and he thought that this was a great reception. When they started putting him into a boiling pot, he said, "What are you doing?" They said, "In just a few minutes you will see."

When the water started getting too hot, the fat missionary with just his head showing out from the big pot, started trying some way to persuade these people: "I have come here to give you a taste of Christianity and you are killing me."

They said, "Don't be worried. Once we have made a soup of you, we will have the first taste of Christianity. That's why we are boiling you – to have a taste of Christianity."

I think there is no other way of having a taste of Christianity! These are the most primitive people: they were three thousand at the beginning of this century, but because it is very rare to find anybody passing in their area – they look all around but nobody goes even close – then finally they have to eat their own people. In the beginning of this century there were three thousand; now there are only three hundred. They have eaten twenty-seven hundred of their own people. Every day food is needed. If they can get somebody from outside, good – just a little taste of some Chinese, some Japanese, some German, some Indian. Just as you go once in a while to the Chinese restaurant, they also want some taste – some change once in a while.

But it is very difficult because people remain miles away from them. Everybody knows that that area is dangerous; people have gone there but they have never returned. Whoever has gone there, has gone forever. Once they catch hold of you, you are finished…soon you will be cooked – maybe stuffed with grapes, spices. You may enjoy it! I am not saying that you will *not* enjoy it, you *may* enjoy it! The whole thing will be such an adventure.

But as you go backwards you will find more and more unintelligent, more and more retarded, more and more barbarous people. So this idea that is being used by all religions – that people in the beginning were great and now everybody has fallen – this is not true. This is absolutely wrong. There is no historical basis to it and no logical support. And I want to say to you that you are the highest pinnacle of consciousness up to now – although your highest pinnacle is not much.

You have immense potential undeveloped. But those primitive people were even more undeveloped than you are. You have at least some consciousness, they had no consciousness at all. They were just close to the animals.

Our true buddha-nature has no shape. And the dust of affliction has no form. How can people use ordinary water to wash an intangible body?

He goes on repeating the same stupid things. Yesterday he was saying how can Buddha drink ordinary milk – now, how can people use ordinary water? – as if there is some extraordinary water available somewhere!

To wash an intangible body… That which is intangible need not be washed. Only the tangible gets dirty. The invisible, space, never gets dirty; the sky never gets dirty. The silence beyond mind never gets dirty. And even if it gets dirty – which is impossible but just for argument's sake, even if it gets dirty – then we will find some invisible soap, some invisible shampoo which you cannot see. You will just see the empty bottle but inside there is invisible shampoo.

I have heard in a New York shop they were selling a certain commodity, so much of it that all the women of New York were immensely excited and wanted to purchase it. It was invisible hair pins. I think no woman can remain without temptation if invisible hairpins are available. There were queues before the shop and women were taking the packages, giving money and going away. One woman opened the box and could not see anything there. How can you see invisible hairpins? So she said to the shopkeeper, "I don't see anything." He asked, "How can you see invisible hairpins?"

She said, "That's right. I want to come again tomorrow to purchase a few more for my daughters and my friends to send as presents, because this is something so new. Will you have enough stock for tomorrow also? because I see so many customers and I had to stand for almost one hour in the queue." He said, "Don't be worried. We have been out of stock for fifteen days but it is an invisible thing. It does not matter whether it is there or not. You can come anytime – it will be always available."

Bodhidharma is saying something which is absolutely illogical, irrational. It is not even common sense.

It won't work. When will they wake up? To clean such a body, you have to behold it. Once impurities and filth arise from desire, they multiply until they cover you inside and out. But if you try to wash this body of yours, you will have to scrub until it is nearly gone, before it is clean.

He is saying you cannot clean this body that is visible. If you try to clean it you will have to scrub it to the point when the whole body is gone. Then you will be clean. That means there is no need to clean this body. It is useless; it will mean committing suicide!

But you know that there is no need to scrub the body to the point that it disappears. You can scrub the body to the point that you don't have a body odor, that your perspiration is not creating a disgusting smell around you, that your mouth is washed clean, that your breathing is not disturbing anybody else. You can use soap, you can use shampoo, you can use deodorants. There is no need to scrub the body to the point that it is completely gone. Then what is the point of cleaning it? Nothing is left.

Bodhidharma thinks he is giving you an argument that shows Buddha does not mean the ordinary bath for your body, he means cleaning your soul.

But Bodhidharma has forgotten completely that in his own sutras he said that the soul is always clean – it has never been unclean – that your buddha-nature is always pure, it has never been impure. Can you remember his sutras? He says that you are already enlightened, just you are asleep. There is no question of cleaning or doing any worship, or any ritual. All that you need is to behold your mind, and slowly, slowly that beholding of the mind will wake you up. To be awake is to be enlightened.

But now he has completely forgotten all those sutras. He has made such a tremendous mistake he should have stopped the moment the ultimate question about ignorance was asked. He did not stop. One has to know where to stop, otherwise one gets into a trap. Now he is going on and on and he does not know where to stop and how to stop.

From this you should realize that washing something external is not what the Buddha meant.

Only the external needs washing; the internal needs no washing. And if Buddha meant what he is saying, then Bodhidharma is also driving Buddha to the same point of stupidity at which he is. Only the external gets dirty and needs washing. The internal never gets dirty and hence needs no washing.

The disciple asked: *The sutras say that someone who wholeheartedly invokes the Buddha is sure to be reborn in the Western Paradise. Since this door leads to buddhahood, why seek liberation in beholding the mind?*

The disciple's continuous insistence is because if Bodhidharma's emphasis on beholding the mind is enough, then why does Buddha talk about other things? And Bodhidharma does not have the courage to speak against his own master. He could have said, "It is not my business to sort out his things. My understanding and my realization is that just beholding the mind is enough. Perhaps Buddha wanted to create an outer discipline also, side by side with an internal discipline. That is his business. That is none of my concern." Just a simple statement like this would have saved him from falling down from the sunlit peak where he was, into small things which he cannot solve.

His answer is again the same kind of foolishness. *Buddha means awareness...*which he has said so many times.

Buddha means awareness, the awareness of body and mind, that prevents evil from arising in either. And to invoke means to call to mind.

If invoke means to call to mind, then why should Buddha not say, "Call to mind?"; why say, "Invoke Buddha?" Why make things unnecessarily complicated when they can be made simple? And Buddha is not a man to make things complicated; he is not a philosopher. He is a realized sage. He speaks only in the simplest way and the clearest way, not using any jargon that can create disturbances in people's minds. His whole effort is to pacify the mind so that you can go beyond it more easily.

And to invoke means to call to mind, to call constantly to mind the rules of discipline and to follow them with all your might.

And this same Bodhidharma has said again and again that no discipline can lead you to buddhahood, that no rules are needed. The only thing that can help you is simply awareness of your thought process, of your mind.

To invoke the Buddha's name, you have to understand the dharma of invoking. If it is not present in your mind, your mouth chants an empty name.

As long as you are troubled by the three poisons, or by thoughts of yourself, your deluded mind will keep you from seeing the Buddha.... If you cling to appearances while searching for meaning, you won't find a thing. Thus, sages of the past cultivated introspection and not speech.

That is absolutely incorrect, because what is introspection except internal thinking? And what is speech but bringing your internal thinking to an expression? They are not different. One is the inside. First you introspect, you think, and then you bring it out: you can think the word *Rama* without saying it and then you can say "Rama." What is the difference? The difference is only that first you were saying it to yourself. Talking to yourself is introspection and talking to others is speech. Introspection is a silent monologue. Everybody goes on doing it all the time – it has nothing to do with sages. Even sinners have to do it!

What are you doing all the time except introspecting? Sitting, walking, you are continuously thinking of a thousand and one things, but only a few things you bring to expression. Saying that sages of the past cultivated introspection and not speech is not true because if sages were not speaking, then from where have your scriptures come, from where your *Vedas,* from where your *Upanishads?* And there are one hundred and eight *Upanishads.* From where does your holy *Koran,* and from where does your *Holy Bible* come? From where your holy *Talmud,* from where Gautam Buddha's *Dhammapada?* And from where do the words of Bodhidharma himself come? He is speaking and talking about sages who cultivated introspection only, and not speech.

That means all your holy scriptures are written by sinners and not by sages. A sage is one who knows himself and he speaks only that which is in tune with his inner experience. If he cannot find a word to express it, he remains silent. He is not against speech, he is not in favor of silence. He has come to a space which is beyond language, so it is very difficult to speak; but it is difficult to introspect also, because whatever can be introspected, can be spoken.

Just watch: introspection is speaking within yourself – you are using words. If you can use words without speaking, why can't you use the same words in speaking? That which cannot be spoken cannot be introspected either because they are two sides of the same coin.

This mind is the source of all virtues.

Now I am helpless but to say that this is pure nonsense! And it is nonsense according to Bodhidharma. In his own sutras he has said that this mind has to be transcended, that this mind is your bondage, that this mind has to be completely silenced, emptied. In other words you have to attain to no-mind.

No-mind can be the source of all virtues, but not the mind. If the mind is the source of all virtues, then what is the purpose of no-mind? All virtues include all virtues. Only sins remain. Is the no-mind the source of all sin? Is meditation the source of all that is criminal in you, immoral in you, unvirtuous in you? Bodhidharma is not in his right senses. Once he trembled, once he lied, he has not been able to regain his balance.

This mind is the source of all virtues. And this mind is the chief of all powers.
Then what about the buddha-nature and its power?
The eternal bliss of nirvana comes from the mind at rest.
Here he comes a little bit closer to the truth but not exactly to the truth.
The mind at rest is still mind.

Nirvana happens on the death of the mind, not just at the resting of the mind, because the mind that is at rest can any moment become restless. The mind simply has to go. Then only can you be certain of your absolute peace. The troublemaker is completely gone.

The troublemaker at rest does not mean you are free of trouble.

The troublemaker may be simply resting to gain a little energy to create more trouble again. He may be tired – everybody gets tired.

I used to live in a house with a friend and his child was a continuous nuisance. His father was tired, his mother was tired but he was an only child so they loved him very much. Only I was not tired of him. They asked me, "What is the matter? He never harasses you."

I said, "I harass him. I call him and he never comes close to me."

He said, "How do you harass him? Because he is such a constant worry, never at rest, always doing something, dropping something, breaking something, jumping from the sofa onto the table. He cannot sit silently."

I said, "I will show you how he can sit silently."

As I went in he said, "I will sit silently."

His father said, "What is the matter? You have not said anything – just your coming and he is saying, 'I will sit silently.'"

I used to live in half of the house and they used to live in the other half – but both were connected from inside. The child used to come once in a while to my side and I used to tell him, "If you want to come in you have to pay for it."

He said, "What?"

I said, "Money is not the issue. I will tell you what you have to do: first you have to go and run around the house seven times" – it was a big house, four acres of land – "seven times exactly, no cheating, no deceiving. Then you can come in."

After seven rounds he was so tired, he would come in and just flop on the sofa. I would say, "How are you feeling?"

He said, "I am still alive." And then I would continue my work and he would just rest.

So his father said, "This is strange... you never told me – and he has been torturing us."

I said, "I have found my way with him. Whenever he wants to see me or come to me, he has first to pay. And seven rounds of the house are enough. Then he does not ask for anything, then he is not in a position to ask. He is so tired he just sits on the sofa and most often falls asleep, and I continue my work."

Mind at rest is not reliable. Mind has to go completely to the point that it cannot come back...to the point of no return.

Rebirth in the three realms also comes from the mind. The mind is the door to every world. And the mind is the ford to the other shore.

This is not right because if mind is also the ford to the other shore, then what is the use of meditation? All powers belong to the mind, all words belong to the mind, all eternal bliss of nirvana comes from the resting of the mind. The ford going to the other shore is of the mind – then what is the use of meditation?

In fact, mind is not the ford to the other shore: meditation is. And meditation always means no-mind. When the mind is extinguished, the same energy that was involved in the mind becomes your meditation.

Those who know where the door is don't worry about reaching it. Those who know where the ford is don't worry about crossing it.

The people I meet nowadays are superficial. They think of merit as something that has form. They squander their wealth and butcher creatures of land and sea.... They see something tangible and instantly become attached. If you talk to them about formlessness, they sit there dumb and confused. Greedy for the small mercies of this world, they remain blind to the great suffering to come. Such disciples wear themselves out in vain. Turning from the true to the false, they talk about nothing but future blessings.

If you can simply concentrate your mind's inner light, and behold its outer illumination, you will dispel the three poisons and drive away the six thieves once and for all.

I have told you that in English there is no one word which can translate *dhyan*. There are three words: the first is concentration, which is the lowest. It means focusing your mind on one thing or one thought. It is useful in science; in fact without concentration there would be no science at all. Science is the by-product of concentration.

The second word in English is contemplation, which is higher than concentration. Contemplation means thinking about a certain subject matter – not a single thought, but a stream of thoughts confined to the same subject matter. For example, somebody is thinking about light. Then he goes on thinking about light, its speed, its division into seven colors and all its possibilities – the whole physics of light. Philosophy arises out of contemplation, just as science arises out of concentration.

And the third word in English is meditation, which is the highest. But still it is not an equivalent to *dhyan,* or the Chinese *ch'an,* or the Japanese *zen* which are different pronunciations of the Sanskrit word *dhyan.*

Dhyan means no-mind. In concentration, mind concentrates. In contemplation, mind contemplates. In meditation, mind meditates. But in dhyan, mind simply disappears. Dhyan is a silence beyond the mind. The man who has translated these sutras has used the lowest word in English – concentrate – for dhyan.

This is a problem with linguistic people – those who know the language. They translate books from one language into another, but particularly when it comes to translating poetry it becomes more difficult. And if it is a question of translating the statements of somebody who has attained to enlightenment, then it becomes even more difficult.

But the problem is that people who have attained to enlightenment are no longer interested in translating anybody's book. They are not even interested in writing their own book, they are enjoying their silence and their ecstasy so much. If they want to convey anything at all, they use the spoken word, because the spoken word has the warmth and the liveliness. And the spoken word has something of the person who is speaking it. It comes from his heart. It carries some flavor of his being. It also carries some light, some profundity which is lost in the written word. Hence, no enlightened person has ever written a single word.

If you can simply concentrate your mind's inner light and behold its outer illumination, you will dispel the three poisons and drive away the six thieves once and for all.

Just change the word concentrate. If you can meditate – and the meditation has to be understood in the sense of *dhyan* – if you can bring your no-mind to function, then all is light, then all is delight.

And without effort you will gain possession of an infinite number of virtues, perfections and doors to the truth. Seeing through the mundane, and witnessing the sublime, is less than an eye-blink away.

Finally at the end he comes back again to his original status. In this sentence he is again the Bodhidharma we started with.

Seeing through the mundane, and witnessing the sublime, is less than an eye-blink away. Realization is now. Why worry about gray hair?

Why worry about tomorrow and old age?

But the true door is hidden, and can't be revealed.

This is all that he needed to say at the time he was asked from where ignorance arises. Going round and round and round, at the end he manages to come to the point. The door, the true door, is hidden and can't be revealed.

I have only touched upon beholding the mind.

If he had only said these two sentences at that moment – and whatever he has said in between would have been dropped – Bodhidharma's sutras would have remained absolutely pure, impeccably pure. But I have made it clear to you, so you can choose what is right and what is just so much prose.

That which is going to help you in meditation is right, and that which is just unnecessarily metaphysical, philosophizing, has no validity and is of no use to your meditation.

In a way I feel happy that by coincidence this sutra came to be discussed and you have seen both sides. It will help you to remain aware – aware that even at the highest peak of your enlightenment you can still commit mistakes, you canstill go astray, you can still say things which are stupid. The problem is that I cannot tolerate anything which is not the best. I want you to know only the best, to experience the best, only twenty-four carat gold, no pollution, no mixture, just utter purity.

It was good to talk about these sutras, because I could go on telling you what is not right and what is right. You may be reading many books, you may be hearing many people. Just watch clearly. Every day I receive letters from sannyasins saying, "I have been to see some saint, some guru"...and I know those people are just idiots. They write to me, "We are very impressed," and I simply say, "My God!"

I have been working with these people so hard to make every small point completely clear, and any idiot can impress them! They don't seem to have the awareness and the clarity and the capacity for discrimination.

One of the greatest Indian scriptures is Badarayana's *Brahmasutra*. He prescribes a clear-cut capacity for discrimination as the first thing needed by the disciple. I can see why Badarayana has made discrimination his first point – to see what is false and to see what is true, to feel what is real and to feel what is just hypocrisy. Have you seen the Catholic pope? Perhaps many of you have seen him or met him and most of you must have seen his photographs. Do you see anything that gives you an indication that this man is the representative of God? He can be a salesman of any shoe company...but a representative of God! He should look at least once in a mirror and he himself will realize, "My God, why have you chosen me? Can't you find some other idiot? In this big world, why have you chosen poor me?"

I have heard about an old Jew dying. He was muttering something, so people of his family came close to hear what he is muttering at the time of his death. He was saying to God, "God, just only one request. We have been your chosen people for four thousand years. It is enough. Can't you choose somebody else now? If you had not chosen us we would not have suffered so much. Now be merciful; listen to a dying old man's last words. It is time that you choose somebody else as your chosen people and relieve us of that great burden. We are being continuously crushed."

Look at your popes, look at your shankaracharyas, look at your Ayatollah Khomeini, look at your Jaina monks, Buddhist monks, and you will be surprised that these people don't have the presence of the awakened person. Neither do they have the words that come from an experienced source of authority, but you become impressed by any kind of nonsense.

And this has been going on for centuries. It is time it should stop. At leasteverybody should be meditative enough that he can discriminate between the man who is an arrow towards the ultimate truth and its realization, and the man who is simply pretending.

These sutras were a good exercise for you to see how to discriminate. Be very alert. To be impressed easily is to be gullible. Don't be gullible, otherwise you will be exploited. Not to be gullible is what Badarayana means by being discriminative, alert, aware. There is no hurry to be impressed by anybody. Wait, watch, look at it from every aspect, and if your heart starts ringing bells, then it is a different matter altogether. But if it is just your mind saying, "I have found the right master," beware of your mind.

Your mind is your greatest enemy.

Okay, Maneesha?

Yes, Bhagwan. .

**Worldwide Distribution Centers
for the Works of
Bhagwan Shree Rajneesh**

Books by Bhagwan Shree Rajneesh are available
AT COST PRICE in many languages throughout the
world. Bhagwan's discourses have been recorded
live on audiotape and videotape. There are many
recordings of Rajneesh meditation music and
celebration music played in His presence, as well
as beautiful photographs of Bhagwan. For further
information contact one of the distribution centers
listed on the next page:

EUROPE

Denmark
Anwar Distribution
Carl Johansgade 8, 5
2100 Copenhagen
Tel. 01/420218

Italy
Rajneesh Services Corporation
Via XX Settembre 12
28041 Arona (NO)
Tel. 02/8392 194 (Milan office)

Netherlands
Rajneesh Distributie Centrum
Cornelis Troostplein 23
1072 JJ Amsterdam
Tel. 020/5732 130

Norway
Devananda Rajneesh Meditation Center
P.O. Box 177 Vinderen
0386 Oslo 3
Tel. 02/123373

Switzerland
Mingus AG
Asylstrasse 11
8032 Zurich
Tel. 01/2522 012

United Kingdom
Purnima Rajneesh Publications
95A Northview Road
London N8 7LR
Tel. 01/341 4317

West Germany
Rajneesh Verlags GmbH
Venloer Strasse 5-7
5000 Cologne 1
Tel. 0221/57407 43

Also available from nationwide
bookshop distributor VVA Vereinigte
Verlagsauslieferung GmbH
An der Autobahn - Postf. 7777
4830 Guetersloh

ASIA

India
Rajneeshdham
17 Koregaon Park
Poona 411001 M.S.
Tel. 0212/60963

Japan
Eer Rajneesh Neo-Sannyas Commune
Mimura Building 6-21-34
Kikuna, Kohoku-ku
Yokohama, 222
Tel. 045/434 1981

AUSTRALIA

Rajneeshgrad
P.O. Box 1097
160 High Street
Fremantle, WA 6160
Tel. 09/430 4047

Rajneesh Foundation Australia
203 Hargrave St.
Paddington, NSW 2021
Tel. 02/327 4948

AMERICA

United States
Chidvilas
P.O. Box 17550
Boulder, CO 80308
Tel. 303/665 6611
Order Dept. 800/777 7743

Also available in bookstores
nationwide at
Walden Books and B. Dalton

BOOKS BY BHAGWAN SHREE RAJNEESH

ENGLISH LANGUAGE EDITIONS
RAJNEESH PUBLISHERS

Early Discourses and Writings
Beware of Socialism
A Cup of Tea *Letters to Disciples*
From Sex to Superconsciousness
I Am the Gate
The Long and the Short and the All
The Silent Explosion

Meditation
And Now, and Here (Volumes 1&2)
Dimensions Beyond the Known
In Search of the Miraculous (Volume 1)
The Orange Book
The Meditation Techniques of Bhagwan Shree Rajneesh
The Perfect Way

Buddha and Buddhist Masters
The Book of the Books (Volumes 1–4) *the Dhammapada*
The Diamond Sutra *the Vajrachchedika Prajnaparamita Sutra*
The Discipline of Transcendence (Volumes 1–4)
On the Sutra of 42 Chapters
The Heart Sutra *the Prajnaparamita Hridayam Sutra*
The Book of Wisdom (Volumes 1&2)
Atisha's Seven Points of Mind Training

Indian Mystics:

The Bauls
The Beloved (Volumes 1&2)

Kabir
The Divine Melody

Ecstasy – The Forgotten Language
The Fish in the Sea is Not Thirsty
The Guest
The Path of Love
The Revolution

Krishna
Krishna: The Man and His Philosophy

Jesus and Christian Mystics
Come Follow Me (Volumes 1–4) *the Sayings of Jesus*
I Say Unto You (Volumes 1&2) *the Sayings of Jesus*
The Mustard Seed *the Gospel of Thomas*
Theologia Mystica *the Treatise of St. Dionysius*

Jewish Mystics
The Art of Dying
The True Sage

Sufism
Just Like That
The Perfect Master (Volumes 1&2)
The Secret
Sufis: The People of the Path (Volumes 1&2)
Unio Mystica (Volumes 1&2) *the Hadiqa of Hakim Sanai*
Until You Die
The Wisdom of the Sands (Volumes 1&2)

Tantra
The Book of the Secrets (Volumes 1–5)
Vigyana Bhairava Tantra
Tantra, Spirituality and Sex
Excerpts from The Book of the Secrets
Tantra: The Supreme Understanding
Tilopa's Song of Mahamudra
The Tantra Vision (Volumes 1&2) *the Royal Song of Saraha*

Books about Bhagwan Shree Rajneesh

Bhagwan Shree Rajneesh:
The Most Dangerous Man Since Jesus Christ
(by Sue Appleton, LL.B., M.A.B.A.)
Bhagwan: The Buddha For The Future
(by Juliet Forman, S.R.N., S.C.M., R.M.N.)
Bhagwan: The Most Godless Yet The Most Godly Man
(by Dr. George Meredith M.D. M.B.,B.S. M.R.C.P.)

OTHER PUBLISHERS

UNITED KINGDOM

The Art of Dying (Sheldon Press)
The Book of the Secrets (Volume 1, Thames & Hudson)
No Water, No Moon (Sheldon Press)
Roots and Wings (Routledge & Kegan Paul)
Straight to Freedom (Sheldon Press)
The Supreme Doctrine (Routledge & Kegan Paul)
Tao: The Three Treasures (Volume 1, Wildwood House)

Books about Bhagwan Shree Rajneesh

The Way of the Heart: the Rajneesh Movement
by Judith Thompson and Paul Heelas, Department
of Religious Studies, University of Lancaster
(Aquarian Press)

UNITED STATES OF AMERICA

The Book of the Secrets (Volumes 1-3, Harper & Row)
Dimensions Beyond the Known (Wisdom Garden Books)
The Great Challenge (Grove Press)

Het Mosterdzaad (Mirananda)
The Mustard Seed (Volumes 1&2)
De Nieuwe Mens (Volume 1) (Zorn) Compilation on
The New Man, Relationships, Education, Health,
Dutch edition only
De Nieuwe Mens (Volume 2) (Altamira) Excerpts from
The Last Testament (Volume 1), Dutch edition only
Het Oranje Meditatieboek (Ankh-Hermes)
The Orange Book
Psychologie en Evolutie (Ankh-Hermes)
The Psychology of the Esoteric
De Tantra Visie (Arcanum)
The Tantra Vision (Volumes 1&2)
Zoeken naar de Stier (Ankh-Hermes) *10 Zen Stories*
Totdat Je Sterft (Ankh-Hermes) *Until You Die*
Priesters & Politici: De Maffia van de Ziel
(Rajneesh Publikaties Nederland)
Priests & Politicians: The Mafia of the Soul

Books about Bhagwan:

Een Tuin der Lusten? Het rebelse tantrisme van
Bhagwan en het nieuwe tijdperk by Sietse Visser
(Mirananda) *A Garden of Earthly Delights?*
Oorspronkelijk Gezicht by Dr. J. Foudraine (Ambo)
Original Face
Bhagwan, Notities van een Discipel by Dr. J. Foudraine
(Ankh-Hermes) *Bhagwan, Notes of a Disciple*
Bhagwan, een Introductie by Dr. J. Foudraine
(Ankh-Hermes) *Bhagwan, an Introduction*

French

Je Suis la Porte (EPI) *I am the Gate*
La Meditation Dynamique (Dangles)
Meditation: The Art of Inner Ecstasy
L'Eveil a la Conscience Cosmique (Dangles)
The Psychology of the Esoteric
Le Livre des Secrets (Soleil Orange)
The Book of Secrets (Volume 1)

German

Und vor Allem: Nicht Wackeln (Fachbuchhandlung fuer
Psychologie) *Above All Don't Wobble*
Der Freund (Sannyas Verlag) *A Cup of Tea*
Vorsicht Sozialismus (Rajneesh Verlag)
Beware of Socialism
Bhagwan Shree Rajneesh: Ueber die Grundrechte
des Menschen (Rajneesh Verlag)
Bhagwan Shree Rajneesh On Basic Human Rights
Komm und folge mir (Sannyas/Droemer Knaur)
Come Follow Me (Volume 1)
Jesus aber schwieg (Sannyas) *Come Follow Me (Volume 2)*
Jesus – der Menschensohn (Sannyas)
Come Follow Me (Volume 3)
Sprung ins Unbekannte (Sannyas)
Dimensions Beyond the Known
Ekstase: Die vergessene Sprache (Herzschlag)
Ecstasy: The Forgotten Language
Vom Sex zum kosmischen Bewusstsein (New Age/Thomas
Martin) *From Sex to Superconsciousness*
Goldene Augenblicke: Portrait einer Jugend in Indien
(Goldmann) *Glimpses of a Golden Childhood*
Sprengt den Fels der Unbewusstheit (Fischer)
Hammer on the Rock
Ich bin der Weg (Sannyas) *I am the Gate*
Meditation: Die Kunst, zu sich selbst zu finden (Heyne)
Meditation: The Art of Inner Ecstasy
Mein Weg: Der Weg der weissen Wolke (Herzschlag)
My Way: The Way of the White Clouds
Nirvana: Die letzte Huerde auf dem Weg (Rajneesh Verlag/
NSJ) *Nirvana: The Last Nightmare*
Kein Wasser, Kein Mond (Herzschlag)
No Water, No Moon

Dieci Storie Zen di Bhagwan Shree Rajneesh: Ne Acqua, Ne Luna (Mediterranee) *No Water, No Moon*

Philosofia Perennis (ECIG) *Philosophia Perennis (Volumes 1&2)*

Semi di Saggezza (Sugarco) *Seeds of Revolution*

Tantra, Spiritualità e Sesso (Rajneesh Foundation Italy) *Tantra, Spirituality & Sex*

Tantra: La Comprensione Suprema (Bompiani) *Tantra: The Supreme Understanding*

Tao: I Tre Tesori (Re Nudo) *Tao: The Three Treasures (Volumes 1-3)*

Tecniche di Liberazione (La Salamandra) *Techniques of Liberation*

Il Libro dei Segreti (Bompiani) *The Book of The Secrets (Volume 1)*

L'Armonia Nascosta (ECIG) *The Hidden Harmony (Volumes 1&2)*

Il Seme della Ribellione (Rajneesh Foundation Italy) *The Mustard Seed (Volume 1)*

La Nuova Alchimia (Psiche) *The New Alchemy To Turn You On (Volumes 1&2)*

Il Libro Arancione (Mediterranee) *The Orange Book*

La Rivoluzione Interiore (Mediterranee) *The Psychology of the Esoteric*

La Bibbia di Rajneesh (Bompiani) *The Rajneesh Bible (Volume 1)*

La Ricerca (La Salamandra) *The Search*

La Dottrina Suprema (Rizzoli) *The Supreme Doctrine*

La Visione Tantrica (Riza) *The Tantra Vision*

Japanese

Shin Jinkensengen (Meisosha Ltd.) *Bhagwan Shree Rajneesh On Basic Human Rights*

Seimeino Kanki – Darshan Nisshi (Rajneesh Publications) *Dance Your Way to God*

Sex kara Choishiki e (Rajneesh Publications) *From Sex to Superconsciousness*

Meiso – Shukusai no Art (Merkmal) *Meditation: The Art of Inner Ecstasy*

My Way – Nagareyuku Shirakumo no Michi (Rajneesh Publications) *My Way: The Way of the White Clouds*

Ikkyu Doka (Merkmal) *Take it Easy, Volume 1*

Sonzai no Uta (Merkmal) *Tantra: The Supreme Understanding*

Tao – Eien no Taiga (Merkmal) *Tao: The Three Treasures (Volumes 1-4)*

Baui no Ai no Uta (Merkmal) *The Beloved (Volumes 1&2)*

Diamond Sutra – Bhagwan Shree Rajneesh Kongohannyakyo o Kataru (Meisosha Ltd./LAF Mitsuya) *The Diamond Sutra*

Koku no Fune (Rajneesh Publications) *The Empty Boat (Volumes 1&2)*

Kusa wa hitorideni haeru (Fumikura) *The Grass Grows by Itself*

Hannya Shinkyo (Merkmal) *The Heart Sutra*

Ai no Renkinjutsu (Merkmal) *The Mustard Seed (Volumes 1&2)*

Orange Book (Wholistic Therapy Institute) *The Orange Book*

Kyukyoku no Tabi – Bhagwan Shree Rajneesh Zen no Jugyuzu o Kataru (Merkmal) *The Search*

Anataga Shinumadewa (Fumikura) *Until You Die*

Korean

Giromnun Gil II (Chung Ha)

Giromnun Gil Ih (Chung Ha) *Tao: The Pathless Path (Volume 1)*

Haeng Bongron II

Haeng Bongron Ih *Tao: The Pathless Path (Volume 2)*

Joogumul Yesool (Chung Ha) *The Art of Dying*

Mit Wurzeln und Fluegeln (Lotos)
Roots and Wings (Volume 1)
Die Schuhe auf dem Kopf (Lotos)
Roots and Wings (Volume 2)
Spirituelle Entwicklung und Sexualitaet (Fischer)
Spiritual Development & Sexuality
Tantra, Spiritualitaet und Sex (Rajneesh Verlag)
Tantra, Spirituality & Sex
Tantrische Liebeskunst (Sannyas)
Tantra, Spirituality & Sex
Tantra: Die hoechste Einsicht (Sannyas)
Tantra: The Supreme Understanding
Das Buch der Geheimnisse (Heyne)
The Book of the Secrets (Volume 1)
Die Gans ist raus! (Rajneesh Verlag) *The Goose Is Out!*
Rebellion der Seele (Sannyas) *The Great Challenge*
Die verborgene Harmonie (Sannyas) *The Hidden Harmony*
Die verbotene Wahrheit (Rajneesh Verlag/Heyne)
The Mustard Seed
Das Orangene Buch (Rajneesh Verlag/NSI) *The Orange Book*
Esoterische Psychologie (Sannyas)
The Psychology of the Esoteric
Auf der Suche (Sambuddha) *The Search*
Das Klatschen der einen Hand (Gyandip)
The Sound of One Hand Clapping
Tantrische Vision (Heyne) *The Tantra Vision (Volume 1)*
Alchemie der Verwandlung (Lotos) *The True Sage*
Nicht bevor du stirbst (Gyandip)/*Until You Die*
Was ist Meditation? (Sannyas) *Compilation about
meditation, German edition only*
Yoga: Alpha und Omega (Gyandip)
Yoga: The Alpha and the Omega (Volume 1)
Der Hoehepunkt des Lebens (Rajneesh Verlag)
Compilation on death, German edition only
Intelligenz des Herzens (Herzschlag)
Compilation, German edition only

Kunst kommt nicht vom Koennen (Rajneesh Verlag)
*Compilation about creativity,
German edition only*
Liebe beginnt nach den Flitterwochen (Rajneesh Verlag)
Compilation about love, German edition only
Sexualitaet und Aids (Rajneesh Verlag)
Compilation about Aids, German edition only

Greek

Bhagwan Shree Rajneesh Gia Ta Vasika
Anthropina Dikeomata (Swami Anand Ram)
Bhagwan Shree Rajneesh on Basic Human Rights
I Krifi Armonia (PIGI/Rassoulis)
The Hidden Harmony

Hebrew

Tantra: Ha'havana Ha'eelaeet (Massada)
Tantra: The Supreme Understanding

Italian

Bhagwan Shree Rajneesh parla Sui Diritti dell'Uomo
(Rajneesh Services Corporation)
Bhagwan Shree Rajneesh On Basic Human Rights
Dimensioni Oltre il Conosciuto (Mediterranee)
Dimensions Beyond the Known
Estasi: Il Linguaggio Dimenticato (Riza Libri)
Ecstasy: The Forgotten Language
Dal Sesso all'Eros Cosmico (Basaia)
From Sex to Superconsciousness
Guida Spirituale (Mondadori) *Guida Spirituale*
Io Sono La Soglia (Mediterranee) *I am the Gate*
Meditazione Dinamica: L'Arte dell'Estasi Interiore
(Mediterranee) *Meditation: The Art of Inner Ecstasy*
La Mia Via: La Via delle Nuvole Bianche
(Mediterranee) *My Way: The Way of the White Clouds*
Nirvana: L'Ultimo Incubo (Basaia)
Nirvana: The Last Nightmare

Tantra: Sexo E Espiritualidade (Agora)
Tantra, Spirituality & Sex
Tantra: A Suprema Compreensao (Cultrix)
Tantra: The Supreme Understanding
Arte de Morrer (Global) The Art of Dying
O Livro Dos Segredos (Maha Lakshmi)
The Book of the Secrets (Volumes 1&2)
Cipreste No Jardim (Cultrix)
The Cypress in the Courtyard
A Divina Melodia (Cultrix) The Divine Melody
A Harmonia Oculta (Pensamento) The Hidden Harmony
A Semente De Mostarda (Tao)
The Mustard Seed (Volumes 1&2)
A Nova Alquimia (Cultrix)
The New Alchemy To Turn You On
O Livro Orange (Pensamento) The Orange Book
A Psicologia Do Esoterico (Tao)
The Psychology of the Esoteric
Unio Mystica (Maha Lakshmi) Unio Mystica

Russian

Bhagwan Shree Rajneesh On Basic Human Rights
(Neo-Sannyas International)

Serbo-Croat

Bhagwan Shree Rajneesh (Swami Mahavira)
(Compilation of various quotations)
The Ultimate Pilgrimage

Spanish

Sobre Los Derechos Humanos Basicos (Futonia, Spain)
Bhagwan Shree Rajneesh on Basic Human Rights
Ven, Sigueme (Sagaro, Chile) Come Follow Me (Volume 1)
Yo Soy La Puerta (Diana, Mexico) I am The Gate
Meditacion: El Arte del Extasis (Rosello Impresiones)
Meditation: The Art of Inner Ecstasy
El Camino de las Nubes Blancas (Cuatro Vientos)
My Way: The Way of the White Clouds
Solo Un Cielo (Collection Tantra) Only One Sky
Introduccion al Mundo del Tantra (Rosello Impresiones)
Tantra: The Supreme Understanding (Volumes 1&2)
Tao: Los Tres Tesoros (Sirio, Espana)
Tao: The Three Treasures
El Sutra del Corazon (Sarvogeet, Espana) The Heart Sutra
El Libro Naranja (Bhagwatam, Puerto Rico)
The Orange Book
Psicologia de lo Esoterico: La Nueva Evolucion
del Hombre (Cuatro Vientos, Chile)
The Psychology of the Esoteric
Que Es Meditacion? (Koan/Rosello Pastanaga)
What Is Meditation?

Swedish

Den Vaeldiga Utmaningen (Livskraft)
The Great Challenge

RAJNEESH MEDITATION CENTERS

There are many Rajneesh Meditation Centers, Ashrams and Communes throughout the world which can be contacted for information about the teachings of Bhagwan Shree Rajneesh and which have His books available as well as audio and video tapes of His discourses. Centers exist in practically every country.

For further information about Bhagwan Shree Rajneesh please contact:

Rajneeshdham Neo-Sannyas Commune
17 Koregaon Park
Poona 411 001, MS
India